Melancholic Modalities

MELANCHOLIC MODALITIES

Affect, Islam, and Turkish Classical Musicians

Denise Gill

OXFORD
UNIVERSITY PRESS

Oxford University Press is a department of the University of Oxford. It furthers
the University's objective of excellence in research, scholarship, and education
by publishing worldwide. Oxford is a registered trade mark of Oxford University
Press in the UK and certain other countries.

Published in the United States of America by Oxford University Press
198 Madison Avenue, New York, NY 10016, United States of America.

© Oxford University Press 2017

Library of Congress Cataloging-in-Publication Data
Names: Gill, Denise.
Title: Melancholic modalities: affect, Islam, and Turkish classical musicians / by Denise Gill.
Description: New York, NY: Oxford University Press, [2017] |
Includes bibliographical references and index.
Identifiers: LCCN 2016045244| ISBN 9780190495008 (hardcover) |
ISBN 9780190495015 (pbk.) | ISBN 9780190495039 (oxford scholarly online)
Subjects: LCSH: Music—Turkey—History and criticism. | Melancholy in music.
Classification: LCC ML345.T8 G55 2017 | DDC 781.6909561—dc23
LC record available at https://lccn.loc.gov/2016045244

To my parents,
Jane and Douglas

Sabredin! Hüzünsüz bir neşe ve darlıksız bir bolluk olmaz.

Have patience! There is neither joy without melancholy
nor abundance without scarcity.
                    —Abdülkadir Geylâni Hz. (1077–1166)

CONTENTS

LIST OF FIGURES

LIST OF EXAMPLES

PREFACE

In this book, I explore how a particular artistic community sounds out, embodies, narrates, and experiences melancholies in their music making. In my focus on Turkish classical musicians, I resist solely approaching musical meaning by analyzing "music" itself. This type of sonicist approach to the study of affect would not fit the ethnographic evidence that emerged in my extended fieldwork in Turkey's western urban centers of Istanbul, Ankara, Izmir, and Konya. I instead maintain integrity with my experiences as an observant researcher, archival and oral historian, student, and concert-hall performer of Turkish classical music. I claim that melancholy is an affective practice mindfully engaged by musicking individuals in collective community. This book delves into the rich and complicated world of musicians' ideological beliefs, pedagogical histories and practices, forms of listening, and subjectivities. It uses the concepts and diverse iterations of "melancholy" to offer an ethnography of how affective practices translate musical meaning for a community of Turkish classical musicians.

Why Turkish classical music? My interest in this music genre began primarily as an aesthetic pursuit. I am fortunate to have the economic, racial, and citizenship privileges that allowed me to pursue my interest in this music genre through higher education in the United States. Increasing my knowledge of Turkish classical music was made possible only through the extended mentorship of multiple teachers in my path, beginning with my undergraduate education at the University of Illinois at Urbana-Champaign. Ethnomusicologist and virtuosic *kaval* (Bulgarian end-blown flute) master Donna Buchanan first opened my ears to this genre, and in my junior year, she bought her Balkanalia UIUC ensemble a *kanun* (Middle Eastern trapezoidal zither) that I coveted and taught myself on before I could travel to Izmir and purchase my own in 2003. My graduate years at the University of California Santa Barbara fortunately immersed me in *ustad* Scott Marcus's remarkable Middle East Ensemble and exposed me to diverse collectives of Turkish, Jewish, Arab, Greek, Armenian, and Persian musicians in southern and northern California. There too I had the privilege of studying under Sonia Tamar Seeman, whose teaching and scholarship greatly influenced early theoretical formulations of this project. In San Francisco in 2004, I first met and played *kanun* for the musician who was to become my primary teacher: Necati Çelik (b. 1955), a master virtuoso on the *ud* (short-necked lute). Necati Hoca ("Necati teacher") to this day continues to open doors for me in Turkey, musically and socially. Since I first began fieldwork for this project in 2007, innumerable musicians in Turkey have welcomed me into their studios, ateliers, workshops, rehearsals, and homes. It is their voices, musics, expressions, stories, opinions, and feelings that make up the core of the book you hold in your hand.

My interest in affect—and specifically, the multiple iterations and diverse melancholies named and espoused by Turkish classical musicians—was initially peaked in my master's thesis on multivalent interpretations of musical transmission in this music genre. In the course of that project, I realized that moments of music transmission—especially in the context of master-apprentice frameworks—were ultimately critical processes of inculcating correct "feeling rules" (Hochschild 1983). In my fieldwork for the dissertation, I came to understand that affect was not only that which bound the community of Turkish classical musicians together—beyond their affinity for the music—it also bound together entire groups of amateurs, patrons, and lifelong students of the genre. In other words, communities making Turkish classical music not only perform and listen together; they also "feel" together. While my initial enthusiasm led me to attempt to cover a spectrum of affective practices beyond melancholies, I quickly realized the scope of such a project was too broad. I hope that future work will consider the additional affective particularities of Turkish classical musicians as well as issues of audience reception and diverse modalities of listening to this genre of music.

I was able to access the affective circulation and socialization of Turkish classical musical meanings as someone who was inculcated into a master-student relationship with Necati Hoca. I was deemed proficient enough on *kanun*, thanks to the lessons I received from *kanun* masters Celaleddin Aksoy and the late Halil Karaduman. That Necati Hoca and I did not play the same instrument was unimportant, as I was primarily learning the arts of instrumental improvisation (*taksim*), melodic ornamentation, and repertoire from him. To Necati Hoca, I am a cherished student, albeit not a full apprentice, as I could not immerse myself in sequential years (a decade or more, preferably) of living and making music by his side. As with many ethnomusicologists, bi-musicality (Hood 1960), or becoming "fluent" in a "different" musical tradition, was a central aspect of my fieldwork process. Indeed, bi-musicality has been as a necessary method in my understanding of the intersections of affective practice and embodiment.

However, I found that my greatest insight came not from bi-musicality, but rather with a shift in the way I listened to sound, musical structure, meaning, and historicities in music making and discourse. I have named this process *bi-aurality* and explore it further in chapter 3. My rhizomatic approach, explained in the book's introduction, and my focus on bi-aurality allow me to identify the fundamental problems of translating sonic, affective materials and practices from the musicians producing it to the normatively secular and academic format our books take. Developing bi-aural horizontal and rhizomatic listening practices was necessary for me to develop the ears to both hear Turkish classical music enough to produce it myself and to effectively listen to the diverse voices and multiplicity of opinions of Turkish classical musicians themselves. I attempt to translate these rhizomatic listening practices and use my sketch of rhizomes to oscillate between different registers of explanatory writing.

Rhizomatic analysis and listening practices make sense as an approach in both literal and figurative terms. Literally, the central instrument of the Turkish classical music canon is the *ney*, an end-blown reed flute that is itself crafted from the rhizome *arundo donax*. The *arundo donax* is a tall perennial cane that rhizomatically sprouts in the marshy regions of Southeastern Turkey. The *ney* itself rhizomatically surfaces in multiple places throughout this book: in chapter 2 I discuss how *ney*-s are constructed and the sound (*Hû*) with which one produces music on the *ney*. Famous *neyzen*-s, or master *ney* players, make appearances in moments of analysis and storytelling throughout the text. In the Conclusion, I describe my journey with a reed collector to a reed bed in the Antep region, where I witnessed and participated in the separation of botanical reeds that would eventually become *ney*-s.

Rhizomatic analysis and listening practices are also figurative. They help me identify how multiple, diverse communities of Turkish classical musicians identify, circulate, and socialize affective particularities through sound and musicking. "Melancholy" is the central rhizomatic affective practice I grab in this text, but my method of tracing how musicians perform, embody, hear, and articulate melancholies is purposefully rhizomatic to allude to the emptiness and lack of other feeling practices I do not consider in this book. With rhizomatic analysis and listening, I hope other scholars may grab, take apart, and follow different affective practices in alternate or syncretistic ways.

This book is built upon firsthand archival research and ethnographic fieldwork conducted in Turkey in major urban centers, mostly located in the western part of the country during 2004–2005, 2006, 2007–2009, 2011, 2013, and 2014. It draws on interviews—life stories, oral histories, and dialogic listening—with individuals of highly differentiated intersectional identities (in terms of race/ethnicity, class, age, gender, sexual orientation, geographic location, socioeconomic class, religious affiliation, political party affiliation, and able-bodiedness). I have recorded and analyzed over two hundred hours of music making and have detailed notes from over three dozen other events I attended for which recording was prohibited. I include insight from my own participant-observational experience and as a performer of this music genre on *kanun* who has concertized professionally in Turkey and Europe. My participant-observation settings included regular rehearsals for two State Ensembles and less frequent visits to other professional ensembles, municipal amateur ensemble rehearsals, music lessons, intimate professional music gatherings, and performances sponsored by private industry. Accompanying consultants to a variety of locations and engaging in political events and religious rituals, I gained extensive insight about the practices of mourning, healing, historicizing, and memorializing that contribute to the crafting of melancholic modalities.

The consultants who fill these pages are professional instrumentalists and vocalists of Turkish classical music. The interpretations of my teachers' and consultants' statements and any possible inaccuracies are completely mine. Most individual musicians go unnamed in the book, per their requests. After all, interviews about music and emotion often led to retelling lessons and recalling memories and sounds that are themselves intimate. In these moments, consultants generously shared their vulnerabilities as musicians and as people. Respecting consultants' boundaries, I have chosen to identify most musicians anonymously, sometimes referring to their primary instrument or role as a vocalist. Often anonymity surfaces simply because my recorded evidence included music making in large groups that flowed in and out of talk as well as musicking (Small 1998), and I could not pinpoint the specific speaker of a given statement. In other cases, consultants have directly requested anonymity as our discussions often got into the sticky terrain of disparate political party affiliations, critical judgments about other musicians, and passionate interpretations of Turkish civil life. Some key musicians are named in particular encounters: my two beloved primary teachers, Necati Çelik (b. 1955) and Celaleddin Aksoy (b. 1961); celebrated and renowned vocalist Melihat Gülses (b. 1958); prominent *neyzen* and unarguably one of the central musicians of the current century, Niyazi Sayın (b. 1927); my first *kanun* teacher Halil Karaduman (1959–2012); and esteemed composer and violinist Ünal Ensari (1938–2016). Losing Ünal Hoca while this book was in its final editing stages rendered a feeling of urgency to share his interpretations of affect and embodiment in music. Remembering Ünal Hoca, I mourn our collective loss of a great musician, composer, teacher, and storyteller.

My own positionality in the social worlds of Turkish classical musicians simultaneously offered and disavowed particular understandings of affective practices. Necati Hoca will speak candidly about the fact that I came to him already a musician. Perhaps the most important aspect of my situatedness beyond my foreignness was that I am a heterosexually practicing cisgender woman. I spent quality time with professional women Turkish classical musicians, but as an instrumentalist first and foremost, I spent most of my time with men. I was also unmarried during ethnographic fieldwork, though I fit into gendered social structures as a student of my teacher and was treated with respect because of my association with him. Yet I often found myself in intimate musician gatherings at which I was either the only woman or one of two women who were actively playing. The care labor that supports these music gatherings—from the preparation of the rooms to the making of the treats and deserts, to constant tea service and refilling water glasses, to clean up after our dispersal—is largely done by the wives and daughters of musicians or hired staff. In other words, much of the material in this book—from the music making to the practice of affect itself—is made possible for musicians by the women who perform domestic tasks that allow musicians the time and space to engage in their creative, artistic, and affective practices. My own teacher's wife, Ayşe Çelik, is a stunning example of an incredibly hardworking, sacrificing, and cosmopolitan hostess whose talents, food, gifts, and conversation enabled my teacher to develop a wide global network of devoted students and listeners.

As I explain in the book's conclusion, selfhood is rhizomatic as well. While most of the Turkish classical musicians with whom I work locate me primarily as a *kanun* player, this book is the interpretive manifestation of my intellectual work in Turkey in dialogue with the wide array of disciplines with which I engage, such as ethnomusicology, anthropology, Islamic studies, feminist and queer theories, and cultural studies. This book is a multilayered ethnography of sonic melancholies that result from loss on many levels (spiritual, cultural, social, political); these melancholies are affective practices experienced and enjoyed by Turkish classical musicians today. Yet the book's larger intervention lies in the rhizomatic analysis I utilize to avoid the construction of binaries and allow for the multiple—and often conflicting—interpretations of discourse and meaning. This book pushes new ground for bi-aurality: thinking and listening in nonlinear, horizontal, and spectral ways.

Melancholy remains current, almost permanently affixed to understandings of Turkishness. Turkish writers devote entire books to melancholy (Temelkuran 2016 and Pamuk 2004) and scholars unravel specific musical or sonic articulations of melancholy, suffering, and loss (O'Connell 2013, Erol 2007, Özbek 2006, Özgür 2006, Stokes 1992 and 2010). I am finishing this book in the immediate aftermath of the failed attempted coup in Turkey of July 15, 2016. The effects of the coup attempt have left some Turks with a "familiar melancholy" (Arango 2016), while other Turks voice pride because of resistance to the attempted coup and also express a vulnerable, tentative hopefulness for Turkey's political future. In the end, the failed coup has produced new forms of listening (Gill 2016) and engendered an urgency of how attentive we must be to the intersections of feeling, sound, and national belonging. It is my hope that this book elucidates the importance of listening closely to what musicians can teach us about the ways affects are practiced, domesticated, managed, performed, and cherished.

CONVENTIONS

After the founding of the Republic of Turkey in 1923, a number of national reforms enacted profound transformations in civic life. Turkey's 1924 constitution established a secular nation-state, and removed Islam as the official religion. In 1928, the Ottoman script, based on an Arabic alphabet, was replaced with the Latin alphabet. These changes were institutionalized, and effectively taught and transferred through generations in state-sponsored educational structures. However, music reforms did not take full effect with Turkish classical musicians who continued to learn through master-apprentice relationships on the basis of oral transmission. As such, there are a number of terms, categories, expressions, and names in this book that are referred to interchangeably by my consultants in Turkish, Ottoman, Persian/Farsi, and Arabic.

In this book I adopt the following conventions. All translations from Turkish, Ottoman, Persian/Farsi, and Arabic are my own unless otherwise designated explicitly. Names and terms employ the modern Turkish spellings found in Redhouse (1997), and I use the modern standard Turkish spelling system for religious terms and place names. Following O'Connell (2013), I further do not employ the Turkish plural suffixes (-lar, -ler), choosing instead to append the English (-s) to the singular form. If the plural form occurs in a direct quote, I maintain the original spelling.

The musical transcriptions I offer in this book are all my own, based on multiple live versions observed and engaged. My transcriptions follow the conventions set in Öztuna (1990). These transcriptions reflect standard notation practices for Turkish art and classical musics, meaning that they are typically presented an octave above performance pitch and notated on a tonic according to standard representation for a given *makam* (microtonal melodic mode).

Importantly, Turkish classical *makam*-s are generally not conceived as collections of pitches (*dizi*-s) but are rather understood as groupings of microtonally inclusive intervals (*aralık*-s) that make up *makam*. The primary unit that makes up any given interval is a microtonal *koma*. A *koma* is essentially one of nine divided parts between two consecutive whole tones. Many Turkish music theorists tend to argue that the Turkish *koma* is itself the Pythagorian comma (cf. Arel 1952, Ezgi 1953, Özkan 1984, Öztuna 1990, Yektâ 1922). Readers new to *makam* in Turkish classical and art musics specifically will notice the unique Turkish accidentals developed throughout the twentieth century to designate *koma* microtonal intervals with flats (*bemol*-s) and sharps (*diyez*-s) (Table C.1).

Any given *makam* is therefore a collection of *koma* that, combined together in particular arrangements (of trichords, tetrachords, and pentachords), have specific idiomatic melodic contours and patterns (*seyir*-s) as well as particular directionalities (descending, ascending). Musicians require a deep knowledge of *makam* to improvise (*taksim etmek*) and understand idiosyncratic microtonal inflections—themselves often learned in a master-apprentice system—that standard Turkish notation practices cannot fully represent. *Makam* should thus be understood as a complicated set of rules that govern pre-composed improvisational forms, including intra-*makam* or multi-*makam* modulations.

However, readers should know that there are many microtonal systems in operation in Turkey today; for example, Turkish folk *makam* systems differ vastly from the multiple microtonal systems used by Turkish classical musicians. In contemporary practices of Turkish classical music, *aralık*-s and *koma*-s may have different usages based on a given musician's educational background, aesthetic preferences, and performance practices. Furthermore, intonations of intervals may differ substantially—even when performed by the same musician—on the basis of the social context of performance (concert

Table C.1 STANDARD TURKISH NOTATION OF FLAT (*BEMOL*) AND SHARP (*DIYEZ*) SYMBOLS ACCORDING TO *KOMA* INTERVALS

Number of *koma* in the interval	Flats	Sharps
1	ᵈ	‡
4	♭	♯
5	♭	‡
8	♭	♯
9	♭♭	x

hall, religious ritual, radio performance, entertainment venue, recording studio, intimate music gathering) and when one is playing or singing as a soloist, as opposed to performing as a member of an instrumental orchestra or singing within a chorus. For English-language sources on Turkish classical and art music *makam* systems in theory and in practice, see M. Aydemir 2010 (translation by Erman Dirikcan), Beken and Signell 2006, Bozkurt et al. 2009, Ederer 2015, Signell 1997, Stubbs 1994, and Wright 1990.

In my transcribed music examples of compositions, I additionally notate the rhythmic mode (*usul* or *usûl*) utilized in the piece. I indicate the basic beats of a given *usul* in the top left corner above my notated musical examples. Within parentheses, I transcribe the basic form of the named *usul* by marking lower pitched beats (*düm*) with stems down and higher pitched beats (*tek*) with stems up.

Additional transcriptions of the pieces offered in this book can be accessed online, either through the national archives for Turkish Radio and Television (TRT) at http://www.trtnotaarsivi.com/ or at http://www.neyzen.com. I have chosen to focus most of my musical examples on well-known pieces, and encourage readers to do internet wandering on various music sites to find alternative versions and live performances of the works I write about. I additionally supply a suggested discography at the end of the book to help readers shape their ears to the sounds of Turkish classical music by some of its greatest artisans.

ACKNOWLEDGMENTS

Writing this book has been a long process that incurred many debts to consultants, teachers, guides, and institutions. I completed a draft while in residence at the Center for the Humanities at my home institution, Washington University in St. Louis. Internal and external readers were brought to campus to read my manuscript and offer constructive criticism to me as the Center for the Humanities' First Book Fellow. The workshop that was held at the Center for the Humanities in December 2015 was one of the most profound and humbling moments in my scholarly career; thoughtful changes were suggested by my readers, Center for the Humanities director Jean Allman, external readers Judith Becker and John Morgan O'Connell, and internal readers Nancy Reynolds and Patrick Burke. I am particularly grateful to John Morgan O'Connell for unreservedly sharing his extensive knowledge with me, and whose monumental works on *alaturka* and on loss have deeply informed this project. The faculty in my home Department of Music has supported this project in all of its parts, and I am especially thankful for the careful attention to my work given by Pat Burke, Dolores Pesce, Alexander Stefaniak, Todd Decker, Paul Steinbeck, Ben Duane, Craig Monson, and our former chair Peter Schmelz.

In recasting this book, I was supported by an ACLS Fellowship from the American Council of Learned Societies. I am deeply grateful to ACLS and to the competitive leave funding provided by Washington University in St. Louis, which gave me the time away from teaching needed to complete this book. Preliminary ethnographic fieldwork for this project was supported by the American Research Institute in Turkey (ARIT, 2005) as well as Fulbright IIE Fellowships (2007–2008, 2008–2009). The manuscript additionally received a publication subvention from the AMS 75 PAYS Endowment. I thank these institutions for their support of this project.

I was fortunate to do the doctoral work on which this book is based at the University of California at Santa Barbara; the Music and Feminist Studies departments were both stimulating environments that supported my early thinking. In particular, I thank the members of my dissertation committee:

co-chair Scott Marcus, co-chair Barbara Tomlinson, Timothy Cooley, and Sonia Tamar Seeman. John Hajda, Stefanie Tcharos, Eileen Boris, and Laurie Oaks also shared their support and wisdom. My final year of dissertation writing was completed at the College of William & Mary while I served as a visiting instructor of ethnomusicology. I especially thank Anne Rasmussen, Gül Özyeğin, and Sibel Zandi-Sayek for their encouragement, feedback, and friendship. I finally thank Donna Buchanan, my advisor from my undergraduate work at the University of Illinois at Urbana-Champaign, for her mentorship of my scholarly trajectory from the beginning.

This book has been made possible only by the generosity and graciousness of dozens of Turkish classical musicians who willingly shared their time, ideas, sounds, beliefs, and spaces with me. I am particularly grateful to the following professional ensembles for allowing me to work with their members and attend their rehearsals: Cumhurbaşkanlığı Klasik Türk Müziği Korosu, İstanbul Devlet Türk Müziği Araştırma ve Uygulama Topluluğu, Konya Türk Tasavvuf Müziği Topluluğu, and Ankara Devlet Klasik Türk Müziği Korosu. I also wish to thank the helpful individuals who supported my work in the libraries and archives I visited in Turkey. I am especially grateful to the staff at the Istanbul University Library (Istanbul), the Atatürk Library (Istanbul), the Turkish Radio and Television Archives (Istanbul), and the National (Milli) Library (Ankara).

My deepest gratitude goes to my master-teachers who generously shared their time and brought me into their lives. Necati Çelik dedicated countless hours to teaching me, performing with me, and sharing his life with me. I care for and respect him more than he will ever know. Necati Hoca's wife, Ayşe Çelik, is like a second mother, and I am deeply grateful for her hospitality, attention, love, and wisdom. As my primary *kanun* teachers, Celaleddin Aksoy and the late Halil Karaduman served as immensely helpful teachers and guides.

I would like to additionally thank the following master musicians who also kindly mentored me personally and professionally: Memduh Cumhur, Aylin Şengün Taşçı, Melihat and Necip Gülses, the late beloved Ünal Ensari, and the late beloved Selma Sağbaş. I hope this project brings visibility to some of the rhizomatic musical meanings that these exceptional musicians hold dear, even as it fails to communicate the full richness of the emotional terrain of their musicking.

Many other individuals in Turkey—musicians, academics, and friends—shared their ideas and helped me in various ways during the course of ethnographic fieldwork. I would like to especially thank Muharrem Aktuğlu, Meral Altan, Halil Altınköprü, Oytun Aren, H. Nur Artıran, Dilaver Aydın, Dr. Savaş Barkçın, Burcu Baysal, Mustafa Bekmez, Dr. Şefika Şehvar Beşiroğlu, Hasan Çalkan, Sıtkı Çalkan, Celaleddin and Selcen Çelik and family, Esra Çelik, Dr. Timuçin Çevikoğlu, Mustafa Copçuoğlu and family, İbrahim and Emine Ersoy and family, the late Melek Fersan, Enise Gümüşoğlu, Selçuk and Senem

Gürez, Dr. Songül Karahasanoğlu, Gözde Kırgız, İpek Metz, İpek Orhon, Abdurrahim Öztürk, Alper and İrem Peker, Niyazi Sayın, Jale Şengün, Ahmet Taçoğlu, Yasemin and Salih Tahir and family, Dr. Murat Salim Tokaç, Tuncay Tuncay, Necdet Yaşar, Cem and Burçin Yılmaz, Şifa Yılmaz, and the entire Yücebıyık family.

Fatma Erdebir deserves special thanks: she has been a sister and close companion while I was doing fieldwork and living in Istanbul. My extended family in Turkey entered my life during final stages of this book's completion: I especially thank S. Mehmet and Gülseven Moralı, Hatice Kaya, Gülüm Moralı Ertan and Ali Uğur Ertan, and Hüseyin and Piraye Ertan for their love and support of my research.

Early ideas informing this book were presented in several academic conferences, and I am especially thankful to the following panelists with whom I exchanged my work: Shalini Ayyagari, Judith Becker, Harris Berger, Jonathan Glasser, Max Katz, Dard Neuman, Tony Perman, Anne Rasmussen, and Christina Sunardi. I thank Tony in particular for being a wonderful sounding board and sharing his ideas and approaches to the study of music and emotion. I am grateful to a number of additional academics, friends, and guides who have continued conversations about the project and inspired me, especially Christine Abbott, Maggie Adams, Hulda Alarcon, Ozan Aksoy, Theresa Allison, Joe Alpar, Nicole Aldrich, Duygu Altuntaş, David Anderson, Angie Archer, Christine Armistead, Kara Attrep, Kristin Aylesworth, James Armstrong, Jamie Bartlett, Daniel Barolsky, Carol Clark Boyer, Josh Brown, Zeynep Bulut, Jason Busniewski, Revell Carr, Emily Chamlee-Wright, Shefali Chandra, Amy Cimini, Judah Cohen, David Coll, Beth Currans, Amy Cyr, Kim Daniels, Sonja Darlington, Ann Davies, Richard Deja, Lamis Diab, Beth Dougherty, Sonja Downing, Eric Ederer, Kate and Bill Engler, Jaleh Fazelian, Caroline Finkel, Andrea Fishman, Jennifer Fraser, Paul French, Lily Frierson, Stuart Folse, Dave Fossum, Jason Gabriel, Jennifer Gartley, Angela Glaros, Jim Grippo, Denver and the late beloved Ida Hamman, Paul Hahn, Eduardo Herrera, Christine Hicks, Jon Hollis, Lavina Jadhwani, Michael and Ayşe Kilfoy, Katrina Kimport, Stephanie Kirk, Deborah Kapchan, Alex Kregor, Tanya Lee, William Lenihan, Charlie Lockwood, Ralph Lowi, Rohina Malik, Ian MacMillen, Debra Majeed, Irene Markoff, Joseph Martorano, Alyssa Mathias, Anthony McCann, David (Davy) McDonald, Anne-Marie McManus, Tanya Merchant, Terry Meyers, Deidre Moore, Craig Morphis, Katherine Meizel, Timothy Moore, Ruth Mueller, Philip Murphy, Pat Orf, Bahram Osqueezadeh, Michael O'Toole, Wendell Patterson, Marc Perlman, Deniz Peters, Melanie Pinkert, Tess Popper, Öykü Potuoğlu-Cook, Andre de Quadros, Megan Rancier, Susan Rice, Elizabeth Rosner, Ann Rothery, Kendra Salois, Roger Savage, Justin Scarimbolo, Gibb Schreffler, Jessica Schwartz, Aisha Shaheen, Zoe Sherinian, Rohan Shirali, Brad Short, Tes Slominski, Robert Snarrenberg, Roy Spicer, Yona Stamatis, Chris Stark, Linda Sturtz, Jane Sugarman, Nasir Syed,

Barbara Taylor, Christopher Trapani, Ioannis Tsekouras, Takahiro Yamaguchi, Sherrie Tucker, Hayrettin and Mukadder Yücesoy, Rachel Vandagriff, Robert Wallace, Sarah Watkins, the late beloved Peter Weismiller, Dave Wilson, Jeff Wirtz, Rick Worth, and Judith Zwelling.

Massaging my text into a finished book was a collective effort. I thank my editor, Suzanne Ryan, for her focused feedback and gift of time. I am grateful to my research assistant and colleague at Washington University in St. Louis, Kelsey A. K. Klotz, who dedicated hours to formatting my transcriptions for publication and generously supplied me with her cheerfulness and cookies. Jamie Kim has been a kind and tireless editorial assistant. Copyeditor Leslie Safford graced this text with her masterful edits. Alphonsa James followed this book through to production with precision and attentiveness. I am also grateful to the two anonymous reviewers for Oxford University Press, who provided excellent feedback to help sharpen my arguments. Needless to say, any shortcomings or errors in this book remain entirely my own.

I thank those close friends who remind me of aspects in life beyond writing, especially George Blake, Dr. B., Pamella and Mark Henson, Farrokh Shehrbano Namazi, Anne R., BT, Kathryn Weber, Jasmine Weiss, and Mary and Jim Wertsch. My dearest friends Marisa Bass and Lillie Gordon read portions of this manuscript and continuously supplied me with encouragement and support. I further benefit from a tightly bound extended family network, and thank my many cousins (especially Rita for a timely visit to St. Louis), aunts and uncles (especially Val and Chuck, Ty and Deanna, Mary Beth and Joe, Judy, Rita and Garrett, and Clayton) and my beloved grandmother Jeannette Dainko for their love and foundational care.

My numerous siblings deserve special thanks. Matthias constantly models how to work for justice; he and Heydi are the first I turn to for advice. Idania Alvarez is my cherished sister who teaches me strength and how to persevere with elegance. Nephews Kai, Max, Harlan, and Lincoln keep me laughing and curious about the world. Dr. Pete has extended his smile, kindness, and goodness to me in challenging times more than he knows. John and Cara help remind me to play, smile, travel, and keep it light. Andrew D. Gill, my colleague in academia, has truly been my peer: I am eternally grateful for the moments when we share what is in our hearts. Luke E. teaches, by example, the importance of silence and sacrifice: may he always know his immeasurable value and see his gifts. Grace has lightened the hardships of writing a book with her storytelling, jokes, and infectious laughter.

My beloved husband, E. Mehmet Moralı, came into my life in the last years the book came into fruition—I thank him for his devotion, hard work, selfless love, and encouragement. I save my final appreciation for my parents, Douglas A. and Jane D. Gill, for giving me unconditional support over the years of pursuing this research. I have benefitted from their work ethic, optimism, love, and integrity more than I can adequately express here. I dedicate this book to them.

Melancholic Modalities

Introduction

Allah derdini arttırsın.
May God increase your pain.   *what?*

I first heard these words spoken in 2007 while I was doing ethnographic fieldwork in Istanbul, Turkey. I watched as my friend smiled and embraced his music teacher after his teacher voiced this expression. It was, at the time, a jarring scene, punctuated by an expression that—in my first hearing of it—I believed to be wholly incongruous to the moment of intimacy to which I was witness. Why would a teacher wish grievances upon his student?

Today, I can no longer recall the embodied and cognitive impact of my first hearing of the expression, which may be said in parting: "may God increase your suffering." Yet I have found myself returning to the expression over the decade of fieldwork and ethnographic writing that have produced this book, because it helps me call attention to the work of translation. Translation— the labor of listening, reading, sounding, and writing across difference—can itself be painful. Acts of translation are processes of making legible a different symbolic order, moving across and between disparate dimensions of language, habitus, religion, and experience in the elusive search for mutual understanding. This book engenders many translations: from Turkish and Ottoman to English, from contexts informed by Islamic philosophies to those of secular normativity and academic analysis, from linear conceptions of history to understanding multiple rhizomatic iterations of the past, from musical material of diverse microtonal melodic and rhythmic modes to the representational mode of western standard notation, and from epistemological frameworks of music as an affective object or mood toward a new method of rhizomatic analyses of sonic, affective practices. One of the most poignant acts of transfer that surfaces throughout this book is my analysis of Turkish classical musicians' distinctive sonic practices of *hüzün, kara sevda, melankoli,* and *keder,* the key Ottoman-Turkish words that translate to the singular, bumbling, and messy label "melancholy." Translation is perilous work.

"May God increase your pain" requires an engagement with rhizomatic listening, interpretation, analysis, and writing, an approach I develop through this book. Unlike the metaphor of the tree—which implies a solid vertical and unidirectional origin—the rhizome, a botanical root, confounds any search for linearity, sprouting multiple shoots and offering numerous entry and exit points (Figure I.1). It is poetically appropriate to engage rhizomatic analysis in considering Turkish classical music: the reeds (*kamış*-s) that are cut from the wet reed beds of eastern Anatolia and turned into the primary instrument of Turkish classical music, the *ney* (end-blown reed flute), are themselves botanical rhizomes.

Rhizomatic interpretation resists binaries and offers us a way to conceptualize knowledge production in multiple, non-hierarchical lines. If broken at any point, a rhizome will sprout anew along old lines or create new channels. Offering a method of rhizomatic thinking, Deleuze claims that

> [t]he rhizome is reducible neither to the One nor the multiple. . . . It is composed not of units but of dimensions, or rather directions in motion. It has neither beginning nor end, but always a middle from which it grows and which it overspills. (1993: 35–36)

A rhizomatic reading of "may God increase your pain" disavows singular translation. This expression points to the valuing of a particular Islamic selfhood—in this case, associated with the Mevlevi Sufi order—while it also

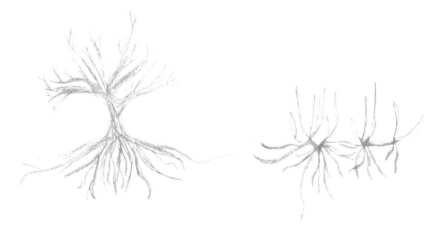

Figure I.1 The tree metaphor versus the rhizome metaphor (illustration by the author).

surfaces in a contemporary Turkish public sphere rife with a pull toward secular Turkish nationalism, on one hand, and political Islamism and neoliberal processes on the other. Voicing this expression elucidates the celebration of, and mourning for, an idyllic Ottoman past while simultaneously acknowledging that past as an impossible point of return. Hearing this expression highlights the intimacy of a dyadic master-apprentice relationship, in which years of hardship and loyalty are required payment for musical mastery and philosophical depth of self. "May God increase your suffering" points us towards an ontological modality that celebrates pain as important, life-affirming, community-giving, and ultimately pleasurable. This expression is a middle ground and hails us into a space where labor, memory and history, and artistic practice flood into a central plateau of affect shared, circulated, and practiced by musicians.

Pain has pleasure for Turkish classical musicians because pain demands that we attend to our embodied existence as human beings. In wishing that God increase your pain, musicians reference a discourse celebrating pain in Sufism; pain reminds individuals of their separation from and mutual need for God. This valuing of pain embedded in the realm of the sacred manifests in Turkish classical musicians' discourses and practices more generally.

The expression "may God increase your pain" helps me call attention to the impossible erasures and precarious excesses this book contains. Rather than treating "Turkish classical musicians" or "Turkish classical music" as sets of subjects for analysis, I concern myself far more with cultivating new ways of listening to and thinking together with the musicians who collaborated with me on this project. The ideas I present here are never completely mine: they are compiled from a chorus of voices and shared experiences, shaped—or twisted—into this book through my hands and ears, both uneasy sites of conformity.

I do remember the first time that a musician wished me "may God increase your suffering." I was packing up my things and about to take my leave from an interview. My consultant and guide, having passionately engaged me in debate about Turkish musical histories, had correctly guessed that I was familiar with the expression. I smiled and immediately voiced gratitude.

Yet my experience does not authenticate me. I am implicated everywhere in this text even though my intention is to amplify the thoughts, performances, and feeling practices of the musicians with whom I work. These musicians are both like me and unlike me in ways that may not always be clear to myself or to you, my readers. While I resist speaking for others, I do speak about them, and grapple with the complications that arise as I frame their voices and sounds in a text of my own creation. I continue to listen, interpret, and write, knowing that there are traces of alternative hearings and other sounds. I am responsible for how I have translated and compiled these sounds, conversations, expressions, and stories. You have infinite ways to read, apply, resist, and experience them. *Allah derdini arttırsın*: "may God increase your pain."

This book is an ethnography of Turkish classical music making in the early twenty-first century, with a focus directly on musicians themselves. I interrogate the work that various melancholies do for musicians, and I trace how musicians' melancholic modalities uncover new insights about Turkish classical musical meanings and Islamic spiritual practices. The term *melancholic modalities* is my way of identifying a constellation of affective practices engaged by Turkish classical musicians in which various iterations of melancholies are performed and experienced as deeply pleasurable, pious, and reparative. Musicking melancholy, I argue, is a practice that creates a form of sociality for musicians, acts as a mechanism for differentiation and boundary marking, and potentially heals. I investigate broader issues in Sufi and Sunni Islamic thought, examining the consequences of a particular sonic, artistic application of the concept that suffering brings believers closer to God in present-day neoliberal Turkey. I examine, rhizomatically, different sonic and social surfacings of melancholy to illustrate its complexity—in healing, in gender and class differentiation, in marking Ottoman from Turkish, in the formation of the fields of musical meaning, and in the constitution of individual and communal selfhood in musical lineages. I tell stories, and share moments of deep music making, to elucidate how melancholies are brought to bear as a method of sociality. I study how suffering and loss—voiced, narrated, sounded and resounding—rhizomatically create and organize communities of musicians, giving them senses of purpose and anchoring their philosophies of sound.

This book also offers an approach to understanding affective practice in music and the performing arts by using rhizomatic analysis. *Melancholy* and *Turkish classical musicians* are the specific terrains from which I project a rhizomatic methodological framework linking ethnography, analysis, and theory. I deploy rhizomatic analysis throughout the book in multiple case studies, in my theoretical structure, in the diverse scholarly landscapes in which I locate myself, in moments of music making, and in the structure of the chapters themselves. I believe that rhizomatic analysis is the only way to understand melancholy in Turkish classical musicians' sonic and social lives, because there is no single origin point from where musicians cultivate melancholies in sound. I move through different levels of examples—from the polyvocality of a single sound; to the work of tears; to horizontal imaginings of musical genealogies; to sites such as tea houses, music therapy hospitals, and musicians' studios or ateliers; to modes of historical memory and commemoration. Through the rhizomatic tropes offered by musicians' own sense experiences of melancholies, I bring a specific rhizomatic approach to the center of debates about affect, emotion, and feeling in ethnomusicology and music's sub-disciplines more generally.

The rhizome is more than a metaphor: it is the method I utilize to most honestly uncover how melancholies constitute, in nonlinear fashion, communities of musicians. Rhizomatic analysis allows me to uncover Turkish classical musicians' melancholic *modalities*. Most literature on Turkish musics—regardless of genre—tends to reify particular essentialisms to interrogate musical meanings, relying on archetypal binaries central not only in Middle Eastern scholarship but also in the discourses of musicians themselves (eastern versus western, Islamism versus secularism, Ottoman versus Turkish). In focusing on affect, however, these bifurcations and the usefulness of national belonging as a primary category of understanding fall away. The consultants who fill these pages are smart, strategic, passionate, and kind individuals who, while courteous to other musicians with different political options, cannot be easily placed into a category of "Islamist" or "secularist." Musicians have diverse social relations—unfixed collages of networks—that organize their musical community of individuals who possess conflicting political opinions and civic engagements.

I found that beyond a career in and love for Turkish classical music, the primary binding agent of this community is the way its members practice affect. I locate musicians' multiple melancholies in the process of musicking: people's active, lived, embodied, transient experience of music making (Small 1998). Melancholic modalities, as a term, describes the collection of unique affective practices through which musicians understand and experience their lives, meaning, and social world. Musicians' melancholic modalities are deeply rooted in Sunni Islamic devotional practices and deployed in resistance to political polarities in present-day Turkish public life, and comprehensively serve as a form of self-fashioning that connects individuals to one another. The melancholic modalities cultivated by Turkish classical musicians are not necessarily painful: descriptions of ecstasy, joy, and elation accompany philosophical articulations of separation and suffering. My aim is to understand the kinds of social politics that enable contemporary Turkish classical musicians to generate particular affective practices, and to explore how ideas and expressions of pain, sadness, and loss are experienced by them as deeply gratifying.

"Modality" indicates the dynamic space in which melancholy is practiced, while the term simultaneously points to musical structures, "mode" (in Turkish, *makam* for melodic mode and *usûl* for rhythmic mode), within which Turkish musicians compose and improvise sonic material in process. Interrogating the divergent and mobile patterns of affective practice as a kind of becoming, I argue that the voicing of melancholic modalities through music and discourse emerges as a primary strategy through which Turkish classical musicians constitute and understand themselves and their agency in their social, cultural, and spiritual worlds. The internal chapters of the book unfold unique iterations of melancholic modalities as social identity, as a method of memorialization, as spiritual labor, as pedagogy, as embodiment, and as a

music to understand and express themselves

process of reparation and healing. My focus on melancholic modalities illustrates the sociality of melancholy: the way melancholy surfaces to make individuals feel together as a group.

When we place melancholic modalities in the center of our studies of musicians, we learn more about affect as well. Rhizomatic analysis is also a critical mode for understanding musicians' music making and explicit articulation of feeling and emotion as a mindful *affective practice*. As I explain later, the literature on affect, emotion, mood, and feeling in music has tended to reify the music object: we assume object-oriented affect, or that music produces emotion, or that music creates a mood. Focusing on musicking melancholy as affective practice means that asking "does music elicit emotion?" or "does music express emotion?" are wrong questions. These frameworks and sonicist approaches, which would give "music" agency to create or produce, do not map onto what I witnessed in Turkey. Turkish classical musicians are precisely articulate about how musical transmission is the central site in which a student is trained in manners (*edep*), morals (*ahlak*), and the appropriate ways of feeling (*duymak*) and transmitting feeling in sound. In other words, in the context of learning music itself, students are shaped to learn how to feel and express that feeling in musical performance. The rhizomatic analysis I present here serves as an intervention into music studies on affect/feeling/emotion, as I offer a new method for ethnographers studying affect in musical communities.

Affect is not something one has; rather, it is an embodied process that one *practices*. In this introduction, I practice rhizomatic analysis in leading you through the primary tricky, interconnected elements that tell a story of present-day Turkish classical musicians and their affective practices that make up melancholic modalities. Rhizomes are unfixed, often unmoored, and seizing hold of one of these elements immediately can lead you to a knotted nexus of another rhizome under the surface. Our first rhizome is the viscous, invented tradition of Turkish classical music itself, a music canon crafted in the beginnings of the Turkish nation-state and contested and reinvented ever since. Our second rhizome is the archive of melancholies that inform this book. Turkish musicians who speak about melancholy know as much about Freud's assumptions that melancholy is about repression as they do about Islamic philosophers' beliefs that melancholy is a way to practice religious piety through experiencing suffering. Our third rhizome attends to the rich academic landscape of affect theory and music studies of affect/emotion/feeling, as I demonstrate why a focus on affective practice is the most appropriate and necessary approach to understanding Turkish classical musicians' emotional and musical lives. Our final rhizome seeps deeply into the reed bed, illuminating the long-standing, sticky aspects of Islamic belief and spiritual practice that are affixed in musicians' senses of musical meaning. Even the most secular musicians I worked with were devoutly attached to a belief and practice that melancholy brings insights and challenges to lead a better moral, ethical, and more just life. Weeding through winding, crossing, nonlinear rhizomes requires the analytic frame that the rhizome itself provides, and has helped me develop new ears for rhizomatic listening.

RHIZOME ONE: TURKISH CLASSICAL MUSIC

Approach this book with care: I do not claim that Turkish classical music is melancholic. I refute the possibility of locating melancholy or Turkish classical music solely as objects of analysis. Diverse iterations and experiences of Turkish terms (specifically, *hüzün, keder, melankoli,* and *kara sevda*) resist being flattened into a single term or object named "melancholy." Rather, musicians' active music making, affective practices, and discourses about musical and emotional meaning take center stage in this book.

To hear Turkish classical music as "melancholic" would simply be incorrect, as musicians locate entire emotional spectrums in musical meaning, most notably joy, sorrow, happiness, elation, ecstasy, cheer, and hope. I approach melancholy as an *affective practice* that musicians engage that informs the social, political, and spiritual value of their musicking. Second, hearing Turkish classical music as "melancholic" would not make sense for a large portion of the musical canon named "Turkish classical music" by musicians and audiences in modern Turkey; these pieces are fast paced and rhythmic, often in dance forms. Arguing that there is only one primary affect that surfaces in this music genre is simply not an accurate description of the musical meaning ascribed by musicians or audiences. Finally, to hear Turkish classical music as "melancholic" would further an orientalist ideology that positions Turks as sentimental, emotional "others" as well as (from an orientalist perspective) regional and religious others. As Edward Said reminds us, "the East" is a fundamentally European invention that renders the Orient as "a place [far away, over there], [with] exotic beings, haunting memories and landscapes, [and] remarkable experiences" (2003: 1).

Marking some Turkish cultural practices as sentimental excess and antithetical to authoritative ideas of Turkish citizenship is not only a product of western orientalist discourses, scholarship, and imaginaries: it was also produced in the early Republican era after the founding of the Turkish nation-state. In his studies of "eastern" style of Turkish musics called *alaturka* (from the Italian *alla turca,* "in the Turkish style")—a styling that was eventually subsumed into the naming of the genre "Turkish classical music"—John Morgan O'Connell details the debates about musical aesthetics during the monumental political shift from the Ottoman Empire (1299–1922) to the Republic of Turkey after its founding in 1923 (O'Connell 1996 and 2013). During the formative years of the new nation-state, negotiations about musical style reflected ongoing political debates about citizenry, nation, and belonging. Music was directly implicated in these debates, as the founder of the Turkish Republic, Mustafa Kemal Atatürk (1881–1938), and his ideologues framed Ottoman court and Mevlevi musics as decrepit reminders of an archaic imperial past, while western-influenced musics (*alafranga*) represented "civilized" and "modern" articulations of Turkishness as an antidote to outmoded Ottomanness. The following decades required Turkish musicians to craft what composer Adnan Saygun described as "a new art for a new society [*yeni sosyete, yeni sanat*]" (Saygun 1965: 45).

The genre "Turkish classical music," crafted through harsh nation-state institutional changes and reforms of the twentieth century, is itself an invented tradition. What is currently named *Klasik Türk musikisi* ("classical Turkish music") is a unique splattering of diverse repertoires including instrumental and vocal works patronized by and heard in the Ottoman court, beginning in the fourteenth century, repertoires of Mevlevi and other Sufi orders, and late-nineteenth and twentieth century light art (*sa'nat* or *sanat*) pieces heard in urban and nightclub (*gazino*) settings. Turkish classical music generally features the voice (often in chorus) and instruments important in Ottoman court music, such as the *ney* (end-blown reed flute with deep associations to the Mevlevi Sufi order), the *tanbur* (long-necked plucked lute), and the *kudüm* (double kettle drum played with mallets). It also includes instruments that gained popularity in urban entertainment environments in the late Ottoman period, such as the *ud* (short-necked plucked lute), the *kanun* (trapezoidal zither played with finger picks), and, by the twentieth century, the *kemençe* (short bowed fiddle played vertically on the knee). Generally heterophonic and based in melodic modes (*makam*) and rhythmic modes (*usûl*), the genre of Turkish classical music denotes a canon—fabricated and shaped by Republican ideologies of the early Turkish nation-state—that continues Ottoman musical practices for instrumental improvisation (*taksim*). The political ruptures that shaped and codified Turkish classical music as a genre are explored throughout this book's internal chapters.

For many audiences in present-day Turkey, the genre of Turkish classical music represents an archaic past that does not give voice to the modernist, civilizing politics of the nation-state's founder, Mustafa Kemal (Atatürk). Yet for other listeners, the genre represents the nation-state itself, as Turkish classical music's primary patronage today lies in state-sponsored television and radio programs (TRT, Turkish Radio and Television) or in state ensembles' live performances, which attract few audience members. For these listeners, the only lifeline supporting these artists and the genre is the nation-state; the music would have died off long ago without live performances funded by the Republic of Turkey and positioned as a kind of historical sonic archive. For still other listeners, the genre of Turkish classical music represents the glory of an archaic Ottoman past, in which music was composed, improvised, performed, and

(margin note, left:) what is associated with Turkish classical music

(margin note, left:) nationalistic

patronized as great art. Finally, for another group of listeners, Turkish classical music represents a sonic materialization of Islamic practice, as foundational ethnic and multi-religious composers and performers of the past are reimagined as homogenous representatives of Islamic art, connections heightened by the fact that contemporary Turkish classical music soundscapes are most ubiquitous in television programs and media outlets during the holy Islamic month of Ramazan. All in all, Turkish classical music is a complex genre that engages multiple ideologies of listening entwined with local Islamic and Mevlevi Sufi philosophies, understandings of Turkish modernity, nostalgia and cultural memory, secularization and nationalism, and neoliberalism.

In many interviews, Turkish classical musicians provided an ostinato of statements like "after all, we are a people in love with melancholy [*sonunda hüzüne aşık bir milletiz*]." In such an utterance, melancholy emerges as the narrative practice through which musicians view themselves and their artistic production. Yet these statements also raise questions of genre and uniqueness: (are the melancholic modalities I describe unique to Turkish classical musicians?) Indeed, one could attempt to cut and paste theories of melancholy and affective practice onto other Turkish musics, such as art (*sanat*), folk (*halk*), and religious (*cami* and/or *tekke musikisi*), vernacular genres produced by marginalized communities (Roman, Kurdish, Greek, Armenian, and Jewish), as well as a variety of popular musics. Scholars writing about *arabesk*—a popular urban music developed in Istanbul beginning in the 1970s and associated with working-class urban migrants from Turkey's southeastern communities—have examined *arabesk* lyrics, musical signs expressing *yanık*, or "burning," and the intense emotionality, pain, suffering, and loss articulated in the genre itself (Erol 2007, Özbek 2006, Özgür 2006, Stokes 1992). Perhaps melancholy is specifically Turkish (Temelkuran 2016, Pamuk 2004, Akcan 2005)? Or perhaps melancholy is something that is cultivated by all Turkish musicians? I suggest we ask different kinds of questions.

Rather than treating the melancholic modalities of diverse musical genres and communities of musicians as unified under the rubric of "Turkish," I argue that scholars must attend to the ruptures between diverse musical iterations of melancholy, pain, and suffering in a rhizomatic frame. When Turkish classical musicians claim "we are a people in love with melancholy [*hüzüne aşık bir milletiz*]," and clarify the "we" as national community of Turks or homogeneous cultural Turkishness, these same musicians leveraged *their* understanding of *hüzün* as "correct" over other Turkish perceptions. Ethnography discloses that melancholy surfaces as the practice in which Turkish classical musicians define and separate themselves from other Turkish musicians.

In other words, melancholy is about othering. Naming affect and locating the boundaries of affective practices is dirty work: identities are forged through "structures of feeling" (Williams 1977) that validate particular emotions and expressions as more valued and more valid than others. Subtle

melancholy more valued to Turkish classical musicians

divisions regarding class, geographic location (being İstanbullu, "of Istanbul," over Turkey's other urban or rural areas), race, gender, nationalism, and secularism surface in all of my conversations with musicians about melancholies in Turkish classical music. If one were to claim that melancholic practices are inherent to all Turkish musics, one could accurately do so only by not reifying an essentialized notion of Turkishness. Further ethnographic studies on diverse musicians' affective practices, perhaps even in comparative terms, would enhance our understanding of how Turkish musicians and audiences differentiate and authenticate themselves through sound and emotion.[2]

Previous scholarship on Turkish classical music and musicians has tended to gloss over the emotional or affective qualities of this music as residual Ottoman nostalgia. This perfunctory gesture neither considers the crucial opportunity for analyzing how and why particular pasts are brought in to comment on the politics of the present, nor interrogates how affect is deployed and shared between individuals through artistic, sonic processes. In this book, I make a commitment to focusing on the intricate constellation of meanings that surface in the unique melancholic practices of a particular community: Turkish classical musicians in present-day Turkish urban centers. This book does not offer an exhaustive study of Turkish classical music or of music and affect. It is first and foremost a book about coming to grips with a particular philosophy of how specific communities of musicians experience and celebrate suffering.

RHIZOME TWO: REPERTOIRES OF MELANCHOLIES

Before melancholy was pathologized as a psychological medical condition of the individual after the founding of the Republic of Turkey in 1923, Ottomans employed diverse terminologies, music therapies, and expressive visual and sonic arts that rendered melancholy as a positive, reparative communal experience. In the current era of biomedicine, "melancholy" is an insignificant category, of little interest in the international debates of specialists in fields of cognition, medicine, or psychology. Yet our preferred preoccupations of the present day—especially our understandings of clinical depression, social anxiety disorder, and a host of other named affective disorders and psychological diseases—hide within them histories of thinking and writing about melancholy. Melancholy surfaces throughout most of western European history as a central cultural idea that focused, explained, and organized the way people understood themselves in the medical, social, and epistemological norms of the era.[3]

These centuries-old histories solidified shifting assumptions about melancholy in "the west" around some central themes: melancholy was a result of the four bodily humors being out of balance; melancholic symptoms include fear and sadness without direct cause; melancholy may be associated with genius, creative energy, or intellectual refinement; and finally, melancholy may be linked with the state of idleness and aristocratic or courtly boredom. Themes of melancholy abound in western European court music traditions in songs, musical dramas, and lyric poetry, mingling and influencing people's ideas about economic and social class, leisure, gender, narcissism, genius, love, and lovesickness. During the eighteenth and nineteenth centuries, Ottomans in port cities—especially Istanbul—were exposed to popular western performing arts, and some of these western themes of melancholy in the arts were viewed as having parallels in Ottoman cultural practices as well, especially in poetry. By the late nineteenth century, however, western epistemologies of melancholy shifted from melancholy as a subjective mood with potentially social class origins to the individualized pathology of clinical depression that we largely observe in biomedicine globally today.

Yet not all forms of melancholy are negative, disabling, or depressive. Often, melancholy is discursively constructed as life affirming and construed as productive. In his 1621 multi-volume *Anatomy of Melancholy,* Robert Burton touched on this argument when he wrote "[t]hey get their knowledge by books, I mine by melancholizing" (Burton 1867 [1577]: 22). In his study of melancholy and modernism in literature, Jonathan Flatley argues that melancholy can function "as the very mechanism through which one may be interested in the world" (2008: 1). The melancholic affective practices of Turkish classical musicians I study in this book are ultimately experienced as positive processes, offering spiritual growth and new forms of knowledge (like Burton's "melancholizing," which rendered melancholy as an active process of thinking).

Generally speaking, western philosophical and epistemological trajectories about melancholy were made possible in the medieval period because of the circulation of Latin translations of key Greek and Arabic Islamic texts. Derived from the Greek *melan-* (dark or black) and *cholē* (bile), melancholy has been viewed by scholars, doctors, and philosophers of the Middle East and western Europe since the Middle Ages as a humoral imbalance caused by an excess of black blood. The four humors (melancholy, or black bile; choler, or yellow bile; phlegm; and blood) of Hippocratic medicine were both physical and metaphysical manifestations reflecting these communities' neo-platonic understandings of the body, mind, and soul, and the properties of the natural world. The idea that melancholy suggested any condition resulting from an imbalance of black bile is drawn directly from two key scholars of Hippocratic medicine: the widely read Greek physician and philosopher of the Roman Empire, Galen (129–200/ 216), and Ibn Sina (980–1037), a crucial classical Islamic philosopher whose central importance in the west is highlighted by the Latinization of his name (and found in both historical and contemporary scholarship) as "Avicenna." In sum, medicinal and musico-medicinal practices of Europe were made possible

[handwritten margin note: how? if one is in such a depressed state.]

due to the appropriation of Muslim medicinal philosophies and development of shared traditions with the Islamic Middle East.

"Melancholy" nonetheless acquired exceptionally unique and distinctive qualities in the Ottoman Empire, which differ vastly from the trajectories, narratives, and practices developed in "the west."[4] Examining contemporary manifestations of melancholies in diverse artistic and cultural practices offers us a truly rich and unique view of vibrant melancholic practices today. While in chapter 5 I outline the specific contours of melancholies in medicine and music in the Ottoman era through early Turkish nationalism to the present day, I concern myself primarily with the philosophies, experiences, and sonic practices of musicians in Turkey who deploy melancholy as a framework for being in the world. Melancholy today, for the Turkish classical musicians with whom I work, emerges from a nexus of Islamic philosophies; institutionalization practices of secular Turkish nation-state; Ottoman nostalgia; local understandings of health, healing, and self-care; ideas of musical meaning and music making; and trajectories of memory established in the master-apprentice relationship between music teacher and student. Furthermore, an entire archive of lexicons of melancholy provide these contemporary musicians with a vast linguistic toolbox from which to explain, voice, and sound out their distinct experiences of melancholy.

The very diversity of words for melancholy in the Turkish language attests to the variety of affective modalities that Ottoman and Turkish communities have historically employed and continue to feel and name. I engage archeological attention (to use Foucault's terms) in considering the subtle enacting of discourse in the collection of musicians' sounds and narratives.[5] Following important scholarly works that examine the relationship between emotion and language, especially from my own field of ethnomusicology (Gray 2013, Perman 2010, Berger 2009, Meintjes 2004, Turino 1999, Feld 1990), I detangle the words, the social work these words do, and the ontological consequences of these categories that we translate into the singular, flattened word "melancholy." The four most commonly used Turkish words used distinctively by my consultants are *hüzün, keder, melankoli,* and *kara sevda* (Figure I.2).

One of the most visible words denoting melancholy in the contemporary Turkish public realm is the aforementioned Turkish word *hüzün*, a term that has relatively recently been refashioned as a type of culturally situated melancholy specific to urban Turks. In his book *Istanbul: Memories and the City*, Orhan Pamuk explains that for the residents of Istanbul in particular, the ruins of the Ottoman Empire serve as ". . . reminders that the present city is so poor and confused that it can never again dream of rising to its former heights of wealth, power, and culture" (2004: 101). Pamuk sees melancholy as a constituent element of Turkishness; he writes that *hüzün* gives Turks "poetic license to be paralyzed" (2004: 104). While Pamuk is speaking of the general abundance of melancholy in Istanbul that arises from living in and among

melancholy to Turkish peoples

"melancholy"

Hüzün	From the Arabic *ḥuzn* (حزن) meaning sadness, sorrow, grief, and melancholy. As in *hüzünlenmek*: to dwell in *hüzün*.
Keder	Care, grief, and melancholic affliction that occurs as a result of a particular event. As in *keder çekmek*: to "pull" *keder*, to suffer with grief and melancholy.
Melankoli	From the Greek *melancholia* (Μελαγχολία) meaning "black bile," one of the four humors (basic body liquids) of Hippocratic medicine.
Kara Sevda	Literally "black love," a particular state of melancholy that occurs when one cannot unite with the loved object/person. Believed to result in death.

Figure I.2 The four most common Turkish words used by Turkish classical musicians all translate simply to "melancholy" in standard Turkish-English dictionaries.

geographically specific melancholic objects—the architectural ashes of the Ottoman Empire—the Turkish classical musicians I work with understand the practice of melancholy as the correct way to be in the world as social and spiritual beings.

But musicians' melancholies are not practiced outside of the elements of power and subjection. What we feel is inextricable from power; issues of safety and intimacy have long been determined by frameworks of colonialism, imperialism, and nation-making. Building on recent scholarship that elucidates melancholy, sadness, and depression as indicative of the lived experience of neoliberal capitalism (Cvetkovich 2012, Berlant 2011, James 2015), this book expands global debates on melancholy in the context of post-imperialism and postcolonialism (Gilroy 2005, Žižek 2000, Cheng 2000) with research for the particular communities of Turkish classical musicians with whom I work on how melancholy emerges as a pleasurable and spiritually redeeming modality to inhabit.

Instead of focusing exclusively on demarcating where one definition of melancholy ends and another begins, I am more interested in understanding the social, cultural, political, spiritual, and aesthetic work that melancholies do for the musicians who practice melancholy in musicking. After all, *hüzün, keder, melankoli,* and *kara sevda* are untranslatable and do not necessarily overlap onto or fold into one another. In stating these Turkish archives of melancholy are untranslatable, I am not only offering a humble acknowledgement of both the necessary pitfalls of ethnographic experience and of my inability to shift the poetic systems informing these terms into English. Rather, claiming *hüzün, keder, melankoli,* and *kara sevda* are untranslatable is itself a rhizomatic settlement. I believe that what may be lost in this linguistic, philosophical, and cultural transfer can ultimately help me in the task of testifying to the challenge of—and critical urgency for—academic investigation of the slippery terrains that we name and locate as affect, emotion, and feeling.

This book disrupts questions about the relationship between music and affect that prioritize the sonic object and assume its capacity to act. "Music" is not an object with agency that can produce, elicit, or express. Turkish classical musicians themselves are quick to explain that melancholy lies in a person, is practiced in a person's faith ideologies, and surfaces in a person's intimate ways of listening—not in the uncanny or ethereal sounding of a disembodied music object or vibrations of sound.

At the initial utterance of terminology, "feeling"—when rendered in the Turkish language—is already intimately linked to what is sensed, lived, and perceived. The primary word used in Turkish to denote "emotion" (*duygu*) translates as sensation, sentiment, perception (Redhouse 1997: 316). Thus in a Turkish context, the terminology already reflects the claim that emotion has to do with impressions, surfaces, and boundaries. Furthermore, the Turkish verb indicating "to feel" (*duymak*) is the same verb used in the following actions: "to hear, to learn (of), to perceive" (Redhouse: 315). The other Turkish verb in general circulation indicating "to feel" (*hissetmek*) also means "to perceive, to understand, to notice" (Redhouse: 487). At these critical linguistic-cognitive levels where language shapes worldviews, native Turkish speakers engage a perception that "feeling" is embodied in physical touch, in perceiving sound, in experiencing and sharing vibrations with other objects and bodies, in considering the porousness of the body itself, and in cognitive understanding and awareness. The philosophical slipperiness and connectivity between "feeling" and "hearing" and "knowing" (and, by extension, between the objects "affect" and "sound" and "thought") are validated in the very language used to explain it. Turkish language practices could be described, by using arguments from western philosophical epistemologies, as promoting an ontological framework grounded in the assumption that feeling is linked to historical consciousness and intentionality.[6]

Our English-language terms disclose similar ontological assumptions. "Affect" comes from the Latin *affectus*, which implies being acted upon,[7] and "emotion" comes from the Latin *emovere*, which refers to moving and moving out. Both terms, affect and emotion, seem to point to a powerful disembodied force (Brennan 2004) or phantom (Navaro-Yashin 2012) that touches, moves, or acts upon us. These terms recover an idea that we are acted upon ("being affected," "being moved") by "*something* throw[ing] itself together in a moment as an event and a sensation" (Stewart 2007: 1, her emphasis). Yet in contemporary transdisciplinary or interdisciplinary scholarship on affect/emotion—drawing from diverse fields from psychology to neuroscience to cognitive studies to anthropology to philosophy to social sciences to feminist and cultural studies—the terms "affect" and "emotion" are increasingly hard to differentiate and make sense of. Basic approaches to the study of emotion,[8] for example, generally categorize emotional experiences into six (often five or seven) universal primary human emotions (fear, anger, sadness, happiness, surprise, and disgust) and a range of secondary emotions.[9] These academic discourses generally perpetuate assumptions of the autonomous individual, rendered able-bodied and universal. Yet historians and literary scholars have convincingly pointed out that particular societies and historical periods may have unique sets of norms guiding how affect should be expressed collectively (termed "emotionology" by Stearns and Stearns 1985, studied as "emotives" or specific "emotional regimes" by Reddy 2001; see also Harré 1986).

Let me offer an example from Ottoman Turkey to demonstrate these debates. In their historical studies of Ottoman poetry between 1550 and 1622 in what Andrews and Kalpaklı name "the age of the beloveds" (2005: 22), scholars claim that the development of aristocratic court culture in Istanbul, the expansion of Sufi orders throughout the Ottoman ecumene, the explosion of new entertainment houses throughout the empire (especially the *meyhane*), and the consolidation of Ottoman power in southeastern Europe led to new and unique representations in Ottoman poetry. During this era, poets penned verses focusing on the senses (deploying music, sound, food, spices, wine, smells, perfume), times of day (especially nighttime), places (gardens), and intense emotionality (Abacı 2013, Andrews and Kalpaklı 2005, Holbrook 1994). In this particular "emotional regime," if we follow Reddy's terminology (Reddy 2001: xiii and 129), the Ottoman-Turkish term *hicran*—a bittersweet state of loneliness and vulnerability—and extensive poetry describing the suffering of lovers and beloveds reflected and shaped narratives of love and ecstasy circulating in Sufi centers and attached to (homoerotic, mystical) love discourses of the Ottoman court (Andrews 1984). The idea that civic life reflects and shapes what kinds of feelings are meant to be had is generally the topic of focus for scholars promoting social constructivist views of affect.

Social constructionist scholars—often anthropologists—considered situated "feeling rules" (Hochschild 1983) and discourses (Abu-Lughod and Lutz 1990, Lupton 1998) that shape what kinds of feelings, affects, and emotions can be experienced and named in diverse "emotional communities" (Rosenwein 2006) or "affective communities" (Walkerdine 2009 and 2010). The argument here tends to be that emotions and affect *are themselves* social and cultural practices; they are that which binds society or the collective together (Berlant 1998, Marcus 2002, Abu-Lughod and Lutz 1990, Lutz and White 1986, and Rosaldo 1984). Scholars working on affect and emotion from feminist and queer studies perspectives have further identified how dominant social forms and norms work through hegemonic power structures and repetition; it is through repetition that worlds materialize and that boundaries are produced (the most significant works in this trajectory informing my project on melancholy include Muñoz 2000, 2006a, and 2006b; Kristeva 1992 and 2014; Spelman 1998; Spillers 1983 and 1996; Brophy 2002; Cheng 2000;

Gordon 2004).[10] Yet simultaneously, scholars writing from another end of cultural studies argue that affect is *not* discourse, but rather that affect indexes a pre-verbal realm beyond talk, texts, epistemic regimes, and cognition (Clough 2009, Massumi 2002, Sedgwick 2003, Thrift 2004 and 2008). For the musicians in this book, it is often the discursive experience of speaking, performing, and musicking that frequently makes affect powerful and facilitates its practice, circulation, socialization, and embodiment.[11]

I do not preoccupy myself with offering new theoretical models for scrutinizing affect from feeling or emotion. Said differently, I am not interested in locating exactly what melancholy "is," as it is vastly richer to approach melancholy with a rhizomatic analysis, studying instead what melancholy "is *for.*" Asking "what is melancholy for?" means questioning how people use melancholy to help make sense of, understand, explain, and evaluate objects or events in life. I argue that Turkish classical musicians mindfully use melancholy *as a practice* to evaluate and give meaning to their music and sonic productions. I take special care to attend to how the potential ontological qualities of melancholic practice intersect with the fraught political conditions of the everyday (Kandiyoti and Saktanber 2002, Özyürek 2006, Stokes 2010) that render possible Turkish classical musicians' diverse forms of subjectivity.

In my own experiences piecing different theoretical trajectories and assumptions together, I have struggled with the taxonomies and literatures that tend to treat affects, moods, sentiments, and emotions as subsets of one another or as interchangeable. It is not my goal to rewrite these (western) epistemological analyses per se; my intention here is to demonstrate the terms and perspectives that most closely articulate and translate how I witness melancholies working in Turkish classical musicians' lives. In this book, then, I treat "feelings" as sensations pointing to systems of reception, whereas "emotions" are the bodily response to outward signs that gives shape to our sense of "self" as a unique, bound object. I follow Sara Ahmed's insightful study of how objects of emotion—such as some dissected sonic objects (texts, songs, collections or archives, lyrics, recordings, performances)—"involve the transformation of others into objects of feeling" (2004: 11). I argue against a perspective that would psychologize or individualize emotions as something "we have." Rather, emotions differentiate the boundary between the "I" and other objects in our social worlds. Ahmed calls this her model of the "sociality of emotions":

> [I]t is through emotions, or how we respond to objects and others, that surfaces or boundaries are made . . . [T]he surfaces of bodies "surface" as an effect of the impressions left by others. (Ahmed 2004: 10)

Ahmed's work is helpful for understanding how public feelings (such as pain, hate, fear, disgust, shame, and love) circulate (like capital) and accumulate value and intensity for an emotional/affective community. Yet Ahmed's

Social media exacerbates this then

model—rooted in the importance of the bodily boundary and border—focuses on emotion as a disembodied force that circulates in texts, not located in specific social actors or particular bodies. ——— music

I proceed with the argument that musical performances, sonic practices, and cultural products can *appeal* to emotions *without necessarily producing them* in individuals.[12] More accurately, in my people-centered, practice-oriented approach, I am explicitly interested in studying how *particular people* claim that they actively *use* processes of music making, performance, and teaching to make themselves, and potentially their listeners, "feel melancholy." I oscillate between a consideration of how musicians speak about melancholy as a thing that "acts on us" (affect) or "moves us" (emotion) and a sustained focus on how melancholy itself is a *practice* or *process*—something musicians "do" and actively pass on or inculcate in students. Said simply, in deploying the rich, diverse terminology from Turkish into the singular English word "melancholy," Turkish classical musicians already leverage a belief that melancholy is a process and a practice. Melancholy-as-sonic-object is culturally heard, shared, and understood, and can circulate through a variety of texts. Yet melancholy-as-process is a lived sense experience, and that experience is itself dependent on and constructed by social contexts and the ways melancholies are learned, embodied, and *practiced*.

By "affect," I mean the appraisal and cognitive effects of emotion and feeling. Affect is the large-scale way that emotions—as effects of objects pressing upon us and the sensations that pressing produces—are practiced, transferred into value, and assessed by individuals and communities. In other words, affect is the subjective and conscious aspect of feelings and emotions. Affect refers to the multivalent and complex ways that feelings and emotions are produced and generate knowledge. In this constellation of terminology, it is thus possible to theorize "melancholy" as feeling, emotion, and affect while simultaneously accounting for melancholy as an object or a thing that presses upon us and also a process of evaluation by specific people in a particular time and place. Melancholy is thus best understood, as it is deployed and experienced by contemporary Turkish classical musicians, as an affective practice.

My notion of practice is indebted to practice theory work in ethnomusicology that extends Pierre Bourdieu's analyses of practices (1990),[13] Deleuze's conceptions of "becoming" (1993), Deleuze and Guattari's use of rhizomatic analysis (1987 [1980]), and Judith Butler's work on performativity (1988, 2004). The term "affective practice" is also deployed by Margaret Wetherell, who argues that for the study of affect,

[a] practice approach focuses on processes of developmental sedimentation, routines of emotional regulation, relational patterns and "settling." These routinely embed patterns of affective practices as a kind of potential. The individual

[handwritten margin note: Very important paragraph that describes "affect" in the context of this book]

is a site in which multiple sources of activation and information about body states, situations, past experiences, linguistic forms, flowering thoughts, etc. become woven together (2012: 22).

Practice, as both a noun and a verb, can account for the repetition, improvisation, discipline, domestication, inculcation, and coercion that I identify in tracing Turkish classical musicians' melancholic modalities. Considering melancholy as an affective practice allows me to point out musicians' process of "emotional quotation" or "affective citation," which aids in the circulation and reaffirmation of their affective practices through the genre of music they play and transmit (Berlant 2008).

Understanding melancholy as an affective practice enables me to focus on how people deploy and experience melancholy in a way that accounts for what melancholic musicking sounds, feels, and looks like, as opposed to presenting melancholy or music as circulating forces with universal value in and of themselves. Turkish classical musicians' affective practice—like melancholic musicking—recruits material objects, institutions, nostalgic pasts, and anticipated futures as what Raymond Williams calls "structures of feeling" (1977: 134). However, the main things that musicians' affective practices fold or bring together are sound, bodies, historicity, and meaning making. Melancholy as affective practice thus lines up with what Flatley names "affective mapping," or how individuals become the (historical) subjects we are through the structuring of our affective attachments (2008: 4 and 76–84). In the context of Turkish classical musicians' melancholic musicking, processes of embodiment meld with the process of making meaning from the raw materials of conflicting ideas of Turkishness, understandings of the genre Turkish classical music, debates about secularism and Islamisms in the Turkish public realm, and Islamic spiritual discourses about sound, separation, and melancholies.

RHIZOME FOUR: THE ISLAMIC ROOTS OF MUSICIANS' MELANCHOLIC ROUTES

As melancholy is an affective practice, it extends to communities beyond Turkish classical musicians. This book broadens and nuances extensive debates about religion and Islam, both inside and outside of Turkey. Much of the book deals with the ways melancholies are learned in the intimate, dyadic master-student relationship today, and I argue that these foundational relationships are not necessarily repetitions of the (Ottoman) past practice. My work on genealogy in relation to rhizomatic analysis intervenes in literature on the Islamic transmission of religious truths (Ar. *isnad*) and offers a framework for understanding contemporary transmission of religious truths in practice (Starrett 1998, Messick 1993, Mitchell 1991). Saba Mahmood has argued that suffering is a way to produce piety (2005, 2001) In many ways, she has offered a complementary argument to mine: hers about Sunni political Islam in Egypt, mine about Turkey and branches of Sufism, hers about subjectivity, mine about affect. We both share the fundamental observation that in Islamic devotions, Muslims believe that repetitive outward action creates faith, and we argue against assumptions in religious studies that would posit that faith itself produces the drive toward devotional labors. Yet this book poses a challenge to Mahmood's study of the outward performance of piety in its interrogation of the emergence of the very idea of an autonomous individual (*birey*) that surfaced in Turkish political discourse in the mid-twentieth century. Mahmood takes "the subject," individuality, and selfhood as an given—my work elucidates how Turkish classical musicians' practices of piety are fundamentally about rejecting individual iterations of selfhood in preference of fashioning communal identities. This book intervenes with case studies demonstrating how scholarship invested in "the subject" contain secular assumptions about human action. Listening to, playing, singing, or otherwise engaging Turkish classical music is a practice that allows individuals to collective "feel together" as a community and fashion communal identification. While melancholic modalities emerge as a tool to shape inner life, they make inner and outward senses of communal selfhood sonorous. My focus on affective practice, in the complex world of Turkish politics and diverse Islamic practices in Turkish urban centers, demonstrates the deep instrumentality of musicking.

Turkish classical musicians' affective practices challenge defined categories of subject-centered national, modern, secular, and religious categories in Turkey. In extending critical anthropological research on secularism in Turkish public life (J. White 2014, Navaro-Yashin 2002 and 2012, Özyürek 2006), I challenge scholastic trajectories that would treat "religion" in Turkey according to western liberal epistemologies of secularism. Studies of Turkish music often maintain a definitive relationship with the category of the secular, a relationship that implies an understanding of religion as something distinct and separate from other categories such as politics, law, or society (see Kusić 1997). With my focus on musicians, I suggest that scholars take the Islamic roots of melancholy seriously simply because most Turkish classical musicians in the present-day do not understand themselves or musical meaning outside of Islamic frameworks. Musicians often justify their understanding of melancholy or ideology of hearing melancholy in their musicking through recourse to Turkish forms of Sunni Islamic—especially Sufi—philosophies.

Musicians' celebration of melancholy often surfaces as resistance to national forms of Turkish citizenry in which happiness and joy—perceived as melancholy's opposites—were leveraged as the appropriate affects for the newly created Turkish citizen after 1923. Melancholy as *hüzün* emerged in

Collective nostalgia? ritual wailing?

riding the lion?

public speeches made by Mustafa Kemal in his attempt to leverage musical and cultural products in developing a new "modern" and "civilized" Turkish culture. Melancholy was, in Mustafa Kemal's view, indicative of a "morbid" past and "eastern" otherness. In his speech at the Sarayburnu Gazinosu (August 10, 1928), Mustafa Kemal proclaimed that

> [i]n truth, the Turks are essentially joyous [şen] and vivacious [şatır]. If ever this beautiful character were to be altered at any time, it would not be done by them. Melancholy [hüzün] is the result of calamitous events. Not to perceive this difference is intolerable. [. . .] By their nature, Turks are joyous. Because, the [Turkish] spirit does not relish in that state which has so disturbed its memory. The maintenance of this predicament must continue to be a desirous goal. (Atatürk 1961, vol. 1: 252–253; translated and quoted in O'Connell 2013: 59–60)

O'Connell argues that as *alaturka* (and, by extension, what we today name "Turkish classical music") served as a sonic reminder of the tragedies of the imperial past and recent experiences of war; "the melancholic character of the music reflect[ed] the forlorn attitude of the people" and melancholy was rendered "alien to the innate sensibilities of the Turkish people" (O'Connell 2013: 202). Today, particular forms of melancholy are rendered valid in the Turkish public realm after Pamuk's writings on *hüzün*, largely due to his own celebratory status as a Nobel Prize–winning author. But this valuing of some forms of melancholy is an utterly new phenomenon, influenced by the rise of neoliberalism and the influx of Ottoman nostalgia with political Islamism in Turkey since the late 1980s. Contemporary Turkish classical musicians engage this Pamukian embracing of melancholy-as-Turkishness (and specially, being of Istanbul) while they also qualify their valuing of melancholy with Islamic rhetoric and discourse.

In particular, Turkish classical musicians deploy Mevlevi Sufi philosophies that justify individuals' feelings of melancholy as a product of the human condition of separation from God. This articulation of melancholy has a nationalist countermelody, as projects of modernization and secularization have historically displaced Islam and the genre of Turkish classical music in various ways in the Turkish public sphere. In 1925, the 105 Mevlevi lodges within the newly formed Republic's borders were closed, Mevlevi sacred books were burned, practitioners were criminalized, and the practice of the Mevlevi turning ritual (*sema*) went underground. It was not until 1953 that the *sema* was resurrected by the Turkish Ministry of Culture as a "historical artifact" for the explicit purpose of tourism. While practicing Mevlevism is still technically illegal in Turkey, Mevlevi philosophies and ideals—especially those codified in the poetic works of Mevlana Celaleddin Rumi (1207–1273)—are highly central, visible, and normative elements of Turkish public life (see chapter 2).

Out of the seventy-three formal interviews I conducted with Turkish classical musicians for this project, sixty-nine of the musicians turned to Ottoman Sufi authors, poets, or Islamic philosophers to justify and interpret their position to me, and thirty-eight interviewees (with some crossover) turned to references of melancholy in the Qur'an or by reputable Islamic scholars. I routinely documented three references to verses from the Qur'an in these interviews, in which melancholy is presented as ḥuzn (حزن), the Arabic version of the Turkish hüzün (and generally translated in English versions of the Qur'an as "grief" or "sadness," as opposed to "melancholy"). The first verse cited by musicians was about Jacob, father of Joseph (Yusuf) who, when being informed that Joseph had died, is described as such: "his eyes were whitened [with tears] with the sorrow [ḥuzn] that he was suppressing" (Qur'an 12: 84). The second most cited portion of the Qur'an by musicians describes the way melancholy binds an individual to the divine: "praise be to God, who has put grief [ḥuzn] away from us. Surely God is all-forgiving, bountiful" (Qur'an 35:34). The final Qur'anic verse recited by a few of my consultants was interpreted as a description of the afterlife, in which for believers "there will be no fear concerning them, nor will they grieve [ḥuzn]" (2:38). In the readings of the Qur'an by Turkish classical musicians, hüzün emerges as a path to practice piety through the acceptance of melancholy as an innate aspect of living.

Beyond the Qur'an, other Turkish classical musicians referred to Sunni exegesis of the hadith, or statements of the Prophet Muhammed and his companions. The tenth century scholar Abdülkerim el-Kuşeyrî's Risâle and the Müfterat of eleventh century scholar Rağib el-İsfâhani were the texts I witnessed being pulled out of bookshelves the most, as my consultants and I examined passages together. In four different interviews, musicians and I allocated long periods of time to the story of Ebû Osman el-Hirî. One of his followers asked el-Hirî "What is melancholy [hüzün]?"; he replied, "First work on searching for melancholy, then ask [hüznü aramaya çalış, sonra sor]" (see Kuşeyrî 1966: 269). Indeed, my own theoretical preference for interrogating "what is melancholy *for*?" over the question "what is melancholy?" is, in a way, indebted to el-Hirî and my many conversations about him with musicians.

The larger ramifications of the linkage between melancholies, musicking, and Islamic texts and ideologies are explored in this book's internal chapters— for now, let me offer a brief interpretation of the overall feedback that musicians offered while quoting these definitive Islamic texts. Musicians argued that ḥuzn/hüzün—grief, sadness, pain, and melancholy derived from loss—are fundamentally parts of being human. Melancholy is all about loss and separation, and also all about spiritual richness and maturity. Melancholy compels believers to align their innermost selves with God, and makes them pure of heart. Musicians often added a hadith wherein the Prophet Muhammed was reputed to have informed believers that God said, "I am near those with broken hearts." If musicians believe that melancholy brings them closer to God,

what is melancholy for?

then framing their own musicking with melancholic terms ultimately grounds their musical meaning as embodied spiritual practice and as a form of spiritual labor. Thus it makes sense to overhear a teacher tell a student, "May God increase your pain."

FOLLOWING THE RHIZOMES OF *MELANCHOLIC MODALITIES*

As an ethnographer, I suspend my processes of analysis in the processes of listening.[14] Instead of "gazing out" from one fixed perspective, I use a methodology that discloses a commitment to a dialogical meeting of "receiving in" (Soyini Madison 2012 [2005]). I do not present "findings" in this book; rather, I present a way of knowing. What is at stake is an understanding of the constitutive affective practices that Turkish classical musicians undertake to anchor subjectivity, build communities, fashion collective identity, and create boundaries between self and other. This book analyzes socialization and identity construction as processes of learning how to feel and express that feeling in sound. The question "who am I?" is already a question of how one feels, especially in the sense that some feelings should be had and that some affective modalities are understood, articulated, and lived as the right way to inhabit the world. The experience-centered analyses I craft are "true" to the logical constellations of meaning for the individuals with whom I work.

My insistence on evaluating melancholy as affective practice and a modality—in the true sense of modality as a method, way, and process—is not drawn from western theories and scholarship on affect/emotion/feeling. As the initial discussions above about musicians' use of Islamic theologies and discourses may suggest, my ethnographic study of contemporary Turkish classical musicians decenters and provincializes the assumptions, aims, and frameworks of western epistemology. Important western theoretical understandings of affect/emotion/feeling help me translate and explain musicians' melancholic musicking and melancholic affective practices in the linguistic and cultural frameworks available to me as a native English-speaking scholar. Nor do I suggest that Sufi-influenced Islamic philosophy in urban centers of Turkey offers a unique "other" against western theory. Yet western theories and frameworks represent one frame among many diverse and alternative epistemological structures available to people. For the Turkish classical musicians with whom I work, issues of Islamic spirituality, ideas of morality and manners, values drawn from master-apprentice relationships, and Ottoman historicities of melancholy as a reparative mode for healing converge to form an epistemological and ontological process that I name melancholic modalities.

In its ontological and epistemological claims, approach to musicking and affective practice, and careful ethnography of a particular community of musicians in Turkey, this book rhizomatically reorients ethnomusicological studies of musical and cultural practices of emotion and affect. Ethnomusicologists have considered the connections between affect/emotion/feeling and music through ethnographic, reflexive, semiotic, phenomenological, and psychological approaches.[15] I offer a unique study of one affective practice (melancholy) situated in a particular community (Turkish classical musicians) in established locations (Turkish urban centers of Istanbul, Ankara, Izmir, and Konya) to push ethnomusicological investigations of affect/emotion/feeling to a consideration of how particular affective practices are mobilized in iterations of subjectivity (melancholic modalities).[16] As this book offers a singular ethnographic analysis of the embodied, affective practices of Turkish classical musicians, it contributes to the excellent archive of previous scholarship on Turkish music generally[17] and challenges some ingrained assumptions about the relationship between music and affect. In my conclusion, I lay out the specific contributions this book makes to ethnomusicological debates, and outline several points of departure for music scholars who work with sound and emotion and affect theory.

In my writing, I weave ethnographic anecdote with theory and interpretation, offer visual texts and my transcriptions of particular moments of musicking,[18] and pull together the rhizomatic routes of experience that give shape to musicians' melancholic modalities. This book's internal chapters trace the processes wherein melancholy appears as a natural, invisible, and essential affective practice for Turkish classical musicians. The architecture of this book also presents itself as a kind of rhizomatic engagement—the chapters unfold to tell a story but have also been written to read in isolation.[19]

My first chapter brings to life a vast history of institutional reforms, politics, and performances practices that were affected by—and also facilitated— massive political changes from the seventeenth century of the Ottoman Empire to the founding of the Republic of Turkey in 1923 through the various coups in Turkey (1960, 1971, 1981, 1997, and the 2016 failed coup attempt) and in contemporary shifts that Turkish classical musicians experience under privatization and neoliberalism. I argue that one of the most central binding elements of the genre Turkish classical music is a loss narrative that positions the music as "dead" (see also O'Connell 1996).

My second chapter is a foundational section of the book, as I demonstrate the depth to which rhizomatic analysis can be utilized with a single sound and word: Hû. This chapter additionally challenges secular discursive and theoretical frameworks that scholars tend to replicate in analyses of Turkish classical music as I focus on Hû as a case study to demonstrate how we can identify spirituality and melancholies in something as small as a single sound.

In chapter 3, I analyze the pedagogical underpinnings of affective practice and melancholic musicking in the context of oral music transmission (meşk). I argue that as meşk works to recreate a master's sensibility and knowledge

Ch. 1

Ch. 2

vocable!

Ch. 3

anew in the apprentice, master musicians inculcate feeling practices and spiritual discourses alongside music techniques in lessons with students. I observe that students, in turn, validate their experiences of melancholy through religious discourse and the memorializing of their musical lineage (*meşk silsilesi*). In chapter 3 I also introduce my concept of *bi-aurality* as an approach for ethnomusicologists to develop new geographies of listening to musics, and particularly to music genealogies, outside of western epistemological frameworks.

In chapter 4, I ground my claims about musicians' melancholic modalities in a multifaceted study of embodiment in Turkish classical musicking. After an investigation of how musicians describe the sensations of bodily melancholy to explain sonic melancholy, I study the way melancholic affective practices demarcate specific kinds of boundaries: boundaries demarcating gender difference, weeping and tears and elucidating bodily boundaries, and theologies of listening and turning (*sema*) that dwell in the interstitial boundaries between the spiritual and the mundane.

The final chapter of my book maps the way melancholy becomes lived as reparative by musicians today. I outline five centuries of Ottoman musico-medicinal treatises on melancholy as disease and melancholic musics that aided physicians in the task of healing patients suffering from melancholy. This chapter oscillates between melancholy as affective practice and objects of melancholy—specific musical modes (*makam-s*) and the illnesses affecting one of the four bodily humors. I expose how contemporary Turkish classical musicians have resurrected Ottoman notions of the positive effects of melancholy after the medicalization of physiological states in the early years of the Republic. Today, Turkish classical musicians deem melancholy a position to dwell in because it is pleasurable and connects individuals to one another.

Identifying and interrogating one affective particular—"melancholy"—in Turkish classical musicians' historicizing, narrative, sonic, artistic, performative, and transmission processes, I argue that melancholy must be understood as an affective practice. In my conclusion, I offer important departure points for ethnomusicology as we push ahead with the study of music, emotion, feeling, sound, and affective practices.

As I scrutinize aspects of melancholic modalities in multifaceted ways, each chapter interrogates different elements inherent in musicians' melancholic modalities. I analyze melancholic modalities as historicized social identity (chapter 1), as spiritual states (chapter 2), as transmitted pedagogical practices (chapter 3), as embodied in musicking (chapter 4), and as specific objects (such as recordings of instrumental improvisation) as they are related to dis-ease (chapter 5). Turkish classical musicians practice melancholy as a tool in the construction of memory, as the sound of separation from the divine, as a sonic emblem of loss, as embodiment, and as a reparative, healing process. Arising from a constellation of Ottoman nostalgia, secular Turkish nationalism, spiritual labor, and neoliberal market processes, melancholy is an indispensable affective practice for these musicians because it is pleasurable, healing, spiritually redeeming, and it socializes them as a group while grounding them as artists of their own history. And rhizomatic analysis is the only way to understand how Turkish classical musicians' melancholies surface in their affective practices to make them a singular community that plays together, sings together, and feels together.

CHAPTER 1

The Melancholic State of Turkish Classical Music

Çok insan anlıyamaz eski musikimizden
Ve ondan anlamıyan bir şey anlamaz bizden.

Not many people can understand our old music
And those who cannot understand that music
can understand nothing about us.
> —Yahya Kemal Beyatlı (1884–1958)

M y teacher Necati Çelik and I passed the hours waiting to eat *suhur*, the last meal before the fast begins during the holy month of Ramazan, making small talk, and playing *taksim*, or instrumental improvisation.[1] I had been staying with my teacher (*hoca*) and his wife, Ayşe Çelik, for weeks now, and the three of us had settled into days rich with music making, laughing, and storytelling. Though I had been disappearing during the day to do interviews and work with other musicians, Necati Hoca had not yet asked me about the research component of my trip.

"So, *kızım* [my daughter], you are writing a book?" he asked, lighting his pipe in the balcony. "You know my dream was that you found a Turkish music school in the USA and perform our music, not occupy yourself with words." He paused, taking some drags from his pipe, before launching into his narrative on music as a language, a concept he had shared with me many times.

"God gave humans a very special gift. You know that birds, whales, and wolves speak like humans speak. But the gift of music was only given to particular people—it is the highest ability God can bestow on a *kul* [servant]. This is why the Greeks named it as 'music,' the language of the *peri* [lit., "fairy" or muses]. Why write a book when you can speak without words?"

Ayşe Abla[2] joined us on the balcony, bringing slices of fresh watermelon and a pile of red grapes. Theirs was a relationship of gender complementarity; separate tasks, separate responsibilities, separate domains. I was accepted wholeheartedly by Necati Hoca before I met his wife, Ayşe Çelik (Figure 1.1); however, my status as permanently welcomed guest and figurative "daughter" was largely because she generously reciprocated my affection. While she defers to her husband, Ayşe Abla is a fierce, perceptive, and strong woman whose sharp command of the politics of socializing in the Turkish classical music world was matched only by her talent as a chef. Ayşe Abla's care and domestic labors, themselves situated in a patriarchal marriage structure, decisively supported Necati Hoca's abilities to dedicate time to his many students, including me. I enjoyed every minute with the two of them, and while I call only Necati Çelik *Hocam* [my teacher], I made it clear to Ayşe Çelik that I constantly learn lessons from my *Ablam* [older sister] as well.

I divvied up the slices and clusters of grapes onto plates as Necati Hoca continued speaking.

"So, *kızım*, tell me. What story will you tell about our music?"

I sipped my tea and smiled. I did not launch into a summary of my theoretical interest in music and affect or my fieldnotes full of conversations, stories, utterances, and moments of musicking that point to the impossibility of a single story about Turkish classical musicians. Instead, I spoke to my

Figure 1.1 Ayşe and Necati Çelik, July 2013 (photograph by the author).

teacher as his diligent student, echoing in simplicity the philosophical training I had received alongside my musical apprenticeship. I had been inculcated enough into Turkish classical musicking to know that musician-ness emerges at the moment of a particular admission, in an assertive testimony of avowal.

"The story I tell of Turkish classical music, *hocam*, is a story of death [*ölüm hikâyesi*]."

Ayşe Abla was the first to respond.

"*Bak bak bak* [lit., "look look look," a verbal construct used playfully, in this case, to tease my air of authority]. "Our *kız* speaks well."

"I have a good teacher," I quickly answered, a remark that brought laughter to the table as we delighted in the game of *edep* (being well mannered), besting one another in compliments.

Necati Hoca paused and picked up his *ud* (short-necked lute). He played an instrumental improvisation, or *taksim*, in the musical mode (*makam*) Uşşak. Much more than a collection of pitches or intervals, *makam*-s are musical modes that include general tendencies for direction (where one should start an improvisation and move up or down), unique musical phrasing or turns, origin stories, and, historically, associations with specific emotions and feelings.[3]

The original term for this mode, Uşşak makamı, was the Arabic 'isq, or "love," a signifier made heavy by centuries of classical Islamic philosophers' discussions of divine love. Since the Ottoman period, musicians have described Uşşak as "the lovers' mode." As one of the primary *makam*-s, Uşşak was a mode in which Ottoman court and Mevlevi (Sufi) composers set countless compositions (see Example 1.1, the standard mapping of the collection of pitches for Uşşak). It was not a coincidence that a discussion of death often led to the sonic utterance of love. After all, discourses of death in Mevlevi terms inspire immediate connections to rebirth.

Example 1.1 Pitches (*dizi*) for the ascending mode (*makam*) Uşşak.

After improvising, Necati Hoca relaxed his hands on the top of his *ud* and began to speak.

"So many listeners today don't know that what I just played was in *makam* Uşşak. That is because most Turks who hear [Turkish] classical music on the radio or television do not hear the difference from one *makam* to another. Our old music and our folk music have *makam* as you know, but unless you are a musician or have tried to become a musician in Turkish classical music you cannot tell *Uşşak* from *Rast* from *Suzinak*."

While I knew the mode well, he followed through with a few idiomatic expressions that signal the beginning of a *taksim* focusing on the lower tetrachord of *Uşşak makamı* (Example 1.2):[4]

Example 1.2 Lines of improvisation introducing *Uşşak makamı*.

Necati Hoca paused and asked me, "*Kızım*, in my *taksim*, after I was satisfied with my wandering through *Uşşak*, where was my first modulation?" Modulation is a normative feature of instrumental improvisation, and demonstrates—to informed listeners who understand the intricacies of *makam*—the skill and creative capabilities of the soloist. As I am accustomed to, Necati Hoca takes care to shape my ears to these shifting melodic flavors so that I might be better able to hear—and thus understand—the idiosyncratic aptitude required to elegantly modulate in my own *taksim*.

"It was to *Eviç, hocam*" I quickly responded. "From *Uşşak* you pivoted into *Rast* briefly to ascend into *Eviç makamı*" (Example 1.3).

Example 1.3 Outline of the basic pitches for the descending mode *Eviç* into *Uşşak* (from left to right): *eksik Segâh* pentachord melds with a *Rast* pentachord, which pivots into an *Uşşak* tetrachord

He smiled and returned to his *ud,* playing through a modulation from the upper pentachord of *Uşşak* to the descending mode of *Eviç*, a modulation that was similar, but different from the one I had recorded a moment earlier (Example 1.4). I was accustomed to hearing many possible variations on specific modulations; this was one of the ways a teacher instills the idea of multiple possible routes for modulations in students.

Example 1.4 Example of an improvisatory modulation from *Eviç* to *Uşşak makamı*.

Necati Hoca then put down his instrument, needing to do so in order to make the shift back to using words, rather than music, to explain his meaning.

He slowly sipped his tea.

Then he said, "Many listeners today do not know anything about *makam*. No one in the audience will say, 'Oh! How beautifully you modulated to *Eviç makamı* at this moment!'[5] That is because you are right; our music is a death story. If a tree, our music tells the story of a tree whose roots have been cut."

This chapter traces the ways in which the genre of Turkish classical music has "roots that have been cut." I delineate a number of social and political shifts that have constituted and shaped Turkish classical music as a canon, a repertoire, or as an idea. These changes can effectively be described as top-down reforms made to musical practices by either the Ottoman Empire or the Turkish nation-state. Such a contextualization is needed to understand the ideologies of listening to the genre we today discursively name "Turkish classical music." I scrutinize contemporary musicians' central loss narrative of the death of this music genre, a narrative that I argue functionally surfaces as the primary constitutive aspect defining the genre for the people playing it.

The articulation, admission, or avowal of this loss narrative—saying, "Turkish classical music is dead"—functions significantly to name and constitute the genre of Turkish classical music itself. Narrating its death includes the loss narrative of the musical genre itself as well as narratives of nostalgia for the performance practices, patronage, and repertoire of imagined pasts.

I claim that contemporary musicians' repeated voicing and circulation of this loss narrative on the death of Turkish classical music is not an endpoint: articulating the so-called death of this music genre is significantly productive (O'Connell 1996).

Contemporary Turkish classical music (*Klasik Türk müziği* or *Klasik Türk musikisi*)[6] traditions can be defined as a disputed continuation and transformation of music genres historically performed in and patronized by the Ottoman courts. The genre includes some of the musical products of the Mevlevi Sufi order, as well as some urban and nightclub (*gazino*) repertoire and contemporary art (*sanat*) music compositions based on the Turkish modal system (*makam*). This music is heard as monophonic or heterophonic (as opposed to polyphonic), and was historically performed primarily by solo singers with a varying number of instrumentalists supporting them.[7] The two main components required for composition within this genre are *makam*, or melodic mode, and *usûl*, or rhythmic mode. The genre's musical canon was solidified beginning in 1926, when a national committee (*Türk Musıkisi Tasnif ve Tesbit Heyeti*) transcribed select works into modified forms of western standard notation. In adopting the word "classical" (*klasik*) to legitimize the genre in parallel with western epistemological discourses, Turkish writers concerned themselves with crafting terminology and editions to explain Turkish classical music history and its lexicons (see especially Gazimihal 1961 and Ezgi 1953). All in all, Turkish classical music denotes a large body of repertoire that is centuries old, with distinct compositional forms, high standards of performance, and intricate practices of improvisation.

The performance of a complicated legacy of defining music genres is produced in the very term *music*. In Turkish, using the term music is always already a political statement that identifies and places the speaker in particular discursive and ideological domains. The two words that Turkish musicians most commonly use to denote music are the Arabic-derived *musiki* and the French-derived *müzik*. An individual's choice of *musiki* or *müzik* immediately places her or him within dichotomous discourses (e.g., "east" versus "west," "modern" versus "antiquated") and may also indicate a person's class background and age. The politics of naming genres of Turkish music echoes and signifies heavy debates of the early Republican leaders who discursively reified an "east" and a "west" and aimed to bring all forms of musics produced by the new nation-state in line with the contemporary art music discourses of western Europe.

The genre of music I describe and discursively recreate in this book is also referred to with a plethora of names: Turkish art music (*Türk sanat musikisi* or *Türk san'at musikisi*), Turkish learned music (*Türk ilmi musikisi*), Ottoman art music (*Osmanlı sanat musikisi*), Ottoman classical music (*Klasik Osmanlı musikisi*), and finally, Turkish classical music (*Klasik Türk müziği* or *musikisi*). This genre is additionally named *Fenn-i Musiki* ("the science of music") in many Ottoman sources. In the Turkish public realm, other expressions are also heard: *Şark Musikisi* ("eastern music"), *Divan Musikisi* ("palace music"), *Türk Müziği* ("Turkish music"), and, more generally, *alaturka* (music "in the Turkish style"). The distinctions and boundaries between these genre names emerge as more transparent, more ambiguous, and more fragmented when used by non-musicking Turks. The performance in terms of choice, spelling, and even pronunciation of these names reveals one's aesthetic preferences and ideological attitudes rooted in discourses that are at the very least two centuries old.

In his exceptional book *Alaturka: Style in Turkish Music (1923–1938)*, John Morgan O'Connell outlines the commodification of musical style during an important period of transformation in the early years of the Turkish Republic. Focusing on the life and works of composer and singer Münir Nuretin Selçuk (1899–1981), O'Connell's historical ethnography elucidates the way Turkish classical music was simultaneously national ("Turkish") and respectable ("classical," linking the genre via reference to the privileged discourses of western classical music). O'Connell's work does not focus on Turkish classical music in the present, as he takes on a project that instead interrogates the consolidation of the style *alaturka* ("in a Turkish style") historically. O'Connell's significant text calls us to consider stylistic musical change in Turkey "as evolutionary and revolutionary at the same time" (2013: 18). In his earlier work, O'Connell presents the debates of the early Republic era as

> a cognitive display of Republic consciousness: a consciousness which has attempted to colonize its Ottoman counterpart but which is unsuccessful precisely because its cognitive dominion no longer exists as discourse. (1996: 172)

O'Connell points to musicians' expression "everything has finished [*hepsi bitirdi*]" to explore musicians' alternative constructions of history. Expanding O'Connell's work (1996, 2000, 2005a, 2013, 2015) in analyzing how past musical changes are narrated and reaffirmed, I elucidate the constitutive affective practices that contemporary Turkish classical musicians draw on to make themselves and their artistic practices intelligible in the present day.

This chapter sets the precedent for a historical understanding of the genre of music on which this book is based. In considering how Turkish classical music functions in the ethnographic present, I claim that the changes of institutional reform—from the Ottoman Empire to the Turkish Republic to emergent neoliberalism and political Islamism—that have affected this music genre are conceptualized as losses by the musicians who cultivate musical meaning for this repertoire and its associated practices today. I argue that the avowal of loss is a built-in and necessary element of Turkish classical music as a lived, performed genre by the individuals and communities that currently cultivate it. Musicians' avowal of loss is a key faction of what I call *melancholic modalities*, musicians' dynamic processes of subjectivity that render feelings of loss and suffering as beneficial modes of existing in their social worlds and

[handwritten margin note: drawing on past to reaffirm present]

productive material for their music making. To demonstrate how the avowal of loss is a primary element in Turkish classical musicians' melancholic modalities, I contextualize the genre Turkish classical music and trace its discursive creation from the Ottoman modernization reforms of the seventeenth century through its reconfigurings by the Turkish nation-state. In telling a story about the homogenizing of multiple genres under the banner of the name Turkish classical music, I begin each section with particular ethnographic moments during which contemporary Turkish classical musicians participate in performing the avowal of loss as repetitive melancholic voicings of loss are announced, affirmed, and asserted.

[handwritten margin note: historical time period]

REFORMS AS ROOTS

By participating in contemporary Turkish classical music worlds as a musician, I found myself constantly surrounded by articulations of Ottoman and early national reforms in contemporary music production. I was a regular witness to the ways telling of losses of the past function to memorialize the death of the genre of Turkish classical music in the present. On one occasion, an afternoon when I played with eight prominent male Turkish classical musicians ranging in age from thirty-eight to sixty-two, our post-musicking conversations over tea turned to the relationship between melancholy and certain reforms of the Ottoman era. The catalyst for this particular conversation happened to be gossip that the Turkish Ministry of Tourism and Culture might partially curtain funding for state-sponsored ensembles, which employ most Turkish classical professional musicians as full-time state employees.

"All Turkish classical music has melancholy [*hüzün*] because the people in seats of power restricted our music. Mustafa Kemal [founder of the Turkish Republic in 1923, referred to most commonly as 'Atatürk'] was really no different than Mahmud II [the Ottoman Sultan from 1808 through 1839]" one *kemençe* (small, pear-shaped fiddle) player claimed.

"Our music died long ago," an *ud* player added, "and that's why we are melancholic [*hüzünlü*]."

"Was there a time when the music wasn't dead?" I asked.

A singer and published poet quickly said, "Yes," which gestured a chorus of head turns.

"There is no melancholy in Buhurizade Mustafa Itri's music [a prominent composer, 1640–1712] because there was little suffering in his lifetime. Itri wrote at a time when the Ottoman Empire was shining [in glory]. Dede Efendi [Hammamizade İsmail Dede Efendi, 1778–1846], however, saw his music die and his circle [*mekan*] die. Everything died . . . court life, *yeni çeri* [the Ottoman military class, transliterated into English as "Janissary"], *mehter* [the musical genre of the *yeni çeri*]. . . ."

[handwritten margin note: golden age / nostalgia]

His voice trailed off. I had been long enculturated to the practice of listening to events of the past as if the individual speaker had lived in those periods as well.

The *kudüm* (kettle drum) player joined in. "There were no listeners left [*dinleyici kalmadı*]."

The singer-poet continued, "And so for centuries now, our music is dying."

The *kemençeci* broke the conversation with a small, slow musical motif on his instrument, in *Segâh makamı* (Example 1.5):

Example 1.5 A brief line of *taksim* (improvisation) indicating *Segâh makamı*.

The singer-poet decided to take the musical line as an invitation, and began singing three rounds of the "*Tekbir*," Itri's most famous composition (Example 1.6):

Al - la - hu ek-ber Al - la - hu ek-ber   La   i - la   he -il - lal - la -

hu Al - la - hu ek - ber   Al - la - hu   ek - ber ve lil-la - hil___hamd

Example 1.6 The loosely rhythmic "*Tekbir*" by Buhurizade Mustafa Itri in *Segâh makamı*.

Picking up instruments, we all joined in playing Itri's second most well-known composition, the "*Salât-ı Ümmiye*" (Example 1.7):

Al-la-hüm-me Sal-li A-la___   Sey-yi-di-na___   Mu-ham-me-din in-ne-biy yil_üm

miy-yi ve a - la   A - li - hi____ ve Sah-bi - hi_____ ve Sel-lim

Example 1.7 Buhurizade Mustafa Itri's "*Salât-ı Ümmiye*" in *Segâh makamı*.

After finishing the piece, the singer-poet looked at me and said, "Do you see the depth of our composers? The depth lies here: this beautiful composition only has five notes. What depth Itri made in only five notes! Itri wrote one of the most beautiful musical lines in the whole world. It became the music for an important Islamic prayer, which is now heard throughout the world. Muslims in [Central] Asia, in India, in Indonesia, in Palestine sing this, and they often do not even know that Itri, an Ottoman-Turkish composer, wrote it."

He paused.

"You see? Not knowing is itself a kind of death. I am glad Itri didn't see these deaths of music in his lifetime."

For these musicians, knowing and placing Itri in an Ottoman-Turkish musical trajectory—in their own legacy—means activating a border between perceived knowledge and ignorance, and celebrating loss as a point of pride. As one of the primary functions of melancholic modalities, melancholic utterances—linguistic or musical—surface to draw a border between *inside* and *outside*, constituting a social body of Turkish classical musicians and differentiating them from others. While melancholy is therefore about othering, melancholy is also regenerative because it distinguishes between Turkish classical musicians and informed listeners from the perceived general Turkish population, a group that may not have nor seek this knowledge. Loss emerges not only as the material for identification, it provides pride and pleasure. The border of Turkish classical musicians' sense of themselves is organized through narrating the death of the genre vis-à-vis institutionalized music reforms of the late Ottoman Empire and early Turkish Republic. Musical reforms during the Ottoman era occurred simultaneously with large-scale political reforms. These reforms were embedded in Ottoman political events as a means to accommodate the various changing currents of the Ottoman Empire: consolidating power over subjects, land, resources, and economic practices. Ottoman historiographers have demonstrated that the loss of territory is more often attributed to European and capitalist aggression than to inner decay that reportedly led to imperial decline (cf. Itzkowitz 2008, Doumani 1995, Peirce 1993, Quataert 2005). The borders of the Ottoman Empire began narrowing in the seventeenth century after a number of failed attempts to seize major European cities. Throughout this period, interest in European culture, especially in education, government, and military affairs, rapidly grew among the Ottoman elite. This elite deployed modernization measures not in an effort to "become western," but rather to protect and consolidate power by adopting western enlightenment rhetoric that emphasized the idea of the priority of the state. Changes in musical practices can be regarded as a series of legislated accommodations to external influences and as a reinvestment in older Ottoman styles and repertoire.

Unlike many modernization projects throughout the world, Turkish modernity did not necessarily begin in a formally colonial or postcolonial context. Rather, it was initiated by the elite of the Ottoman Empire, beginning in the reforms (*Tanzimat*) of 1839 through the early decades following the founding of the Republic of Turkey in 1923. European lifestyles and institutions were not perceived as a challenge or threat to the Ottoman imperial tradition, since Ottoman forms of identification were based, in part, on Sunni Muslim cultural and religious practices. In the context of musics of the Ottoman court, the first steps toward "modernization" occurred during the reign of Sultan Selim III (1789–1807). During Selim III's rule, an Italian opera house was founded in Istanbul in 1797. A composer and *ney* (end-blown reed flute) player himself, Selim III introduced "Europeanisms" into Ottoman classical music, seen in his own so-called invention of the melodic mode *Suzidilârâ makamı*, which is heard by many Turkish classical musicians today as "modern" simply because it resembles, in their ideologies of hearing, a western major mode (Example 1.8):

Example 1.8 The pitches (*dizi*) of the ascending *Suzidilârâ makamı*.

Turkish musicologist Bülent Aksoy tells the story of a concert in the palace, where Selim III requested a specific composition in *İsfahan makamı*, yet none of the musicians present knew of the piece (1985: 1228). Selim III was apparently so upset about this that he commanded a search for musicians who did know the *makam*, and only one single musician was found (Aksoy: 1229). Thus at this time, *meşk*, a practice of oral transmission that was the primary system of music transmission, was found to be inadequate, as it created the conditions for losing or forgetting the repertoire. After this incident, Selim III reportedly commissioned the Armenian composer Baba Hamparsum (1768–1839) to create a practical notation system for Ottoman court music, which was eventually referred to as Hamparsum notation (Ezgi 1953: 535).

Selim III's successor, Mahmut II (1808–1839), initiated a series of reforms that appropriated western European administrative and military models into Ottoman structures, setting the trend for several reforms throughout the nineteenth century that were referred to as the *Tanzimat-i Hayriye*, lit., "auspicious reorderings," which scholars today refer to simply as the *Tanzimat*. Most importantly for Ottoman musical production, Mahmut II abolished the military *yeni çeri* in 1826 (see O'Connell 2010). The military band of the *yeni* çeri, known as the *mehterhane*, was disbanded, as *mehter* (military music) did not adequately fit the newly westernized military training and outfits (And 1984: 1214).[8] The loss of this military ensemble led to the diminishing of the genre of *mehter* itself. In the place of the *mehterhane* ensemble, Mahmut II ordered the creation of the Imperial Band (*Muzika-i Hümayun*), a musical group that played repertoire that generally mirrored western European court music conventions. Giuseppe Donizetti (1788–1856) was invited to Istanbul from Italy to train the Imperial Band, in order to shape the ensemble's repertoire toward European-style marches, and later gained the Ottoman title Donizetti Paşa (see Aracı 2006).

Even though the Imperial Band did not play *mehter* repertoire, the ensemble did occasionally play traditional musical forms of the Ottoman court such as the *peşrev* (an instrumental introduction), *fasıl* (a kind of Ottoman musical suite), and the instrumental compositional form known as *saz semaisi* (Aksoy 1985: 1215). Eventually, the Imperial Band became part of the Enderun, a significant palace school that trained statesmen in the sciences, military tactics, and, importantly, the arts. In the institutional structure of the Enderun, the band was enlarged to include a chorus and orchestra, and an educational branch that included training for *muezzin*-s, or the public reciters of the Islamic five-times daily call to prayer (*ezan*). Over time, the band split into two factions: one played *Fasl-i Atık* ("classical *fasıl*") and the other played *Fasl-i Cedid* ("new *fasıl*"). The latter group consisted of western flutes, mandolins, and guitars in tandem with the traditional *ud, ney,* and *kanun* (trapezoidal zither), all under the baton of a conductor. The *Fasl-i Atık* ensemble performed repertoire that was based in the melodic modes (*makam*-s) that were most similar to the major and minor modes of western concert music traditions. This nineteenth century structuration epitomizes a primary—and preliminary—attempt to cultivate musical texts and practices harmonizing Ottoman classical music with European polyphony, while simultaneously creating a synthesis of "eastern" and "western" instruments.

Today, contemporary Turkish classical musicians narrate this history as a story of loss—as opposed to a story of development or progress—even though a bound, singular genre of Turkish classical music was neither named nor conceptualized during this period of Ottoman history. In the context of contemporary Turkish classical musicians' melancholic modalities, narrating a loss of Turkish classical music is distinctly related to a kind of Ottoman nostalgia that fronts the loss of imperial power as the loss of the Ottoman cultural practices writ large. During the nineteenth century, Ottoman public space proliferated with borrowings from Europe, manifesting in architecture (evident in the Victorian style of Dolmabahçe Palace), painting (seen in era depictions of the palace life, especially the activities of the women of the *harem*), and heard in the musics patronized by the court.

During the reign of Abdülmecid (1839–1861), Ottoman classical music was still officially patronized by the court while interest from the patrons and audiences moved from a preference for the cyclical concert suite (*fasıl*) to the short, light classical song form (*şarkı*). This shift further marked the Ottoman elite's preference of western-influenced genres and performance styles and additionally points to shorter attention spans of listeners. Particular established Ottoman musical forms, such as the *kâr*, were replaced by *şarkı* (Klaser 2001, Feldman 1996) or experienced a significant revival and refashioning (O'Connell 2013). Abdülmecid additionally established a women's orchestra of women musicians of the *harem*, a move that validated Sunni Muslim women's musical production and promoted their visibility and circulated their composed musical works beginning in the mid-nineteenth century.

Abdülmecid's heir, Abdülaziz (1861–1876), did not have the same affinity for western musics promoted by his predecessor. Abdülaziz himself was a *ney* player and composer of numerous works, including a *Hicaz Sirto*, and several songs (*şarkı*-s) in *Muhayyir makamı* that are still heard in present-day Turkey and parts of the Arab world. Abdülaziz even dismantled the ballet, opera, orchestra, and women's harem orchestra that the Sultanate previously patronized. He evidently believed that too many funds were being wasted on westernized art forms, and used the funds to instead support the traditional (men only) arts.[9] While Abdülhamid II (1876–1909) deviated strongly from his uncle Abdülaziz's aesthetic tastes, he continued a long tradition of Ottoman leaders who actively performed or composed music. Abdülhamid II preferred western musics, explicitly supported opera, and played piano and violin himself. Furthermore, his public statements gave voice to a particular ideological narrative that positioned the system *makam* as "foreign" inventions of Arabs, Persians, and Greeks (Aksoy 1985: 1224). This origin discourse perpetuates a belief that the musical systems governing Ottoman musical production were, in essence, non-Ottoman.

We can trace the Ottoman court's move away from celebrating Ottoman classical musics to validating western musical forms through the life narratives of key musicians during this time. Walter Feldman describes the "hostile contexts" that had to be negotiated by Ottoman classical musicians (1996). Composer Zekai Dede Efendi (1825–1908), for example, left Istanbul for Cairo, as he found better patronage from an Egyptian ruler.[10] Zekai Dede's teacher, İsmail Dede Efendi (1778–1846), also experienced great sadness at the changes in musical life in the Ottoman court, and was the individual musician singled out by the singer-poet in the conversation I described above in circulating loss narratives. One of the greatest musicians of the early twentieth century, Tanburi Cemil Bey (1873–1916), was invited to perform at court only once: a performance that ended when Abdülhamid II fell asleep (Feldman 1996: 16). These stories are currently narrated and retold as part of the loss narrative that I argue is both constitutive of musicians' melancholic modalities and an inherent component in the very definition of the genre of contemporary Turkish classical music.

Large-scale national transformations, facilitated by the deposition of Abdülhamid II by the Young Turks in 1908, eradicated the primary institution of patronage for music: the Ottoman court. The political conditions that ensued—namely, the Balkan Wars, collective violence and genocide, World War I, and the Allied occupation of Istanbul—did not facilitate conditions for the maintenance of the musical practices of the Ottoman Court. Military leaders created the modern Republic of Turkey (*Türkiye Cumhuriyeti*) in 1923, under the leadership and vision of Mustafa Kemal (1881–1938).

CULTURAL POLICIES AND THE POLITICS OF NAMING

While I spend most of my time during ethnographic fieldwork engaging Turkish classical musicians and their social worlds, I occasionally find myself in the role of cultural translator to non-musicians. My response to queries tend to be uneasily drawn from a collection of experiences from which I author and produce loss narratives of my own. I spent a lovely night enjoying dinner with a number of academics in Istanbul in the summer of 2013. All of my friends identify as Turks, born in Turkey with Turkish as their first language. Our table boasted an architect, an art historian, a poet, a physician, a literature professor, a physics professor, and me. Besides the poet, I was perhaps the only scholar "of Turkey," as all of the others at the table had received their advanced degrees in the United States, United Kingdom, or Canada and were specialists of methodologies and debates of the English-language humanities and social sciences.

After I was asked about my book project and explained it a bit, I was immediately peppered with questions:

"What is Turkish classical music? I don't think I've ever heard it," said the literature professor, who grew up in Izmir, Turkey's third largest city.

"I'm sorry, what is the *sema* turning ritual of the Mevlevi?" asked the architect, who was interrupted by the physics professor, who shouted, "Slow down! Do we have Mevlevi-s in Turkey?" Both were born and raised in Istanbul.

After answering these and other questions, the poet leaned into me and whispered, "You see what Turkey is? Ignorance [*cahillik*]." He winked at me as he settled back into his seat.

The physics professor continued, "Denise, I've heard Turkish classical music before on the state television channels [Turkish Radio and Television, or TRT]. But it is not Turkish, is it? I mean, Ottomans just stole Greek Orthodox music and put words to it."

I paused and sipped my water. The origin discourse birthed by Sultan Abdülhamid II and reified during the early years of Republic nationalism has been so widely adopted for generations that it is constantly present for non-musicians.

I was about to give value to my physics friend by discussing his interpretation and offering examples of shared traditions, but the poet rushed in with his own ideological discourse. "You fool! You'll say it is Greek, she'll say it is Arab, she'll say it is Persian. Is there nothing left for us? Have we not created anything?"

"That's true," the architect chimed in. "Everyone in Greece and Lebanon and Israel think baklava [a rich, sweet filo pastry] is theirs. What can be named 'Turkish?'"

There were some snickers of laughter around the table, as the poet continued, "The truth is, in forty years Denise will be the one of the only ones left knowing Turkish classical music."

"American imperialism!" the physician piped in.

More laughter.

I switched to speaking English. "You're welcome to send your children to study in America to learn about this aspect of your intangible heritage."

Laughter, louder still.

Moving back to Turkish, I finished with, "But really, there are great musicians and scholars of Turkish classical music right here in Istanbul. I wish they were not inaudible to you all."

The poet got the final word.

"What does it mean to think about a name, though? This is Turkish music. It's ours, even if we don't listen to it."

He wiped the corners of his mouth with his napkin.

"And so it is the same with baklava. Shall we order some, and truly make it ours?"

Knowledge and the performance of knowing in this anecdote are directly related to the practice of naming. To lay the foundation for the new Turkish Republic, Mustafa Kemal and his associates worked to create an identity for the Turkish people rooted in Turkism, an ideology that began in the nineteenth century and grew out of the political reforms of the Ottoman court with the *Tanzimat*. Mustafa Kemal and his associates with political power strategically crafted the identity of Republic citizenry to be distant from the identities valued during the Ottoman Empire. State agents sought to reshape individuals' senses of identity as Turkish citizens through the control and manipulation of cultural practices. Self-definition, naming, and performing historical knowledge have, in a way, always already been projects of self-knowing.

With the founding of the Republic of Turkey in 1923, a number of top-down strategies were implemented that challenged previous iterations of self-fashioning and instantiated new citizen-selfhood models derived from emergent Turkish nationalism. Along with nationalism, modernization

developing Turkish identity

became an important part of the Kemalist doctrine established by Mustafa Kemal and his allies. Founders of the nation-state articulated Turkey's goal to be the attainment of the level of contemporary civilization, which for Mustafa Kemal and his associates meant western civilization. Mustafa Kemal's acclaim as a strategic Ottoman military figure allowed him to easily transition into a highly visible political figure. In the reformation of the judicial, legislative, and economic realms of the nation-state, a primary goal was secularization. Two important legislations to enact secular reforms and ensure the silencing of religious perspectives were the abolition of the Caliphate in 1924 and the suppression of the Kurds in 1925.[11] Significantly, Mustafa Kemal also presided over the effort to decenter the practices of Islam in public life. His reforms crafted a contemporary Turkish public sphere that continues to be rife with normative categorizations. The initial modeling of Turkish citizenry was concentrated on the bifurcation between sacred and secular and the privileging of secular iterations of selfhood and individual autonomy. In short, Mustafa Kemal legislated a transition wherein the proud member of the Turkish nation was to be both a secular nationalist and thoroughly westernized.

In 1925, early in the cultural policies of the nation-state, the *fez* was banned, a head garment for males that symbolized one's place in Ottoman class hierarchy. In its place, the western European hat (*şapka*) was declared the official head garment of a Turk. One year later, series of paintings and statues of Mustafa Kemal were visible in public places, a practice that strongly went against Sunni Muslim beliefs about visual representations of individuals. In 1927, Ottoman and Islamic symbols were removed from public places, an action that heralded the end of governmental support for Islamic religious law (*şeriat*). In 1928, Islam was declared no longer to be the official religion of the nation-state. Essentially, top-down national reforms acted on the body of Turkish citizens; leaders believed that Islamic and Ottoman cultural heritage could simply be removed, slipped off, and replaced. But Ottoman customs were polysemic, and represented an entire web of social relations that had to be transformed on the road to secular nationalism and a new modern Turkey.

This polysemy was reflected in Ottoman naming practices, evident in the reinterpretation and application of the term *Türk*. The act of naming—whether it be through your choice of terms for "music," "Turkish classical music," or "Turkishness"—continues to be a critical and inherently political practice in contemporary Turkey. We know that Ottomans, especially members of the educated elite, had two main focuses of loyalty and identity during their recorded history. One of these was Sunni Islam, adopted by Ottoman leaders as their empire expanded to include key Muslim trade routes and holy lands. The other focus of loyalty was to the Ottoman Empire itself, as Ottomans were the "champions of Islam in the world" (Kushner 1997: 219). An Ottoman gentleman would thus identify as a Muslim and an Ottoman, never as a Turk (Kafadar 1995). History was narrated simultaneously as Ottoman and Islamic history, evident in the fact that the Ottoman language itself was infused with multiple Persian and Arabic words. Ottoman sultans ascended not only to positions of political and military leadership, but also claimed the caliphal authority of Sunni Islam. The Ottoman caliphate remained within the dynasty of sultans from 1362 until the founding of the Republic.

Given the importance afforded to Ottoman forms of identification, who are the "Turks"? Where did this word *Türk* come from, and what did it (does it) denote? What does the "Turkish" in Turkish classical music signify? During the Ottoman era, the word *Türk* implied an impolite and crude individual. It was essentially a derogatory reference to the reportedly ignorant peasant or nomad of Anatolia (Mardin 2002: 118). In contrast, identifying as Ottoman marked an individual as elevated, civilized, intellectual, cosmopolitan, and cultured (Mardin: 116). Beginning in the 1880s, the signifier *Türk* was appropriated by some individuals in Ottoman circles, imbuing the identification with an anti-authoritarian resonance. Thus the revolution of 1908–1918 unsurprisingly was named the "Young Turk" movement. *Türk* had already acquired new symbolism that enabled the nationalistic ideology of the Turkish Republic under Mustafa Kemal's command to be framed as Turkism. In his Republic Day speech to the nation on October 29, 1933, Mustafa Kemal uttered a phrase that eventually became the nation-state's motto: *ne mutlu "Türküm" diyene*, or "how happy is the one who says 'I am Turkish.'" Mustafa Kemal's complete embracing of the term at the level of national citizenship constituted the major ideological, wide-spread shift in Turkishness from signifying crudeness to connoting patriotism, heroism, and secularism.[12] The term *Türk* was refashioned as the proud mascu-linized title of an individual in an independent nation spread over vast areas. Sociologist and political scientist Şerif Mardin argues that "[t]he image of the Turk as the country bumpkin was transformed into that of the bronze-bodied, strong, serene and silent farmer carrying his load of grapes door-to-door in the stifling heat of summer" (2002: 122). The basis of the Republic of Turkey was located in loyalty to the homeland (Anatolia) and to the reportedly homoge-neous communities couched therein. The founding of the Republic ushered a broader political meaning to the signifier Turk: all citizens of the Turkish nation-state were deemed Turks in the 1924 constitution. The designator Turk ignored the daily experiences of people who had, for centuries, understood themselves as belonging to different nations (*millet*) divided by ethnic lines and religious affinities (see Andrews 1989).[13] At the same time, naming the new citizen Turk in the constitution naturalized a division of citizenship agreed upon with Allied powers in the 1923 Treaty of Lausanne that recognized Turkish sovereignty. As previously mentioned, the 1924 constitution also stripped Islamic political and social functions away; Islam was no longer the religion of the nation-state.

In Ottoman Turkey, the gulf between the educated elite and the masses was linguistically performed, symbolized, and maintained in the gulf between the languages of Ottoman (*Osmanlıca*) and "crude" (*kaba*) Turkish (*Türkçe*). In

1926, the founding of the Turkish Language Society (*Türk Dil Kurumu*) initiated official movement toward bridging this gulf. The largest language change occurred in 1928, when the Ottoman alphabet was replaced with the roman script. The significance of the change in script not only meant individuals read text with different characters. The act of reading required an embodied reconfiguration of space: while reading Ottoman (and Arabic) engendered movements from right to left, the newly-imposed Turkish script shifted the flow of reading from left to right. Similar shifts dramatically reorienting embodied practices happened on many levels, such as changing the division and experience of time from the nine-month Islamic lunar calendar to the twelve-month Gregorian calendar.

But the reforms affecting speech, texts, and time—like reforms affecting sound in the public sphere—could not simply be enacted, policed, and domesticated by a decree of the nation-state. The result of the language reforms was not the displacement of some terms with others, or with one script or alphabet over another. Instead, Ottoman language practices coexisted with the modernized Turkish language that the nation-state aimed to create. An individual's choice and manipulation of language practices opened up the space for subversive discourses to be voiced and heard, a space that still exists and is played in today. Language practices were additionally met head on with the politics of familial names and the cultivation of genealogies. As the term *Türk* came to new signification, so too did the names of each individual living within the boundaries of the nation-state. In 1934, all individuals were required to adopt a last name. Mustafa Kemal, the founder of the Republic, was given the name *Atatürk* by the elected assembly. Most English-language texts translate Atatürk as "father of the Turks." However, the prefix *ata* has deeper signification than "father:" *ata* denotes "ancestor" and it resonates a discourse of roots. We can see that by being named Atatürk, Mustafa Kemal embodied the new zero point of Turkish history: ideologically speaking, there was no history beyond him, no direct reference to other histories than those beginning with the nation-state.

OTTOMAN MUSIC AND THE TURKISH NATION-STATE

A professional singer: "Other people in the world can be sad or have depression, but melancholy is ours."

Me: "Yours, the Turks?"

The singer: "Yes. Well . . . not all Turks. Mostly us, the artists who play Turkish classical music."

Diverse traditions of music making in multi-ethnic Ottoman places were eventually consolidated and renamed "Turkish classical music" by the early founders of Turkish musicology. Multiple practices were homogenized under this title and structured by national institutions, especially at radio houses and in music conservatories. Yet national legislation affecting the arts represented a reformulation, rather than a total reformation, of laws passed during the previous century with the *Tanzimat*. As a continuation of previous reforms, republican leaders' formulated ideas in the field of music production drew on established divisions to solidify and anchor representational power in the emerging secular nation-state.[14] Turkish theatre historian and folklorist Metin And explains that

> Mustafa Kemal knew that if his new state was to have a durable basis he had to change the way people thought *and felt*. All Ottoman religious and cultural elements had to be eliminated, so that the people would identify with the Republic and its higher aims unselfconsciously. (1984: 216, my emphasis)

The radio replaced the Ottoman court as the new source for music patronage. Because of the great political power of Mevlevi Sufi orders and their religious and political influence on the masses, on April 20, 1925 Mustafa Kemal announced that "all dervishes, fortune-tellers, witch doctors . . . [and other] primitive [Islamic] callings" would henceforth be banned. Sufi lodges [*tekke*-s] were officially closed, gathering places were razed, sacred texts were burned, sonic rituals and musical repertoire was forbidden, and this legacy and a narrative frame of "destruction" continues to resonate in the Turkish classical music world today.[15]

Early architects of the Turkish nation-state drew on the writings of Ziya Gökalp (1876–1924) to shift the way people conceptualized Turkish music: they sought expunge Ottoman elements and associations, affirming a sense of the Ottoman as backward and lacking in progress. Gökalp was a Turkish sociologist who interpolated the sociological principles of Émile Durkheim (1859–1917) and the philosophical writings of Auguste Comte (1798–1857) in crafting his statements about Turkish musical meaning. Gökalp was not the only model of nationalism produced in the era; Holly Shissler examines Ahmet Ağaoğlu's formulation of philological nationalism, which posited language as the basis of national belonging and recognized the diversity of Anatolia (2003). However, Gökalp's 1923 publication *Türkçülüğün Esasları* (*The Principles of Turkism*) influenced Mustafa Kemal so profoundly that Martin Stokes describes the text as "a blueprint for the entire revolution" (Stokes 1992: 26). In it, Gökalp articulates a distinction between "culture" (*hars*) and "civilization" (*medeniyet*), and positions "culture" as synonymous with language and education as that which binds the nation together (Gökalp 1923: 27). "Civilization," by contrast, is the product of individual will, consisting of theology, philosophy, technology, and science.[16] For Gökalp, the split between "culture" and "civilization" can be illustrated by the existence of three

— distinct from either?

musics: Eastern, Western, and Folk.[17] In Gökalp's narrative, the music of the Ottoman elite was a product of the Arab and Persian civilizations, based on the civilization of the Byzantines. The music of Anatolia was the true culture of the Turks.[18] The "new Turkish culture" was to return to what it supposedly always had been before the destructive introduction of foreign elements by the Ottomans, while the "new Turkish civilization" was to move from an ostensibly eastern to a western focus. Folk music was the untouched raw material from which civilized Turkish culture could be fashioned. The new national music of Turkey needed to be a synthesis of Turkish folk music with the techniques and esteemed ideals of western civilization.[19] It was necessary that the Republic of Turkey produce musical genius of the caliber of western musical masters; Gökalp claimed that musical genius can occur only when the culture and the civilization of a nation are "in unison" (1923: 51). This period of musical and ideological reconfiguration coincided with the introduction of the idea of "the (autonomous) individual" (*birey*) and the expansion of a virtuosity discourse among Turkish classical musicians, which I discuss in chapter 3.

Yet bifurcated discourses were not new. During his reign from 1876 to 1909, Abdülhamid II viewed Ottoman classical music a foreign import and appropriation, a narrative that continues to circulate in the present day. Gökalp was dipping into discourses already available to the elite of his era, providing the sociological framework for the analysis of music history into separate epochs divided into pre-Ottoman, Ottoman, and Republican. These teleological temporal partitions supported dichotomous discourses about Turkish musical practice. These bifurcations emerge when present-day individuals in Turkey interpret musical sounds—and sounds heard as spiritual (chapter 2)—into established dualisms of eastern versus western, sacred versus secular, and traditional versus progressive.

Turkish classical musicians occupy a particularly interesting liminal space for Ottoman historiography: as vocalists and instrumentalists for a music genre with Ottoman language lyrics, they experience the purported rupture from the shift of the Ottoman to the Turkish intimately in daily life. Furthermore, as many musicians have continued oral transmission in the context of the master-apprentice relationship—either separate from or in conjunction with state music conservatories—multiple methods, terminologies, and ideologies have been passed down to musicians from lineages that were the center of cultural artistic production during the height of the Ottoman Empire.

Yet while I present and analyze Turkish musical discourse in terms of discursive separation, we should not assume that there are always clear divisions for contemporary Turkish classical musicians today. For example, musicians today playing a sixteenth century Mevlevi *ayin* (music suite) may throw in extended techniques in performance—such as arpeggios, brief passages of chromatic ornamentation, and particular kinds of vibrato—all techniques or musical minutiae that, while indicating the heavy appropriation of "wester-nisms" in reinterpreting Ottoman musics, are not heard problematically by contemporary musicians and listeners. Central musicians composing and performing in the periods before bifurcated discourses were naturalized, especially renowned virtuoso Tanburi Cemil Bey (1873–1916), engaged these music techniques in their individual practices. In other words, the dichotomies of classical versus folk, eastern versus western, and Ottoman versus Turkish are far-reaching ideological concepts that, while discursively performed, may still be uncritically adopted by musicians. As such, individual musicians' strat-egies, lifestyles, and negotiations of self-presentation challenge these pre-sumed dualisms as productively synchronistic, not contradictory. Consider, for example, the following anecdote offered by Karl Signell about an improvi-sation by Niyazi Sayın, one of the most important *ney* players today:

> ... Niyazi Sayın, ever the experimenter, once caused an unfavorable reaction by subtly inserting the chorale tune from Beethoven's Ninth Symphony, the "Ode to Joy," into a traditional *taksim* improvisation in *makam Rast* ("that's what Atatürk wanted, wasn't it?" he later said). (Signell 1980: 168)

The music reforms and cultural policies enacted by political leaders since the seventeenth century have significantly affected the way individuals in Turkey conceptualize Turkish classical music. These same policies also created the institutions and the discourses that became authorized to lay claim to diverse ideologies and authorize particular musical practices and texts. The effects of these reforms were far reaching, and have created fragmented understand-ings, interpretations, and practices in a kind of colonization of consciousness.

"SHAPING EARS AND HEARTS": EMERGENT MEDIA PRACTICES

Radio was a tool to create national sensibilities: music's efficacy as a vehicle for nationalism could work only through repeated experiences that fostered feelings of national solidarity for individuals in all villages, towns, and urban centers of Turkey. Important individuals and institutions of the nation-state reconceived and re-presented Turkish civility and national identity and moni-tored its repetitive inculcation. Print, sound, and visual media were employed by the government and its institutions to control and shape Turkish national consciousness, as it was considered crucial for fostering unity among citizens. In the early years of nation building, radio emerged as the most influential medium for "shaping the ears of the new nation" (Seeman 2006: 3). The first radio broadcast from Ankara and Istanbul took place on May 1, 1927; at this time, radio was operated by a private French firm. While the Turkish nation-state supervised radio broadcasts during this time, Mustafa Kemal did not initiate the government's monopoly over radio until 1935. In an opening speech to the Turkish Parliament that year, Mustafa Kemal claimed radio was crucial in building national culture. He allocated the administration of radio waves to the government, claiming that radio would aid in raising Turkey "to the level of a contemporary civilization" (Öngören 1986: 179).[20]

Mustafa Kemal's most active legislation regarding Ottoman musics was passed after a speech he delivered on November 2, 1934, when he banned Turkish classical music from the state radio, a decision that was not overturned until 1936.[21] Even though Turkish classical music had been silenced from the radio, by 1938 the genre had found a generous patron in radio stations in the nation's capital, Ankara (O'Connell 2000: 136). The government also supervised the issues of the radio's newspaper in 1941, a publication that worked to both disseminate national consciousness in print form and popularize state artists. Radio became the "mouthpiece of the government" (Öngören 1986: 186). New radio ensembles facilitated the ideological categorization of Turkish nationalism and civility outlined by Gökalp and appropriated by Mustafa Kemal. Ensembles were divided into two categories: "national" music (*milli musiki*) ensembles and "western" music (*batı müziği* or *garp musikisi*) ensembles, which performed music of the western concert tradition and popular musics such as jazz and tango. The category of national music was further divided between Turkish folk music (*Türk halk müziği*) and Turkish art music (*Türk sanat müziği*). These seemingly fixed categories continue to be reified in the present day in television programming and conventional naming practices of music genres.

At the height of the reforms of the nation-state in 1935, there were 4,834 registered radio sets in rural Turkey (Güngör 1990: 55). These radios were generally kept in state-run "People's Houses" (*Halkevleri*). Founded in 1911 (as *Türk Ocakları*, or "Turkish Hearths") and reinvented in 1923, People's Houses were designed to fill leisure hours with the goal of engaging and entertaining communities by bringing musical and other cultural practices—filtered through Kemalist principles—directly to the people all over the country (Karpat 1963). Educational programs disseminated the proper expression of the Turkish language, history, folklore, and approved musical genres. These sound waves, representing Turkey's westernizing, civic identity, became property of public space in rural areas at this critical phase of Turkey's nation building. In 1961, the national Turkish Radio and Television (TRT) was established, and eventually oversaw radio and related medias.[22] After TRT's founding, radio power doubled in kilowatts, and a second station was added that solely broadcast western European music (Öngören 1986: 188–189).

Turkish classical music radio productions were filtered through performance practice models heavily influenced by western European models. Turkish classical music was maintained by TRT and the government precisely because it was adapted in the 1930s through the 1950s in such a way that it appeared westernized, modernized, and stripped of particular signifiers of Ottomanism and Islam. Mesud Cemil (1902–1963), son of Tanburi Cemil Bey, is credited for having introduced the "choir concept" (*klasik koro*) to Turkish classical music: he presented music that was typically sung by a soloist and staged large mixed choruses singing monophonically, creating a heterophonic choral line replacing a single voice. Mesud Cemil was also responsible for habituating the role of conductor to the ensemble, a feature that was not typically used previously, as individual musicians were generally accustomed to keeping time through the percussion (Beken 1998: 18). Yet the practice of choirs, conductor, and similar western appropriations had been already initiated to some degree in musical practices of the Ottoman court during the *Tanzimat* era. The mechanisms of the nation-state worked to expand, codify, and amplify these elements as normative musical practice. TRT was additionally the dominant institution of folk music research and dissemination.[23] The study of music and establishing authoritative collections, sanctioning performances, and regulating the circulation of media texts became tightly interconnected under national control.

INSTITUTIONAL CHANGES FOR PRACTICES OF MUSICAL TRANSMISSION

A singer and former conservatory educator: "I think we lost Turkish classical music because of large classes. Master-apprentice lineages were replaced with one of us teaching thirty children at a time. Many musicians give private lessons today, but it's not the same."

The fields of musical education and performance were also part and parcel of the nation-state's project to shape Turkish citizenry. Music education institutions, founded and supported by the government, operated both as discursive and practical mechanisms for domestication. The physical spaces for the education and performance of genres homogenized under the term Turkish classical music were eradicated during the early years of the nation-state; the Ottoman court was closed with the defeat of the Ottoman Empire at the end of World War I and Sufi lodges (*tekke*-s) were abandoned per Mustafa Kemal's order in 1925.

The process of inculcating new Turkish civic identity was in part achieved by institutions that melded western European and Turkish musical practices. The first public institution to offer a comprehensive system of instruction in Turkish music, the Darül'elhan, was founded in 1912, closed in 1918, and reopened in 1923. The Darül'elhan offered a system of music education that imitated western practices of music transmission through an emphasis on notation (musical literacy) over oral transmission (*meşk*). Students were taught solfège, notation, and transcription and offered classes in religious genres, voice, and instrumental performance (see chapter 3). The Darül'elhan also organized concerts, sponsored the publication of a journal (*Darül'elhan Mecmuası*), and promoted notation in a musical series (*Darül'elhan Külliyatı*). The Darül'elhan strategically added western musics to the curriculum in 1923, the same year of the founding of the Republic. Despite these efforts, by 1924, the eighteen full-time staff members at Darül'elhan were dismissed, and only three were retained as musicologists for the explicit purposes of putting repertoire into western staff notation (O'Connell 2000: 134). When the *tekke*-s were closed in 1925, the Darül'elhan was the only official institution of music education remaining that housed the repertoire that was eventually filtered and codified as Turkish classical music.

Upon Mustafa Kemal's request, Osman Zeki Üngör (1880–1958), the composer of the Turkish national anthem, founded the first state conservatory for western music in the new capital, Ankara, in 1924 (Beken 1998: 19). This conservatory started as the Music Teachers' School (*Musiki Muallim Mektebi*), training high school and elementary school teachers for western music instruction in Turkey's schools (And 1984: 220). To make the switch to a music curriculum focusing on western and folk musics as seamless as possible, Mustafa Kemal canceled all music programs in Turkish high schools until the first-year-entry graduates of the Music Teachers' School had their diplomas and could immediately be deployed to teach (Ayvazoğlu et. al. 1994: 10). In Istanbul, the Fine Arts Academy (*Güzel Sanatlar Akademisi*) was founded in 1926, and replaced both the Darül'elhan and the Ottoman palace school (Enderun). The Fine Arts Academy restructured and remade previous music institutions into a single academy; O'Connell argues that

> . . . the Fine Arts Academy not only provided a focus for defining and debating Turkish aesthetic preference according to the dualistic structures of discursive practice but it also enabled individual commentators to validate distinctive cultural positions by co-opting the formalized language of a dominant republican perspective. Through their manipulation of the discursive realm, supporters of the new Academy were able [to] change and control Turkish taste by promoting *alafranga* ["foreign/western style" music] in the new music curriculum and by discriminating against *alaturka* both institutionally and economically. (2000: 118)

The first leaders of music education institutions concentrated on music education as a focus for defining acceptable *alafranga* practices over what was viewed as aberrant *alaturka* practices.. Music education institutions operated both as ideological and practical mechanisms for republican control.[24] By 1927, the nation-state began to actively recruit young Turkish musicians to study abroad in Europe on national scholarships (And 1984: 220). In 1932, foreign musicians, teachers, conductors, and composers were invited to Turkey by Mustafa Kemal and tasked to develop curriculums at the primary music institutions in Istanbul (the Fine Arts Academy was later renamed and restructured as the Istanbul Municipal Conservatory, or İstanbul Belediye Konservatuvarı) and in Ankara (Devlet Konservatuvarı and Gazi Enstitüsü). Among the European guest musicians were Joseph Marx (1882–1964), Paul Hindemith (1895–1968), Béla Bartók (1881–1945), Carl Ebert (1887–1980), and Eduard Zuckmayer (1890–1972), foreigners who significantly influenced the Turkish music education institutions that are still in operation.

The first entering class from Ankara State Conservatory (Devlet Konservatuvarı) celebrated their graduation on July 3, 1941. The head of the Ministry of Education at this time, Hasan Ali Yücel (1897–1961), was invited to give a speech at the momentous occasion. Yücel called the audience to recognize that a conservatory's focus on opera was equally important as a university requiring classes on World War I in their curriculum, as opera was a matter of civilization (Ali 1983: 1532). Yücel claimed that even though the composers who wrote the operas were not Turkish, western operas—when translated into Turkish—still promote Turkishness, because Turks understand the larger meaning of civilization and of national pride (Ali: 1533).

The reforms to music institutions concretely worked to codify Turkish musics in notation and classicize genres according to western standards; Turkish classical music was marginalized through the use of a bifurcating musical discourse that sedimented musical practice. In short, Turkish and western classical musics were interpreted within contrasting ideological categories (Turkish versus western) by emphasizing the use of melody (monophonic versus polyphonic), use of musical texture (heterophonic versus polyphonic), and compositional techniques (significant knowledge-based forms of improvisation versus memorizing compositional pieces produced by a single composer). In doing so, Turkish classical music practices—practices that were highly heterogeneous and pluralistic—were essentially recreated, homogenized, and rearticulated through the discourses of the nation-state and its various institutions. Music reforms did not simply replace preexisting practices in existing musical circles, especially those outside of music institutions.

The Istanbul conservatory, or İstanbul Teknik Üniversitesi Konservutuvarı located in the Maçka campus of İstanbul Teknik Üniversitesi (hereafter, İTÜ), is a central institution that inherited the bifurcation of musical discourses. Founded in 1975, İTÜ was the first state-sponsored conservatory opened for teaching Turkish musics, and included a curriculum that taught western classical music, Turkish classical music, and Turkish folk music through the pedagogical tools of western classical music education. It is significant that this conservatory, the first that included training in Turkish music, was founded in Istanbul, the center of the Ottoman Empire, as opposed to Ankara, the capital of the Turkish Republic.[25] When conservatories in Turkey eventually introduced Turkish musics into western-music-focused curriculum, teaching Turkish music was first divided according to the ideological categories of folk (*halk*) and art (*sanat*) music. Curriculum reflected political bifurcations: conservatories were shaped to emphasize the melodic over the poetic, words over lyrics (in Turkish, *söz* over *güfte*), the secular over the religious, and the literate over the oral. Contemporary conservatories inherited a structure of education that teaches Turkish classical, Turkish folk, and western classical music through pedagogical techniques of the west, relying on musical notation, standardization and codification of theory, and bounded lessons in space and time.[26] Today, faculty members in the ethnomusicology division at İTÜ masterfully interrogate the discourses they have inherited, and actively model exemplary critical critique in their classrooms and research.

Some contemporary Turkish classical musicians today perceive the music conservatory system as one of the reasons for the ostensible loss of Turkish classical music. In the place of the Ottoman model of master-apprentice relationships discussed in chapter 3, conservatories are reportedly required to be in the business of what one musician claimed was "creating academic graduates, not necessarily musicians." Yet while dissenting voices against the larger tide of westernization may be loud, musicians deeply value İTÜ, its esteemed internationally-recognized faculty, and the opportunities it provides for legitimation in Turkey and transnational music institutions. As with TRT production, contemporary conservatories magnify the political processes and ideological frameworks that maintain early nation-state iterations of official history. As "history" is produced and organized, the ongoing presence of Turkish classical music provides an interesting glimpse of this historical narrative due to the recently increased interest in Ottoman arts in the Turkish public sphere. While the musicians who learn, teach, and perform Turkish classical music claim that the genre has died, the genre also functions as a resource for nostalgia of Turkey's former political power and Ottoman strength and, for increasing numbers of new audience members, public interest in sonic products that resonate elements of Islamic spirituality.

I was wandering around Kadıköy, one of the prominent districts on the Anatolian side of Istanbul, with a good friend and professional instrumentalist of a state chorus specializing in Turkish classical music. Arm in arm, we walked around in the light Istanbul drizzle, not talking about music, but rather about broken hearts. She had recently ended a relationship, and squeezed my hand as she made sense of it all.

"God saw me as unfinished, Denise. This pain and this sadness are teaching me. I need these lessons. It's all learning."

"*Hamdım, piştim, yandım* [I was raw, I was cooked, I was burned]" I replied, restating a famous line of Islamic philosopher and poet Mevlana Celaluddin Rumi (1207-1273). My chorus to her refrain was intimately and immediately recognized: suffering ostensibly effaces the ego (*nafs*), rids us of our assumptions and expectations, and brings us closer to burning, divine love and union with God.

She looked at me and smiled. "Exactly. My loss will make me a better person."

At home that night I found myself examining my field notes of the previous months. I examined dozens of interviews in which contemporary musicians claimed that the so-called death of their genre gives them a sadness that, in due time, increases their spiritual knowledge or moral depth. That night, I wrote a field note about my field notes: I found twenty-seven iterations of musicians claiming that the effect of this loss "makes them better more ethical people." Twelve interviewees deployed the poetic line *hamdım, piştim, yandım* in their justifications. Losses fold into one another, and I find myself dutifully producing the same performative narratives that I had received from others.

NEOLIBERALISM, ISLAMIC MOVEMENTS, AND THE PRIVILEGES OF PRIVATIZATION

The historical district of Istanbul known as Sultanahmet is an influential location for the contemporary production of official Ottoman history for Turks and for Turkey's international visitors. It is a central tourist spot, facilitating global and local cash flows directly into Turkey's economy. This sacred and imperial place, home of the Ottoman Topkapı Palace, Aya Sofia (Hagia Sophia), and Sultan Ahmet Camii (known as the Blue Mosque), comes alive in the Islamic month of Ramazan. When I had first started fieldwork in Istanbul in 2004, the municipality funded an impressive and exciting book fair in the Sultanahmet area during Ramazan.[27] Families from Istanbul and beyond came with their relatives of all ages and attended large gatherings of Ramazan nighttime prayer (*teravih*) in the mosque and its gardens, looked at the hundreds of versions of the Qur'an and religious texts, snacked on fruit, and drank tea. Since 2012, that book fair has been replaced with another kind of commercial exchange: selling Islamic mementos, crafts, and souvenirs. Families still come, the soundscape is still rich with the recitation of the Qur'an in a variety of *makam*, but the books are down from hundreds to dozens. Texts have been replaced with artifacts: *tesbih*-s (prayer beads), *ebru* (water-marbling) art, Islamic calligraphy, toys, headscarves, jewelry, and prayer rugs. The fair embodies a kind of neo-Ottomanism supported by the historical frame of the current ruling Justice and Development Party (AKP), flattening seven centuries of Ottoman rule onto material artifacts of Turkish Sunni Islam, and leveling symbolic markers of the Ottoman and the sacred as superior to traditional Kemalist symbolic markers of a secular Turkish nation-state. Ottomanism is consumption at the fair. Buying Islamic artifacts serves, as political scientist Alev Çınar has argued, "to construct an alternative national identity which is Ottoman and Islamic, evoking a civilization centered in the city of Istanbul, as opposed to the secular, modern Turkish Republic centered in the capital city of Ankara" (2001: 365).

The Fatih Book Fair is funded both by the Istanbul municipality and by a variety of private organizations that also support the artisans and crafts-women and men who sell their products. Public Islam in Sultanahmet during Ramazan had, in the past, required the particular kind of a consumer who engaged with reading, who paid for the specific sense experiences of literacy and cultural prestige afforded to the visibility of one's library. Now, public Islam is consumed and traded in the accessible forms of trinkets, tokens, and material artifacts.

To wrap my mind around this considerable shift, I purchase a few items: wooden prayer beads (*tesbih*), a plastic figurine of Sultanahmet Camii itself, a headscarf with embroidery on its edge, and a plastic tray for serving tea with an imprint of the Bosphorus on it. Later that evening, in the bright light of my bedroom, I notice that the mosque figurine, the tray, and the small tag at the edge of the headscarf share the same inscription on the back: "made in China."

Since the 1980s, indicators of notions of Turkishness are increasingly impli-cated in the language of neoliberalism, and Turkish identity markers are expressed through the means of consumer goods. Emergent symbols of neo-liberalism substitute market-oriented terms and participatory frameworks in the place of the nation-state. As "public Islam" in the rise of political Islamism in Turkey meant that Sunni Islamic terms, norms, and habits gained visibility in public life, symbols of secular Kemalism were, to some extent, privatized according to market terminology (Özyürek 2006). However, observing that habits of consumption in everyday life are markers of personal and political identity also demonstrates that Turkish Islamists have more in common with secular Kemalists and with western neoliberal democracy than they do with an imagined Islamic or Ottoman past. Furthermore, Ottoman events are now celebrated by the nation-state along with the habits secularists engage in to venerate Mustafa Kemal that resemble religious ceremony. Anthropologist Jenny White articulates that "[r]eligion in Turkey has become secularized and the secular sphere sacralized" (2014: 5).

The emergence of neoliberalism and particular instantiations of political Islamism in Turkish public life in the 1980s and privatization in 1992 ultimately afforded Turkish classical musicians new avenues of negotiation and visibility.

Recent representations of Turkish classical music have materialized amid significant political turmoil, as privatized forms of patronage now exist alongside state-sponsored institutions. After Mustafa Kemal's passing in 1938, the Republic went through decades of political transformation that produced narratives and naming practices for the past that speak worlds about the political present. In 1950, the first full democratic elections ushered in the Democratic Party (*Demokrat Parti*) and a period of significant rural-urban migration and ethnic violence. In 1960, Kemalism rose to center stage again with a coup d'état by the army, which set the stage for a long-standing atmosphere of cynicism for most of the musicians I work with. One musician expressed the scale of structural turmoil claiming, "political action is rarely productive, as the army stages a coup in this country every ten years." Such contemporary narratives validating political inaction were produced by memories of the military coups of 1971, 1980, and 1997, all of which (save the "postmodern coup" of 1997) violently marked the large gulf between a militarized authoritarian secular government with a top-down approach against a call for modes of diverse citizenship made manifest from bottom up. The latest failed coup of July 15, 2016 was a watershed moment in Turkish civil history, as people flooded the streets to resist the attempted coup after hearing the *ezan* (call to prayer) projected from loudspeakers throughout Turkey's main urban centers (Gill 2016). In other words, sounds of Islamic devotions—combined with an invitation to the streets by President Erdoğan during the coup—organized and inspired people to pour into public spaces and resist the coup attempt.

Various iterations of "Islamist movements" began after Turkey's economic and industrial transformations of the 1980s, which resulted in privatization in the 1990s and supported a fast-growing Muslim middle class. The first Islamist political organization in the post-1980s environment, the Welfare Party (*Refah Partisi*), emerged in 1995 to lead the Istanbul Metropolitan Municipality before the "postmodern coup" of 1997, when the party was closed on the legal grounds of working against the Turkish Republic's principle of secularism. Two political parties emerged in the aftermath, *Saadet* and *Adalet ve Kalkınma Parti*, the most successful of which was the Justice and Development Party (*Adalet ve Kalkınma Partisi* or *Ak Parti*, hereafter AKP) which still maintains and expands political power at the time of writing this book. The vast and diverse communities supporting Islamist movements writ large, with the power of new political representation in the AKP and neoliberal capital flows entering Turkey, participated in crafting a lively (Sunni) Islamic public presence within the generally secular public sphere that included private universities, new visibilities in consumerism, rising economic stability, and significant additions to national cultural practices in the realms of television, literature, fashion, and music (see Frishkopf 2010 and 2012 for analyses of similar trends in Egypt). The individuals and communities supporting Islamist representation in Turkish political, economic, and cultural

[handwritten marginal note: coups attempting to prioritize public religion instead of secularization]

circles articulately countered claims of Islam as antithetical to the projects of Turkish modernity, nationalism, and intellectualism. Turkish public life since the 2000s has often directly challenged the neatly parsed binaries of center versus periphery, secular versus sacred, reason versus tradition, and west versus east that continue to pervade everyday discourse.

The rising Islamist control of state apparatus was joined by major global transformations of the city of Istanbul and the social life produced by neoliberalism, which delegates the state's role to that of managing markets and facilitating global capital movements. One of the primary effects of neoliberalism in Turkey is the dismantling of the center-periphery model of the nation-state, in which Kemalist secular, modernizing authority is dwarfed by social media, the internet, privatized radio and television, and satellite channels. Iconic national images and claims of nationalism that promote Kemalist visions are no longer solely produced by the state, but rather by private institutions such as banks (Özyürek 2006). Similarly, additional forms of public civil Islam have been generated to fit models of democratization, albeit in what is experienced as uncomfortable and destructive ways for many Turks. The market-driven priorities of neoliberalism effectively produce and regulate the relationship between citizens and the nation-state, and privatized institutional structures have emerged as perhaps even more powerful in shaping notions, performances, and claims of citizenship than government agencies. White argues that in such a context, Islam does not challenge the structure of the nation-state, but that in a urban, cosmopolitan, mass-mediated globalized context, "religious and national identities, like commodities, have become objects of choice and forms of personal expression" (2013: 4). The performance of Muslim identity is constantly in flux, shaped by the market and emergent communities (Mandaville 2011: 23–26). This condition returns us to my anecdote about changes in the Fatih Book Fair and how tokens of Islamic material culture—often outsourced for production to China because of cheaper labor costs—reflect the public, popular, and highly commodified materialization of "Islam" in Turkish life.

For contemporary Turkish classical musicians, the emergence of privatization, neoliberalism, and political Islamism has primarily increased their public visibility and economic possibilities. On one hand, TRT still maintains active employees to play Turkish classical music, and municipal state orchestras performing the genre can be found in all major Turkish cities. On the other hand, the privatization and neoliberal global flow that began in the 1990s allowed for a massive increase in transnational touring circuits for Turkish classical musicians, most of who traveled to Europe on contracts that they themselves put together. Musicians who toured in the 1990s and continue to manage these contracts today find themselves most employable if they play Mevlevi *ayin*, or the musical suite to accompany the *sema* ritual featuring "whirling dervishes." The long-lasting popularity and manufacturing of a world music category of "Sufi music" in international festival and concert circuits reflects non-Turkish audiences' fascination with Sufism and expectation of the kinds of transcendental experiences that consuming sacred music might afford (Frishkopf 2012, Kapchan 2008). The privatization of music and media in Turkey and the eventual rise of cable and satellite television further allowed musicians distinct freedoms in terms of copyright and arguing for royalties, and created a context wherein musicians could support themselves as performers of Turkish classical music outside of the institutional frameworks of TRT and music institutions. Interestingly, this prosperity did not usher in a change in narratives about the meaning of the genre that these musicians performed—rather, discourses narrating the "death" of the genre of Turkish classical music grew only louder as privatized media markets joined the state as institutions of patronage.

Like Sultanahmet, the historical district of Eyüp Sultan is of immense importance for Muslim Turks not only for celebration in Ramazan, but also for pilgrimage to the tomb of Abu Ayyub al-Ansari (576–672 or 674), one of the companions of the Prophet Muhammed. Tourists visit to drink tea at the idyllic Pierre Loti café, which is accessed after a hike through one of the most famous graveyards of Istanbul. Like Sultanahmet, Eyüp Sultan has changed its appearance and soundscape in recent years during Ramazan to a commercialized, hyped-up performance of Muslimness that features musical entertainment (usually electrified *ilahi*, or religious hymns), guest speakers (usually representatives of the AKP), and merchants selling Islamic crafts and tokens.

I often frequent the restaurants near the center of Eyüp Sultan to meet with friends and conduct interviews. One particular restaurant is a popular feasting place for the head religious leaders of Eyüp Sultan's mosque and tomb. Most of my conversations here have revolved around the effects of privatization and capitalism on this sacred site. In the early 1990s, my friend, an owner of this prominent restaurant near Eyüp Sultan mosque, had tried many times to bring a few Turkish classical musicians to play *ilahi* in the garden of his restaurant after the breaking of the fast during Ramazan. One of the musicians was a close friend of his who was finishing a Ph.D. in religious studies. All were respectable young men, practicing Sunni Hanafi (Tr. *Hanefi*) Muslims, and strategically mindful of the specific repertoire of Turkish classical music that would be most appropriate during the holy month.

"I tried for years and years to have some religious music here. I thought our classical music, as a kind of art, brings a different sacredness to our holy month of Ramazan. But I had so many complaints by officials. I was told, 'You can't turn a pilgrimage site into a pavilion.' Three times I tried and ended up cancelling the program."

He paused and swept his hand around. "Look at this, listen now." The electrified music and pumping bass line amplified his gesture.

"I was going to have classical musicians. Now we have pop stars coming to perform here. It is not my place to judge who should sing sacred songs—what do I know of these pop stars' religious life? But I ask you, is this Ramazan?"

A young woman in a headscarf who worked as a television producer of a popular Islamist network joined our conversation.

"This is the dilemma of being Muslim today in Turkey, with all of this capitalism. I walk through these graveyards but because of language change of the 1920s, I no longer can read the tombstones as I cannot read Ottoman. If you play me the old Ottoman music or most of what art musicians play on the TV and radio, it has no meaning for me because I cannot understand the lyrics. And so we produce Islam in buying small things to adorn our houses because we can relate to it, we can understand it, and we can hold it. I wish I could relate to other things, but I cannot."

This professional Muslim woman articulates an inability to "no longer" read Ottoman, as if there existed an Ottoman primordial state she should be able to access but has been denied by the rupture between empire and nation-state. The experience of religion has been mediated by capitalism, because in the normative contexts of neoliberalism, relations are experienced in market-oriented processes of consumption. The restaurant owner remains gazing upon and listening to the glitzy performance of "Ramazan," wondering out loud about his own capacity to enact change in this commercialized environment. These are different loss narratives, newly emergent and facilitating the visibility, social exchanges, and performances of "Islam" in Turkish public life.

DEATH OF A GENRE

A Turkish classical music composer: "We are melancholic because our music has died, but we are not sad people."

Me: "What is the difference between sadness [üzgünlük] and melancholy [hüzün]?"

The composer: "Sadness comes and goes, but melancholy is our essence. Melancholy stays. Life—for me as a musician, playing this Turkish classical and Ottoman music—life is melancholy."

While most contemporary Turkish classical musicians may not know the detailed history of reforms and institutionalization that I have outlined, they all tend to mourn the melancholic state of the music genre they play by announcing the death of the genre, testifying to its loss. For some of the musicians I work with, to even call Turkish classical music "Turkish" legitimizes this music as devoid of a past, as non-Ottoman, and as non-Islamic.

Singer and author Savaş Barkçın (b. 1966) articulated this process to me in claiming that "what was at first a reification over time became the real."

The large majority of loss narratives I recorded musicians articulating contain detailed historical moments they have memorized and memorialized. Some of these include the legislation of June 15, 1826, when Sultan Mahmut II closed the military music house of the *yeni çeri* and set into motion the most dramatic change of the *Tanzimat* in Istanbul's overall soundscape. Other musicians cite September 17, 1828, when the new palace orchestra (*Muzikayı Hûmayûn*) was established and Donizetti Paşa was brought in to compose and lead the group in *alafranga*. These contemporary musicians recall particular moments when patronage of the Ottoman elite began shifting toward an interest in western aesthetics, and see a direct correlation between the fate of past Ottoman court musics and the present state of Turkish classical music. Contemporary Turkish classical musicians have, in a way, become agents of "duty-memory" as theorized by historian Pierre Nora. Nora claims that "[t]he less memory is experienced collectively, the more it will require individuals to undertake to become themselves memory-individuals" (1989: 16). As agents of memory, who understand their responsibility as protecting memory itself, Turkish classical musicians constantly negotiate their positioning vis-à-vis conflicting political ideologies supported by the nation-state and neoliberal circuits.

Melancholy is inextricably linked to musical meaning for these musicians, as feelings functionally constitute a social world (i.e., Turkish classical music) that effects a mandatory set of losses: if you make Turkish classical music, you are necessarily bound by a particular instantiation of melancholy that directly implicates your ideas, practices, and habits of the self. In other words, to be a competent, participating musician of this genre, one must adopt and circulate a narrative discourse of loss that constitutes one's personhood as a melancholic modality.

Turkish classical musicians have struggled for decades to make music, but their music making can occur only when filtered through the complicated—and often conflicting—ideological mechanisms of Turkish nationalism. In such a context, contemporary musicians' remembering of an Ottoman past often tells us more about the present than anything else. Many musicians claim that their greatest problem being musicians today is "historyless-ness" (*tarihsizlik*). The impossibility of return to an idyllic pre-republic world abounds in contemporary Turkish classical music narratives. Some musicians I work with identify not as Turkish but rather as Ottoman, defining Ottoman-ness itself as an emotional state (*hâl*) in which one finds that "there is nothing to hold onto."

But narrating the "death" of Turkish classical music is not simply a product of national politics, privatization, or emergent neoliberalism. Ethnomusicologist Karl Signell outlined his thoughts on the state of

Turkish classical music during the time of his fieldwork in the 1960s, writing that

> Turkish classical music lingers on today in a state of siege, with ideological rocks being rained on its head and the artistic sustenance slowly giving out. Defensive because of its archaic texts, Oriental techniques, and historical liabilities, Turkish classical music is still searching desperately for a niche in modern Turkey. (1976: 81)

Signell paints a dreary picture of the possibility of the very existence of the genre of Turkish classical music. In a later work, he explains that in 1972, Recep Birgit, a leading singer of Turkish classical music, predicted that the genre would not last another decade (Signell 1980: 167). Feldman also writes that he heard that Turkish classical music would not last another decade when he was doing his historical research in the late 1980s (Feldman 1996: 16) as did O'Connell during his dissertation research in the early 1990s (O'Connell 1996: 95). I too heard the same when doing my own fieldwork. And claims that after Mustafa Kemal's death, Turkish traditional music beyond folk music slowly became tolerated again, but by then it was too late:

> What is broadcast today by the state radio and television as "Traditional Turkish Art Music" shows Turkish taste at its very worst: indifference to aesthetic values, degrading capitulation to commercialism, blatant disregard for discriminating tastes, and deliberate pandering to the vulgarity by imitation of the pop music of the Middle East. (1984: 222–223)

Signell reports that 1971, a controversy erupted in the newspapers when the prominent academic and Minister of Culture, Talat Sait Halman, decided to present a concert of Turkish classical music for the first time in the State Concert Hall in Ankara. Self-appointed musical progressives, led by the European-trained violinist Suna Kan, were violently opposed to allowing this "primitive, monophonic" music to be heard in the official showcase stage of the Republic (Signell 1980: 166). The concert was canceled.

In his insightful analysis on loss and Turkish musics, O'Connell traces the expression he documented many musicians saying, "everything has finished [hepsi bitirdi]." O'Connell argues that the claim "everything has finished" is a "discourse beyond discourse" for Turkish musicians that categorically points to diverse conceptions of modernity itself. He argues that "[b]y bracketing the past as a past, my Turkish friends are able to practice their past in the present—a past which has never ended and a present which has never begun" (O'Connell 1996: 214). O'Connell's tracing of musicians' utterance is another metaphor of loss that folds itself into the death narrative at the heart of Turkish classical musicians' melancholic modalities. The loss narrative articulating the death of the genre thus emerges as a critical identity practice and requisite form of self-fashioning. The discursive trope at work is that Turkish classical music has died and no longer exists, even though the weavers of these loss narratives are themselves the musicians whose very livelihood comes from performing this music. To play Turkish classical music today means claiming the music has died. Yet the avowal of the loss of this genre is not a recent phenomenon.

I argue that more than instrumentation, more than repertoire, and more than performance practice techniques, the narrative of the death of Turkish classical music *is* the constitutive element binding the genre. Indeed, claiming that this music genre is lost may be the very thing that allows us to speak about this genre as a bound entity at all.

What do we make of these incessant references to death and loss when we talk about this genre of music? How can we understand the logic driving individuals and communities to play and support a music genre that many believe to already be lost? If Turkish classical music has died, I suggest its death marks the very possibility for its continuation. In one of my interviews, a TRT vocalist explained the way the practice of melancholy functions as a particular type of cultural remembrance:

> We don't remember [*hatırlamıyoruz*], because to remember would mean that we have forgotten and need to recall. We live with memory, so much so that we cannot call it memory. It is something else. . . . It weighs on the soul, to live without forgetting the feelings that those before us also lived.

Philosophers of the psyche, particularly those engaging Freudian analyses, argue that melancholy is itself the effect of unavowable loss. Melancholy not only stems from the loss of another or object to consciousness: the social world in which such a loss became possible is also lost. Melancholy itself is, in part, the refusal to acknowledge or accept the impossible loss of that social world, and in doing so preserves this lost object as a psychic effect. The vocalist above articulates not a separation of past and present, thought and feeling, memory and history—he instead sees his self-understanding, experiences, poetry and music as a living of loss of the Ottoman that he does not acknowledge as "lost" to begin with.

While being framed by the loss of the Ottoman and the death of the genre of Turkish classical music, melancholy is actually not a form of loss. Melancholy is precisely the refusal to account for loss. Melancholy is an affective practice that validates living with loss. It makes sense then that Turkish classical musicians would circulate loss narratives and "hear" the death of their beloved music genre, because citing its death ultimately opens up the possibility for its continuation and future.

[handwritten margin notes: "the difference between melancholy and nostalgia?" and "restorative nostalgia?"]

CHAPTER 2

Separation, the Sound of the Rhizomatic *Ney*, and Sacred Embodiment

In the last fifteen years of his life, the renowned Islamic saint Mevlana Celaluddin Rumi (1207–1283) dictated 50,000 lines of poetry in couplet format to his scribe Husameddin Çelebi, in a work that eventually became known as his *Mesnevi* (lit., "masterpiece"). Turkish classical musicians today refer to this preeminent theologian simply as "Mevlana," which means "our master." English-speaking audiences know this figure as "Rumi," a designation that locates Mevlana as an individual from the Asia Minor or the Anatolian peninsula, a region historically named "Rum."[1] While Mevlana continues to be a bestselling author in the United States and the United Kingdom eight centuries after his death, much of his poetry, in its original Persian, has been committed to memory by the contemporary classical musicians in Turkey with whom I work. The most devout of these musicians dedicate significant time and energy to the study of Mevlana's philosophies, and utter his name as "Mevlana, *quddisi sirruh*," attaching the Ottoman title, "the keeper of the secrets." This chapter seeks to share a small aspect of one of Mevlana's spiritual secrets: namely, the belief that it is appropriate—indeed, it is spiritually necessary—to experience feelings of pain and separation and funnel these cries into sound.

Mevlana began his six-volume *Mesnevi* with this text (in its original Farsi calligraphy in Figure 2.1):

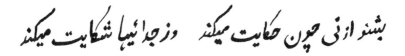

Figure 2.1 First line of poetry in Mevlana Celaluddin Rumi's *Mesnevi*, Book I, written by calligrapher Farrokh Namazi.

Mevlana begins his masterpiece with a command to listen:[2]

> *Bişnev in Ney....*
> Listen to the Ney....

Whereas the Qur'an calls practitioners to recite, Mevlana asks his readers to listen. Listening is beyond hearing: Mevlana both invites us to critically tune into sound and engage in its interpreting meaning. Turkish classical musicians today argue that Mevlana's call to listen to the end-blown reed flute, the *ney* (Figure 2.2), is profoundly significant, as it was the primary instrument in a variety of musics patronized by the upper classes of the Ottoman Empire.

The *ney* is the chief instrument of Ottoman court music because of the deep ties between the palace and the Mevleviyye, the Mevlevi Sufi order founded by Mevlana's followers in Konya after his death in 1273.[3] It was Mevlevi philosophy, based on the teachings and poetic utterances of Mevlana himself, that positioned musical sounds, and in particular the tone of the *ney*, as inherently spiritual. The preeminent *neyzen* (*ney* master) Niyazi Sayın (b. 1927) speaks a definition of music that I have heard from him and from countless other Turkish classical musicians: "music is the spiritual relationship between two sounds [*musiki iki ses arasındaki manevi münasebettir*]."

Figure 2.2 *Ney*-s on display in Mevlana's Museum in Konya, Turkey (photograph by the author).

Eight centuries after Mevlana invited followers to listen, my interviews with Turkish classical musicians brim with repeated references to the *ney* and Mevlana's first stanzas of his *Mesnevi* as musicians explain how sounds of sadness, loss, separation, and death are inherently part of their ideologies of listening. Of course, the Turkish classical musicians with whom I work do not think their music is only about loss and separation: discussions of joy, ecstasy, commensality, and pleasure have equal weight in responses to queries about musical meaning and philosophies. Yet one crucial component that unlocks these musicians' sense of meaning lies in the way positively-qualified emotions, feelings, and affective practices associated with music that are intimately and necessarily linked to loss, separation, sadness, and death. Instead of thinking of these latter elements as negative, Turkish classical musicians perceive them as fundamentally positive. Thus emotions and sensations that, in isolation, many individuals would qualify as negative or destructive, Turkish classical musicians embrace as beneficial. Throughout this book, I call such practices *melancholic modalities*: Turkish classical musicians' forms of subjectivity that render a spectrum of feelings (loss, suffering, pain, separation) as correct modes of existing in their social worlds, as productive material for their music making, and ultimately as spiritually rewarding.

Listening to the *ney* is one of the ways that contemporary Turkish classical musicians' melancholic modalities are shaped: the act of listening emerges as a dynamic form of accomplishing, experiencing, and practicing melancholies that arise from many forms of separation. "Listen to the *ney*," Mevlana spoke:

> . . . *çün hikâyet mîküned.*
> . . . how it tells a tale.

Listening to the *ney*, for Mevlana and the countless others who have drawn on his spiritual ideologies through the centuries, necessitates interpreting the sound of the *ney* as a kind of story. On one hand, listening to the *ney* telling its tale requires an embodied anthropomorphism: seeing the *ney* as a kind of human being, and for Mevlevi devotees, seeing yourself as a kind of *ney*. For the Mevlevi, the *ney* stands in as metaphor for the human body and the human experience, and the instrument is often referred to as *insan-ı kâmil*, which translates to a "perfect, completed human being."

Most Turkish classical musicians' understanding of the concept *insan-ı kâmil* is comprehensively situated in narrations of the *ney* through Mevlana's point of view. Yet the philosophy of *insan-ı kâmil* embraced by Turkish classical musicians today is as thoroughly drawn from the writings of the Spanish Muslim theologian Ibn al-'Arabi (1165–1240) as it is from Mevlana. Al-'Arabi was writing intellectually rigorous texts that solidified Sufi ideas about God's being, humanity, and the cosmos around the same time Mevlana spoke his ecstatic verses. He formulated a theory that emphasized the absolute oneness of God's being, arguing that the absolute existence of God is opposed to the passing existence of living creatures, a doctrine that was later called *wahdat al-wujud* (lit., "oneness of awareness/ experience/being"). William Chittick argues that "Ibn al-'Arabi's teachings come together on the issue of human perfection, which is none other than for human beings to be fully human" (1998: xxiii). Al-'Arabi cultivated the doctrine of *insan-ı kâmil* that, when paired with Mevlana's teachings and statements, has become the archetypal spiritual goal to which many Turkish classical musicians claim to aspire.

What are the embodied, sonic, and linguistic links between a *ney* and *insan- ı kâmil*? Musicians today, when speaking of emitting sound out of the *ney,* breathe hot air into the *ney* "to bring it alive" (*can vermek*). Other musicians participating in different or multiple Sufi orders argue that our souls (*ruh-s*) are the product of God breathing into our own organic bodies. Some musicians I interviewed further name the act of blowing into the *ney* by using the expression *neye ruh vermek*, "to give [a] soul" to the *ney*.

For the individual contemporary Turkish classical musicians who define music itself as inherently spiritual and not only sonic, music making may thus be intoned as spiritual practice. In justifying their interpretation of sound as sacred and their understandings of the *ney*'s sounds as about separation, these musicians cite Mevlana: "Listen to the *ney*, how it tells a tale...."

> ... *Ez cüdâyîhâ şikâyet mîküned.*
> ... *Complaining about its story of separation.*

The *ney*'s story of separation is as follows: it is a rhyzomatic plant, which has multiple reeds shooting out from a watery reed bed. One of the reeds gets cut from the marshy reed bed and dried. In a process that can take contemporary *ney* makers in Istanbul up to three days, the dried reeds are slowly placed above fire at their joints to be straightened out. This process of burning until hot and straightening the *ney* by rolling it with pressure over a maker's upper legs crafts not only a "cooks" (*pişmiş*) a *ney* but also creates heavy calluses on the maker's hands and thighs. Hollowing the reed out requires cutting the ends, as the reed "has died" (*öldü*) in the process of drying. Six finger holes are burned into the front of the instrument and sanded to smoothness. The ends of the reed are cut down and affixed with silver rings, and the *ney* is then soaked in almond or sesame seed oil to curb the drying and ready it for playing. A small mouthpiece (*başpare*) made of carved water buffalo horn, ivory, or heavy plastic is affixed at the top before it is fitted to the individual client's preference for left or right positioning and hand size which determine the placement of the back thumb hole. The *ney* makers who have let me watch this process explain that the act of crafting a *ney* requires physical and spiritual cleanliness according to Islamic tenets (*abdest*) and regaled me with stories about how the *ney* is like a human body. A cyclical symbolism of *insan-ı kâmil* emerges: a *ney* maker, a human being, crafts an instrument, a *ney*, which metaphorically stands in spiritual narratives as a human being itself for these instrument makers.

The *ney* has seven finger holes, a mouth, and an end hole, all which have iconographic significance in Mevlana's writings about how sound and air enter in and out of the body (Çetinkaya 2006). The nine holes in total amplify the correlation between the holes of the *ney* and the porous holes in the (male) human body itself. Finally, for Turkish classical musicians and musical-instrument makers, the *ney*, this *insan-ı kâmil*, embodies the full story of human life. Humans, too, are separated from their source; the reed bed stands for the divine, for God. Like the process an anthropomorphized *ney* purportedly experiences in its making, humans also endure pain, burning, and hardship throughout their existence. The *ney* is breathed into existence in the act of making music, as humans' souls are breathed into the corporeal body for life. The *ney* cries, wails, and laments because of its separation from its source. The sounds of enlightened, aware, and intelligent humans, Mevlevi practitioners argue, should reflect this separation and agony, as humans are detached from God.

Thinking about the *ney* as a person and a person as a *ney* means grappling with how listening to sounds of wailing and music making activates melancholic modalities that engage loss and separation as inherently spiritual and, therefore, appropriate, innate, positive, and natural.

The story of the *ney*'s separation from the reed bed is one of many tales I share in this chapter to demonstrate the spiritual discourses that shape and validate melancholic modalities for contemporary Turkish classical musicians. Mevlana instructs us to "listen to the *ney*, how it tells a tale complaining about its story of separation." Turkish classical musicians today listen to the *ney* with ears shaped for interpreting sound as embodying angst, death, loss, and lament. Feelings of pain that surface with narratives of separation and death are feelings meant to be had. When we consider the melancholic modalities of contemporary Turkish classical musicians, separation and loss are heard in the acts of listening and music making. They are celebrated because they connect individuals and communities to the philosophical underpinnings of a deep-rooted spiritual ideology.

Listeners throughout the Ottoman Empire exposed to Mevlevi institutions understood the metaphoricity of the *ney* ostensibly in the same way Turkish classical musicians do today. But historically, Ottoman listeners also intrinsically heard the *ney* as the sound of death. As musicians today speak of playing as "giving the *ney* a soul" or "bringing a *ney* alive" with their breath, narratives about the *ney* resonate with Ottoman debates about the Islamic concept of the separation between physical and spiritual worlds, the (Ar.) *barzakh*. The *barzakh* is the "obstacle" or "barrier" encountered by the soul's separation from the body after death. In understanding the *ney-as-object* (as a soulless form) and the musician's breath producing the *ney* wail (as the separation of the soul from its origin), discourses of the *ney* reverberated in and poetically structured the contour of Ottoman Islamic eschatology.

The metaphoricity of the *ney* as a kind of human being was also deployed to explain dying, and the sound of the *ney* was interpreted as a longing for death. Wanting death inscribed death itself as a celebratory return to your source, a reunification with God. The multivalent themes of death are ubiquitous in the symbolic practices and beliefs of individuals who follow a number of Sufi paths. In Mevlana's works, for example, death is an inevitable and beautiful part of transition, from matter to mineral to vegetable to animal to human, and then back to the earth for the cycle to begin again. Furthermore, the Mevlevi concept of death is definitively about shedding one's ego (*nafs*) and dying to oneself before one's life ends and one is reunified with God, an idea that references a *hadith*, or statement of the Prophet Muhammed, "die before you die" (see chapter 5). As such, death in Sufism is a sign of spiritual life or awakening, one step in a path toward knowledge of and union with God. This is why Mevlana's own death on December 17 is annually celebrated as his "wedding night" (*Şeb-i Arus*), an acclaimed and highly visible celebration within the Mevlevi order, and a festivalized ritual that continues today. Taking these perspectives seriously means viewing the Mevlevi *sema* turning practices (e.g., the "whirling" of the "whirling dervishes," discussed in chapter 4) as primarily death rituals (O'Connell 2015). In this worldview, life is pain—a journey of separation and suffering—and death is pleasure—the end of separation and becoming one with the divine.

While hearing these references to death-as-pleasure in the *ney*'s wailing tone might be lost on most non-Mevlevi listeners in Turkey today, the narrative of the instrument's sound as voicing loss and pain due to separation from its origin point is generally known in Turkish public life because of the widespread circulation of Mevlana's most accessible and understandable ideas. As Mevlana is translated, appropriated, and consumed throughout the world in international markets, his ideas are revered in Turkey and interpreted as a safe and acceptable way for Turks of all backgrounds to engage with one branch of Islamic philosophy that is often assumed to be apolitical in contemporary public life.

A reputable expert on Mevlevi philosophy, Emin Işık (b. 1936), argues that Mevlana's *Mesnevi*—and Mevlana himself—function as a kind of commercial commodity. Engaging the Mevlevi tradition of metaphor to unfold larger meanings, he told me, "you wouldn't go to buy bread in the market with a 100 lira bill . . . you would go with change [*bozuk para*]." His point was clear: smaller items require smaller exchanges. Significant ideas are simplified to allow for use by individuals of all backgrounds. Işık explains that *the ney's journey parallels the human journey*

[s]ome people cannot engage the Qur'an, but every drunkard, every individual of any religious background, and every person despite their racial, national, or linguistic background will love Mevlana. He was not a prophet, but God gave humanity a gift through him. (personal communication, 26 July 2013, Istanbul)

One of the most circulated ideas from Mevlana's *Mesnevi* is the story told within the first three lines from Book I: the sound of the *ney* wailing and complaining after separation from its source. As a kind of simple "change" exchanged between people, Mevlana offers a highly accessible story that clues us in to how listening to musical sounds, when interpreted according to these spiritual ideologies, produces melancholic feelings of separation that are positioned as pertinent and germane. *Quddisi sirruh*, one of the many secrets Mevlana conserved, was that melancholy is something to be embraced.

The musicians who specialize in the *ney* speak in terms of pain, of how playing *ney* requires one to "tear a bit of their soul off and give it away" (*kendi canından kesip vermek*), and "fill the *ney* with a burning piece of your soul" (*neyi kendi yanmış ruhundan bir parça ile doldurmak*).[4] Playing *ney*, for these musicians, is an active process that translates sacred instrument sound to subjectivity as a melancholic modality. To play the *ney*, one does not simply breathe into the reed. Instead, a musician shapes the mouth, purses the lips, tucks the chin down, and slowly says "Huuuuuuuuuuuuuu" into the mouthpiece. One word, one sound, one hot soul breath. *Hû*.

To understand the intersections of affective and musical practices for contemporary Turkish classical musicians, we must begin with an understanding of Sufism (Tr.: *tasavvuf*; Ar.: *tasawwuf*)[5] and Islamic religious tenets that embrace loss and suffering as constructive aspects of humans' existence as spiritual beings. Sufism, generally understood as the major expression of mysticism in Islam, took root in the tenth century and had a significant role in large-scale conversions to Islam that happened during the period 1000–1800. The term Sufism most often manifests as a process or path (*tariq*) that is guided by the direction of a spiritual leader or mentor (*shaykh* or *pir*) with the goal of union with God. "Walking" a Sufi path generally involves practitioners subduing and erasing their base impulses and ego (*nafs*) to experience annihilation (*fana'*) and reunification with God.

Ethnomusicologists have long called attention to the ways in which Sufi or mystical Islamic belief systems center on music as an expression of and means to transcendence. Scholars working with Turkish Sufism and sound in particular have focused on analyses of musical form or performance as ritual event (And 1977, Feldman 2000 and 1996, Friedlander 1975, Markoff 1986). In this chapter, I cast an analytical eye on how Mevlevi Sufi philosophies about music are made manifest in sound itself rather than in music structure or ritual, and how sound subsequently recreates and reorganizes these understandings and worldviews in Turkish classical music today. I focus on a single sound—*Hû*— to examine the processes in which contemporary Turkish classical musicians create and comprehend sound experience as sacred and how this approach, in turn, shapes their subjectivity, considering the following:

- *Hû* as sound
- *Hû* as a word
- *Hû* as an essence or quality
- *Hû* as *zikir*, or "divine remembrance"
- *Hû* as a technique for playing the instrument *ney*
- *Hû* as sacred embodiment

My case study of *Hû* foregrounds an experience-centered approach that rhizomatically discloses how truth claims and spiritual structures are made logical among the individuals and communities of Turkish classical music that cite *Hû*'s importance. Previous musicological and ethnomusicological studies of Turkish classical music have generally portrayed the genre "Turkish classical music" in purely secular terms, with little focus on the way spirituality makes the sound world intelligible (cf. Aksoy 1985, Ali 1983, Bates 2010, Klaser 2001, O'Connell 2000, Oransay 1983 and 1986, Signell 1977 and 1980, Stokes 1995 and 1997). Scholars have generally tended to insist on a politics of an autonomous subject with a lens that has rendered discussions of musical meaning so secularized that we have paid very little attention to the ways in which spiritual knowing is primarily a project of self-knowing. It is easy to fall into a nationalist or neoliberal trap and adopt the categories constructed during the nation-building policies of the Republic of Turkey (established in 1923). From the modernist gaze produced within the politics of the early nation-state, "Islam" appears as fixed and redolent of backwardness. In the contemporary AKP governance in a neoliberal era, Sunni Islam is presented as a monolithic power and nuances of practices and politics are ignored. I argue that in maintaining these secular and neoliberal frames of analysis, we overlook critical moments in which musicians' emotional and ideological experiences are absorbed into sonic and artistic products and practices. I present this case study of *Hû* to demonstrate how spiritual ideology binds musical meanings and affect together for contemporary Turkish classical musicians.

Scholars who persist in reifying the categories and terminology of sacred versus secular, Islamism versus Kemalism, private versus public, "oriental" versus "western," and more generally eastern versus western perpetuate these dualisms often because they are taking seriously the dualistic, bifurcated categories of the language and discourses of the everyday of contemporary Turkey. These problematic bifurcations are linguistic and conceptual frameworks crafted in the Ottoman *Tanzimat* (reforms) and the early days of nation-state formation that have, over time, been rendered natural and invisible in public life. Foundational studies of modernization in the Ottoman Empire and Turkey have located a modernist historical trajectory, wherein the construct and bifurcation of "secularity" and "religion," "past" and "present," "tradition" and "modernity" was habituated (Itzkowitz 2008, Quataert 2005, Mardin 2000, Doumani 1995, Peirce 1993, Lewis 1969, Berkes 1965). Early works set the terms of academic discourse on secularism, which produced a linear teleology of history that told a story of Turkey's "development" on a trajectory from archaic to modern. Postmodern scholars studying the Middle East, following Michel Foucault's interrogation of history as a disciplining mode of power, have often ended up reproducing the same binaries—religion versus secularity, tradition versus modernity—that they simultaneously critique, as these terms and categories are interpreted as belonging to distinct domains of *habitus*. From these academic perspectives, Turkish classical musicians' discourses, narratives, and practices tend to be immediately placed by academics in a category of neo-Ottomanism or assumed to be potentially representative of political Islamism. As the case study of *Hû* demonstrates, Turkish classical musicians' understanding of their selfhood and their artistic practices evade, resist, and confront simple reduction according to these categories.

In recent political turns in Turkey, we see that even the so-called everyday of Turkish public life (Kandiyoti and Saktanber 2002) is filled with individuals and communities that simultaneously affirm and reject these bifurcations of Muslim/Islamist, Islamism/Kemalism, east/west, traditional/modern, sacred/secular as well. In simplistic terms, these compartmentalized dualisms do not adequately explain Turks' social lives. The political unrest of the Gezi Park (*Gezi Parkı*) protests of the summer of 2013 significantly demonstrated the challenges Turks can levy against state and government structures and discourses that simplify issues as Kemalist or Islamist. The Gezi protests were not about Islam or secularism; rather, the protests crossed these lines. Protesters from all forms of profession, religious orientation (from Islamist to atheist), ethnic background, gender and sexual identities, and age gathered to confront the government's use of green public land, the increase in violence in civil society (often against women), policies on Syria, treatment of the Kurds, changes in the constitution to give particular political leaders more power, and the imposition of values by force. These issues, raised in protest, crossed secular and pious lines, and allowed for ethnographers of modern Turkey to immediately account for the political urgencies that require us to shed labels assumed to be helpful in the past.

Joining recent interrogations of secularism and religiosity in Turkish society, I argue that we must not study secularism or spiritual ideologies according to the terms set by modernist paradigms (J. White 2002 and 2014, Navaro-Yashin 2002a and 2012, Özyürek 2006, Çınar 2005). Going beyond analyses of social institutions or state leaders that tend to be privileged in academic studies of power, the site for this case study is the everyday (see especially Stokes 2010), a category that enables "the study of the political in its fleeting and intangible, transmogrified forms" (Navaro-Yashin 2002a: 3).[6] Public life emerges as a central domain wherein ideas of nationality, civility, piousness, and religiosity are appropriated, produced, and made meaningful by individual musicians who craft selfhood in relational ways. National subjectivity is highly situational and context driven; the stories I share problematize the terms "Islam," "Muslim," "Sufi," and "secular," taking them to task both because they have emerged as the most dominant discourses that form the basis of public life in Turkey, and because they are categories that are challenged and played with by the musicians whose beliefs, practices, and narratives have informed this study. In the context of emergent neoliberalism, mass-mediated commercialization, and transnational globalization, Muslimness and Islamic practices have become personalized—often picked up and found fashionable by some individuals. In short, "Islam" in contemporary Turkish public life has become unfixed from formal groups that claim to represent Islamic ideas and practices.

Turkish classical musicians are active agents who playfully and creatively engage Islamic rituals, practices, or philosophies and resist dualistic categories of Islamism versus Kemalism, Islamist versus Muslim, pious versus secular, and even Ottoman versus Turkish as they mindfully engage in acts of sacred embodiment. The collective body of Turkish classical musicians exists in a political in-between in Turkish public life, in the interstices of a normalizing Kemalism or secular versus Islamism or pious Muslim debate.[7] While "individual strategies fit a cultural logic" (J. White 2014: 16) of pious Muslim or secular identity frameworks, Turkish classical musicians cannot be grouped as representative of these categorizations, nor can musicians' ideologies fall into easy classification. Turkish classical musicians' national identities and subjectivities are not either/or; their senses of themselves as citizens are but/and. They demonstrate White's claim that in Turkey, Muslim identity "is not a homogenous category . . . and also offers a code for expressing political ideas, social class position, or general life philosophy, in addition to specific religious beliefs or affiliation" (2014: 38). What unifies Turkish classical musicians beyond the music they make, I argue, are particular affective practices that are based on voicing loss, separation, pain, and suffering: a living of melancholy that stands in as a practice of selfhood. I have named this pattern of identity practices based on affect *melancholy modalities*, and trace the way musicians engage their philosophies about sound as spirit and spirit as sound in dissent of the divisive discourses of Turkish public life. The voicing of melancholy through sound and spiritual discourse about sound, as in the case study *Hû*, emerges as a strategy through which Turkish classical musicians constitute and understand themselves and their agency in the social and political worlds. Studying musicians' engagement with *Hû* offers one crucial insight into musicians' melancholic modalities: loss and pain are validated, justified, and celebrated through recourse to spiritual ideologies in Sufism and Islam more generally.

The word *Hû* manifests in devotional hymns (*ilahi*-s) and music ritual, in Ottoman and contemporary Turkish proverbs and poetry, as an incantation for trance, as a greeting or other form of social exchange in Sufi orders, and as a vehicle for musical and spiritual transmission. *Hû* written in Ottoman Islamic calligraphy (*hüsn-ü hat*) is ubiquitous in Turkish sacred spaces, written on musical instruments (especially *def* frame drums), in art and ornaments hung on walls in businesses and homes, and in personal items such as jewelry.[8] Figure 2.3 depicts an example of *Hû* done in *ebru*, a water-marbling art developed during the Ottoman era and still popular in Turkey today. The calligraphy of *Hû* is done in the *müsenna* (Ar. "duel"), or mirrored style, which symmetrically represents the Islamic belief that when one looks to the west and to the east, that person can witness and experience God in both directions:

Figure 2.3 *Hû* in *ebru* by Cem Yılmaz from the author's collection (photograph by the author).

Musicians claim that the repetition of *Hû* as sound both articulates and bridges the human condition of separation from the divine (i.e., God). It is at these crossroads of subjectivity and collectivity, normative frameworks of Islamism and secularism, challenges of popular culture and sacred embodiment, body and spirit, sound and silence that I interrogate how sound creates and gives shape to the spiritual practices that musicians engage in their social worlds.

SUFISM AS SEPARATION

Hû as word, sound, and spiritual practice manifests in all Sufi orders in contemporary Turkey and in the seemingly simultaneously secularized and Sunni Islamic Turkish public sphere. While contemporary Turkish classical musicians may draw mostly from Mevlevi Sufism, some musicians foster close bonds with more than one order, even participating in rituals of diverse Sufi paths (Tr. *tarikat*). Generally speaking, Sufis throughout the Middle East, North Africa, and South Asia have historically differed from other Sunni Muslim communities in their emphasis on the knowledge of interiority and the inner meaning of religious texts (Ar. *'ilm al-batin*). Early Sufi authors of theoretical works focused on issues of practice, ethics, and morality. The writings of Ibn al-'Arabi mark a watershed moment in Sufism because he solidified a shift to focus on dialectics and alterity. Al-'Arabi articulated that Islam's holy book has two names, *Qur'an* (lit., "bringing together") and *Furkan* (lit., "separation" or "differentiation"). These names signify the two basic principles in which God created the universe and reveals him/herself in three manifest domains: the universe, the soul, and the Qur'an. God is "one" through his/her essence and "many" through his/her differentiated knowledge.[9] Such a theoretical, theological accounting of alterity is one of the reasons that some contemporary scholars have focused on eminent medieval Sufis as the first postmodern and poststructural thinkers, centuries ahead of those in western Europe (Frishkopf 2003, Terzioğlu 2002).

Sufism is often framed by practitioners as the "essence" (*jawhar*) of Islam. Primary to this essence is the devotional love (*aşk* and *muhabbet*) Sufis have for God, the Prophet Muhammed and his family, saints such as Mevlana, and other human beings, ostensibly regardless of boundaries based on race, gender, sexuality, class, or language. This spiritual love functions dialectically: love is simultaneously the experience of separation from God (*firak*) and union of living in God's presence (*wisal*). Thus to be a Sufi means to be one who welcomes both pain and joy. The closing of the ontological gap between separation and union led some Sufis historically to make bold expressions of this paradox, statements that Sunni Islamic theologians construed as blasphemous. Perhaps the best known of these Sufis was Mansur al-Hallaj (858–922), who reportedly claimed, while in a state (*hal*) of ecstasy, "I am the Truth!" (*ana al-Haqq!*),[10] an utterance for which he was put to death. Al-Hallaj's admission, indicative of the mystical annihilation of *fana'*, was heard by his community as a statement equating oneself with God and thus negating the unity of God

(Ar. *tawhid*), a basis or pillar of Islam. By performing devotions, Sufis aim to raise the soul (*ruh*) toward its origin in God, while purifying the self or ego (*nafs*) from its baser longings. Many believe that poetry brings God's presence into the direct awareness of the listener, and love for God requires "remembrance" (Tr. *zikir* or Ar. *dhikr*). For many Sufis, especially those in the Mevlevi order, the hearing of love through the audition of music (Tr. *sema* or Ar. *sama'*) often encourages a state of devotional ecstasy (Tr. *vecd* and Ar. *wajd*) brought about in particular by "turning" (Tr. *sema*), which is experienced as a generative spiritual practice. The anticipated end result is the complete obliteration of ego and the self, understood and experienced paradoxically: a simultaneous cessation of being and absorption into God (*fana'*).

When we consider the diverse social and political histories of ethnic and religious communities in Turkey, the term *Sufism* itself tends to be unhelpful, because multiple sects grouped under the umbrella term of Sufism have vastly different beliefs and practices. Equally complicated are these various Sunni and Shia orders' histories in the Ottoman Empire. The Bektaşi, a Sufi order, and the Alevi, a heterodox sect, can be traced back to the Babai movement of the thirteenth century. Members of both sects revere Hacı Bektaş Veli as a patron saint and share roots in Shia Islam.[11] The Alevi-s and Bektaşi-s were in favor of the Persian Safavid Empire and Qizilbash Islam (*Kızılbaş* in Turkish, understood in language practices today as a pejorative). As avid supporters of the Persian Shah İsmail I (1487–1524) and the proselytizing efforts that surfaced in his poetry (written under the pen name Hatai), Alevi and Bektaşi communities were viewed by Ottoman Sunni bureaucrats as separatists. If we view Ottoman histories broadly, Alevi and Bektaşi communities were generally secluded societally in the Ottoman Empire, often located in rural Anatolia and, after 1826, in southeastern Europe (Markoff 1986, Dressler 2003). Despite the political discord, Bektaşi-s played an especially significant role in the lives and activities of the Ottoman military class, the *yeni çeri* (transliterated as "Janissary" in English).

As previously mentioned, the most politically powerful Sufi order throughout the duration of the Ottoman era was the Mevlevi, or Mevleviyye (Ar. *Mawlawiyah*). An extension of their authority in social realms, the Mevlevi also dominated in the institutions of Ottoman aesthetic practices, including music, calligraphy, and *ebru*. Mevlevi discourse became the dominant discourse of Ottoman cultural and artistic production because of their political power in the Ottoman government. The legacy and hegemony of the Mevlevi continues to resonate today, as most contemporary Turkish classical musicians' understandings of the philosophies of Sufism more generally are themselves Mevlevi-based. Mevlana's son, Sultan Veled (d. 1312) established the Mevlevi order in Konya. Its first permanent lodge (*tekke*) in the Ottoman capital of Istanbul, the Galata Mevlevihânesi, was founded in 1494. Elsewhere in Istanbul neighborhoods, the Yenikapı Mevlevihânesi opened its doors in

1597, and Mevlevi *tekke*-s in Kasımpaşa and Besiktaş were opened in the early seventeenth century, with an influential lodge founded in Üsküdar in the late eighteenth century. The Mevlevi were necessarily a transcultural institution, as there were major centers in other parts of the Ottoman Empire as well, such as Aleppo, Damascus, Hims, Tripoli, Beirut, Jerusalem, and Cairo, and in Greece, Bulgaria, and Bosnia.

The history of Mevlevi Sufism in the nineteenth and twentieth centuries reflects the consequences of Ottoman *Tanzimat* (reforms) and the appropriation of European philosophical thought. Mevlevi-s themselves benefited from the reforms in some ways that other Sufi orders did not.[12] For example, they participated in the new public sphere, as indicated by the increase of Mevlevi-s writing and publishing in Ottoman journals during the nineteenth and twentieth centuries, such as *Muhibban, Hikmet, Tasawwuf,* and *Mahfil.* Mevlana's highly circulated *Mesnevi* was studied within the framework of many Ottoman institutions, and writers such as Abidin Paşa, Tahir ul-Mevlevi, and Kenan Rifai wrote commentaries on the *Mesnevi* in dialogue with their readings of western political thought as well as science paradigms we might today term biomedical (see chapter 5). Yet Mevlevi political privilege was brought to a halt with the decline of the Ottoman Empire, World War I, and the establishment of the nation-state. With the foundation of the Republic of Turkey in 1923 and the goal of leader Mustafa Kemal (Atatürk) to create a nation-state vastly different from the Empire that preceded it, the political power held by Mevlevi-s during the Ottoman Era came to an end.[13] The architects of the new nation-state understood that they needed to shape modern Turkish citizenry away from—and in opposition to—previous Ottoman iterations of power. Sufi orders were altogether abolished and the *tekke*-s were closed in 1925. Mevlevi texts were burned, and practitioners fled to Syria and other locations while the Mevlevi who stayed in Turkey either stopped practicing or took their gatherings underground. The subsequent changes in the republican period cultivated an environment today in which Mevlevi artistic practices are presented and taught as archaic and esoteric historical artifacts of the past, a trend that feeds into popular discourses about Sufism as a "spiritual"—not "religious"—commodity in the secular "world music" market (Kapchan 2008, Shannon 2011). Mevlana's international posthumous reach has allowed for the celebration of the spiritual in the sanitized form of neoliberal commodities, the desacralization of Islam in representations of Sufism globally, and Turkish tourism, trends that reached their height when UNESCO declared 2007 as the "Year of Rumi and Global Peace."

While benefiting from the increase in tourism and commodification of "Rumi" as politically representing Turkey as a tolerant, arts-loving nation in international discourse, the official national position on Mevlevi rituals remains staunchly secular. The movement to sterilize any political potency

Figure 2.4 The entrance to Mevlana's mausoleum and museum in Konya (photograph by the author).

remains secular?

remaining after the closing of the *tekke*-s was a decades-long endeavor that the Republic undertook. For example, Mevlana's mausoleum in Konya reopened in the 1930s as a national museum rather than as a functioning *tekke* (Figure 2.4). While most Turkish classical musicians today are not alone in undertaking a visit to Mevlana's tomb as a religious pilgrimage, Turkish official narrative frames this space as a place of historical artifacts and as a museum emblematic of Turkish history.

It was only in the 1950s, with a relaxation of state anti-religious measures, that Turkish authors writing about Mevlevi philosophies were able to publish in publically circulating texts. *Şeb-i Arus* was presented for the first time since the dissolution of the Mevlevi order as an official, national, and secular ceremony in Konya in 1955. In 1973, the Turkish government authorized these performances of the so-called historic past to be given annually; this same year they financed the creation of a state orchestra playing Mevlevi *ayin* (musical suite) and *iluhî* (religious hymn) to tour internationally (And 1977: 84). Taken together, these institutionalized mechanisms helped fix and secure normative frameworks, not only bifurcating sacred versus secular, but also privileging secular over sacred and establishing a framework wherein Mevlana's ideas found an acceptable place as quaint, historical artifacts of culture in secularized public life.

Today, while the practices and rites of the Mevlevi order officially exist as museum pieces or historical artifacts, the beliefs and philosophies of the Mevlevi, specifically those concerning sound and music, have continued to influence Turkish musical texts and practices to the point that discernment between "Ottoman-Turkish musical texts" and "Mevlevi musical texts" is difficult, if not impossible. Indeed, the overwhelming majority of the musicians I work with know, articulate, and embrace the tenets of Mevlevi Sufism even if they do not identify as Mevlevi themselves.[14] In contemporary Turkish classical music practices, an astounding example of the fluidity between Sufi realms and the discourses, practices, and worldviews of Turkish classical musicians is the word and sound *Hû*.

HÛ AS SOUND

Sound is a critical mechanism for the cultivation of spirituality, and *Hû* provides a clear example of how individuals and communities perceive and come to understand themselves and the sacred through sound. Most individuals in Turkey first recognize *Hû* as a name for God, a perspective shared with Persian/ Farsi-speaking communities.[15] In Arabic, *Hû* manifests as *huwa*, or "he," the third person masculine singular personal pronoun (Wehr 1994: 1215).[16] But for Turkish classical musicians, *Hû* is just as likely to be translated as "essence" as it is to be translated as a name of God, which resembles the Arabic *huwīya*, which also connotes "essence" or "nature" (Wehr 1994: 1215).

Hû has a place in Turkish Sufi interpretive discourses about the "beautiful" names of God (*esma-ül hüsna*). The commonly known ninety-nine names or attributes each describe a quality of God (*sıfata müteallık*—lit, "dependent on quality"). There are two words or names of God, however, that are believed to combine all of the ninety-nine attributes within them (*zata müteallık*—lit., "dependent on individual essence"). The two words that connote all of the ninety-nine attributes are *Allah* and *Hû*. When collected with the ninety-nine attributes, *Allah*, *Hû*, and *Azam* (the hundredth name of God), they collectively are called *cami-ül esma*, or "collection of names." It should not be a surprise, then, that when we look at nearly a century and a half of texts from various Sufi orders in the Ottoman period. *Hû* becomes a preferred word for the naming of God. *Hû* is a word that combines all of the attributes in one syllable, making it both a paintbrush and a sonic instrument in a poet's toolkit.

As *Hû* simultaneously connotes God's name and God's essence, it appears in the daily language practices of various Sufi orders as well. Abu Bakr Shibli (d. 945) for example, is said to have heard and rendered the name of God as

"*Hû, Hû*" in the "koo, koo" of the dove and nightingale (Nurbakhsh 1976: 8). Anthropologist Francis Trix notes that *Hû* is uttered as a type of incantation at the end of most stanzas of Bektaşi religious song (*nefes*), and intoned at the end of meals (Trix 1993: 10 and 169). Sheikh Muzaffer Ozak (1916–1985) of the Halveti-Cerrahi order recommended the lengthy and repeated chanting of *Hû ya Hû* as meditation practice for his disciples in order for them to take on a quality or essence of God (Ozak 1991: 29 and 34). In addition, Ozak writes that English-language prayers for Halveti-Cerrahi practitioners should always end with this formula:

> In honor of our saint Sultan Nureddin al-Jerrahi, heir of Haydar al-Karrar, the Cupbearer of Divine Love. Let us join his circle and say *Hû*. By your grace accept our prayers Lord Ya Allah Hû. (1991: 62)

Hû is valued not just for its various meanings as a word but also because of the spiritual potency of the sound *Huuuuuuuuuu* itself. Ottoman Sufi writers, such as the seventeenth century Halveti poet Niyazî Mısrî, purposely deployed *Hû* as sound in poetry not only because *Hû* both names God and evokes God's essence, but also because *Hû* as sound "does" *zikir*. *Zikir*, or "divine remembrance," is prayer and trance through sound, breath and movement. Niyazî Mısrî was well known for playing with *Hû* as word and as sound in his poetic texts (Uludağ 2001: 172). Many musicians I work with know Niyazî Mısrî's poetry well and have committed many of his verses to memory, especially as his poems were frequently set to music by the Ottoman composer Hafız Post (otherwise known as Mehmed Efendi, d. 1693). One of Mısrî's classic poems deploying *Hû* is the following:

> *Gir semâa zikr ile gel yana yana Hû deyû*
> *İr safâ-i aşk-ı Hakk'a yana yana Hû deyû*
> *Zat-ı Hakk'ı buldular buluştular bir Hû ile*
> *Dost göründü her taraftan yana yana Hû deyû*

> Enter the *sema* doing *zikir* burning and saying *Hû*
> Into Truth [*Hakk* is also a name of God] with pleasure, peace, and
>   love burning and saying *Hû*
> The individual essence found truth and was itself in Truth with *Hû*
> Friends appear from every direction burning and saying *Hû*

In this brief poem, Niyazî Mısrî engages in wordplay with the word *Hû*, using it to seamlessly invoke different meanings and simultaneously indicate the sound *Huuuuu* and *Hû* as God. In utilizing *Hakk*, one of the ninety-nine attributes naming God as "Truth," Niyazî Mısrî engages wordplay with another name of God and the name's essence. Wordplay also occurs with the word *yan* in the last line, which complicates the translation to mean that friends appear from all directions and say *Hû*, that friends simultaneously say *Hû* as they come into the presence of *Hû* (i.e., God), and that friends "burn" (from the verb *yanmak*) in the saying of *Hû*.

Hû proliferates in dozens of commonly known religious hymns (*ilahi*-s) in contemporary Turkey, and there are a few *ilahi* that specifically focus on *Hû*. In the singing of these *ilahi*-s about *Hû*, one singer explained to me, participants are effectively reminded about the lessons of the poetic text, they benefit from the collaborative music making in singing *ilahi* together, and also they have the opportunity to engage in a particular kind of prayer by "pulling *Hû*" (the meditative practice named *Hû çekmek*). Let us take the *ilahi* with the title "*Hû Demek İster*" (lit., "[To] Want to Say *Hû*") as an example. While some novices of *ilahi* cite two different *ilahi* with the title "*Hû Demek İster*," Turkish classical musicians who regularly perform this kind of simple, strophic religious repertoire name and differentiate between the *ilahi*-s by the first line of text. One of the texts of an *ilahi* whose topic celebrates the desire to "say *Hû*" is attributed to the fifteenth century sheikh Ahmed Kûddûsi and anonymously composed in the melodic mode (*makam*) *Hicaz makamı* (Example 2.1). While the first stanza of this *ilahi* tells a well-told narrative about a Sufi practitioner denouncing a comfortable life in commitment to spiritual richness, the last stanza allegedly references the poem's author:

> *Mestü hayranım*
> *Zarü giryanım*
> *Her dem lisanım*
> *Hû demek ister*

> *Hû ismi Azam*
> *Hû Hû der hocam*
> *Kûddûsi her dem*
> *Hû demek ister*

I admire the [thin, worn-down] boots
With misery I weep
With every breath my tongue
Want to say *Hû*

The name *Hû* is the Greatest[17]
My teacher says *Hû, Hû*
With his every breath Kûddûsi
Wants to say *Hû*

Example 2.1 The *ilahi* entitled "*Mestü hayranım*"—often also referred to by the name "*Hû demek ister*"—in *Hicaz makamı*.

A second version of an *ilahi* that is often also called "*Hû Demek İster*" is better known by musicians according to the first line of the lyrics: "*Yüce sultanım derde dermanım.*" Its text, which was purportedly written by the beloved thirteenth century Turkic folk poet Yunus Emre, explains the subject's experience of every aspect of his/her being as a desire to "say *Hû*":

> *Yüce sultanım*
> *Derde dermanım*
> *Bedende bu can*
> *Hû demek ister*

> *Her derde derman*
> *Ey gani Sübhan*
> *Bedende bu can*
> *Hû demek ister*

> My exalted sovereign
> My cure to suffering
> This soul inside this body
> Wants to say *Hû*

> The remedy to every pain
> O God, the one without fault
> This soul inside this body
> Wants to say *Hû*

reference to music healing physical ails? like in Greek thought?

While a few separate compositions have been written for this text, notably a modern setting by composer Sadun Aksüt (b. 1932) in the melodic mode *Hüzzam makamı*, contemporary Turkish classical musicians' most beloved version was written by prominent composer Zekai Dede (1825–1897) in a highly classical setting in a different mode, *Suzidil makamı* (Example 2.2):

Usûl: slow and heavy sofyan

Example 2.2 The *ilahi* entitled *"Yüce sultanım derde dermanım"* by the nineteenth century composer Zekai Dede in *Suzidil makamı*.

In a way, *Hû* maintains an efficacy in contemporary Turkey simply because of the ubiquity of the shared tradition of *ilahi*-s. Cem Behar has documented that since the seventeenth century, there continues to be no clear formal or stylistic differences between the *ilahi*-s sung in Mevlevi, Halveti, Cerrahi, or Kadiri *zikir* ceremonies in Istanbul, and that any of these hymns could be sung in other *tekke*-s in regions of Southeastern Europe, North Africa, and the Middle East (2006: 60).

Hû is not only a subject of *ilahi*-s, but is also used as devotional remembrance and trance (*zikir*) itself. In a variety of practices, *Hû* is generally coupled with *zikir* with the use of the incantation *Lâ İlahe İllâ Hû* (lit., "There is no God but 'Hû'"). This pairing is precisely why *Hû* tends to be interpreted as more effective or heavier than another name of God, as *Hû* is a way of doing *zikir* in one sound, an idea deployed by Niyazî Mısrî in his poem above. *Hû* working as *zikir* is clearest when it is chanted in long breaths with repetitions of the exhale of *Huuuuuuuuuuuuuuuuuuuu*, a chanting practice known as "pulling *Hû*" (*Hû çekmek*) that continues to be ubiquitous in Sufi lodges throughout urban centers in contemporary Turkey.

Furthermore, some Muslims are quick to extol the importance of the sound *Hû* as "naturally occurring" in all types of Sunni religious practice. One blogger of the Kadiri order points out that whether or not Muslims are aware of the importance of the sound *Hû*, they end up voicing *Hû* 229 times a day if they observe the Islamic five-times daily ritual prayers (Tr. *namaz*, Ar. *salat*) because of the number of times *Hû* occurs, such as in the statement "God is great" (pronounced and interpreted, in this creative misspelling, as "Alla-Hû-Akbar").[18]

In Mevlevi sects, *Hû* has been also used as a greeting and request. For example, a Mevlevi may ask "*Destur*" (lit., "permission") or "*Hû*" as a call and request to enter a particular space, and hear permission granted with the response "*Yamen Hû*" ("enter Hû"). The individual in charge of the *tekke* (the *Meydancı Dede*) then calls out "*Buyurun ya Hû*" ("come, o Hû") or "*Ye ya Hû*" ("eat, o Hû") to call others from the order in for a meal (Tanrıkorur 2003: 111–112). Here *Hû* as sound names God, invokes God's essence, and effectively "does *zikir*" (*zikretmek*), a critical act of remembrance. Voicing "*Ya Hû*" in calling fellow Sufis together fulfills another deep spiritual exchange beyond invoking God's essence and doing *zikir*, because naming others around you with a name of God functions as a way in which a Sufi sees God or divinity in all fellow human beings. This practice reflects and recreates Mevlevi beliefs about the sacredness in each human being, as individuals themselves are named and name others as *Hû*. Indeed, the act of writing *Hû* in calligraphy (see Figure 2.3) embodies the belief of the human in the divine itself, as the vowel of the word *Hû* is the letter "vav," or و. While Arabic and Persian speakers throughout the world experience this letter sounding "ooooooooooooooo" in thousands of words, Ottoman artists separated this single letter out and produced hundreds of calligraphic representations of the letter standing alone (Figure 2.5).

In typical interpretation, the letter "vav" resembles the human fetus in utero. Islamic calligraphers in present-day Turkey verbosely articulate how hanging a "vav" on your wall reminds a viewer of their smallness, insignificance, and dependence on God. Seeing yourself as infantile, preborn, and on a long spiritual path is one of the ways calligraphic renderings of the "vav" stich together spiritual ideologies and situated histories of artistic representation. Multiple calligraphic representations of "vav" and of *Hû* abound in Turkey,

Figure 2.5 The "vav" letter inscribed on the author's finger rings (*yüzük*) that hold picks (*mızrap*) in place for playing the trapezoidal zither, the *kanun* (photograph by the author).

cementing a slippage of meaning between the letter "vav" and the word *Hû*. Seeing a visual representation of *Hû* can thus be an encounter with yourself. As another manifestation of an embodied "vav," calling those around you "Ya *Hû*" emerges as a way of seeing and naming God both in the self and in the others who make up your social world.

HÛ AS INSTRUMENT TECHNIQUE

While many Sufi practitioners in Turkey readily articulate a knowledge of *Hû* as essence, name, and sound, not as many will be as informed to speak about the affiliation between *Hû* and the Turkish classical reed flute that opened this chapter, the *ney*. The web of meaning residing in *Hû* as sound may be most apparent in the philosophies of the Mevlevi order, which elaborately outline a cosmological belief system involving the *ney*. The fifteenth century Halveti sheikh Cemâl-i Halveti (d. 1494) attested to the importance of a call-and-response interactive experience of sounding and hearing *Hû* in the *sema* ritual, penning the following:

> *Nâleden ney deldi bağrın*
> *Hû deyü nalân ider*
>
> The cry of the *ney* pierces his breast
> He lets out a wail with *Hû*

As the Mevlevi valued the *ney* and its web of symbolic associations, and as they held authority in many Ottoman institutions of artistic production, the *ney* today maintains this historical legacy and continues to hold a central place in the rituals of many Turkish Sufi sects.

Scholars argue that the development of the instrumental improvisational practice known as *taksim* from the sixteenth through the nineteenth centuries in urban Ottoman musical centers can be attributed to the Mevlevi order (Behar 2006, Feldman 1996). While multiple forms of improvisation coexisted, the Mevlevi did not invest as much in elaborating on vocal improvisation forms (*kaside* and *gazel*) but rather developed a highly specific style of *taksim* for the *ney*. Part of the aesthetic that the Mevlevi developed features an emphasis on the overtones emitted from the *ney* and the use, audition, and function of the breath of the player (the *neyzen*). In his substantial manuscript on Ottoman musical practice, Feldman writes that *neyzen* Aka Gündüz Kutbay (1934–1979) "... viewed the breath of the *neyzen* as a symbol of the mystical syllable Hu ..." (1996: 97). Feldman's statement is left as a passing remark because a study of the sound *Hû* was not in the realm of his particular project. Yet his observation of a *neyzen* breathing *Hû* into his instrument emerged in my own fieldwork as the most important detail in the layers of meaning embedded in the sound *Hû.* The *neyzen*-s I work with in Konya, for example, will not even use the word "breath" (*nefes*) to describe how they send air into the reed flute to produce sound: they constantly corrected my questions by reminding me that I should know that a true *neyzen* does not breathe but "prays *Hû*" (*Hû dua ederek*) or "recites *Hû*" (*Hû okumak*), or "pulls *Hû*" (*Hû çekmek*) to play the *ney*. For these contemporary Turkish classical *neyzen*-s, *Hû* functions not just as word and sound, but also as the primary technique for playing the *ney*.[19]

Turkish *neyzen*-s literally blow into the *ney* by saying *Hû*—when *Hû* is voiced and sounded into the instrument the lips take the correct position needed to play the Turkish *ney* with its specific mouthpiece (*başpare*). *Hû* is then sounded into the *ney* to produce music. *Hû* is not only a metaphor of the *neyzen*'s breathing into the reed as God breathes soul into the human body—*Hû* is also, for these contemporary musicians, a literal act that replicates and mirrors divine processes as acoustic distribution. It is a performance practice that does not simply reflect spiritual ideology: *Hû* itself is evidence of musicians' understanding of inherent sacrality in musical practice. *Hû* as sound names God, evokes God's essence, does *zikir*, and serves as a music technique for playing the *ney* that links the contemporary world to the divine. *Hû* thus reveals the processes through which spirituality is shaped and brought into being through sound. *Hû* also helps us understand the philosophical legacies with which contemporary Turkish classical musicians engage, and the connection between Turkish classical music and Sufi realms. How does sound, understood as sacred, assist individuals in the task of making themselves intelligible to others?

HÛ AS SACRED EMBODIMENT

Hû works as a sacred embodiment that musicians take on to ground the sacred in their individual and social bodies. The spiritual is no less social than the political, and also becomes a mediator of the traffic between the personal and the political, the individual and the community. When we investigate the voicing of *Hû* and discourses about its meaning as a sacred embodiment, *Hû* surfaces as a tool individuals use to make sense of their selfhood and larger community, especially in the context of public life, in which assumptions about the antagonistic discord between Kemalism and Islamism and secular and sacred ideologies converge. Turkish classical musicians connect their senses of spirit-in-body to their social identities by deploying *Hû* to explain embodiment and also to sound out resistance to hegemonic dualistic normative power structures that circulate alternative meanings of *Hû*.

Sacred embodiment entails a particular engagement with body praxis, which positions the body not as an accomplished fact but rather as a process.[20] Embodiment concerns all of the ways in which people inhabit their bodies— eating, sleeping, grooming, tending to illness, making sound; all are forms of body praxis and expressive of dynamic social, cultural, and political relations. The processes through which contemporary Turkish classical musicians become habituated to the spiritual through the body, such as playing the *ney* or otherwise mindfully engaging with and producing the sound *Hû*, become forms of sacred embodiment wherein they make the connection between body, sound, and spirit. Insisting on a (communal) selfhood situated in sacred embodiment, Turkish classical musicians labor against secularizing frameworks by validating all aspects of their embodied lives as sacred.

An elementary level of sacred embodiment emerges in a larger creation myth that reflects Mevlana's introductory call to "listen to the *ney*" in his *Mesnevi*. The musicians with whom I work often tell the story that when God created the human body from earth, God had difficulty getting "Spirit" (*Ruh*, lit., "soul," anthropomorphized as Spirit in this story) to enter into the human body. Spirit refused to reside in the human body because it did not want to be separated from God. So the angel Gabriel brought a double-*ney* flute (*koşney*) from heaven and began to breathe the sound *Hû* into the *ney*. Spirit immediately fell into ecstasy and chased the sound *Hû* through the end of the double end of the *ney* Gabriel was playing. The *ney* became the human body, and Spirit found itself confined to that body. The material body remains on and of the earth, separated from God. But the body retains its state as an instrument that produces *Hû*, which is interpreted as a mournful sound of longing to be reunited with God. The Spirit inhabiting that body has the immaterial sound *Hû* to remind us from where we came and to where we will return.]

Like this creation myth, which frames and recreates a poetic core of Turkish classical music practices, many musicians believe sounding *Hû* to be an antidote to separation from the divine, a rift inherent in the human condition. Sonic and musical articulations of sadness, loss, and pain are justified when philosophies of *Hû* abound: one should feel pain and sorrow because of the human condition of separation from God. Yet *Hû* also becomes a way musicians draw social boundaries, creating the surfaces that divide and separate diverse social worlds. A musician may effectively deploy *Hû* against mainstream Islamist or Kemalist categories of selfhood by engaging spiritual embodiment discourses. In this way, the evocation of *Hû* reproduces and nuances frameworks wherein individuals construct social identity. For Turkish classical musicians, performances of social identity are collectively tied to senses of separation, whether voiced as a separation from God, from the Ottoman, or from a public life that relegates spiritual beliefs into categories cemented in the political present. In evoking *Hû* as sacred embodiment, musicians make statements such as "Hû is a veil" (*Hû örten bir şeydir*), or "when Hû occurs there is nothing else [to comprehend]" (*Hû olduğu yerde başka bir şey yok*). For these musicians, in *Hû* we become one with God and thus cannot discern where we or God begin or end. One *neyzen* explained this through metaphor:

> When a drop of water falls into the sea, there is only sea. The drop of water is silent in becoming the sea, and the sea becomes the drop of water. It is not until you pull the drop of water back out of the sea that it becomes a drop of water again [*Damla denize düşünce sadece deniz vardır. Damla deniz oluyor. Ancak denizden çıkınca tekrar damla kimliğine kavuşur*].

Like a drop of water being pulled from the sea, this musician articulated a feeling of separation from God and longed for a way back. Similar statements emerge in discussions of bifurcating political debates, and show how individual musicians name *Hû* as a political antidote to vehement debates about Kemalism versus Islamism, clashes between political parties, and discussions about "Turkishness" based on exclusionary narratives. In this interpretive frame, *Hû* as sacred embodiment becomes a critical vehicle wherein musicians make sense of their lives and their identities as inconsequential in the grand scheme of things. The perception of one's life as impermanent and one's identity as transient bleeds into a sense of separation that these musicians experience in their contemporary social world, and further discursively outlines the social boundaries of their alienation within the context of public life rife with dichotomies.

In the context of widespread contemporary Turkish language practices, *Hû* is regularly heard and used by Turks but has been rendered secular, stripped of the deeper Sufi meanings that present-day Turkish classical musicians vehemently defend and reinstate in their own daily practices. Take, for example, the commonly heard Turkish proverb "*Hay'dan gelen Hû'ya gider.*" This proverb originates as a Sufi expression, or *derviş deyimi* in Turkish (Os. *ıstılahat-ı sofiyye*). Here, *Hay* connotes "alive" and is also a name for God, denoting the "living, everlasting God" (Redhouse 1997: 465). Thus the proverb reads, "That which comes from *Hay* goes to *Hû.*" I regularly witnessed many situations in which musicians purposefully deployed the proverb (often alternatively spelled "*haydan gelen huya gider*") when they wanted to impart a belief that the values and ideas of mainstream Turkish politics were temporary and fleeting. These musicians translate this proverb as "that which comes from the everlasting God returns to the essence of God." As musicians iterate *Hû*, they recreate the Sufi practice of producing multiple renderings that may shape alternate readings and perspectives. *Hû* levels the sacred as a critical identity practice to make sense of the pain of life and celebrate the ultimate end and reunification with the divine that death inevitably brings.

Often musicians mobilized the proverb "*haydan gelen huya gider*" directly to protest the ways Turkish classical music remains invisible or unappreciated in contemporary Turkish public life. The proverb metaphorically points to the ways musicians are silenced in Turkey today, as musicians tend not to deploy the proverb as other Turks do. Contemporary Turkish classical musicians voice sacred interpretations against secular usage, which has stripped interpretations of proverbs and of musical meaning of their ostensibly original spiritual weight. For example, in contemporary Turkish vernacular language practices, the proverb "*haydan gelen huya gider*" connotes "easy come, easy go" and is used primarily when talking about making money. Thus musicians' understanding of and engagement with *Hû* acts as a way for them to both name their estrangement from Turkish public life and justify their position as one originating from an informed place of higher spiritual authority. Voicing *Hû* emerges as a subtle act of resistance, wherein Turkish classical musicians labor to maintain Sufi orders' religious content in mainstream Sunni, non-Sufi, or secular contexts.

While the depth of understanding *Hû* in Sufi orders outlined in this chapter may be lost for non-musicians or Turks in general, *Hû* still maintains a place in Turkish popular culture. Children utter games of wordplay that feature *Hû* as a kind of calling out and naming others as *Hû*, as in the two-voiced poem "*Komşu Komşu Hu*" [lit., "Neighbor Neighbor Hey"]. Stripped of religious context, *Hû* is a call to any individual as a way of getting his or her attention. Email and Facebook message exchanges between individuals who identify themselves as atheists will often begin with "Huuu." A well-known German rap artist of Turkish heritage named himself *Ya Hû*, adding another layer of potential interpretation, as many of his European fans believe he is primarily parodying the search engine company Yahoo. Yet in the vernacular, "*Ya Hû*" is also an expression of the Turkish everyday that most Turks claim simply means "Hey there" (Redhouse 1997: 491) and is used as a greeting by many secular Turks who do not identify with any iteration of Muslimness. Another Sufi expression from the Ottoman period, "*Edep Ya Hû*" (lit., "Manners, o *Hû*"), also has a particular meaning in Islamic circuits, namely, that God watches us, and it is with this knowledge that we should live our life. Today "*Edep Ya Hû*" is used in vernacular Turkish to simply mean "shame on you." Yet during the course of fieldwork in 2013, I witnessed a number of statements from different Islamic organizations that boldly printed "*Edep Ya Hû*" on 8.5 × 11 fliers, pasting the expression repeatedly over the uncovered arms, neck, and legs of models and actresses in large commercial advertisements that proliferated bus stops and newsstands in Istanbul. Many of the musicians I work with verbalized disgust toward this deployment of a Sufi phrase—literally plastered on women's bodies—as a kind of public protest in defense of specific Islamic covering practices (*tesettür*). Secularized usages of *Hû* are not the only kinds of emergent meanings that may irritate Turkish classical musicians.

These types of shifts are indicative of twentieth century nationalistic processes that implicated private identity practices throughout Turkey, such as language and music, that worked to separate individuals and communities from Islamic institutions and draw allegiances toward the new nation-state. *Hû* is a classic example of language change: there was a word imbued with specific meaning in a heavily prestigious context (*Hû* in Sufi orders); through time, the context becomes less privileged (the Republic's institutional formations that rendered Mevlevi orders disempowered), yet the word remains in present day. Contemporary musicians cite their disparate interpretations of *Hû* and the expressions in which *Hû* is couched to articulate their modes of self-fashioning as lying outside the boundaries of mainstream Turkey; their utterances of *Hû* are performances of refusal to engage norms that would render their particular, situated, spiritual, and sonic understanding of *Hû*'s meanings obsolete.

HÛ AS ISTANBUL

The following story directly ties musicians' poetic and spiritual structures to power, history, and social identification, especially for the artists who strongly connect their sense of self to identifying with Istanbul. On the morning of November 13, 1918, the well-known Ottoman Islamic calligrapher (*hattat*)

Necmeddin Okyay (1883–1976) rose and went to his balcony in Istanbul, over-looking the Bosphorus. What all Istanbul residents saw that morning caused a panic to fall onto the city like a thunderstorm, but this panic did not reach Necmeddin Okyay, musicians told me, "because his faith in God was vaster than the power and violence of this world." While his neighbors let out shrieks that morning as they witnessed British ships sailing into the Bosphorus, begin-ning the Allied occupation of Istanbul that was to last from November 13, 1918 through September 23, 1923, Okyay calmly performed his *abdest* (Islamic ritual of washing parts of the body before prayer, handling the Qur'an, or engaging religious devotion). After cleansing his body, he sat down at his writing desk and wrote in Ottoman calligraphy, "*Bu da geçer ya Hû*," which means "even this will pass, o *Hû*." The saying "*Bu da geçer ya Hû*" had apparently been spoken by Sufis of Istanbul for centuries. Even at the time Necmeddin Okyay memorial-ized the statement in calligraphy (*hüsn-ü hat,* lit., "beautiful hand"), it was con-sidered a common spoken Sufi expression like the others mentioned above. Yet while it had been used in daily verbal discourses, when Okyay put calligraphy tool to parchment, this expression's meaning became grounded in a particular historical moment and today continues to be associated with the Allied occu-pation of Istanbul after World War I.[21] Turkish classical musicians claim that at this very moment, *Hû* no longer stood for Sufism; it was brought to bear in representing Istanbul at a time when Istanbul and the remnants of Ottoman communities were both under siege.

Today, some musicians claim that hanging a calligraphic representation of the saying "*Bu da geçer ya Hû*" is a way of showing one's pride in Istanbul and the Republic of Turkey, as the occupation of Istanbul ended when the Turkish nation-state came into existence. Others told me that hanging the expression on one's wall was one of the most powerful ways to silently protest something. Some musicians embracing this perspective hung the same proverb on their walls in protest against the Turkish nation-state. Still others hung the proverb as a demonstration of secular pride and their commitment to Kemalism, as it was Mustafa Kemal who brought an end to the occupation. Many people I spoke with agreed that this saying was the most classic phrase a person could use when trying to comfort another (*teselli etmek*) and hope that difficulty passes. There are other musicians still that see the expression "*Bu da geçer ya Hû*" as one that does the important cultural work of linking Istanbul to its ostensibly authentic Sufi roots. Often, these individuals do not make a distinc-tion between the Ottoman Istanbul of the past, infused with expressions that focused on *Hû* in all of the meanings outlined in this chapter, and the Istanbul of today, where many of those meanings have been forgotten or transformed.

How can hanging a single phrase in Ottoman calligraphy include such diverse intentions and divergent interpretations of supposedly contradictory political perspectives? The polyvalence of hanging *Hû* on your wall indicates the creative play engaged by Turkish classical musicians to resist any normative statement of Turkish identity that would tend to support a singular interpretation of "*Bu da geçer ya Hû.*" Musicians' acts of voicing *Hû*, sounding *Hû*, and displaying *Hû* on their walls resist bifurcated assumptions and demonstrate the central aspect of crafting selfhood based on affinities beyond political categories that are assumed to be oppositional. It could be argued that these protests against a kind of dualistic normativity are passive, as the protest only entails simply hanging calligraphy on your wall. This form of resistance may alienate or be inaccessible for most viewers in contemporary Turkey, who cannot read Ottoman, Persian, or Arabic. It is significant that Turkish classical musicians' resistances of this kind in public life are often presented as visual artistic representations: two-dimensional icons that are silent and require particular readerly subjects. For these musicians, silence has the possibility of being activated as politically meaningful because of the deep value that silence is given in the same spiritual ideologies that imbue *Hû* with sacred significance.

FROM LIFE TO DEATH AND SOUND TO SILENCE

Silence is the language of God,
all else is poor translation.

> —Mevlana

When *neyzen* Niyazi Sayın defines music as "the spiritual relationship between two sounds," he not only emphasizes a belief that sound is inherently spiritual but he also speaks back against other kinds of meanings related to sonic and musical production that permeate Turkish public discourse. Engaging the sacred in narrating musical meaning is a critical tool that contemporary Turkish classical musicians use within broader Turkish public life, especially when it comes to alternate narratives of their musical ideas that emerge in popular and vernacular music production.

While the wide audibility of *ney* permeates Turkish urban centers during the holy month of Ramazan and contributes to an ideology of hearing that positions the *ney* as spiritual and Islamic, you are just as likely to hear the *ney* in popular music products that are situated as secular, such as electronica, dance hall, commercial marketing advertisement jingles, and hip-hop tracks. For many general listeners in contemporary Turkey, this popular circulation means that the sound of the *ney* is not interpreted with the weighty Mevlevi philosophies involving the cosmology of the reed bed and human life. The silences that occur in the public sphere about the *ney*'s origins, for many of the musicians with whom I work, is felt as a deep loss. These musicians cite the well-known electronica musician Mercan Dede (aka DJ Arkin Allen, b. 1966), who plays *ney* over electronic tracks he lays out. Many complain about the ostensible audacity of this popular artist who chose to name himself "Dede," an honorary title given to spiritual masters in the Mevlevi Sufi order (such as İsmail Dede Efendi and his student, Zekai Dede, whose *ilahi* is offered above).

Beyond the vernacular pop music realm, some contemporary Turkish classical musicians also voice anxiety about the massive popular interest in playing *ney*, attested to by the nonprofit *vakıf*-s and musical clubs (*dergah*-s) that have popped up in Turkey's urban centers over the last decade. Privatization and the emergence of neoliberalism in the 1990s gave rise to the growing Muslim middle- and upper-middle classes in Turkey. Simultaneously, hundreds of young people began to foster a desire to play *ney* as a hobby, leading to an increased audience and consumer group interested in the sounds and philosophies about the *ney*. For Turkish classical musicians, the economic benefits were immediately enjoyed. Yet the problem with this visibility and interest in creating an amateur class of *ney* players was also acute: musicians found themselves in the business of creating *ney* players, not cultivating *neyzen*. Turkish cities are now filled, one musician complained to me, with people who "breathe into a *ney*" to produce *sound* instead of *neyzen*-s who "recite *Hû* into a *ney*" to produce *music*. It may take only a few years to teach someone to "play" the *ney*, but musicians argue it takes decades of study and discipline in the context of a master-apprentice relationship to become a *neyzen*. A *neyzen*, I am told, is first an artist of great depth, and *ney* is only his (and, rarely, her) tool. Adversely, a *ney* player simply plays the *ney*, and is assumed to be a person who lacks artistry and depth. Musicians point to a difference between identity (*neyzen*) and activity (playing *ney*), a distinction of crucial importance for constructing notions of selfhood for Turkish classical musicians.

If the *ney* is rendered as "just a musical instrument" in public life, as one *neyzen* told me, this trend surfaces an experience of loss for musicians who name themselves *neyzen*. If the *ney* simply produces musical pitches rather than music formed out of a spiritual relationship, to paraphrase Niyazi Sayın, some Turkish classical musicians believe that the increased visibility and audibility of the *ney* in Turkish public life can ultimately undermine the very spiritual discourses that center around the *ney*. The narrative trope about separation reemerges here again, but not perceived as the kind of separation from the divine, a separation that is seen as spiritually productive for people. This emergent, uncomfortable separation manifests when Turkish classical musicians experience the dissonance between their beliefs about the sacredness of sound against the challenges brought by normative mainstream music production that positions sound production as a commodity, an *object* to be purchased and enjoyed rather than a spiritual *practice* that requires intentionality and cultivates awareness of sacred embodiment in everyday life. In such a context, the *ney* no longer sounds death and separation that is positioned as a happy reunion with the divine. For contemporary Turkish classical musicians, the *ney*, utilized in popular contexts, sounds a death of the *ney*'s spiritual discourses of embodiment.

How do contemporary Turkish classical musicians respond to these emergent musical meanings and practices that render the *ney* as a musical instrument rather than a spiritual vehicle? Evoking *Hû* is one primary strategy Turkish classical musicians have to deal with the ostensible spiritual poverty of musical meanings they confront in public life. On one occasion, debating the proliferation of *ney* players who were not or could not be *neyzen*, a musician said, "Oooof ya Hû. All I can say is Huuuuuuuuu." He gestured for us to pick up our instruments and he began playing an *ilahi* in *Nihavend makamı*, which calls us all to say *Hû* (Example 2.3):

> *Ya Rabbi aşkın ver bana efendim*
> *Hû diyeyim Allah Allah döne döne*
> *Aşkın ile yana yana efendim*
> *Hû diyeyim Allah Allah döne döne*

> O Teacher [God], give me your love
> Let me say *Hû* while turning, turning
> Burning side by side with your love
> Let me say *Hû* while turning, turning

Example 2.3 The *ilahi* entitled "*Ya Rabbi aşkın ver bana efendim*" in *Nihavend makamı*.

Beyond this particular anecdote of one moment of musicking, contemporary Turkish classical musicians respond to vernacular musical meanings and practices that render the *ney* as a musical instrument rather than a spiritual vehicle in another, more profound way. Musicians move from saying *Hû* to saying nothing, from sound to silence. As with the case study of *Hû*, feelings of loss, pain, and separation are made into musical sound and justified through recourse to Islamic and Mevlevi theologies. The circulated philosophies and narratives about *Hû* and sound in general pedagogically instruct Turkish classical musicians to value their perceived abject social position and welcome it with silence. Sound itself is, after all, intelligible only in relation to that which it is not. But the silence *Hû* imparts works as a site of potential: it is the recognition and rationalization of one's state of relative isolation in his/her social world. At the end of one of his poems, the sixteenth century Ottoman poet Hayâlî (d. 1557) writes thus:

> *Cûylar ki vardılar*
> *Deryâya hâmûş oldular*

> Rivers running to the sea make a lot of noise
> When they flow into the ocean, they become silent

Other musicians I worked with who did not read or speak Ottoman imparted a similar corrective with the following Turkish expression:

> *Bilenler söylemez*
> *Söyleyenler bilmez*

> The ones who know do not speak
> The ones who speak do not know

Many musicians extended this injunction to me as well. On a few occasions, for example, musicians offered the following wish: "May God grant that what you reflect in writing be transformed into that which you silently reflect in your soul [*Allah satıra aksettirdiğin halini sadra inkılab ettirsin*]."

Listening critically to *Hû*, to silence, and to the musicians who move placidly between sound and silence demands a particular set of ears. Studying the melancholic modalities that contemporary Turkish classical musicians cultivate, I developed—with the help of my teachers—the critical rhizomatic listening skills necessary to understand musicians' silences as much as their sounds. While interrogating melancholy and musical meaning, musicians answered my interview questions about feelings and music by quoting Mevlana and by reciting the Qur'an. For these contemporary Turkish classical musicians, music is a spiritual medium; for them, sound cannot be rendered secular. Listening to the sounds and silences of Turkish classical musicians therefore requires a shedding of methodologies that would silence what is made meaningful to and explanatory for Turkish classical musicians simply because the spiritual is assumed to be biased or based on the unreal. Looking back at the genesis of my early work with Turkish musicians, I did not plan on becoming a scholar of Islam. As an ethnographer who took my teachers' and friends' voices, sounds, and ideologies seriously, I was made a scholar of Islam. Stories I have offered about *Hû* impart a lesson in taking the spiritual seriously. *Hû* is an example of how a single, small sound can pack a constellation of meaning that makes its way into musicians' repertoire, performance practice techniques, narrative utterances, stories, discourses, and political actions. The spiritual ideologies that name and articulate musical meaning are themselves products of individuals' hearing of sound as uniformly spiritual and, in the case of the *ney*, critically about separation, loss, and death (Figure 2.6).

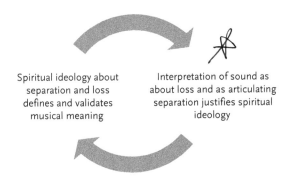

Spiritual ideology about separation and loss defines and validates musical meaning

Interpretation of sound as about loss and as articulating separation justifies spiritual ideology

Figure 2.6 Diagram of the relationship between spiritual ideologies and musical meaning.

In following the movements of *Hû* in Turkish classical musicians' narrative and musical practices, I unraveled one particular process in which sound becomes understood as sacred and how this understanding, in turn, shapes subjectivity. I examined *Hû* as a sound that names God, evokes God's essence, does *zikir*, and functions as technique for playing the *ney*. *Hû* resists classification as only sound, as only word, or as only technique—indeed, *Hû* demonstrates that the lines we draw between word, sound, and music technique are ideological, are context-bound, and resist direct translation. *Hû* as sound illuminates the cosmological underpinnings of a world that uses sacred knowledge as the medium through which musicians understand themselves and navigate their place in their social and political surroundings. Beyond hearing *Hû* as sound, in its artistic representations, *Hû* reminds viewers of God's presence and essence in themselves and those around them (Figure 2.7). By focusing on something as modest and dense as a single sound, we can begin to understand and unpack the social work that music does through spirit, and that spirit does through music.

Figure 2.7 Calligraphy of *Hû* in *müsenna* carved into the entrance of the Yeni Camii of Istanbul (photograph by the author).

CHAPTER 3
Melancholic Genealogies
Rhizomatic Listening and Bi-Aurality in Practice

Interested musicians new to Turkish classical music may immediately witness one commonly held assumption regarding the axiomatic differences between Turkish classical and western art musics: there has never been and ostensibly never will be a child prodigy in Turkish classical music, while there have been many child prodigies in the western art music world.[1] In one of my multiple observations of a music lesson while I was doing research in Istanbul, a master-teacher was quick to raise this point as evidence to support his belief that Turkish classical music is necessarily dependent on melancholic attachments and affect. "It is a fact that children cannot compose Turkish classical music," he announced in the middle of the lesson:

> Children cannot compose our music because they do not know melancholy [*hüzün*] or experience pain [*acı çekmek*] because they are given everything they need by their parents. The beginning of the affective [*duygusal*] is always located at hardship: you want something beautiful but cannot have it because it is far away.
>
> [*Turning to his young adult student*] You and I are here now and separated from God. We see God's beauty and long for it through music. But our music is not music until someone else hears it and understands that we are putting our pain, that separation, into music. Just like God is not God until s/he is praised. This is why God created us and asked us "Am I not your God? [*Ben sizin rabbınız değil miyim?*]"[2] We need to recognize [God] to make [God] real.
>
> We feel melancholy [*hüzün*] because that is how God intends us to feel. It is in our souls. This is why Turkish classical and Mevlevi music is so special, and

why so many people in the world hear our music as emotional. It is not just in our souls, it is in our blood.

This master-teacher discloses a number of conflated romantic and essentialist ideas that coalesce and inform his perspectives. Melancholy is connected to spiritual belief, which, in turn, creates the conditions for emotions to be justified as spiritually occurring, in that they come from God. Furthermore, an individual can begin to understand and live melancholy, and perhaps by default spirituality, only with the experience of pain. Finally, Turkish classical music carries the weight of being an emotional music precisely because it both reflects and recreates a spiritual essence ("it is in our souls") with an essentialized national-ethnic identification ("it is in our blood").[3]

Another master-teacher made similar claims to his student in a separate lesson I observed months later, and additionally argued that child prodigies of Turkish classical music are impossible to find because of the web of experience-based learning necessary to understand the music itself:

It is simply not possible [to consider the feasibility of Turkish classical music child prodigies] because being a musician is about being human. Western music is based in virtuosic repetition, which a talented child can grasp. But that talented child cannot possibly understand sound. Not in the way we understand sound. Ours is a sound that has a different meaning. It comes from the call to prayer [ezan] and from the music of the tekke [Sufi lodge] . . . our sound is different. A child has not yet been taught to feel the longing that is in our sound. It is hard to explain in words.

One of my jobs as your teacher is to teach you about feeling and help let it cut you deeply so that you can be a musician. The most beautiful instruments are made from the harsh, painful cuts against a tree. There is little difference between what a tree goes through to become an instrument of beautiful music and what a human being must go through to become a beautiful artist.

These master musicians' perspectives about music complement each other: a child cannot know and make Turkish classical music because a child has not experienced the longing, pain, and loss needed to understand and thus produce sound, an attitude that is ideologically positioned as a sonic expression of melancholy. This understanding of sound is deeply integrated with belief structures of Islam, especially Sufi discourses and practices. These ideas, beliefs, and assumptions about melancholy, music, and spirituality are instilled in master-apprentice or master-student relationships. The embracing of this understanding of sound is attached to this genre in a way that maps Turkish classical music itself as a genre of relative maturity and depth.

Turkish classical musicians therefore view themselves as primarily affective, and only secondarily musical, beings. In tracing contemporary Turkish classical musicians' melancholic modalities, processes of music transmission emerge as elemental moments shaping musicians' senses of musical meaning and of selfhood. In teaching music details—music theory, repertoire, improvisation technique, and performance practice—processes of music transmission are key sites to witness the formation of individual and collective identities in the sanctified relationship and institutional space of master and student. In the anecdotes shared about child prodigies, we learn that a key feature of Turkish classical music shared by master-teachers and adopted by students is that this music is centrally based on emotional experiences, especially those associated with pain, longing, separation, and sadness. In this way, Turkish classical musicians construct an essentialist dichotomy as they espouse a belief that their music is "nothing like" musics of the western concert tradition. If we take these claims seriously as ethnographers, we must find more appropriate methods with which to understand and interrogate Turkish classical music in the terms musicians themselves use to explain musical meaning.

Understanding musicians' ways of knowing and systems of meaning may require us to develop different ears. I study music transmission as it contributes to the cultivation of musical genealogies, or musical lineages of descent and development traced from the present back into the past. Studying musical genealogies in a Turkish classical music context means understanding the unique specificities of the system of oral music transmission, *meşk*, developed in the Ottoman era. After a brief consideration of how musical genealogies for Turkish classical musicians are primarily *genealogies of affect*, I look at systems of *meşk*, considering histories of music transmission, the importance of the master-apprentice relationship, uses of notation, and lineages established through *meşk* that individuals use to place themselves in positions of authority. I use this specific music tradition to cultivate new geographies of listening for Turkish classical music, and I propose the term bi-aurality to describe this necessary practice. Furthermore, I argue that bi-aurality must be developed because of the impositions western-oriented genealogies might bring to bear on our research, and I end the chapter by offering a new metaphor for bi-aurality in the end-blown reed flute of Turkish classical music, the *ney*, an instrument produced from rhizomatic reed beds.

This study of genealogy makes a particular claim about the *logos*, or knowledge, that we bring to studies of musical lineages and musics of the past, arguing that we must overturn our own situated, western-specific geographies to understand how music is transmitted in diverse musical traditions. From the Greek *genea* (γενεά), or "race," "family," "generation," and *logos* (λόγος), or "word," genealogy is about tracing lineages—often familial—and their histories. Musical genealogies generally entail plotting particular musical traditions in terms of transmission from generation to generation. Analyses of musical genealogies generally focus on the mechanics of music, transmission of music objects, or key individuals whom scholars locate as inheritors or progenitors of musical particulars. Importantly, most analyses of musical genealogies may inconspicuously reify provincial structures of knowledge in studies of *genea:* time is assumed to be linear, lineages of musicians are traced back vertically, chronologically back in time. As my research demonstrates, approaching a Turkish classical music with this frame is utterly unsuitable, as it is incompatible with the understandings of selfhood espoused and articulated by Turkish classical musicians. This chapter unravels the critical temporal and special geographies of knowing their past embraced by Turkish classical musicians to understand themselves, their sounds, their teaching, and their music's meaning.

My own research with contemporary Turkish classical musicians ultimately led to an interrogation of transmission practices as primarily processes of subjection, in which the cultivation and inculcation of self and communal subjectivities occur. Transmission practices are fundamentally about creating affective and musical senses of selfhood in students. For contemporary Turkish classical musicians, shaping students into musicians in the context of music making and lessons are processes rimmed with nostalgia. Codified during the founding years of the Republic of Turkey, the constructed genre of "Turkish classical music" is substantially rooted in presenting the musics of the Ottoman court and elite Mevlevi Sufi lodges as historical, secular artifacts in modern Turkey. Working with the present-day musicians charged with maintaining this genre offers a distinct understanding of how this particular musical community is shaped and defined by the circulation of affect more so than by sonic performance tools. My research inaugurates a consideration of how affect—specifically, melancholy—is practiced and prioritized in music learning contexts as a fundamental aspect of identification for musicians. As transmission produces subjects in the form of new students—a new generation—of Turkish classical music and affirms their affective, melancholic practices, links to the past are collapsed and experienced as rhizomatic iterations. Melancholy is validated, for students, in the act of transmission in which melancholic loss narratives, feelings, and embodiment are simultaneously soldered together in the process of learning music itself.

One key argument is thus that musical genealogies and Turkish classical musicians musicians' diverse constructions of pasts are rhizomatic. The rhizome, a botanical root with multiple shoots pushing through the earth, resists the organizational structure of a branching tree system that assumes vertical, chronological, single-root origins. In *A Thousand Plateaus* (1987 [1980]), philosophers Gilles Deleuze and Félix Guattari propose the rhizome as a new metaphor for narrativizing history. Rather than tracing a linear chronology of things (the tree-like root with original and vertical conclusions), a rhizome metaphor presents history as a map of influences and intersections with no specific genesis. Considering Turkish classical music genealogies as rhizomatic means mapping the intersections of multiple, diverse imaginings of various iterations of a past to make sense of the present. The process of participating in these genealogies is highly affective, meaning that musicians sound out senses of self and belonging in deeply melancholic ways. As musicians understand their musical practices as producing melancholy in sound, their transmission practices bring to bear multiple threads of melancholic utterances—sonic and verbal—as they instill and shape melancholic modalities in students. Transmission emerges as the site where past practices are rendered hopeful iterations of the future, where students experience and adopt melancholy as a common-sense modality as musicians.

I analyze the pedagogical underpinnings of melancholy in the context of aural music transmission (*meşk*). *Meşk* is a packed term—often used differently in diverse discursive domains—that implies learning music in aural tradition in a deeply dyadic relationship with a master (Gill-Gürtan 2011). *Meşk* is a dense performance that musicians engage, as it is equal parts historical narrative and romanticized practice of aural transmission despite the need and use of texts (e.g., music notation, collections). Musicians today nostalgically embrace *meşk* as the primary method of teaching music during the Ottoman period, and actively seek a return to the idyllic musical practices that exist in their imaginaries of the past. Present-day transmission practices through *meşk* place young musicians in binding musical genealogies: musicians shape and pass on melancholic modalities in their very process of learning Turkish classical music and sustaining their lineages. As *meşk* works to recreate a master's sensibility and knowledge anew in the apprentice, master musicians spread spiritual discourses along with "feeling practices" (Hochschild 1983) in their lessons with their students. The students, in turn, validate their authentic experiences of melancholy through religious discourse and the creative memorializing of their musical lineage. Placing oneself in a *meşk silesilesi*, or *meşk* lineage, grounds individuals in a collectivized identity and reifies a "genealogical imagination" (Shryock 1997) validated through the close relationship between master and apprentice.

Exploring the way melancholic modalities are passed down from master-teacher to student allows me to speak in terms of the circulation of melancholy and allow melancholy a kind of material tangibility. Yet melancholy as an object is not something an autonomous individual subject feels but is rather a shared *affective practice* whereby a musician is shaped by a teacher to feel and to pass on to his/her future students. Analyzing the transmission of sound as the transmission of feeling practices from master to apprentice and teacher to student demonstrates that melancholy is not something that one has but rather *something that one does*. Music lessons emerge as a primary site where musicians' melancholic modalities are circulated, validated, and individualized.

Engaging the metaphor of the rhizome and rhizomatic analysis, I trace the changes of musicians' genealogical mapping in the late twentieth and twenty-first centuries to demonstrate how Turkish classical musicians have struggled with their self-understandings as autonomous individuals (*birey*-s)—a concept introduced in the mid-twentieth century—with their self-understandings as part of a communal body of their musical lineage (*silsile*)—lineages that were shattered during the 1920s through the 1940s with the changing institutionalization of Turkish classical music. As we shall see, contemporary musicians' melancholic modalities function, in part, to resurrect and imagine previous (Ottoman) understandings of communal selfhood in relation to music lineages. In other words, lineages now are more constructed than real. Melancholic modalities emerge in simultaneity: rhizomatic iterations of the past, present, and future coming from multiple directions justify melancholy as a common sense link to musical being.

LEARNING MELANCHOLY, LEARNING LOVE

Ruhun en değerli azığı ızdıraptır.
The most important nutrition for the soul is suffering.
                              —Yaşar Nuri Öztürk[4]

Turkish theologian Yaşar Nuri Öztürk (b. 1945) posits that suffering is a fundamental part of maintaining and nourishing one's soul.[5] Musicians make similar statements, justifying the various iterations of their melancholic modalities as spiritually redeeming. If suffering is believed to be nourishing and productive for spiritual and personal growth, as Turkish classical musicians believe it to be, how is suffering ideologically brought to bear on a community of musicians and passed down from one generation to the next?

Many of the feeling practices associated with Turkish classical music making are learned by individuals in the context of learning how to sound out musicking in the master-apprentice relationship. The language and terminology used to name the individuals involved in an intimate, dyadic master-apprentice/student relationship demonstrate the seriousness with which Turkish classical musicians approach music learning. Whereas the common term for "student" in Turkish is *öğrenci* (from the verb "to learn," *öğrenmek*), musicians more frequently call students of their tradition by the Ottoman term for student, *talibeh* (*talibât*). Couched in the verb *talib etmek*—"to want, to desire"—*talibeh* denotes one who actively searches for and eventually depends upon one's teacher. A *talibeh* is perceived as crude or raw material (*kaba* or *ham*) that seeks out a master (*usta*) to shape him/herself.

Turkish classical musicians claim that in *meşk,* or oral music transmission, "it is not the music that is being shaped, it is the person being shaped [*musiki şekillenmiyor, insan şekilleniyor*]." A student does not gain only knowledge from the master: a student gains selfhood. Ideally, a student will not only resemble a master, but also become the master. The process of learning in the master-apprentice/master-student relationship is not about "making music" (*müzik yapmak*) as much as it is about learning how to "influence the soul" (*ruhuna işlemek*), a common expression that explains how a student has mastered being able to affect another human being, and thus become him/herself a master.

For my teachers, shaping a student as a human being means cultivating that student's spiritual roots so that he or she will be able to eventually "influence the soul." The overall melancholy articulated and claimed by Turkish classical musicians lies not only in the loss narratives previously explained, but also in a constant sense of loss or mourning that is assumed to be thoroughly part of the human condition. These individuals strongly believe that "becoming melancholic" (*hüzünleşmek*) is itself a sign of spiritual devotion. Being too comfortable in this life, they argue, is an indication that they are out of tune with God. It is a master's duty, then, to instill in a student the understanding of melancholy as spiritually beneficial. After all, one becomes melancholic only because of deep love—melancholy arises naturally out of the condition of separation from and yearning for the lost love object. Indeed, the master-apprentice relationship established in the Ottoman era for musicians was modeled after the ultimate religious master-apprentice relationship: the relationship between God and the Prophet Muhammed. It makes sense, then, that the system of musical transmission, *meşk,* is propelled by deep, established love relationships between a master and a student.

UNDERSTANDING *MEŞK*

Okumakla, yazmakla olmaz, ta üstaddan görmeyince.
[You will achieve] not by reading nor by writing,
until observing a master.
          —Aşık Paşa (d. 1333)[6]

Contemporary Turkish classical musicians have become agents of "duty-memory," as theorized by historian Pierre Nora. Nora claims that "[t]he less memory is experienced collectively, the more it will require individuals to undertake to become themselves memory-individual" (1989: 16). As agents of memory, who, Nora might argue, understand their responsibility as protecting memory itself, these individuals constantly negotiate their positioning vis-à-vis conflicting political ideologies supported by the nation-state. One of the ways these individuals ground themselves in history and in memory is through engaging, in present day, with Ottoman practices of *meşk*. It is in the process of *meşk* that the avowal of loss narratives about Turkish classical music's alleged death is communicated and passed on to future generations. Beyond instilling certain ways of speaking about Turkish classical music along with the ability to perform music, *meşk* is a system that also cultivates and circulates melancholy.

As the primary method of teaching music during the Ottoman Empire, contemporary musicians valorize *meşk* as the locus of authenticity for linking the present to a nostalgic past. The term *meşk* itself was brought into Ottoman from the Arabic *mashq*, which denotes the repetitive and imitative practice of a given task. The initial use of *meşk* in Ottoman times referred to the training of archers in the Ottoman military class. *Meşk* was also the term used to describe a model of writing and learning the art and practice of Islamic calligraphy, whereby students continually rewrote characters and entire scripts until they received the approval of their master (Jäger 1996a, 1996b). *Meşk* was further used to describe the repetitive training needed for mastering other Ottoman art forms, such as carpet weaving, furniture making, miniature and *ebru* (water-marbling) arts, and, of course, music.

During the Ottoman Empire, the standard and formal relational institution for the transmission of musical knowledge was the master-apprentice, or *usta-çırak*, relationship. *Meşk* in the context of the master-apprentice relationship implies a number of attributes: dedication and devotion between a master and an apprentice, long-term learning relationships (often apprentices worked with their master for over a decade), and regular, lengthy one-on-one lessons in which music was learned by ear. *Meşk* involved all aspects of musical training, meaning that an apprentice learned *makam*-s (melodic modes), *usul*-s (rhythmic modes), *taksim* (improvisation), *beste* or *eser* (well-known compositions), literature (specifically, poetry), languages (Arabic and Farsi/Persian), theory, history (of music, *makam*, and previous master-teachers of one's lineage), *aruz* (poetic meter of texts and lyrics), and repertoire.

Music transmission for instrumental music was focused on the voice and the poetic core of vocal and literary traditions as well as ritual forms of the Mevlevi order. In other words, *meşk* concentrated on a poetic basis of Turkish music and organized the training process accordingly (Behar 2003 [1998]: 47). As John Morgan O'Connell explains, this framework was largely grounded in vocal repertoire, and served to structure the learning experience and aid memorization by collapsing all textual, musical, and stylistic traits into one graspable whole (1996). The beating of the *usul* (rhythmic mode, often transliterated as *usûl*) in a variety of patterns with the hands on the knees and thighs (*usul vurmak*) was critical. That is, repertoire was learned from a master, replicated exactly, and memorized orally with the aid of *usul*. This method of beating musical lines (*dizi dövmek*, lit., "hitting the knee"), not only served to transmit the repertoire from master to apprentice within a structured framework according to levels of rhythmic complexity, but also worked to preserve the compositions for subsequent generations (Behar 1993: 25). Yet as the emphasis was on the poetic and rhythmic structure of vocal repertoire, Ottoman instrumental compositions proved harder to preserve.

The scope of *meşk* was not limited to the study of music, as a student was also thoroughly schooled in ethics, style, mannerisms, and lifestyle. This element of *meşk* remains present today: master-teachers often insist that students follow them to rehearsals, recording studios, and recitals to observe them and learn how to interact in diverse social settings. Necati Hoca, my primary teacher introduced in chapter 1, repeatedly voices that this "other" social education was more crucial than the music elements. "Learning the intricacies of *makam* or ornamentation is simple enough," Necati Hoca explains. "Sitting with me for a few hours, drinking tea, and sharing life and silence is as important for training a musician."

While the two physical institutions that housed the master-apprentice system in the Ottoman Empire were the Enderun (an Ottoman palace boarding school) and the *tekke*-s (Sufi lodges) of the Mevlevi Sufi order, *meşk* also historically took place in the private home of the masters. This practice illustrates the importance of creating and maintaining a deep personal relationship between an apprentice and a master that was informed by familial structures and intimate, private spaces. Master-apprentice relationships, deeply rooted in everyday interactions, were further solidified by their longevity: as *meşk* was an uncodified and unstandardized pedagogical system, there was not a fixed schedule for completing training. An individual's music education varied according to the needs of a student, the type of repertoire that was being memorized, and the nature of the position aspired to. Since musician's accomplishment in the Ottoman era was based upon the breadth of the repertoire she or he had memorized and the depth of philosophy attained, the duration of *meşk* often extended over decades. The processes of transmission through *meşk* were thus intertwined within the relationships between and the intersecting social lives of masters and their apprentices.

The system of reciprocity in the master-apprentice relationship illuminates the personal connection between these two individuals. Monetary or commercial exchange rarely came into the *meşk* system, as Ottoman forms of musical patronage—especially provided by the Court and by the Mevlevi order—created an institutionalized space of financial comfort in which the master-apprentice musical relationship flourished without a pay-for-lesson model. Among contemporary Turkish classical musicians invested in revisiting and instantiating *meşk* into the present, teachers who have the economic possibility to do so refuse money from students.

Necati Hoca, as a celebrated musician with a full-time position as a state employee of the Istanbul State Turkish Music Orchestra (*İstanbul Devlet Türk Müziği Topluluğu*), is in the position to invest in the continuation and reification of *meşk* in the present day without economic exchanges with students. His daily schedule includes a morning rehearsal with the ensemble, after which he drives to the center of Kadıköy on the Anatolian side of Istanbul to his studio, or *atölye*. Mondays through Saturdays from approximately 1 p.m. through 6 p.m. Necati Hoca is available for *meşk*: students, colleagues, friends, and visitors come to experience the conversations and the music making in this space (Figure 3.1).

Necati Hoca uses his salary to fund the upkeep and rental fees of this space, which he has had for over a decade. Before establishing his *atölye*, Necati Hoca had *meşk* at his home, an arrangement that created many visitors to whom his wife, Ayşe (introduced in chapter 1), attended with her care labors (offering snacks, tea, house slippers, conversation). In his *atölye*, Necati Hoca benefits from the Turkish economy of small-business owners in a shared building space, as the renowned *ud* (short-necked lute, hung on the wall in Figure 3.1) maker Mustafa Copçuoğlu has his own instrument-building *atölye* only two floors below. In the basement of the building, tea-maker Ahmet Usta labors six twelve-hour workdays each week to continually make tea and serve it to

Figure 3.1 Necati Hoca's empty *atölye* on an early weekday afternoon before students and other music professionals gather for music making and conversation (photo by the author).

the *atölye* owners and their patrons. Ahmet Usta's tea allows for and sustains the comfortable unfolding of conversation and *meşk*.

Necati Hoca is a privileged recipient of state-sponsored patronage for the arts—music, theatre, and dance—that was first established in the early years of the founding of the Republic of Turkey. While his salary provides a comfortable living for himself and his family, Necati Hoca's worldwide reputation as an *ud* virtuoso means that he also benefits from international touring circuits, giving solo concerts and offering music workshops throughout Europe, North America, and the Middle East. He further profits from the emergent opportunities for income generated by privatization and neoliberalism, as private organizations fund a number of programs featuring Turkish classical music, especially during the holy month of Ramazan. In short, Necati Hoca, like many established Turkish classical musicians I consulted, benefits economically from a number of crosscutting music performance opportunities provided by private industry, the nation-state, and transnational music markets. Because of the intense time commitment, *meşk* today requires master-teachers to have a relative amount of economic privilege.

The divide between amateur and professional musicians is often elucidated by monetary exchange for musical lessons. Necati Hoca vocalizes a distaste for contemporary musicians who charge for lessons—an adversion made possible by his economic status—and would be deeply insulted if one of his students attempted to give him money. "I am not paid, just as my teachers would not have accepted money from me," he claims. However, while currency exchange is not a part of a present-day *meşk* practice, master-teachers ostensibly do "get" something in return, so they purport. For example, Necati Hoca claims that he "receives love" (*aşk alıyorum*) from his apprentices, and expects the reciprocity of "love" to be made manifest in each of their interactions. Necati Hoca also believes that he feeds off the love his apprentice has for the tradition he sees himself passing on: standing witness to this process unfolding is, for Necati Hoca, a tremendous gain.

The discursive claim of doing things "for love" is ubiquitous among contemporary Turkish classical musicians. On one hand, the claim of doing things "for love" is made possible only by neoliberal market flows and the patronage of the nation-state. *Meşk*'s socioeconomic valiance has decreased with the institutionalization of a western conservatory system. The conservatory system, in the eyes of some musicians, represents the loss of Ottoman tradition and thus is a partial cause of melancholy that enters into musicians' narratives about music transmission. As *meşk* was the normative way music transmission was conducted during the Ottoman period, part of the mythology of *meşk* in the present day emerges in vocalizing a death narrative of *meşk* itself (see chapter 1).

At the same time, the *meşk* system, as practiced today, produces the value of intensive, long-term social relationships generally experienced as familial love, trust, and devotion. One musician explained this as a "natural" (*doğal*) result of spending a long time with a teacher:

> *Meşk* meant that you go for a very long time to work with your master, because learning one or two songs at a time means that you need many years to learn and memorize all of the repertoire. *Meşk* means building a link of respect and love. Because the master sees that you respect him, he will love you. Because he loves you, he will take you in as a son or daughter. You are someone he forms, someone he shapes. He gives everything he knows to you, not only through music, but also with music.

In his introduction to the book *Aşk Olmayınca Meşk Olmaz: Geleneksel Osmanlı/Türk Müziğinde Öğretim ve İntikal* ["Without Love, *Meşk* Cannot Occur: Education and Transmission in Traditional Ottoman/Turkish Music"], Cem Behar claims that learning music through *meşk* established moral values in the Ottoman art world (2003 [1998]: 10). According to Behar, the hardship of learning through *meşk*, the required sacrifices, the pride and privilege of working with one's master, and the sense of belonging to a lineage (*meşk silsile*) were well worth the rigorous lifestyle. The moral values of *meşk* are embedded in the proverb "*aşk olmayınca, meşk olmaz*," which means "without love, *meşk* cannot occur" (Gill-Gürtan 2011). *Meşk*, during the Ottoman Empire, created a link of belonging: individuals belonged to the tradition, belonged to the repertoire, belonged to their stylistic interpretations, and belonged to one another in link after link after link of contiguous master-student-master-student-master-student relationships. Iterations of autonomous individuality were virtually non-existent, as forms of identification were necessarily communal and based on one's lineage.

LEARNING FROM A MASTER

Learning from a master means learning how to foster and accept the philosophical, affective, and spiritual assumptions and worldview of that master. Many musicians' lives and experiences demonstrate a boundlessness of musical and spiritual learning and teaching, of the sacred and the secular. This seamlessness demonstrates the mutuality and interdependence of affective and spiritual experiences for several contemporary Turkish classical musicians. In the majority of the interviews I conducted about melancholy, musicians immediately grounded their understanding of emotion in their belief in God. Embracing this perspective, one of my primary *kanun* teachers, Celaleddin Aksoy (b. 1961), saw the capacity to experience emotion, and in particular melancholy, as necessarily coming from God. A prominent musician with the Turkish Sufi Music Ensemble (*Türk Tasavvuf Müziği Topluluğu*) based in Konya and dedicated to the performance of the Mevlevi *sema* turning ceremony throughout the world, Celal Hoca taught me that any discussion about affect and Turkish classical music must be centered on spiritual/religious belief, and in particular Sufism.

Celal Hoca made sure to demonstrate the interrelationship between affect/ emotion/feelings, music, and spirituality to me in almost all of our interactions. Take, for example, our work together on *taksim*. One afternoon, as he was explaining modulations that could happen during an improvisation in *Nevâ makamı*, he paused and explained that modulation, "like most things in life," operated like a crossword puzzle (*bulmaca*):

> When dwelling on *Nevâ*'s upper tetrachord on *Rast*, you may choose to make this your lower tetrachord and, adding a *Bûselik* tetrachord after that, play the *makam* [called] *Acemli rast*. Or you could modulate easily to *Uşşak* because of *Nevâ*'s lower tetrachord.
>
> It is like a crossword puzzle: one letter appears in so many different words, and those words have letters that connect to other words.
>
> The same principle applies to emotion. Longing [*hasret*] could pivot to happiness [*mutluluk*] at any moment, and the very next moment that happiness can turn into another emotion.
>
> But this is all done with God . . . it is God's desire. But it is also your choice. God does not tell you what *makam* to play or what emotion to feel. In a crossword puzzle, there is no rule that dictates you need to fill in this word before another word. You can complete a crossword puzzle successfully no matter where you start. The same thing occurs with music and with feelings. It is the path that you take and the patience that you cultivate that is important.

In this anecdote, Celal Hoca utilizes a modern metaphor—crossword puzzles were invented by Arthur Wynne (1871–1945)—to discuss a conception of emotion in his own perspective.[7] He succinctly narrates his belief that feelings and music not only are interrelated, but can metaphorically stand for each other as well. Spirituality, however, does not shift or pivot; instead, God becomes the space where the event of crossword-puzzle making, emotion, and music making can occur.[8] The voicing of melancholy emerges as an iteration of remembrance of God, especially in the context of hardship. "You must embrace suffering to be a great musician," Celal Hoca once told me:

> After all, our music is all about melancholy, as everything has been lost. Look at this sheet of paper. [*He gestures to the print-out of transcription affixed to the tuning pegs of my* kanun.] I am trying to use this notation to make you feel and play out your feelings. With a piece of paper! We have lost *meşk*.

LEARNING WITH NOTATION

Any discussion of *meşk* with musicians brings up the issue of playing from notation (*nota*) versus playing from memory (*ezberli*), as *meşk* itself is primarily a system of oral and aural transmission in which music is learned by ear. Pointing to universalist claims of music performance, many Turkish classical musicians observe that even in western art musics, the preferred way to perform professionally is always from memory. My own teacher's teacher, Cinuçen Tanrıkorur (1938–2000), believed—as musicians in many different concert traditions do—that the final performance of any piece could never be found in the notes themselves. In my experience, many Turkish classical musicians initially learn through notation but also memorize the repertoire. Notation has therefore codified some features of the repertoire, but the very existence of notation has also been part of a discursive formulation about *meşk*. In other words, the adoption and continued use of western notation has been interpreted ideologically; an individual musician's use of notation may indicate his/her perspectives about an Ottoman past. When *meşk* was an oral transmission-based practice during the Ottoman period, the various lineages of masters and apprentices (*meşk silsilesi*) had different interpretations of the same piece, as musical phrasing, articulation, and ornamentation were often lineage specific. Ultimately, musicians believe that one needs a master-teacher to interpret notation (Behar 2003 [1998], 1993).

Turkish musicians' use of notation is performative (Hall 1989). For example, a typical afternoon lesson early in my studies with Necati Hoca proceeded something like this: before I arrived, Necati Hoca had chosen the *makam* we were to work on. After settling into his studio, we chat, and then I tuned my *kanun* as Necati Hoca talked me through the makeup (tetrachords, pentachords, etc.) of the *makam*, its characteristic melodic phrases, and its common modulations. By the time I was ready to begin, Necati Hoca had chosen which piece we were to start the lesson with (usually a *peşrev* or a *saz semaisi*). He placed the piece on the stand in front of us, and we proceeded to play it. By the middle of the first *hane* (verse-like section), Necati Hoca ceased playing and shuffled through piles of sheet music as he searched for an alternative transcription. If that newfound transcription was also not to his liking, he might find a third or fourth. If any tangibly available transcription continued to be inadequate to him, he consulted his digital archives and printed out another transcription from his computer. In the end, I never received a single piece of sheet music untouched by his pencil—Necati Hoca constantly refigured transcriptions to convey his interpretation of the piece as clearly as possible.[9] Since 2011, Necati Hoca has been notating his own transcriptions specifically to share with his students.

The notation system that Necati Hoca and others tend to rely on today is a product of the early twentieth century at the end of the Ottoman Empire and during the early Republic era. After the founding of the Republic (1923), a few musician-scholars were tasked with inventing and codifying a core repertoire for the newly fabricated genre named "Turkish classical music." However, other notation systems were in use long before. Examples of cipher notation systems abound in the early Muslim world, beginning with notational forms designed by Safi al-Din Ardabili (1252–1334) and extending to the emergent notational system established by Dimitrie Cantemir (1673–1723), referred to as Kantemiroğlu in Turkish (Öztuna 1969 [1955]: 110).[10] These scores were not read for performance, as their purpose was to illustrate a theoretical point, or to simply be a part of a collected record of known pieces (Signell 1977: 2).

Hamparsum notation, created by Baba Hamparsum (Hampartsoum Limondjian, 1768–1839) under the commission of Sultan Selim III, is another prominent cipher system still occasionally used today. An easy, versatile one-line transcription system, Hamparsum notation was easily written on blank paper (e.g., no staff lines needed) from right to left in a script that was easier for Ottomans because of their embodied experience of reading (Ottoman text is, like Arabic or Farsi, read right to left). This notation system was created to preserve compositions for Armenian liturgy, and its role in preserving a large part of the repertoire of Ottoman court music of the eighteenth and nineteenth centuries cannot be underestimated. Turkish scholars argue that large numbers of compositions in untranscribed Hamparsum notation (e.g., not "translated" into western staff notation) still exist in private collections in Turkey (Ezgi 1953: 520; Sözer 1964: 237) and in Germany (Jäger 1996b). While most Turkish classical musicians today might not know Hamparsum notation, those who do share rich anecdotes about their ability to quickly transcribe ideas for *taksim* or compositions on a whim. The acclaimed *neyzen* Niyazi Sayın (b. 1927) recounted an anecdote about one afternoon in the 1960s when, before many of the Jews of Istanbul left the city because of civil unrest and new legislation aimed at restricting minorities, a group of musicians were walking by a synagogue and heard the cantor reciting a beautiful section of the Torah. They were ostensibly so moved by the melody that one of the musicians ripped open his cigarette pack and quickly jotted—in Hamparsum notation—the melody on the inside of the wrapper. "Musicians collect music from everywhere, it does not matter if it is a church or a mosque or a synagogue," Niyazi Hoca explained. "[W]e see it all as a manifestation of One God."[11]

In the Ottoman Empire, western staff notation was first used in the seventeenth century by Ali Ufki (Wojciech Bobowski, 1610–1675), a Polish convert to Islam. His famous collection from 1650, *Mecmua-i Saz-ü Söz* (*Instrumental and Vocal Collection*), holds transcriptions in western notation of repertoire we now denote Turkish classical music.[12] When Giuseppe Donizetti (1788–1856) came to Istanbul to work with the newly formed Imperial Band in 1827, he brought western notation and solfège with him and thus prompted a more widespread usage of western staff notation in a variety of different musical spaces in the Ottoman Empire, even as Donizetti himself additionally used Hamparsum notation. Western staff notation became more widespread in Turkish musical production when Raûf Yektâ (1871–1935)[13] introduced a system in which he adopted western staff notation and developed accidentals to denote the koma-s ("commas," or microtonal intervals) needed for Turkish makam.[14] His notation became the standard notation used in most official publications of the Istanbul Conservatory during the 1920s and 1930s (Signell 1977: 3). Eventually, Yektâ's colleagues, Suphi Ezgi (1869–1962) and H. Sadettin Arel (1880–1995), made the critical revisions to Yektâ's system and produced the standard notation system in use in Turkey today.

Considering the variety of systems of notation that have long existed, how can we understand the fact that notation was consistently unused within the Ottoman meşk system and came into widespread circulation only in the mid-twentieth century? Beyond the importance of the institutionalization of music pedagogy in newly emerging conservatories, the answer lies in notation itself: what can be actually saved and marked down in notation contains only a very small proportion of the piece to be played. In 1867, Ritter von Adelberg, a European musician connected with an embassy in Istanbul, made the following observation:

> Turkish music cannot be transcribed appropriately. Turkish modes allow performers of this music to be flexible and free in their interpretation. This makes it impossible to uncover the secrets this music holds. (In Beşiroğlu 1998: 78)

The critical accidentals indicating the nine to twelve different koma-s needed for notating makam properly were not fully developed in transcriptions until the Ezgi-Arel-Yektâ notation system, which itself has been in use only since the mid-1930s. Yet even this system does not describe the finer subtleties of makam in use by contemporary Turkish classical musicians, especially when we consider the different performance-practice techniques needed for breath instruments (ney) or instruments that are plucked (even here, the fretless ud requires a different approach to koma than that of that kanun, which uses mandal levers to set pitches). Such microtonal details are best learned in the context of oral tradition and within lineages of masters of particular instruments, a requirement that may explain why the meşk system was continually in use during Ottoman times and could be transformed only with the music educational reforms of the nation-state. The notation crafted by Ezgi, Arel, and Yektâ to record existing repertoire was itself, after all, produced within the contexts of these individuals' particular, situated meşk lineages.

Turkish musicologist Bülent Aksoy suggests another reason for resistance to notation; he writes that when individuals attach learning to notation, they simply look to paper to learn music, instead of looking to people to learn (1985: 1229). He suggests that one cannot truly "tie" *meşk* together with notation; there is no comparison to what an apprentice truly learns from his or her master. Thus for Aksoy, notation was resisted simply because individuals valued the personal relationship and socialization offered by the master-apprentice system.

In an interview, esteemed *tanbur* (long-necked lute) master Necdet Yaşar (b. 1930) answered my questions about *meşk* in the present day with a firm statement denying its very possibility. "There is no *meşk* today because of notation," he explained to me. "Now people learn from paper instead of from a master." While my narrative and analysis up to this point seems to celebrate the reification of *meşk* in contemporary Turkish musical life, many musicians articulate exactly the opposite. For such musicians, discussions about *meşk* are folded into the avowal of loss and are manifest in the genre of Turkish classical music itself. *Meşk* becomes another item on the list—alongside patronage institutions, Ottoman performance practices, informed audiences, and the demise of Mevlevi Sufism in the context of the emergence of secular normativity in wake of the nation-state—that is offered as evidence of the so-called death of the genre of Turkish classical music. Musicians' narrative utterances announcing the destruction of *meşk* have a clear role in the linguistic mediation of melancholy modalities.

It is generally undisputed among contemporary Turkish classical musicians, however, that the domestication of western standard notation, along with the codification of repertoire under this notation system, did a kind of "damage" to the genre. The national radio naturalized these new systems as appropriate sounds in the ears of listeners all over Turkey. "By the middle of the 20th century," Walter Feldman explains,

> the acceptance of both musical notation and a consistent form of theory for pedagogical purposes led to the existence of two forms of legitimation, one through conservatory instruction and the other through master-pupil training. These might be combined in a single individual, but this was often not the case. Thus the past forty years have seen significant changes in musical training and composition, which have worked against important areas of both musical vitality and continuity. The situation is by no means resolved, and changes in both patterns are quite possible within the coming decades. (Feldman 1996: 18)

One of the primary ways that individuals find themselves working to reestablish *meşk* and validate their musical practices is by placing themselves in a *meşk silesilesi*, or *meşk* lineage. Espousing a lineage grounds an individual in a collectivized identity. Yet lineages also entail a committed engagement in giving back to others. "As there are links in a chain," one musician explained to me, "each link must give to the other what s/he has taken from before."

Meşk—as a term, discourse, or performance—is used to situate oneself in history, embody one's lineage, and see oneself as actively crafting a future. Contemporary iterations of meşk provide important insights into issues of self and collective identity formation and the maintenance of historical memory. Individual musicians today identify with a specific musical lineage or tradition, referred to as silsile or zincir (lit., "chain"). Significantly, the Turkish term silsile, like the word meşk, is also found in Arabic. The Arabic silsila denotes an iron chain or a series, and is used in reference to the succession of transmission of religious truths, generally referring to the sharing of esoteric knowledge for Sufi sects and the transmission hadith-s, or the sayings of the Prophet Muhammed in Sunni Islam. While meşk silsilesi in the musical sphere were about transmitting sonic knowledge and practices, similar meşk silsilesi with identical methods were used in the Ottoman era for passing on religious and spiritual knowledge, practices, and truths. The secularization reforms that rendered the genre of Turkish classical music a historical artifact devoid of spiritual intonation were thus targeting music transmission practices and musical lineages, which were deeply stitched into the multi-ethnic fabric of religious and spiritual life during the formative years of the nation-state.

With the notation systems and vocal lyric text collections (güfte mecmuası) in circulation during the Ottoman period, meşk was the main means used to pass musical repertoire from one generation to the next. While learning said repertoire, theory, and performance practices from a master through meşk, apprentices were also trained in their master's specific stylistic approaches, techniques, and idiomatic interpretation. While particular religious groups, such as the Mevlevi dervishes, Jewish synagogue cantors, and Greek Orthodox chanters, had distinct lines of musical transmission, none were necessarily closed to outsiders (Behar 1993, Feldman 1996). Individual musicians who had trained with specific masters had highly differentiated and uniquely characteristic styles that placed them within one of many lineages or dynasties.

Many aspects of meşk were never standardized or codified, outside of the cultivation of core repertoire performance practices and the circulation of particular notation systems. However, steps were taken to ensure the life and longevity of these lineages. For example, when a master decided a given student was finished with his/her education and training, the student received a diploma (icazet). Upon receipt of the diploma, the student had a moral obligation to teach, a moral obligation to be a link in the chain. Each link gave to the next what she or he had taken from before, creating a chain much larger than any individual or generation. In 1990, Turkish musicologist Yilmaz Öztuna (1930–2012) published an encyclopedia entry, entitled "Meşk Silsilesi," in which he connected himself through the chains of meşk all the way back to Safi al-Din (Öztuna 1990: 47–52). The existence of an academic article of this sort showcases the importance of the master-apprentice relationship in representing the pedigree of an individual and the cultural capital that comes with it during the twentieth century.

The placing of a contemporary musician in a particular lineage is also a placing in terms of time. While contemporary musicians ground themselves by naming their lineage, this grounding is rarely smooth or even and thus requires musicians to constantly reimagine or remap the past. Throughout interviews, my consultants were quick to align themselves with a specific lineage, and were also able to clearly articulate the historical, stylistic, and aural differences between their lineage and others. However, when I asked the same consultants to diagram their lineage, huge gaps between the 1920s and 1940s consistently appeared, suggesting that the lineage temporarily "died" during this period. In these ethnographic moments of mapping and remapping, individual musicians perform the silencing of their music at the hands of the early nation-state, even though many of them were not themselves alive during that area.

Lineages are muddy and sticky constructs. Some Turkish classical musicians do not claim a lineage, because they were centrally trained in the pedagogical institutions established by the nation-state. Other contemporary musicians do name their lineage, but trace it back only two generations. Others yet espouse a lineage without ever studying with a musician from that lineage, claiming that they learned from recordings. While such a claim may be readily challenged by other contemporary musicians, we must recognize the role recordings have in functioning as a secondary orality, as many musicians learn *taksim* by memorizing those of celebrated musicians of the past (see chapter 5). Performing lineages constitutes an important naming practice, but an individual naming his/her lineage might not necessarily list a chain of masters and apprentices that stretches back through the centuries. As Nora reminds us, history has become "a repository for the secrets of the present" (1989: 18). The past is understood only by an act of the imagination, and made real only to the extent that it is performed.

As processes to create and legitimate memory, *meşk* practices ultimately constitute internalized and habituated processes of remembrance. Naming one's practice as *meşk* discloses one's recognition of the importance of one-on-one learning, the intensity of a relationship between a master and apprentice, and the historical legacy of transmission practices during Ottoman times. Performing lineages shows that musicians' self-grounding in the present directly informs how they narrate the past and maintain a form of communal self-fashioning. Sociologist Jeffery Olick states that "memory is the central faculty of our being in time, the negotiation of past and present through which we define our individual and collective selves" (1998: 385). The struggle over narrating the past is not necessarily to achieve already constituted interests, but to constitute these same interests. Musicians' engagement with historical (self and collective) consciousness vis-à-vis lineages is therefore a critical identity practice that used to situate themselves in a historical narrative.

BI-AURALITY AND THE PROBLEM OF ASSUMED
LISTENING GEOGRAPHIES

Many ethnomusicologists have taken seriously Mantle Hood's insightful expansion of bilinguality in his method of bi-musicality (1960), in which ethnomusicologists learn to play the musics they study to become fluent in more than one musical "language." Hood's approach aims to enable the researcher to learn music "from the inside," and by doing so to directly experience, in a truly participant-observation framework, the aesthetic, technical, conceptual, and embodied aspects of the music traditions she or he seeks to uncover. As a product and inheritor of this academic tradition, for example, I rely on my long-term investment in bi-musicality (and fluency in Turkish), which has only been made possible by the teachers and consultants with whom I work who have given their time and talent freely. Yet while I join many other ethnomusicologists in espousing a bi-musical approach, there remains a process we all may use to some extent that has yet to be similarly named or interrogated. While I needed to have deep, embodied knowledge of the intricacies of *makam* to be able to improvise, while I needed to be adopted as a student by Necati Hoca to understand *meşk* or experience the workings of *meşk silsilesi* in a limited way, and while my own newly situated, embodied, socialized musicking allowed me to understand the role of affective practices in shaping the contours and meanings of musicians' lives, it was not simply learning to *perform* that allowed these transformational insights into Turkish musical meanings, but more significantly, it was learning to *listen* for the new structures of meaning my teachers themselves brought to music listening and musicking. *Meşk* is the system of musical transmission that does not only shape one's hands and voice but also further shapes one's ears and methods of memorialization. I name the process of shifting and shaping one's ears to different axes, geographies, and idioms of listening *bi-aurality*.

Ethnomusicologists are keenly aware that we enter multiple, diverse sonic worlds with our own established ideologies of listening. Often, we spend a great deal of our research in translating one musical system into "our" musical home base, which still, perhaps problematically, remains heavily localized in western epistemological frameworks of musical cognition, analysis, and explanation (for example, transcription and analysis into western standard notation). I suspect that there are many ethnomusicologists who find our work and teaching to be projects of translation: asking our students and our readers—who, we may generally assume, have ears shaped by the standard listening practices of western art and popular musics—to learn to listen differently.

In my own experience, I was not directly trained by my teachers in Turkey to become bi-aural: rather, we were all fixated on the embodied materiality of my performance ability on the *kanun* (trapezoidal zither) and my ability to rearticulate the musical philosophies that influenced and shaped the music I was learning. I found myself invested in becoming bi-aural and experienced it as a project that was separate, yet related, to the project of bi-musicality. In the context of my work with contemporary Turkish classical music and musicians, bi-aurality for me has meant hearing the homologies—material and immaterial analogies or intersections of aesthetics, beliefs, practices, and artifacts—between subjectivity and music making (S. Feld 1990, Hebdige 1979). Listening with the ears that I cultivated to emulate those of Turkish classical musicians has allowed me to perceive and hear how selfhood is reflected in music making, but to also critically hear how music making (the doing, the teaching, the performing, the analyzing, the talking about, and—importantly—the listening) emerges as a collective, non-isolated experience of selfhood that resists easy categorization in western conceptions of listeners and audiences (Negus 1996). Let me offer an example of how Turkish classical musicians listen horizontally, not vertically.

My initial study of *meşk silsilesi* cascaded into one of many nodes in my shift toward bi-aurality. I began my study as many scholars might: trying to locate and pinpoint particular music details—especially ornamentation and patterns of phrasing—that were direct idiosyncratic markers of distinct, separate music lineages. I took an aural genealogical approach. I met with dozens of contemporary musicians and asked them to play particular, iconic moments of a variety of core repertoire (usually the first lines of a *peşrev*, or overture, and the entirety of a *teslim*, or refrain, of an instrumental composition, or *saz semaisi*). I stuck with instrumental music because I knew that in working with vocal repertoire, I would soon find myself investigating the various *silsile* of Qur'anic recitation and the reciters of the *ezan* (Islamic call to prayer) leading me to mapping religious *silsile* more so than lineages of musicians per se. I further located my analysis in instrumental music because, as explained above, I had access to and knowledge of a variety of different notation systems that allowed me some tangible evidence for locating and tracing lineages. My aural genealogical approach meant that I conducted this research and analysis with a vertical metaphor in place: I sought present day manifestations of *meşk silsilesi* traceable through a wide spectrum of articulation and ornamentation in diverse instrumentation for the purpose of finding how far that lineage could be traced back with the material evidence I had in recordings and in transcriptions.

My analysis demonstrated that the only *meşk silsilesi* able to maintain lineage continuity was the *silsile* of *neyzen*-s (musicians who play the *ney*, or end-blown reed flute), who had held the highest cultural capital in the Ottoman Empire as leaders in composition and, importantly, in the social space of the

Mevlevi *tekke*.[15] When examining the canon of Turkish classical music—an invented repertoire shaped by top-down reforms of the nation-state in the 1920s through the 1950s—one sees that many of the great composers of the past happened, not coincidentally, to be *neyzen* and key leaders of the Mevlevi order (as *dede*-s or sheikhs). Despite the efforts by the leaders of the Republic of Turkey to eradicate any influence of the Mevelvi order in new national cultural production, the few Turkish individuals tasked to create and cultivate national repertoire, such as Raûf Yektâ, were often themselves *neyzen* who had been trained by and are assumed—by musicians today—to have still been secret members of the Mevlevi order.[16] At first applying the common model that traced *meşk silsilesi* genealogy vertically "like a tree," I pinpointed particular authors, found definitive gaps in specific lineages, and focused heavily on identifying *silsile* "housed" in individual people who made key recordings, transcriptions, and established institutions.

I thus made a few assumptions about musical lineages that were decidedly rooted in western epistemologies: I assumed teleology (musical transmission is linear, directional, with a singular past flowing directly into a present) and I assumed that locating *silsile* was possible with a focus on the autonomous individual producing autonomous works of art. I was not listening bi-aurally, but rather bringing in a common ideology of listening housed in western music frameworks: (1) we understand musical influence and shared traditions as traceable between bound, separate individuals; (2) we tend to understand musical change in a model of development or linear trajectory; (3) we often espouse a singular notion of a past and reify a teleology of past to present.

Listening and mapping the genealogy of *meşk silsilesi* vertically "as a tree" confined me to making claims about the genealogy of lineages that reified common epistemological assumptions about musical transmission from individual to individual to individual. Often this initial vertical frame of analysis was supported directly through my engagements with my primary teachers. Take, for instance, this statement I recorded during a lesson with Necati Hoca:

> Music communicates and shares something in its existence. I communicate and speak through this language of music. It might, of course, be very possible for people who do not speak Turkish to understand or feel Turkish classical music in their souls. Western music, Turkish music, Hindustani music actually only have differences at the level of technique. We're all saying the same thing because we're all human. It's like these grapes. [*He points to the grapes we have been sharing for the past half hour.*] You can use these grapes to make wine, you can use them to make jam, you can eat them raw. Sound is the same—a musician shapes it for his/her story. Turkish music will tell a Turkish story, Western music will tell a Western story. You know the Turkish expression, "every tree feeds off of its

own scent" [*ağaç kendi kokusundan beslenir*]. Our tree tells our story, and it's our job as musicians to tell the story to society.

In this statement, Necati Hoca's metaphor of the tree as housing essentialized sonic properties that can be mapped on to social difference is mediated first by a claim that music can be "understood" by individuals not socialized in that musical system. Necati Hoca oscillates between music as a universal, humanist tree that all can access, and music as an exclusive or essentialist entity that preserves and tells a specific people's story. It may seem that these two statements are contradictory, but I argue that such contradictions show competitive discursive domains. Said differently, this statement demonstrates the way the vertical tree metaphor is expanded by Necati Hoca to explain his worldview. The contradiction arises because the metaphor he chose did not serve his purposes well. Perhaps he chose it because he was speaking directly to me, and he understood the usefulness of teaching me through naturalized western explanatory frameworks.

Yet Necati Hoca deploys the tree metaphor elsewhere, particularly in the avowal of loss that I argue is constitutive of the genre of Turkish classical music:

> Ottoman civilization [*Osmanlı medeniyeti*] was like a tree. This tree had deep roots and many branches: the palace, the *tekke* [Sufi lodge], the *Mevlevihane* [institution of learning and practice for the Mevlevi order]. Slowly the roots to this tree were cut [by the nation-state]. One by one, each root was torn out and left to rot. Of course, a tree whose roots have been left to rot will lose its fruit. Music was one of the greatest fruits that dropped from the tree. And now I look at you and other young students. You are the new offshoots [*filiz-s*] of this great tree. You are bringing life . . . you are life itself. But you are aware of your connection to the tree that has been slain, remembering what that tree had been, and knowing the reality that the tree will not be again.

In this moment captured in another recording of a lesson, I, as student, am instructed about my own role in both perpetuating the loss narrative about the so-called death of Turkish classical music and seeing myself as an antidote to it. Finding yourself embedded in such a loss narrative does more than weave a nostalgic web around an Ottoman past: through this process students learn that this loss is a loss that is to be personally adopted and endured. This loss becomes the foundation of students' identities and senses of self. It is as much learned from the master as musical ornamentation or the understandings of *makam* are learned. This tree is offered as indicative of the genre Turkish classical music, and Necati Hoca identifies its demise in the piece-by-piece eradication of Ottoman systems of patronage and physical institutions. It would seem, then, that the vertical tree metaphor serves many interpretive purposes for understanding the whole of Turkish classical music making beyond *meşk*. At the same time, shifting our listening geographies horizontally is also indispensable to understand the rhizomatic emergence of contradictory narratives of musical genealogies in Turkey today.

GENEALOGY, ORIENTALISM, AND ORIENTATIONS

Genealogy has been a central concept for ethnographers, having been at the center of early anthropological work on kinship (cf. Rivers 1900; Evans-Pritchard 1940 and 1949, Gellner 1969). The work of Michel Foucault (1972 [1969], 1977, 1978, and 1981), which considers heterogeneity and places the body and power in the center of analyses of genealogy, has offered ethnographers tools for useful alternatives to standard, singular descriptions of narrative history, and provided a way to consider the genealogies that exist in our own disciplinary frameworks through Foucault's theorization of archeological analysis. Anthropological works since the late twentieth century on historicity and mobile diasporic formations in the Indian Ocean (Ho 2006), in Bedouin communities of the Middle East (Shryock 1997), and North Africa (Glasser 2012 and 2016) have fleshed out Shryock's concept of the "genealogical imagination," a distinct historical consciousness in the present. Components of the genealogical imagination—which include the struggle over authoritative transmission, the dialect of embodiment and exteriorization mediated by ways of practice (music) and the archive (written notation), and the movement of a mobile archipelago transcending the map of nation-states that did not come into being until the twentieth century—all find their place in the Turkish classical music transmission practices I describe here.

Scholarship on musical genealogies has also proved incredibly useful in thinking about how genealogical difference can be embedded in sound and listening, and how genealogy can be a frame that lets us understand musical decision-making and musical meaning in the here and now. Genealogical transmission in Turkey bears similarity to genealogical transmission in other settings, especially in the case of North African Andalusi (Glasser 2016) and urban Iranian musical practices (Youssefzadeh 2000, During 1995). In all cases, we see an overlap between musical and sacred discourses and practices. Musical transmission parallels sacred transmission associated with the blessing of an Islamic (Sufi) master infused with divine energy, *baraka* (Grewal 2014). Musical lineage narratives also resemble the way lineages of teaching in Islamic legal thought as well as spiritual oratory traditions linked back to the Prophet Muhammed, his family (his wife Ayşe was ostensibly a spirited, well-respected orator), and his companions, as well as the lineage of the twelve imams of Shia Islam. As previously mentioned, in Turkish classical music discourses on *meşk*, many musicians cite the relationship between God and the Prophet as the best model for master-apprentice relations.

In twenty-first century musical genealogical studies of the Middle East and North Africa, scholars have particularly examined the way music lineages become profoundly localized, attenuating over time, only to be tentatively rescued from disappearance through projects of revival and reform (see especially Glasser 2012 and 2016). Nation-states and private markets function in tandem as neoliberal governmentality supports salvage projects by funding new print media, releasing archived recordings, and promoting amateurization. Angling for "authentication" (Deeb 2006) and privileging one's authority because of one's lineage are always at play—whether the actors be musicians of the nation-state, private industry, or amateur circuits. The discourse of *meşk* lineages paints a fantasy of a clear line of connection from the present into the past, a line of connection I complicate.

There is also excellent academic work on musical genealogies in South Asian traditions (cf. D. M. Neuman 1990, Weidman 2006, Rahaim 2012, D. Neuman 2012, Katz forthcoming). Often focusing on hereditary musical genealogies (e.g., lineages in which musical, embodied knowledge is transmitted, most generally, from father to son), studies on music transmission in South Asia have yielded tremendous insight into the ways in which specific North Indian elite music lineages, or *gharana*, can house competitive collective memories. One of the general characteristics of the genealogical imagination for North Indian or Hindustani classical musicians is that hereditary musicians define the value of their own lineage against those of others. Stephen Slawek astutely describes the *gharana* as

> a mechanism through which one's musical status can be preserved. The stronger the alliance, the higher and more stable the status. Weaken the alliance and you create conditions that will allow the propaganda of rival groups to be taken for historical fact. (1998: 174)

It seems then that in other non-Turkish and also definitively non-western musical traditions, vertical tree-like tracings of musical lineage can emerge as flawed memorializing more aptly telling a story about contemporary politics rather than presenting historical "facts."

Metaphors often arise directly from the political assumptions made by past scholars of genealogy. Scholarship on musical genealogies has demonstrated how genealogy itself is part of an orientalist project, in which "the east" is presented as the exotic and distant other, distinct from the "civilized, modern west." Orientalism, a term first proposed by postcolonial studies scholar Edward Said to refer to western patronizing perceptions and depictions of Middle Eastern and North African societies, arises in an inherently unequal power dynamic wherein imperialist societies produce knowledge about "the

East" (1978). For example, musical lineages of North Indian/Hindustani classical musics were greatly affected and reshaped by the mechanisms of British colonialism, which validated high art Indian music production as legitimate when it could be notated, codified, analyzed, and represented according to the standard representational frameworks of the west (Butler Schofield 2010, Farrell 1997). In the context of postcolonial Indian (Hindu) nationalism, an orientalist project further positioned "classical" knowledge as derived from a "golden-age" past in a pre-Muslim era, reducing thousands of years of shared traditions into a contemporary bifurcated discourse ("Hindu" versus "Muslim") and leading a revival of Sanskrit treatises (Butler Schofield 2010, Bakhle 2005, Katz forthcoming). Zooming out to the Middle East and beyond, we can see that from the nineteenth into the twentieth century, musical discourses seemed to converge on transnational narratives of salvage, preservation, standardization, and reform. In other words, we can speak globally of ruptures in musical genealogies in the twentieth century as connected to histories of orientalist scholarship imperialism, war, class divisions, and the emergence of folklore. In the context of colonialism, nationalism, and new technologies (especially in recording formats and radio), remediated narratives of music analysis proliferated public spheres according to western standards, ultimately rebirthing a discourse of musical salvage (e.g., "we must save music").

My contribution and intervention to studies of musical genealogies calls attention to the ways in which our present analyses of music lineage may indicate a continued and invisible inheritance of orientalist frameworks. While musical genealogical scholarship of non-western musics was produced in dialogue with music scholarship on western musics, the project of legitimatizing non-western music according to western musical terms resulted in methods of analyzing musical genealogies that make it difficult to develop the bi-aural listening skills needed to understand how music is passed along and shared. I view the way disembodied music objects and particular primary authors (autonomous individuals) are centered in genealogical study to be one of the main ways we maintain orientalist frameworks: it collapses musical processes and practices into a music object, removing music making from social contexts of the active agents musicking, who may conceive selfhood in communal, not individual, terms. Furthermore, I argue that a key orientalist assumption—the notion of a teleological past and linear musical lineages that extend backward in time—might inhibit our analyses rather than produce critical insight. Bi-aurality requires an alternate listening geography, one that does not use the ears appropriate for western epistemologies to understand how musics are shared, circulated, and passed from person to person and across time.

I argue that we must change our orientation as we approach musical genealogies in any context. In her book *Queer Phenomenology: Orientations, Objects, Others* (2006), Sara Ahmed foregrounds the concept of "orientation" to understand bodies of knowledge from postcolonialism, critical race studies, and feminist and queer studies. Focusing on the "orientation" aspect of "sexual orientation" and the "orient" of orientalism, Ahmed examines what it means for bodies to be situated in space and time. Bodies take shape as they move through the world, directing themselves toward or away from objects and others. Being "orientated" means feeling at home, knowing where one stands, or having certain objects within reach. Orientations affect what is proximate to the body or what can be reached. A queer phenomenology, Ahmed contends, reveals how social relations are arranged spatially, how queerness disrupts and reorders these relations by not following the accepted paths, and how a politics of disorientation puts other objects within reach, those that might, at first glance, seem awry.

Ahmed articulates how bodies are turned toward the objects around them, and how "direction" matters in understanding orientation. If music scholars perpetuate a focus on music objects, away from the socialization of musicking and the embodied practices of the people signifying those music objects, our orientation will inherently shape our conclusions away from the actual practices of people musicking. In changing my own orientation, I came to understand that vertical analysis and listening ends up replicating and imposing my own normative (western academic) ideologies of listening onto musical meanings and lineages embraced by contemporary Turkish classical musicians. It was, of course, the materials I was engaging to parse out difference in *meşk silsilesi*—notation, interviews, my own lessons and my observation of others', and old recordings—that opened my ears and shifted my hearing to a new aural geography. Instead of setting aside the muddy evidence that did not fit into a vertical tree-like interpretation of lineages, I placed that which did not fit in my model in the center of my analysis.

In redirecting my orientation, I came to understand that the very nature of *meşk silsilesi* is best understood horizontally, or rhizomatically. I discarded a unidirectional time narrative ("the singular past flows linearly into the singular present") that I had previously imposed. This release gave way to listening across *silsile* informed by the very institutions and patronage structures—during the Ottoman era and the early years of the Republic of Turkey—that brought different *meşk silsilesi* together. It was actually the consistency of the musical idioms I was analyzing across *meşk silsilesi* that shifted my cognitive framework and opened my ears to a horizontal listening practice, which changed my ideologies of listening and initiated my integration into a new way of rhizomatic, polydirectional, or spectral listening I have named bi-aurality.

LISTENING LIKE A *NEY*

In my "aural turn," I placed the hindering evidence that did not fit into a tree-like, linear interpretation of lineages in the center of my analysis and located *meşk* rhizomatically. The consistency of the musical idioms I was analyzing across *meşk silsilesi* initiated my orientation into an aural geography not like a tree, but like a *ney*. This nine-holed end-blown reed flute, the central instrument of the Mevlevi order and Turkish classical music, offers a unique spatial framework to understand genealogy that both is more referentially accurate to the workings of *meşk silsilesi* and allows for a multivalent discursive archeology of contemporary Turkish classical musicians' narrative tropes.

Listening rhizomatically allows for an interrogation and understanding of the ruination of fixed, material institutions and their effects on *meşk silsilesi*. While I was interviewing a well-known *neyzen* about listening for differences in *meşk silsilesi*, he interrupted a question with frustration and anger. "*Meşk* was never strictly established or codified," he claimed, "because it was *not* supposed to disappear. Lineages should have continued. The *tekke* should still be standing. We are left with our own recreations because it has been taken away from us." Historical records describe the pedagogical practices of the palace school, known as the Enderun, in the court of Mehmet the Conqueror (1432–1481). The Enderun's curriculum included literature, theology, science, and art. Scholars postulate that the arts in progress during this time, such as calligraphy, miniatures, poetry, and music, were transmitted through *meşk* as early as the fifteenth century (Beşiroğlu 1998: 75). The other primary context for *meşk* was in designated rooms for lessons (*meşkhane*-s), which were located either in the religious houses of the Mevlevi dervishes (*Mevlevihane*-s), in lodges (*tekke*-s), or in the palaces of the Ottoman elite.

The patronage systems and material institutions of the Ottoman Court were disbanded and closed with the founding of the Turkish Republic in 1923. The Turkish Republic's passing of Law 677 on December 13, 1925, however, effectively closed the *tekke*-s. Some contemporary Turkish classical musicians discuss the dissolution of centuries of spiritual, literary, and musical authority held by the Mevlevi-s in the Ottoman Court as if the cultural violence against Sufis and Sufism in 1925 (expressed most profoundly by the public burning of Sufi texts) was something they personally lived. Some musicians know the exact wording of portions of Law 677, which translated reads thus:

> LAW 677: Which prohibits and abolishes the profession of tomb-keeping, the assigning of mystical names, and the closing of *tekke*-s, *zaviye*-s [central lodges], and tombs.
>
> Clause 1. All the *tekke*-s and *zaviye*-s in the Turkish Republic, either in the form of *vakf*-s [religious foundations] or under the personal property right of its sheikh or established in any other way, are closed. The right of property and possession of their owners continue. Those used as mosques and *mescit*-s [small mosques] may be retained as such.
>
> All of the orders using descriptions such as sheikh, dervish, disciple, *dedelik* [working as a person of religious authority], *çelebilik* [leading aspects of the

Mevlevi order; a *çelebi* is a descendant of Mevlana], *seyyitlik* [passing on religious truths; a *seyyit* is a descendant of the Prophet Muhammed], *babalık* [leading Sufi gatherings; *baba* denotes an elder of a religious order], *emirlik* [occupying the status of heading important households], *nakiplik* [working as a warden of a religious order], *halifelik* [serving in high positions in the Caliphate], *falcılık* [telling or reading fortunes], *büyücülük* [practicing magic], *üfürükçülük* [curing illnesses by means of the breath], divining, and giving written charms in order to make someone reach his or her desire: service to these titles, and the wearing of dervish costume [this included *sikke*, an important male headpiece or hat that signaled identity in a various sect or order], are prohibited. The tombs of the [Ottoman] sultans and the tombs of the dervish orders are closed, and the profession of tomb-keeping is abolished. Those who open the closed *tekke*-s or *zaviye*-s, or the tombs, and those who re-establish them or those who give temporary places to the orders or people who are called by any of the mystical names mentioned above or those who serve them, will be sentenced to at least three months in prison and will be fined at least fifty Turkish liras.

Clause 2. This law is effective immediately (adapted and modified from the translation in Friedlander 1975: 117).

Today, the physical buildings of the *tekke* either stand idle or have been reopened in the last decades as museums or pilgrimage sites. Turkish classical musicians describe these empty monuments as "stand[ing] like moonlight [*mehtap gibi kaldı*]." This particular narrative description gestures to a long-established trope in Ottoman poetry in which the moon symbolizes the face of the beloved (one's unreachable lover or God) shining in the distance yet untouchable by any on earth. Positioning the *tekke* as moonlight is a melancholic positioning: a *tekke* today is a historic architectural monument rendered "soulless" (*ruhsuz*) and accessible only as a visual artifact. How might the leveling of the two primary institutions housing *meşk* and patronizing *meşk silsilesi* invite us to listen rhizomatically?

CASE STUDIES: LISTENING RHIZOMATICALLY TO *MEŞK* LINEAGES

Let me give three examples of how *meşk silsilesi* as musical genealogy can be understood rhizomatically like a *ney*. The first example features a key female musician of the early Republic period, *kanun* or zither master Vecihe Daryal (b. 1908 or 1914, d. 1970), who played at the national radio houses in both Istanbul and Ankara. The *kanun* offers a rich example of a musical genealogy of rupture and invention, as the instrument itself was not widely adopted by musicians in the public sphere until the early twentieth century. In other words, the *kanun* did not become a central instrument of the newly constructed genre of Turkish classical music until it had first become an instrument performed by Ottoman men in urban settings. Daryal's *meşk silsilesi* was specifically associated with the musicians of the Ottoman *harem*, exclusively composed of women. Her style of *kanun* playing ostensibly incorporated a method of holding the plectrums and striking the strings that was "different" from that of male performers (Feldman 1996: 159). During fieldwork, I was unable to ascertain what this method might have looked like, as the second- and third-generation inheritors of her style do not have a method differing from that of other (male) performers.

Daryal was a key actor introducing women-only *meşk silsilesi* into early national sound waves, and the fact that her sonic signifiers (ornamentation, articulation, phrasing patterns) were adopted while embodied difference was lost demonstrates the slippage between institutions and lineages discursively articulated as separate today. Perhaps the claim to difference in all-women music lineages was not real; rather, the idea of "difference" in embodied music making was simply mapped onto women's different bodies and iterated or presented as difference in music. Perhaps, too, the embodied difference of playing that Daryal ostensibly espoused disappeared simply when she died; gendered bodies disappear as all bodies do.

When Daryal married and left the radio, she was replaced by the *kanun* player Ahmet Yatman (1897–1973). He was a prominent Roman musician from the *piyasa*, or "live music market" circuit, and his moving to the lofty institution of the state radio challenges the bifurcation assumed today between classical and popular musics. Yatman introduced sonic signifiers from his own Roma family *silsile*, characteristics that allowed him to play with speed and agility previously unheard. The following two transcriptions point to a similar musical descending line on the *kanun* rendered by Daryal (Example 3.1) and Yatman (Example 3.2):

Example 3.1 Descending musical line in the style of Vecihe Daryal.

Example 3.2 Descending musical line in the style of Ahmet Yatman.

By the 1940s, *kanun* players had adopted Daryal's "classical, pure, feminine" style and synthesized it with Yatman's "fast, heart-racing, Roma" styling. So for *kanun* players today, the claiming of a distinct *silsile* in the present emerges as purely ideological and discursive, unmoored from musical difference. Hybridized *kanun* practices indicate how individual selfhood takes precedence over a unified chain of influence.

Case study two considers chains of *meşk* wherein prominent musicians claim they are completely self-taught. In our interviews, master *tambur* player Necdet Yaşar claimed that he never studied his instrument and modal theory, or learned repertoire from a master-teacher. Yet it is well documented that Yaşar studied with Mesud Cemil (1902–1963), son of Tanburi Cemil Bey (1873–1916), a lineage attested to in the liner notes of Yaşar's thirteen albums. These musicians name themselves *alaylı* or *alaydan yetişme*, meaning that their received their music examination "on the streets" (see also Beken 1998). Given the prestige afforded to lineages, why might one disavow a master-apprentice relationship? During the 1930s, when Yaşar was a child, the new concept of the "autonomous individual" (*birey*) was invented and circulated in the Turkish public sphere. It is no coincidence that the birth of this term coincides closely with the increased celebration of the Turkish appropriation of the French discourse on music virtuosity (Tr. *virtüöz*), which focuses on an individual's mastery. Musical genealogies had previously not been conceptualized with an initial emphasis on the individual—indeed, many Ottoman composers wrote their master-teachers' names as the composers of their pieces instead of their own. An emerging political climate that valorized autonomy, individuality, and virtuosity meant that some musicians began identifying themselves as autonomous music producers, a venture frequently replicated by contemporary music ethnographers. *Meşk silsilesi* are rhizomatic—individual musicians learn from many sources but may strategize and situate their musicking as self-engineered products.

The final case study I offer emerges from the late eighteenth century with the celebrated Ottoman musical authority Hammamizade İsmail Dede Efendi (1778–1846). Dede Efendi witnessed the beginning of the *Tanzimat* (reforms) that brought swift modernization to Ottoman musical practices: the military music house (*mehterhane*) of the elite corps of the Ottoman army was closed and a new palace orchestra (*Muzikayı Hûmayûn*) was established by Giuseppe Donizetti. A celebrated composer of Ottoman palace music and lead *ney* player at Istanbul's Yenikapı Mevlevihanesi, Dede Efendi had enjoyed complete support under the patronage of Sultan Selim III, wrote multiple compositions, and invented new *makam*-s such as *Sultanîyegâh, Nev-eser,* and *Hicaz büselik* (İnal 1955 and 1958). With the atmosphere of change at court, Dede Efendi was reputed to have announced to his students "the taste has gone away (*tadı kaçtı*), our music is dead." He ostensibly packed his *ney* and Qur'an and, abandoning Istanbul, set out on the pilgrimage to Mecca (*hac* or *hajj*). A present-day *ney* player articulated to me that it was here, on the hill known as Mina, that "the great Dede Efendi, full of melancholy, finally embraced God in death." While Dede Efendi reportedly died from cholera, most musicians who told this story believed it was the cultural losses he endured that ultimately ended his life.

For the dozens of musicians who remembered and retold this story to me, Dede Efendi's life and passing narrate loss upon loss. Ottoman palace music was lost with the supposed invasion of western music. Dede Efendi's voyage was a loss for Ottoman musicians, for the Mevlevi, and for all of Istanbul. And finally, Dede Efendi's departure from Istanbul, which metaphorically reflected his departure from life itself, is not only symbolically interpreted as the death and loss of a great composer, musician, and spiritual authority figure, but also the death and loss of music.

Nearly all musicians I interviewed today trace themselves back to Dede Efendi's lineage, even though he reportedly had only a few students. As present-day musicians claim in chorus to emanate from his lineage, we witness a rhizomatic affiliation that renders Dede Efendi's losses as more sticky and lasting than the music objects we attribute to him. To understand contemporary *meşk silsilesi* linked to Dede Efendi demands that we prioritize affective practice over the transmission of musical, embodied knowledge. Musicians link themselves to Dede Efendi in a shared sense of loss, calling ethnographers to account for how, as one *kanun* player told me, "feeling [*duymak* also means hearing] multiple generations [together] at the same time (*nesilleri birlikte duymak*)" surfaces as a primary element of transmission.

The collapsing of nineteenth and twentieth century lineages on Dede Efendi offer a historical example, beyond Vecihe Daryal and the rise of the autonomous individual (*birey*), of how musical genealogies for present-day Turkish classical musicians are horizontal—they entail communities coming together to forge collectivity rather than tree-like vertical links of autonomous individuals in separate outstretched branches that grow upward over time. Arguing that the "root," a tree-like metaphor, emblematizes potentially problematic modes of mapping and thinking, Deleuze and Guattari discard this epistemological structure of modernity in preference of the rhizome. I too invite us to criticize our geographies and shift from a vertical aurality in which things are grounded and time is singular and teleological to a sonic metaphor of the unstable, wailing, and limitless "plateau" of the reed bed.

Deleuze and Guatarri argue that the rhizome is "anti-genealogy" (1987 [1980]: 11), but I find in the *ney* a productive model for reorienting (S. Ahmed 2006) our assumptions as we listen past our structures into those engendered by the individuals and communities with whom we work. My first case study of Daryal and Yatman shows that lineages' tangible differences of embodied music making may disappear while the ideological apparatus of naming lineages remains. My second case study disrupts our insistent focus on autonomous individuals, and my final case study demonstrates that for over two centuries, Turkish classical musicians have placed themselves in lineages not because of musical artifacts but because of affective discourses and practices. Before mishearing musical genealogies maintained by western-generated epistemologies of genealogical collectives, we must first listen for how musicians establish and monitor the boundary of their social, communal body across time and space.

LEARNING MUSIC AS THE PRACTICE OF MELANCHOLY

Listening to how musicians talk about music transmission and passing music on from one generation to the next in the context of music lessons is an example of musical metapragmatics, or practice commenting on itself (Feld et al. 2004, Dent 2009). Musical transmission is, after all, the opportunity to witness the emergence of discourse and meaning at the site of embodied sonic practice. As a practice that comments on itself, studying the transmission of music, the transmission of music philosophy, the transmission of music history, and the transmission of "literacies of listening" (Kapchan 2009) between masters and students allows us a glimpse into knowledge construction that elucidate the fundamentally affective character of Turkish classical music meaning. Considering systems of *meşk* and the genealogies musicians craft through *meşk* as metapragmatics allows us to understand how musicians' melancholic modalities are forged in the interstices of learning music itself.

In this chapter, I examined the ways in which melancholy is learned and engrained through practices of musical transmission and associated discursive practices. As practices of *meşk* work to recreate the master's sensibility and knowledge anew in the apprentice, understandings of music, and in particular music's relationship to emotion and spirituality, are inculcated and passed on to future generations. The result is a melancholic subject that mourns the loss of the music she or he plays, and yet also celebrates the mourning and associated feelings of melancholy. Furthermore, embracing melancholy is not only experienced as a common-sense modality for musicians; it is also celebrated as a practice individuals engage to live a spiritually rich life. Yet significantly, this melancholy is anything *but* individual: it has been forged and fixed through chains of masters and their students. Senses of individual selfhood merge with identification with one's lineage and construct a collective selfhood. It is a melancholic subjectivity that extends into all other intersectional identity categories and serves as material for collective self-fashioning. The next chapter continues interrogating melancholic modalities by focusing on how embodiment works to arrange other forms of difference at the level of individual bodily boundaries and borders.

CHAPTER 4

Boundaries of Embodiment in Sounded Melancholy

To the extent that in emotion we are, so to speak, under the spell of our body, we are delivered to mental states with little intentionality, as though in emotion we "lived" our body in a more intense way.

—Paul Ricoeur

Any theorizing of the body must account for exactly how the body actively comes to matter in the process of materialization, or how bodies come into perception and existence. For a book about musicians and musicking, an author must attend to how the materiality of the body is an active, not passive, process. In studies produced by scholars with foundational training in western art music canons, we may tend to examine music as our primary object for analysis, rendering it a kind of ethereal artifact or text that exists outside of embodied particularities of performers or listeners. This is often named the objectivist approach to music analysis, and this framework has three central problems. First, music is stripped of signification given by people making and consuming music, and performance and transmission practices tend to be drowned out. Second, presenting music as a disembodied object renders music itself as having agency; statements such as "music does x or music moves y" renders sounds as having anthropocentric qualities and the capacity to act. And third, valuing music as an incorporeal object neglects the ways musical practices leave traces on the body of musicians and listeners. How many of us have blisters from playing a string instrument, have jaw soreness after playing an instrument dependent on our breath, or have experienced the range of sensations left on the throat after extended periods of vocalizing? How many more of us as participants in live music listening have sustained tinnitus (ringing in the ears) or altered sense experiences of hearing as a result of amplification? We may also be intimately familiar with musicking that involves significant bodily sensations from chills to dancing to sweating to crying. Arguing that our experiences of musicking or listening to music leaves traces on our diverse bodies and bodily experiences is not a new idea.

Valuing the inherent embodied aspect of musicking is embedded in the very language that musicians use in Turkish. Offering an analysis of Turkish classical music as a disembodied object would not only strip away the richness of musical meaning as cultivated in the social lives and discourses of musicians themselves, but it would also be highly inappropriate as an act of translation. In Turkish, many high-art music pieces are named *eser*, or "work." In literature, poetry, visual art, and, of course, music, the term *eser* is reserved for works that are considered significant pieces of human greatness.[1] A musical composition can become an *eser* if it outlives the author and remains in circulation through oral transmission. Thus *eser*-s are works that musicians perceive as having some agency: *eser*-s seem to resist loss.

Importantly, musicians do not name every music composition an *eser*. Instead, musicians generally name pieces by a given composition's musical form and the melodic mode (*makam*) in which it is written: *Acemaşiran peşrevi* denotes an introductory composition (*peşrev*) in *Acemaşiran makamı*, *Uşşak saz semaisi* denotes a suite-like compositional form in *Uşşak makamı*, *Rast şarkısı* denotes a light vocal song format in *Rast makamı*, and so forth. Works deemed deeply important are named *şaheser*-s by musicians: we may translate *şaheser* as "masterwork" or "masterpiece," as *şah* is the princely term for Persian monarchs. While naming a given musical work *eser* or *şaheser* is ultimately subjective and based on the speaker's value judgments and aesthetic positions, these socially sanctioned naming practices, generally solidified in the processes of musical transmission described in chapter 3, share some general characteristics. Like visual monuments that withstand rain, storms, and natural disasters and may share the title *eser*, musical *eser*-s—though nontangible cultural products—are regarded as having the same strength or durability as their physical counterparts. In my observations, Turkish classical musicians label a musical work *eser* when the piece has four main components:

1. It is a composition, a fixed musical work (e.g., not an improvisation) that is an established item in multiple, diverse core repertoires engaged by Turkish classical musicians.
2. The author/composer of a work is an individual (who has passed or is no longer alive) who is also a regarded spiritual leader or authority.
3. A work is interpreted as an excellent sonic example of the character or quality of a composer's own self, even when the composer may not have been known or placed the name of another (for example, his or her master-teacher) as the composer as a sign of respect.

4. Musicians and listeners today claims that a work is very "affecting" (*duygulandırıyor*) or "touches them" (*dokunuyor*).

These four items reveal the importance of embodiment and affect in naming practices. To produce "emotion" (Tr. *duygu*) means to enact change by pressing upon us and moving us in some way. To be touched (Tr. *dokunmak*) implies that an object comes into contact with the surface of one's self, hitting against the boundary between an individual and the outside world. Naming a musical work *eser* means recognizing the way listening to or engaging a sonic musical product calls attention to our boundaries. We note that, in taking music into ourselves, our bodies' surfaces are opened to the outside: our boundaries are rendered porous.

The linguistic significance of the term *eser* is that an *eser* leaves "a trace, sign, mark" such as those left by "the Hadith, monuments, remains" (Redhouse 1997: 347). Importantly, canonical Turkish dictionaries identify Islamic discourse at the ideological center of the word *eser*: the *hadith*-s are the statements and actions of the Prophet Muhammed and his family, and serve as important source material outside of the Qur'an that Muslims look to for modeling lifestyle and attitudes. As contemporary Turkish classical musicians deploy the term *eser* to denote a significant music composition, this naming gesture is first grounded in spiritual discourse (often including Arabic, Farsi, and Ottoman idiomatic expressions alongside modern Turkish) and, second, supported by an understanding that experiencing music has the potential to leave marks and remains. The traces left by music listening and musicking ultimately require something to be left *on*: a surface of some kind. Naming the product of the craft of composition as an *eser* indicates a cultural assumption that music has the potential to leave traces on us in some way. In this chapter, I explore how musicking melancholy in particular aids musicians in understanding their embodied experiences as individuals-in-community; I reveal the way melancholy itself surfaces as a boundary of the body.

One foundational claim of this book is that contemporary Turkish classical musicians actively craft and maintain unique affective practices through which they understand meaning and experience life, a constellation of affective practices I have named melancholic modalities. In investigating musicians' melancholic modalities, I consider how feelings such as pain, loss, joy, and sadness are experienced as beneficial and spiritually rewarding ways of being for these musical communities. Melancholic modalities, while individually felt, are ultimately produced in intimate social situations, from the dyadic master-apprentice relationship discussed in chapter 3 to the large-scale discussions around memory, history, and spiritual labor discussed in chapters 1 and 2.

Arguing that affect is social and not individual means recognizing that bodies and emotions are constructed within shared social and sonic worlds. Melancholy is not an object one "has"; rather, affective particulars like melancholy circulate and create the very effect of the surfaces and boundaries of our individual and collective bodies as we respond to the other individuals, groups, and objects that make up our worlds. We feel, sense, and hear surfaces and boundaries as being there through contact with others as the result of the impressions left by them. Just as an *eser* ostensibly leaves a trace on the body, I argue that melancholy circulates in musicians' musical and discursive practices *as the tension of the boundary* between the individual and her outside world.

Melancholic modalities thus present us with a paradox about bodily boundaries: perceiving, feeling, and hearing melancholy requires the physical instantiation of the individual body, yet simultaneously, this individual body is perceived as individual only in social situations shaped by other bodies and objects. In this chapter, I explore the paradox of the boundary by interrogating the materialization of individual bodies and the processes of embodiment in the context of Turkish classical musicians' melancholic modalities. Again, I do not assume that melancholy, for these musicians, is necessarily an object that necessarily lies in the body; rather, melancholy surfaces as a *practice* that delineates the boundary between inside and outside. I consider how and why musicians deploy melancholy to understand the musical body and name melancholy to generate particular embodied and sonic effects. I ask, what might melancholy feel like, and how is that feeling expressed musically? How is melancholy "made ours" in the process of embodiment? How might melancholy aid in the project of self-fashioning, differentiating individuals from other individuals?

Embodiment entails the ways in which individuals acquire routines that form distinctive dispositional practices. In Bruno Latour's metaphor, the perfumer has to "acquire a nose" and learn how to smell and recognize different perfumes (2004). Individuals' bodies become customized through inculcated cultural processes, processes we may even describe as a kind of growing, setting, naturalizing, and "pruning" (Rose 2004). Bodies are further shaped by being marked by *eser*-s and other works that leave a trace. Turkish classical musicians acquire and develop particular modes of embodiment to not only listen to, qualify, and experience musicking, but to also intimately adopt the knowledge of one's master-teacher and render the philosophies surrounding Turkish classical music "theirs." These processes are ultimately happening across boundaries in a collective: from social to individual and back again (S. Ahmed 2004). This process in biological terms, over time, includes deep neurological and physiobiological processes: central nervous system and autonomic nervous system repertoires, while individual and personalized, are culturally contingent and become entrenched through the repetitive practices of musicking and music transmission.[2] Feelings that Turkish classical musicians name "melancholy" associated with musicking thus emerge as "embodied dispositions," responses and instincts that are apparently autonomic or not consciously performed (Thrift 2000: 36).

In this chapter, I unpack melancholic embodied dispositions by considering four significant sites of embodiment for contemporary Turkish classical musicians. Musicking is not bodily in an easily systematized way: I consider critical aspects of embodiment that intersect, creating a constellation that supports and validates musicians' melancholic modalities. First, I consider how melancholy is sounded through music itself, focusing particular attention on musicians' narratives of how sonic melancholy mirrors bodily melancholy. Second, I turn to musicians' articulation that not all bodies are the same. I investigate the ways melancholy is leveraged in identifying and justifying gender difference, and focus attention on how melancholy is deployed in acts of music transmission to solidify ideas particular to normative performances of gender.[3] While melancholy surfaces in managing a boundary of gender difference, melancholy similarly demarcates bodily boundaries in an intimate and physical way. In the third section of this chapter, I focus on the way tears demonstrate a bodily boundary between the inside and the outside, inviting us to consider the significance that musicians place on Islamic narratives that celebrate the beauty of weeping. In the last section, I turn my attention to the Arabic concept *sama'*, understood by contemporary Turkish classical musicians as an important historical Islamic term to denote "listening." While the rest of the book to this point has largely considered musicians' melancholic modalities as deeply cultivated on a social level through recourse to Islamic iterations of spiritual practice, this chapter narrows in on shared objects in the social world—namely, individual bodies, bodily affective responses, and individual iterations of gender.

RENDERING MELANCHOLY MUSICAL

"What does melancholy feel like?" is indeed an awkward interview question, but one that I found myself effectively asking after musicians spoke about playing music and "rendering [it] melancholic" (*hüzünleştirmek* or *hüzünlü hale getirmek*). Describing the process of rendering music melancholic, musicians generally use expressions that link melancholic sound to melancholic sensations; in other words, musical features deemed melancholic are justified through relation to bodily melancholy. While melancholy is practiced as a natural and essential element of Turkish classical musicians' social identity, musicking melancholy also happens at the level of the individual body. Musical melancholy, as an embodied disposition, is similarly rendered innate, invisible, and instinctive simply because musicians assume that "we all know what melancholy feels like."

The Turkish classical musicians with whom I spoke about the relationship between sonic and bodily melancholy were quick to note that "feeling melancholy" is ultimately qualitative, subjective, and unique. I gathered that most believed that melancholy and other affective particularities were intricately linked to a person's worldview, values, expectations, and dispositions, akin to Bourdieu's concept of *habitus* (1990 [1980] and 2005). In other words, musicians were reluctant to converse in terms that hinged on claims about human universality; they denied that there was one right or singular way to experience melancholy. Instead, they offered lyrics, poems, and stories of famous lovers or spiritual guides who suffered and experienced loss in uniquely Ottoman-Turkish contexts. While they often spoke in generalizing terms, they did so with statements about loss and separation as something all humans may experience, albeit differently according to their social frameworks. If musical melancholy is relatable to the bodily sensation of melancholy of an individual, then I return to the question "what does melancholy feel like?"

In dozens of interviews with Turkish classical musicians, answers about feeling melancholy often shifted into conversations about spirituality and separation (described in chapter 2). Yet nearly all of the musicians I interviewed with this line of questioning offered answers that placed feeling melancholy (specifically *hüzün*) alongside discussions of bodily feeling and physical sensation. One *tanbur* (long-necked lute) player described the feeling of melancholy as if "tears [were] welling up in your eyes, but in [the] tightness you also feel relaxed." A singer noted that if she was about to render a song melancholic, she felt as if her feet "had large rocks tied to them, or roots like a tree." Another singer claimed that he brought melancholy into his singing by simply mimicking the physical sensation of crying in his facial muscles, while delicately disciplining the "look" of his face to not appear as if he were weeping. And a *kemençe* (short-necked fiddle) player stated that for him, melancholy was "feeling both light and heavy in *hal* and *kal*, but neither heavy nor light on its own." [in between] For this musician, feeling melancholy in *hal*, which denotes one's nonmaterial state (e.g., an emotional or psychological state), and in *kal*, which describes one's material and physical state, ultimately indicates that feeling melancholy is about existing in a boundary between experiential extremes. Furthermore, by calling upon the common Sufi expression *hal ve kal*, often translated as "body and speech," this particular musician grounds his experience of feeling melancholy in a wider discourse of ethical comportment, piety, and morality.

Discussions with musicians further demonstrate that musicking melancholy tends to be about balancing qualities assumed to be opposites (as in simultaneously experiencing heaviness and lightness, oscillating within *hal* and *kal*). To demonstrate how a musician might render melancholy sonic on the instantiation of a set musical piece or composition, I turn to one specific interview with master composer and violinist Ünal Ensari (1938–2016). Incredibly articulate about his craft in composition and his understanding of melodic improvisation that he learned from his esteemed teacher Cahit Gözkan (1911–1999), Ünal Hoca (the respectful term for teacher) offered many examples of how he personally understood melancholic musicking. One of his examples he shared with me to demonstrate his perceptions was the well-known piece "*Derdimi ummana döktüm*" (lit., "I shed my pain to the ocean"). The original poem was written by Süleyman Nazif (1870–1927), and Şerif İçli (1899–1956) set it in a light classical song form (*şarkı*) in *Hicaz makamı* (Example 4.1).

> *Derdimi ummana döktüm âsumâna inledim*
> *Yâre de âğyâre de hal-i derûnum söyledim*
> *Âşina yok derdime ben söyledim ben dinledim*
> *Gözlerim yollarda kaldı gelmedin çok bekledim*

> I shed my pain to the ocean and [raised] my moan to the sky
> I opened the inside of my heart to friends and strangers
> No one is familiar [with the level of my pain], I talked [about
>   it], I listened [to myself]
> I kept watching [for your return], you did not come [back],
>   I waited a long time

Example 4.1 Şerif İçli's composition "*Derdimi ummana döktüm*" with poetry by Süleyman Nazif.

Ünal Hoca explained: "now of course, Denise, context is of utmost importance. To render '*Derdimi ummana döktüm*' melancholic [*hüzünlü*] requires an appropriate performance space, where there are not other distractions such as eating, smoking, or drinking. The space is for listening. And then you of course must have listeners who are listening, truly listening. After all, if a man's heart is not open to being affected, how can music affect him? Listeners must be able to be molded by a musician. After that, making this piece melancholic resides in the musicians.

"And what can a musician do? S/he can of course feel melancholy first in herself.[4] And that may change from musician to musician, but of course if you are sad you are able to easily render music melancholic. And if you are not sad, then perhaps by recalling pain and suffering in your body and your heart, your fingers, and your voice take the shape of melancholy.

"And then there are small musical things one can do to express melancholy in music. Let me demonstrate from the perspective of the singer."

Ünal Hoca started singing, and immediately before he opened his mouth, I observed him lower his head, close his eyes, and swallow as he shifted his weight back in the chair. I witnessed the performative moment wherein a musician, in his own terms, "recalls pain and suffering in your body and heart—and in your fingers and voice" to offer a musical recipe for melancholy. He raised his head, and in low and slow tones, recited the first line of "*Derdimi ummana döktüm*" (Example 4.2).

[handwritten margin note: difference between feeling and being able to perform a feeling]

Example 4.2 The first section of Şerif İçli's composition "*Derdimi ummana döktüm*" rendered melancholic [*hüzünlü*].

Ünal Hoca stopped singing and smiled at me, waiting for an indication that I indeed "heard" melancholy. I nodded as he gestured with his left hand, continuing, "And then I can take the same music, the same song by the same composer and poet, and even be the same musician, but not produce melancholy. I can do something like an opposite. Listen to me make the same music joyful [*neşeli*]" (Example 4.3):

Example 4.3 The first section of Şerif İçli's composition "*Derdimi ummana döktüm*" rendered joyful [*neşeli*].

Ünal Hoca stopped singing and smiled even more broadly, opening both of his hands and raising his eyebrows. "You see, Denise?" he asked. "Do not be fooled into thinking that melancholy lies in the music. It lies in us musicians!"

In the first example rendering "*Derdimi ummana döktüm*" melancholic, Ünal Hoca engaged what he described as "reading [a piece of music] heavily" (*ağır okumak*). The original composition's notes are heavily ornamented with upper and lower neighbor tones in a variety of patterns, a quality he describes as making music with "more melodies" (*daha nağmelerle*). Significantly, Ünal Hoca's choice of the older Turkish or Ottoman word for melody, *nağme*, as opposed to the Republic-era Turkish term for melody, *ezgi*, locates him in a particular community of individuals who celebrate Ottoman heritage and espouse the loss narratives characteristic of the genre of Turkish classical music more generally. A component of reading music heavily and with more melodies was part of Ünal Hoca's toolkit for making music melancholic and additionally included pulling words apart into vowels—which are the subjected to *nağme* (see also chapter 5) and ornamentation—and consonants—which are also "sat upon" (*oturmak*) and ornamented.[5] Furthermore, the *aruz*, or the prosaic structure of a vocal piece, provides the rhythmic structure and poetic imprint on the melodic turns and *nağme* themselves. In the case of "*Derdimi ummana döktüm*," the *aruz* of the lyrics allows for the space for melisma on the last foot of the poetic lines. Thus the poetic structure of the words themselves, as collections of long and short consonants and vowels, provide the moments for accentuating "melancholic" musical gestures, tension and release, through *nağme*. Finally, rendering sound and sounding melancholic, for Ünal Hoca, included making music out of silence. "Silences need to be so significant that they reach a musician's own ears," he explained.

Alternatively, rendering the same musical material joyful (*neşeli*) downplayed the poetic text to the point that, as Ünal Hoca explained, "the words are almost not even heard." To not emphasize the text means that consonants are not separated from the vowels, ornamentation and *nağme* fall away, words lyrically connect to other words without silences or intentional pauses, and the pace quickens. The second most significant tell of rendering music joyful was the rhythm: with an increase in tempo, the rhythmic mode (*usul* or *usûl*) of the piece was simplified and pronounced, instead of the serious or "heavy" (*ağır aksak*) slow-paced iteration of the first. These musical qualities would be most appropriate if the song itself was sung on the context of a lively performance of *fasıl*, or "suite," in an entertainment context. Finally, Ünal Hoca offered two separate performances of vocal timbres: rendering music joyful seemed to include a vocal placement more "in the mask" (*kafa sesi*) or face, whereas melancholic presentation featured a thicker, chest voice (*göğüs sesi*).

"And for musicians to make music melancholic," Ünal Hoca continued, "of course it helps when you know about the people from which a musical *question for Denise: (difference between feeling and performing) how do masters teach their students to effectively convey feelings through their performance?*

composition emerged. This poetry, for example, has a story. Most people who know this song think that the poet Süleyman Nazif wrote a love poem and Şerif İçli wrote a love song, but they are wrong. It is not about losing a lover but about losing one's hope and future. Nazif's son had just tragically drowned in the Red Sea. What grief, to lose your child and to not be able to say goodbye and bury him. Nazif was left, waiting, and with that loss. And of course melancholy is about separation and loss. And so he writes a poem:

> "*ben söyledim* [I spoke]"

Ünal Hoca raised his right hand and intensified his gaze at me.

> "*ben dinledim* [I listened]"

He brought his left hand to his ear and closed his eyes, as if listening intensely. Ünal Hoca was not singing, but even in this short poetic recitation of the last lines of the lyrics, he drew out vowels and consonants, and created considerable pauses between words and phrases. He continued,

> "*gözlerim yollarda kaldı* [I kept watching for his
> return {lit., my eyes stayed on the roads}] . . ."

Ünal Hoca opened his eyes and his mouth in this long silence, as if waiting or hoping for someone else to interrupt him or continue. After what felt like minutes, but turned out to only be five seconds in my field recording, he concluded,

> "*gelmedin* [you did not come . . .
> . . . *çok bekledim* [I waited a long time] . . ."

Despite a potential musical recipe for understanding the performance of melancholy as located in the individual musician described above, most musicians argue that connecting music to melancholy lies most centrally in a listener. No matter what sounds musicians may cultivate and in whatever the context, a musician can attempt to elicit melancholy but may not be successful, as invoking affective responses in music ostensibly depends on a listener's background. If we continue considering the case study above, for Ünal Hoca's melancholic performance to be quintessentially successful, a listener needs a number of qualities to listen "correctly." First, a listener should have a working knowledge of Ottoman or "old Turkish" (*eski Türkçe*) to understand the words of the poetic text, which present-day Turkish audiences do not generally have, something that musicians and listeners alike bemoan. Knowing a text includes understanding the meaning of archaic Ottoman terms, but also includes an appreciation of the prosody (*aruz*) along with the poetic imprint on the melody and performance practice of the vocalist as well. Second, a listener should be able to hear—and by extension, appreciate—the distinctions made in the portions of singing with "more melodies" (*daha nağmelerle*). They should have ears attuned and shaped to the creativity and technique a vocalist will deploy with her sounds—and her silences—to join pitch to consonants and vowels. And finally, musicians I interviewed argued that a listener must have experienced pain, suffering, and loss in her own life. "A person who knows no suffering has not matured, and thus cannot understand the beauty that comes from melancholy," a *neyzen* (master of the end-blown reed flute, the *ney*) explained.

Indeed, many musicians explained that drawing from sensations of suffering is the primary way to render music melancholic, no matter how a listener may interpret the sounds she hears. As Ünal Hoca claimed, melancholy lies not in the disembodied music object—sound, silence, lyrics, rhythm, timbre—but in the individual musician rendering sounds and silences melancholic. Yet Melihat Gülses (b. 1958), one of the most celebrated Turkish classical and art music vocalists with over a dozen solo albums to her name, offered me another explanation as to how best she personally renders music melancholic in performance:

"As an artist, when on stage, I must be fully myself, Denise," she explained. "I am honest and my music and my voice do not lie. There is that connection between my voice and my person, my voice and my body. When I sing. . . ." She paused, closed her eyes, lifted her hands, and furrowed her eyebrows as she began to vocalize:

> "*Bir sabah bakacaksın ki birtanem, ben yokum* [one morning you will look [and see], my one and only, that I am gone]."

Within the first three notes, I recognized her chosen musical example for this demonstration. Composer Selahattin İçli (1923–2006) crafted this piece in *Kürdilihicazkar makamı* with a text by the renowned poet Hüceste Aksavrın (1919–2006), author of three volumes of poetry and one of Turkey's many revered women poets. As Melek Abla ("sister Melek," short for Melihat, the intimate name that Melihat Gülses invites me to call her) sang the first line, I scribbled quick descriptions in my field notes, noting her drawn-out consonants, pauses between words, and melodic elaborations.

Melek Abla stopped singing after this first line and I, having expected more, looked up at her. Her eyes welled with tears, and I watched in silence

[handwritten margin note: does a musician's "voice" come from this melancholic rhetoric?]

as one weighty teardrop cascaded onto her right cheek. I felt myself grind to a halt—I did not know what response I could offer to this ten-second unfolding of song and sadness, and was left with the knowledge that I had failed in this opportunity of listening, as I had chosen to suspend my own experience for my description of the moment's sonic contents. I sat, pen in the air, and after a moment Melek Abla readjusted her seating position and, with apparent ease, shook off her facial expression.

"You see how melancholy is music Denise? It is because I tell the truth with my voice, in my heart, and thus my body responds with tears." She wiped her cheek and continued, "You ask me how I make listeners feel melancholy? When I sing this song, every time I sing it in performance, viewers weep." Significantly, Melek Abla used the word *seyirci*—"viewer" or "witness"—as opposed to *dinleyici*—"listener," to demonstrate her point. Such a distinction is crucial, and shifts an understanding of musical interaction from musician-listener to one of musician-witness. She made her proclamation:

"Yes, truly viewers weep, and why? Because after all, I myself am ruined from crying while singing [*çünkü, ben zaten ağlamaktan beter oluyorum*]! And that is how my honesty is my art. If I am feeling melancholy and weeping, and if the audience in the concert hall is with me, how can they not keep from weeping too? It passes from me to them."

Melihat Gülses, in offering an account of being "honest" (Tr. *durust*) in performance, ultimately delivered her own version of what English-language researchers have called "emotional contagion," the psychological phenomenon when people "catch" feelings from one another as they would a cold or spread a yawn. Psychologists pursuing this line of argument claim that if someone close to you is happy, that brightness will infect you, while if she is sad, that gloominess may transfer to you as well (Schoenewolf 1990, Hatfield et al.1993, Van der Gaad et al. 2007). Philosopher and political scientist Teresa Brennan alternatively names this process the "transmission of affect:" how the emotions of one person can be enhanced—in this case study, through music—and thus transmitted to and enter another person (2004). What these two perspectives share is, of course, an interest in how social togetherness and social processes—such as musicking or live-music listening—decisively produce diverse biological and physical results in autonomous individuals. This relatively recent psychological and philosophical literature does not simply explain or account for what Melihat Gülses reported. Rather, she described, in her own specific terms based on lived experiences, what scholars in a variety of traditions, languages, and settings are only recently beginning to grapple with. Melihat Gülses offered a glimpse into how this process plays out in a specific context: her own musicking and professional performance life. Melihat Gülses drew on her own established experiences as a successful "transmitter" and simply espoused a philosophy that if she is truly "honest" in and demonstrative of her inner feeling, her voice and sound and body language will evoke and aid those around her in experiencing similar emotional particulars and, in turn, be "moved" by music.

Later in another interview with Melihat Gülses and her husband, acclaimed *tanbur* master Necip Gülses, the poet who penned the poem that became the lyrics of Selahattin İçli's song *"Bir sabah bakacaksın ki birtanem, ben yokum"* came up again in conversation. Yet this time, Melihat and Necip Gülses brought up Hüceste Aksavrın's name to make a point about the richness, sensitivity, and emotionality that arises in particular from women composers, performers, and (in this case) poets. Melek Abla informed me that singing İçli's song was powerfully informed by her own experiences as a mother as she readied her body to sing by identifying with the (female) narrator of Aksavrın's poem. Aksavrın ostensibly wrote the poem *"bir sabah bakacaksın ki birtanem, ben yokum* [one morning you will look {and see}, my one and only, that I am gone]" to her son while she was near death in a nursing home. Melihat and Necip Gülses explained that they visited the poet herself in the nursing home and spent quality time with Aksavrın in the last weeks of her life.

Of Aksavrın, Melek Abla explained to me, "That woman wrote like a woman. She wrote with woman feelings [*kadın duygularıyla*]. Of course, do not misunderstand, men experience and express suffering and pain and melancholy in art as well as women. But perhaps our emotions [as women] are more intense [*yoğun*]."

Melek Abla was not alone in identifying and expressing ideas about gender difference in conversations about music and melancholy. Here, melancholic music making and listening reveals another kind of border or boundary: articulations of suffering, pain, and sadness surface as a way some musicians distinguish between men and women, masculinities and femininities. Narratives about melancholy and gender norms intersect in contemporary Turkish classical musicians' lives in a number of sites from acts of music transmission to narratives about musical meaning.

EMBODYING GENDER, MELANCHOLY, AND THE BOUNDARIES BETWEEN

"Denise, you should not simply call this composition a *longa* [dance], even though that is its musical form. You should call this an *eser* [work]."

I took the notation handed to me by my first *kanun* (trapezoidal zither) teacher Halil Karaduman (1959–2012). It was 2005, in our fifth month of regular lessons, and he was satisfied with my understanding of basic *makam* and was graduating me to memorizing particular pieces. The goal was of course to not only build memorized repertoire, but importantly to also understand key turns of phrase and musical characteristics of a given *makam* in composed works, the better to improvise with. I had only about a dozen works memorized at this point, and they were all established high-art works of Ottoman palace life, such as instrumental *saz semaisi*. I was handed a *longa*, a light popular instrumental form associated with dance and with the somewhat lowbrow spaces of the *gazino* or *piyasa* (live music market). In short, I was asked by my teacher to place a simplistic musical form associated with merry, light entertainment ideologically adjacent to the dense formality and intricate poetry of the Ottoman court. Furthermore, this *longa* was supposed to become the basis of solo improvisation (*taksim*). And finally, I was being given careful instruction to name this piece as an *eser* as well as a *longa*.

"Why *hocam* [my teacher]? Why must I call this an *eser*?" At this point in my time with Turkish classical musicians, I understood *eser* only as a term denoting a high art compositional form associated with the Ottoman palace. While I understood *eser* was an ideologically weighted term, I had yet to interrogate the signification of an *eser* leaving a trace and pressing upon the surface of individual and collective bodies.

In the conversation that followed, I came to learn that one of the constitutive elements of this particular work's status as *eser* was that it was instrumental composition by a woman who was able to, in my teacher's opinion, successfully articulate her femininity in sound. This work, *Nihavent Longa* by Kevser Hanım (1887–1963), was the first of many pieces introduced to me by many teachers for two separate but intersecting pedagogical purposes: to better my musicianship and to advance my performance of femininity, musically speaking.

Musics are central practices wherein people learn and shape individual and collective iterations of gender subjectivity. In musicking, situated performances of masculinity and femininity (intersecting with other categories such as race, class, sexuality, and able-bodiedness) are learned, taught, debated, consolidated, challenged, and naturalized as a part of social organization. The most simple and longstanding social formations, such as patriarchy, are enduring simply because they are seamlessly woven into our emotional and affective lives. Gender difference is not only a way we make sense of our world—gender also emerges as that with which we learn to emotionally relate to others and objects in our world. Affect materializes as one of the tools we might utilize to relate to others and objects differently. Whole sets of affective practices come into being through intersecting categories of gender, race, sexuality, able-bodiedness, and class.

Femininities and masculinities are not only created and constituted in the circulation of bodily movement, intimate relationships, and embodied language practices: they are also engrained through sound and music making. One of the primary sites to diagnose the process of cultivating gender difference—besides the femininity and masculinity enculturated and normalized in the voice itself in speech or singing—is in examining instrumental music transmission. Through the transmission of music-as-object, teachers pass on gender ideologies through sound, language, and embodied music acquisition. While *Nihavent Longa* by Kevser Hanım helped my teachers shape me as a musician, they additionally deployed this piece to attend to the task of rendering my music feminine in instrumental musics without poetic texts.

This pedagogical experience was not exclusive. Most of the women musicians learning Turkish classical music I had the opportunity to interview reported being instructed by their teachers—both men and women—to focus on the compositions and recordings of Ottoman women vocalists and instrumentalists to develop the necessary "emotional expression" (*duyguların ifade edilmesi*) that is believed to be the vehicle to creating one's own unique style (*tarz*). In the process of deploying normative gender performances to develop musical style, a paradox emerges: a woman supposedly crafts her unique musical voice by knowing and emulating a community of women artists before and around her. In interviews, both women and men musicians claimed that compositions written by Ottoman women are necessary components of contemporary women musicians' education because Ottoman women composers were able to put their "genuine" or "authentic identity" (*gerçek kimliklerini*), "woman-ness" (*kadınlık*), and feminine melancholy into their compositions. Importantly, other consultants completely and utterly dismissed the notion that melancholy or other affective particularities were markers of gender difference. Yet in asking my consultants who supported the notion of separate feminine and masculine sounds to actually identify sonic femininities, I found that the task proved to be quite complicated. As many ethnomusicologists have demonstrated, these types of aesthetic concepts index deeper affective and moral states (Berger 2009, Buchanan 2006, Hahn 2007, Koskoff 2001, Racy 2003, Sugarman 1997).

Historically speaking, musicking while female tended to be celebrated in intimate, all-women segregated spaces among the private lives of the Ottoman elite. There are dozens of Ottoman women composers whose multiple works continue to be performed and circulated in Turkey and in the former Ottoman provinces, especially in Southeastern Europe and the Middle East.[6] Yet Muslim women's musicking in public—outside of the clear economic and religious divisions of Ottoman social life—was not readily available, and women's audibility was a topic of considerable debate within communities espousing Islamic beliefs and attitudes about piety. Should Ottoman Muslim women have performed openly for a mixed gendered audience, they might earn a reputation of being "light women" (*hafif kadınlar*), a pejorative gesture dismissing modes of public femininity as ungrounded and unrooted. As such, most well-known women performers of the Ottoman era were women of minority ethnic and religious groups, generally Greek, Armenian, Assyrian, Jewish, and Roma. With the founding of the Turkish nation-state in 1923, the various reforms to music (and theater and dance) institutions, and leader Mustafa Kemal's own personal aesthetic valuation of a number of women vocalists, Ottoman women—now rendered "Turkish," "modern," "civilized," and "enlightened"—visually and audibly entered the public sphere.

Yet femininity in music is not nor was not, of course, solely a woman's domain of production. O'Connell brilliantly documents the ways (male) composer, *tanbur* player, and singer Münir Nurettin Selçuk developed and mainstreamed a unique vocal style in the early Republic era, often qualified by audiences and music critics as "feminine" (2013). Considering contemporary Turkish popular musics, Stokes offers compelling analyses of musical, aesthetic, and political ideologies of feminine voice and feminine body in the social lives and musical production of popular singers Zeki Müren and Bülent Ersoy (2010). Many musicians further qualify the genre of "Turkish classical music" itself as feminine and opposed to the ostensibly masculine genres of folk musics or popular musics (O'Connell 2013). Such a discursive separation may point to the overall feminization of the Ottoman Empire as "weak," as opposed to the "strong" Turkish nation-state. When we narrow in from genre to minute sonic terminology, particular musical terms to describe timbre or tone color are also often gendered feminine, such as "clean" (*temiz*), "elegant" (*zarif*), and "bright" (*parlak*).[7] And finally, women instrumentalists are praised for their musicality with the expression "you play like a man" (*adam gibi çalıyorsunuz*). This expression is not used to right one's gender but rather to complement, highlight, and celebrate one's "mastery" (*hakimlik* or *ustalık*)—terms that disclose masculinizing gender assumptions—of difficult instruments.

Affective practice offers another opportunity to peel apart the messy intersections of gender norms and "feeling rules" (Hochschild 1983) of musicians' social worlds. Of particular interest considering melancholy is the expression some musicians circulate: "melancholy suits a woman" (*hüzün kadına yakışır*). In such statements, these particular musicians infer an unquestionable acceptance of gender difference—femininity and masculinity, male and female as distinct and oppositional in a closed two-sex heterosexual system—and bring these assumptions about femininity and masculinity to bear in discussions about musical meaning and affective particularities. Yet when I pushed musicians, in formal, recorded interview settings, to articulate in words exactly what "feminine" and "masculine" affects or emotions may be or sound like, musicians did not easily offer explanations. Most of the time, they simply noted that if affective or gendered feelings were easily explainable with words, we would not need things like music, poetry, and other performing or visual arts.

Learning to sound out "feminine melancholy" (*kadın hüznü*) through music emerges as a particularly compelling component of women musicians' education and development. For example, one of the reasons *Nihavent Longa* is a fascinating choice for learning to articulate "feminine" musicality is that the *longa* form includes some formal musical elements that would seem to implicitly render it a non-melancholic piece: it is a dance form with a significantly perceivable, quickly paced tempo. It is also an instrumental piece, and thus lacks a specific backstory with a narrative provided by the subject position from which a vocalist sings or textual-poetic elements open to exegesis or interpretation. Finally, the undulating, rapidly ascending-descending musical lines leaves a performer very little room to use ornamentation, pitch embellishment, silences, and articulations to draw out a musical product deemed more melancholic or emotive. As such, *Nihavent Longa* is a useful case study to follow an interpretation of "feminine melancholy" (*kadın hüznü*): locating, hearing, and producing "feminine melancholy" may surface only in individual musicians' discourses rather than any outward, external markers of difference.

My teacher was not alone in his interpretation of Kevser Hanım's *Nihavent Longa* as a successfully feminine work. Other musicians suggested that playing the piece helps develop a feminine style and "sensitivity" (*hassasiyet*).[8] These select musicians heard femininity in the musical lines, claiming that it was clear that it was written by a woman. When looking at the score or hearing a recording, some musicians explained that they heard femininity in the scalar (directional note-to-note) passages that happen repeatedly in the four sections of the piece. Femininity, for these listeners, was located in this ongoing ebb and flow of the structure (ABCB) of the musical lines.

Example 4.4 *"Nihavent Longa"* by Kevser Hanım (1887–1963).

As I asked after *Nihavent Longa* in interviews, it became clear that musicians conceptualized each of the four sections of this piece as having four musical phrases each, the first two lasting two measures each and the last two musical phrases consisting of four measures. Each of these musical phrases contained highly scalar passages, which musicians believed could be rendered with extreme dynamic contrast to enhance its purported feminine quality. For some musicians, the second section of the piece sounded like a question that was repeated three times. One musician explained that "a woman" may ask a question once (part A). Receiving no answer she may ask again (part B), until, perhaps in frustration or excitement (part C), she will restate the question in a more elaborate and expressive way (return to part A).

Yet as a *longa*, was this *eser* possibly a vehicle for the expression of "feminine melancholy"? Some musicians argued that *Nihavent Longa* could be representative of feminine melancholy, while others dismissed the notion of melancholy having an inherent gendered component altogether. For musicians making the case that *Nihavent Longa* evoked feminine melancholy, the piece was perceived as technically complicated yet melodically simple, full of tonal tension yet resolvedly relaxed. It was the rearticulation of simple musical phrases that sounded out melancholy, almost as if Kevser Hanım were musing on or wallowing in the same feeling that she circulated over and over and over again in her composition. Repetition, reiteration, dwelling, sounding and resounding were heard by musicians I interviewed as sonic movements inherent in melancholic musics.

Importantly, I am not claiming that "femininity" or "melancholy" or "feminine melancholy" lies in these musical elements. If *Nihavent Longa* is inherently feminine, as some musicians may state, than its femininity resides in the ideologies of listening and *habitus* that musicians adopt and craft, through their relationships with teachers, a *meşk* lineage, and political institutions, and in their own diverse social lives.

These subtle listening patterns indicate embodied dispositions—implicating performances and experiences of gender and of affect—that tell a unique story about bodily boundaries. Individual musicians are invited to perceive, sense, and exist within particular mappings of gender difference while they simultaneously activate and deploy affect in their musicking. Thus intimate experience at the level of the individual—gender performance, feelings, and crafting one's unique style and sound—is conclusively rendered possible only in shared social terms. Executing the pieces named above in my own musical performance, I entered a process wherein melancholy and femininity were "made mine" in a social world not of my own creation. Sounding melancholy and femininity offers such experiences in navigating gender borders—between masculinities and femininities— and engages bodily boundaries—between the individual and the social. Melancholic musicking highlights numerous bodily boundaries, and it is to the boundary of the body's surface—specifically, considering the work of tears—that I attend to next.

THE BODY'S BOUNDARY: MELANCHOLIC MUSICKING AND TEARS

Siz benim bildiğimi bilseydiniz az güler, çok ağlardınız.
If you could know what I know
you would laugh little, and cry a lot.

— *Hadith* of the Prophet Muhammed

A few Turkish classical musicians related to me a story about the Persian Sufi Junayd Baghdadi (830–910), who apparently witnessed angels rapidly descending from heaven as they tried to catch something on earth.

Junayd Baghdadi asked them, "What are you trying to catch?"

The angels responded, "A friend of God has sighed here, played music with melancholy, and cried at this place. The drops of his tears fell on the ground like the melancholic sound went out through the air.

"Now we are trying to catch the tears so we can also reap the blessings God gives to humans.

"What divine blessings lie in these tears!"

In 2005, I accompanied friends to the cinema in İzmir in the opening month of Çagan Irmak's film *Babam ve Oğlum* ("My Father and My Son"). I knew enough about the film to expect it to fall in line with my past experiences of great Turkish cinematic dramas: in short, I expected the film to rip the hearts out of its audience. But walking into that movie theater that day, I knew I was underprepared for the emotional weight of the film when, along with our ticket stubs, the woman behind the ticket counter also handed each attendee an individual pack of tissues. After we had seated ourselves, my friends excitedly opened their tissue packets so as to not have to break into the plastic during the show (they aimed to not be the cause of sonic interruptions). One friend turned to me with a broad smile, saying, "Denise, this film is going to be so so so good!" "Good" here, of course, indicates a significant emotional experience, a kind of catharsis that will impact my friends in a dramatic, but ultimately positive, way. Expecting to cry, their smiles, joyous energy, and ecstatic whispers disclosed an idea many Turkish classical musicians easily offer: there is balance in tears, and there is pleasure in the act of crying.

In her work *Deep Listeners: Music, Emotion and Trancing* (2004), ethnomusicologist Judith Becker argues that music can affect us—with significant physiological and psychological effects—by causing or inducing physiological arousal. Becker explains that emotional reactions to music should not necessarily be assumed or described as "peaceful" or "soothing" but rather fall into Damascio's theory of emotions (Becker 2004: 44–52). Emotional reactions to music produce higher degrees of arousal in the automatic nervous system, or ANS. ANS arousal, triggered by our culturally instantiated *habitus* of listening, is motivated by pleasure and the increased participation of opioid and dopamine systems in the brain. Becker suggests that "sadness *in relation to a musical example* can be more arousing than sadness [itself]" (2004: 53, my emphasis). Becker's argument leverages the work of psychobiologists and neuroscientists, such as Jaak Panksepp. Panksepp claims that

[t]he fact that sadness can provoke chills seems outwardly perplexing from the perspective that most people find the experience to be positive emotionally. No doubt, this is only a superficial paradox that disappears when we consider the deeper aspects of human emotionality.... As neurological evidence indicates, the basic output circuitries of grief and joy (as indexed by crying and laughter) are intertwined in the human brain. These powerful emotions, which emerged early in mammalian evolution, were designed to solidify and elaborate the mandates and possibilities of social bonds (1995: 197).

Feeling sadness in music is a highly arousing emotional experience that triggers the ANS and may result in chills, tears, and brain chemistry that ultimately results in "a heightened sense of aliveness, an alertness, and, mostly, a joyfulness" (Becker 2004: 54). In *Deep Listeners*, Becker seamlessly moves from universal questions of biological and physiological arousal to unique, situated, context-specific examples of musicians and audience in diverse cultural, linguistic, and religious settings. Tears play out in the specific context of Turkish classical musicians and musicking in a similar socially bonding way. For musicians drawn to Islamic worldviews and life paths explored in chapter 2, tears and the act of weeping carry particular valence for an individual's spirituality. Junayd Baghdadi's story instructs listeners that tears are so precious that angels scramble to collect them.

How are tears leveled as positive treasures at the level of spiritual discourse? Some Turkish classical musicians locate the answer in the Qur'an, which details moments when weeping is presented as the appropriate response to witnessing truth. Consider this passage, indicating the Prophet's actions:

Those were the ones upon whom Allah bestowed favor from among the prophets of the descendants of Adam and of those We carried [in the ship] with Noah, and of the descendants of Abraham and Israel, and of those whom We guided and chose. When the verses of the Most Merciful were recited to them, they fell in prostration and weeping (Qur'an 19:58).

In passages from the Qur'an and supportive anecdotes from the *hadith*, weeping is necessarily connected with the divine. If experiencing divine presence or having deep spiritual knowledge results in weeping, then Islamic philosophical belief structures validate tears as positive, divinely inspired, and spiritually affirming. If the Prophet—the human being believed to be closest to divine perfection—explains that if we could know what he knows then we would cry profusely, then crying itself may be, for practitioners, always positively coded in spiritual terms and a physical manifestation of piety (Mahmood 2005).

What might these tears indicate, beyond this particular interpretation of spiritual piety? In biomedical terms, tears associated with emotional experiences—as opposed to lacrimation (the term for the physiological act of shedding tears in a non-emotional state)—are densely packed with unique chemical compounds that scientists argue make us "feel better" (Knight 2014, Walter 2006).[9] Like the iterations of melancholy explained in this chapter, tears similarly mark a shift in experience from tension to release. Tears surface and demonstrate individual borders. Tears function as a material manifestation of the boundaries of the human body; they arrive when we are full and our borders overflow. Tears indicate our deep emotional connections to our world in tangible ways and, if flowing in social spaces, tears indicate our vulnerability and openness to show our boundaries to other people. Tears are an invitation to intimacy.

A composer and Turkish classical music *tanbur* player once told me a story to explain his thoughts about the benefits of weeping. In his earliest sermons, the Prophet Muhammed apparently spoke to crowds of new Muslims from a small wood stump. Over time, his followers built an elaborate mosque for these Friday gatherings. On the first occasion of hearing the Prophet speak in this mosque, his voice was largely unheard due to a loud, unearthly wailing that covered the city. No one could tell where the crying was coming from, as it seemed to come from many directions, but the Prophet reputedly left the newly built mosque and walked straight to the small wood stump from which he previously preached. He began to caress the stump, and the wail subsided. "There is no object, living or dead, male or female, believer or non-believer that is outside of God," the Prophet is believed to have said.

At this point in the telling of the story the musician paused to finish his tea. A story is not complete without the storyteller offering his or her individual interpretation. He continued, "But as you know, the story is not about a stump, presumed dead, that is animated and has life in it still. Absolutely not. What we musicians—what we humans—need to take away from this story is the Prophet's *ears*. How he listened—that is the lesson."

In the end, celebrating the Prophet's ears, like celebrating pious tears, meant that this *tanbur* musician both admired and attempted to mirror similar acts of listening. The Prophet's ears are presented as tuned to a different, divine frequency; as a perfected human being, the Prophet heard a wail from an object others assumed inanimate. Furthermore, the *tanbur* musician's telling of this story informs us that the Prophet understood that crying is about separation: this knowledge brought him to the source (e.g., the stump). Islamic philosophers throughout the Middle East have used the Arabic term *sama‘*, "listening," in long-standing debates over the moral and spiritual implications of sound. Since the fourteenth century, Mevlevi Sufis, drawing from this tradition, crafted the *sema*—a Mevlevi turning ritual based on the principles of *sama‘*. As the Prophet remains the primary example for Muslim lifeways, the story above offers a quintessential example of the possibilities of hearing and how we might listen.

SEMA AND SAMA‘

Wherein lies the boundary between hearing and listening? In the ears? In the mind? In an intention? For the Turkish classical musicians who indicate and name (using the Arabic) *sama‘* as the moment that hearing becomes listening, *sama‘* simultaneously emerges as the site at which the boundary of the body between the inner life of intentionality and thought and the outer world of sonic objects is made porous. The body is not a bound, solid, and individualized object. In *sama‘*, the materiality of one's body is active, not passive. The body is simultaneously yours and not yours: yours in that you make the intention to listen, not yours in the way sounds in any social world bombard your ears in cacophony.

Early Islamic philosophers used the Arabic term *sama‘*, which denotes audition, to develop a sophisticated discourse around "the art of listening."[10] Philosophers debated the role of sound—and, in particular, music—in the role of pious Muslim life. In engaging this debate, which contemporary scholars name the *sama‘* polemic (Nelson 1985), we understand that past Islamic philosophers were mindful that our ears are a primary site where bodily boundaries are exposed and uncovered to the rest of the world. We have no control over our soundscapes but may try to be as attentive as we can to attune to nourishing, nurturing sounds. In the early years of Muslim societies, "music" was associated with particular entertainment contexts that were deemed problematic for pious life, while sound produced in the context of spiritual calling or worship—such as diverse melodies of the five-times daily call to prayer (*ezan*) or religious hymns (*ilahi-s*)—were validated in *hadith*-s and the writings of prominent Islamic philosophers.[11]

Importantly, philosophers writing on *sama‘* placed the responsibility of musical meaning on the listener rather than the producer. In his analysis of historical debates over *sama‘*, Shiloah notes that "[a]s to its value and nature [of musical meaning], these are determined chiefly by the listener's virtues, his degree of mystical cognition of God and His revelation" (1995: 40). The acclaimed, prolific philosopher al-Ghazali (1058–1111) wrote, "[We] say here that [the position of] music [with respect to the Law] must be judged by the heart, for music does not bring anything to the heart that is not there; instead, it excites that which is already in it" (Ghazali 2002: 6). If the heart is clean, then sonic practices can apparently facilitate spiritual growth. If musical value hinges on listeners in classical Islamic philosophy rather than the sounds produced by musicians themselves, then *sama'* brings an additional dimension to considerations of Turkish classical musicians and melancholic modalities. While al-Ghazali was writing for Islamic intellectuals ten centuries ago, he indicates that music that "bring[s] tears and increase[s] sorrow in the heart" reputedly offers spiritual rewards (2002: 10). For Turkish classical musicians, engendering sound as melancholic and experiencing sonic melancholy as a positive affect are primarily tasks of listeners, not necessarily the musicians.

How did the classical Islamic term *sama'* move from the Arab peninsula to Anatolia, from Arabic to Ottoman-Turkish? *Sama'* began to have valence as a term indicating a specific, embodied ritual presentation of *zikir*, or divine remembrance, with the founding of the Mevlevi Sufi order in 1273.[12] The origin myth of the Mevlevi *sema* is as follows: one afternoon, Mevlana Celaleddin Rumi, the philosophic center of the Mevlevi Sufi order, was walking through the bazaar in Konya. Wandering in the crowded shopping aisles, he suddenly heard a blacksmith hammering, and in the rhythmic hits of the hammer on metal, Mevlana's astute listening and attuned ears ostensibly heard *la illahe ilallah* ("there is no divinity or reality outside of God"). Entrenched in this moment of intense listening, Mevlana apparently stretched his arms out and did the first *sema*, or turning *zikir*.

As described earlier, the Mevlevi Sufis who practice *sema*, dubbed "whirling dervishes" by early twentieth century orientalists, embrace a ritual that was formalized in the early fourteenth century by the Mevlevi order, centralized in Istanbul and acquired prestige among the Ottoman elite beginning in the fifteenth century, was disbanded and criminalized by the leaders of the new Turkish nation-state in 1925, and in 1955 was reinstated by the Turkish government as a historical artifact. Since the 1990s, *sema* groups from Turkey have benefited from privatization and have toured internationally, where many foreign audiences interpret the turning ritual as a kind of performative emblem of Mevlana's philosophies of love and tolerance. The Turkish Ministry of Culture and Tourism, in turn, has appropriated international interpretations of *sema* as a dance of tolerance and mapped these positive qualities as inherent elements of Turkish nationalism. Several non-Turkish non-Muslim communities that began learning *sema* outside of practicing or converting to Islam formed around the same time in parts of western Europe and the United States (especially in New York and California). Tourists today continue to flock to *semahane*-s (lit., "houses of *sema*") in Istanbul and Konya to view *sema* troupes "perform." What is lost on many tourists is the importance of interpreting *sema* turning as itself a kind of mortuary dance (O'Connell 2015), a turning that symbolizes the bridging of the separation between life and death and reminds us of Mevlana's own death, which is celebrated annually on December 17 as his "wedding night" (Şeb-i Arus). As a turning ceremony, sema renders death itself as a positive reunion with God instead of a loss.

For most Turkish classical musicians who identify as Muslim, sema is not a "performing art" but rather a zikir, an embodied religious ritual of remembrance. It is a highly disciplined and formalized ritual, and like the musical suite (ayin) specifically composed to accompany it, practicing sema requires months, often years, of training. Young semazen-s ("turners") learn the art of sema in deeply embodied ways, as practicing sema entails constant spinning with very narrow, mapped horizontal movements. Eager students new to sema quickly get dizzy and often vomit while learning this demanding practice. The sema is additionally hard on the body when learning in the traditional Mevlevi way with a meşk tahtası, or method board. A semazen student repetitively moves the body on and over this board, which consists of a large, thick nail hammered vertically down into a flat horizontal piece of wood. It is a training tool used for months. Students place their big and second toes around this nail and, with the help of talcum powder and under the watchful eye of a master-teacher, learn the art of sema in corporeal, blistering ways.

Yet doing sema does not only leave traces (through dizziness and presyncope, or lightheadedness) in experiences of a semazen—doing sema is believed to also leave a trace on the world. In short, the symbolism of Mevlevi sema turning is about deploying movement in your body to bring about significant change to your surroundings. Semazen-s begin the ritual in black cloaks, which they formally discard at the beginning of the ceremony when they step into the center of the place of turning in the semahane; this gesture symbolizes the ridding of the mundane and the beginning of the movement into a spiritual space. The sema turning movement symbolizes a divine cosmology of Mevlevi philosophy that includes the movement of the planets and the changing of seasons. There is also the inner, spiritual change that occurs in an individual semazen: a semazen's outstretched arms, either in a straight line or in a ninety-degree angle upward, symbolize the Arabic construction "lâ" (ﻻ), which translates to "nothing[ness]." Indeed, a semazen must become nothing—empty of ego (nafs)—for the possibility of spiritual ascension and potential experience of divine love. The sema is believed to be a ritual that offers and promises such nothingness: the embodied possibility of experiencing the divine and bringing that experience back to the mundane. Musicians believe that the hands at the end of a semazen's arms are active conduits mediating the border between the material and the immaterial. The left hand is opened, palm up toward the heavens, while the right hand, palm down, is directed to the earth, gestures that are believed to allow a semazen to receive spiritual energy (through the left hand) and transfer that divinity, through sema, to the earth (through the right hand). In short, practitioners believe that in doing sema, their bodies leave a trace, enact change, affect the world.

emotives?

The art of listening in Islamic discourse, *sama'*, may leave little physical traces that remain on the body, yet the experience of shifting from passive hearing to attentive, artful listening that the word *sama'* engenders is articulated as a profound experience. In learning *sema*, however, would-be Turkish *semazen*-s have physical marks to bear. Turning for hours on one's *meşk tahtası* can create significant tears in the skin as a student grips the nail between the two toes while perfecting the turning movement. These skin tears, the wound at the site where the body meets *sema* and is changed, develop into thick callouses until a student turns in *sema* without the apparatus of the nail. Like an *eser*, the musical work of art, a *sema* leaves marks, albeit in different ways. In the concept of "work," in the act of listening, in rendering music melancholic or otherwise, in listeners' affective responses, and in the act of turning, embodiment works on many levels and points to specific bodily, affective, and im/material tensions. As the *sema* mitigates the margins between the mundane and the spiritual, this world and the divine, *sama'* extenuates the tension between the individual body and the social world. In short, *sema* and *sama'* are both about inhibiting the interstices and existing within the tension of boundaries. The body, active and permeable, houses boundaries that constantly materialize in actions of crossing over and back again.

LIVING WITH THE BOUNDARY

Western epistemological perspectives—offered by scholars in philosophy, neuroscience, psychology, and ethno/musicology—generally tend to represent bodies in universalizing terms that focus on the workings of an individual body in scholarship on feelings, moods, emotions, and affect. Melancholic musicking and the embodied dispositions that melancholic musicking engender disrupt the notion of autonomous individuality and of potential universality. The case studies presented here demonstrate that in Turkish classical musicking, melancholy circulates in the interstices of boundaries, from investigating the sonic and musical elements of melancholy and how musicians render music melancholic, to how musicians deploy melancholy in understanding gender difference, to interrogating the visibility and audibility of tears as the breakdown of an individual's bodily boundary, to discussions of *sema* and *sama'* as the philosophical embodiment of listening and physical turning beyond the borders of skin. In Sara Ahmed's terms, there is no part of a musician's experience that can be presented as simultaneously individual *and* social, psychological *and* biological, but rather that the "and" itself disappears when we consider how musicians themselves approach, perform, and articulate melancholy (2004). In this analysis, Turkish classical music practices and philosophies invite us to experience and inhabit boundaries, and all of the confusions and joys, discomforts and ecstasies, they might provide.

melancholy exists between these boundaries

After all, the lines and boundaries we draw shape and bind our senses of self and community. Perhaps one lesson to take away from these musicians is that the lines we draw are also meant to be transgressed. Mevlana Celaleddin Rumi articulated this very transgression when he advised, "*Ya olduğun gibi görün, ya gördüğün gibi olun,*" which means "either appear as you are, or be as you appear." For Mevlana, the border—between outward appearance and inner being—demands erasure. The *sema* turning practice itself, developed and formalized by the Mevlevi order inspired by Mevlana's own ecstatic turning, is a purposeful crossing: a turner literally turns to pass beyond the boundary of one's mundane into the possibility of temporary union with the divine. Perhaps the stories offered here demonstrate that the lines we draw are also invitations to cross over, and it is precisely the labor of crossing that makes us who we are.

CHAPTER 5

Melancholic Modes, Healing, and Reparation

I am speaking with a sheikh (religious leader) of an Istanbul Cerrahi Sufi order in his *tekke* (lodge), primarily to understand his methods as he is well known for caring for the sick using sound, breath, and music. I am interested in the relationship between sound and healing, because many musicians link the multiple and diverse Turkish terms for melancholy with contemporary biomedical diagnostic terminology, especially depression and bipolar disorders. Indeed, in interviews, musicians were quick to return to some conceptions of melancholy, especially the Ottoman term from the Greek-derived *melankoli*, and another particularly harsh iteration of melancholy called "black love," *kara sevda*, as medical and psychological diseases that were treated in Ottoman hospitals with music therapy.

As I am long accustomed to, most of my specific questions about his methods of musico-medical healing turn quickly into discussions about Islamic theology familiar in Turkish classical musicians' discourses and considered throughout this book: notions of how sound is inherently spiritual, how experiencing pain can be a form of piety, and how humans suffer in life because of the separation from divine. Yet in my interviews with this sheikh, I seek specifics, having gathered reports from various musicians that this particular sheikh had ostensibly cured forms of epilepsy, autism spectrum disorders, and schizophrenia with his touch, breath, reading, and sonic recitations over inflicted individuals' bodies.

I attempt my line of questioning again. "But *Hocam* [my teacher], how do you use music to cure? What kinds of sounds heal?"

"Where does it come from? Have you not been listening?" He furrows his brow and continues, "You are asking the wrong question."

The sheikh takes his time to answer. I am accustomed to these delicious periods of waiting—silences that offer an opportunity to reframe assumptions brought into an interview setting.

"Your focus is on the sound itself, not the people. And your questions are about the sick. But that is not how this works. Of course, we Turks go to doctors too. Westernized. They ask what is wrong, they try to fix the problem. They see people as collections of problems. They focus on the illness. . ." He pointed to me and smiled, "and you focus only on sound."

In the sheikh's answer, I hear a critique of biomedicine, which would strip patients of personhood and reduce them into diseases: diagnoses instead of people, empiricism instead of individuality, and doctors' structures of "best practices" instead of attentive focus on a patient's full life in context. I appreciate the sheikh's direct challenge to an objectivist approach to sound, which would isolate sound as a disembodied object outside of individual and communal practices. Embedded in both of the sheikh's critiques is a severe evaluation of western epistemological categories.

The sheikh does not disregard biomedicine fully, but rather explains how his expertise and methods are brought in to pick up where medical practices leave off.

"You focus on the illness and on the ill person. You ask about specific sicknesses and seek examples. I do not focus on these things: they are there, they are important, of course, but they are fundamentally unimportant for me. For I focus on the one who gives the sickness."

I respond in an attempt to demonstrate my openness to this perspective. "Of course I understand the teaching that illness ultimately comes from God," I state. "But how does one such as yourself go about making someone feel better?"

"Ah, well here is the problem," he responds. "Feeling better is not the issue. By thinking about the one who gives sickness, you will see that sickness is a line of connection to God. An opportunity to not feel the separation from God. Often, sickness is a test from God, a way to return to God. Do you see?"

I nod my head.

"So if you ask for specifics, I must first explain the nature of sickness. The natural state of every object—every stone, every animal, every person—is to be in constant movement and *zikir* [devotional remembrance]. Sound is an extension of God, and can help in pushing people back on the right movement, the right frequency [*frekans*] in the natural way. The vibration of sound vibrates a body. I remind the sick where their illness comes from." He motions toward my pen and notebook. "You write the most important things down, so as to give yourself permission to forget it. Forget this point now, so you can reflect on it later."

I ready my pen.

He enunciates the following very clearly. "Every illness is something to give thanks [şükür] for. An illness itself is one's connection to God. Inside the pain and suffering [dert] is the very healing remedy [derman]. *Dert dermandır* [Suffering is remedy itself]."

idk... umm... about that

Throughout this book, I have argued that melancholy is an indispensable resource for contemporary Turkish classical musicians because musicians position melancholy as spiritually redeeming and because their voicing of melancholy socializes them as a group while grounding them as history-makers. I have claimed that melancholy, as a central affective practice of musicians, is cultivated within specific modalities: musicians' dynamic modes of agency engaged when they accomplish, perform, and experience melancholy. Often, melancholic modalities are justified by local Islamic spiritual discourses and beliefs, woven in stories celebrating the value of melancholy for those who suffer with it. Yet melancholy emerges as a resource for Turkish classical musicians for two further reasons unique to the situated identities of contemporary Turks who sound out musics of an imagined, idyllic Ottoman past in the present day. First, contemporary Turkish classical musicians draw on over five centuries of Ottoman medical history that reportedly engaged melancholy in various music therapy contexts. Ottoman physicians often viewed melancholy in a positive frame, not necessarily as an illness to be cured. Second, the Turkish classical musicians who are deeply invested in Islamic validations of melancholy extend local Sufi discourses equating suffering and disease with *nimet*, or "blessings" from God.

melancholy viewed positively

In this chapter, I examine musicians' musicking and discourses to understand how they perceive melancholic sound and melancholic music as kinds of healing. I argue that we must weave analyses of music objects—a musical piece, a collection of pitches, or musical mode (*makam*)—with a consideration of musicians' ideologies of listening and descriptions of musicking to understand how melancholy is rendered reparative. Furthermore, the "feeling" of melancholy itself becomes less important in analysis than the ways contemporary Turkish classical musicians understand *what the feeling does for them.*

I first consider musicking in the context of instrumental improvisation, by considering the famous *neyzen* (ney or reed-flute master) Neyzen Tevfik, who was diagnosed as a melancholic during the early years of the Turkish nation-state.[1] Without lyrics to analyze, contemporary musicians are left with recordings of his instrumental improvisations. The musicians today who deeply value Neyzen Tevfik's sound hear his improvisations as evidence of his melancholy, and further argue that melancholy might be a criterion for virtuosity. In my second case study, I consider the reparative aspects of songwriting by a famous Ottoman composer, Hacı Arif Bey, who suffered from a particular medicalized iteration of melancholy after the death of his beloved wife. Finally, my third case study considers a popular, well-known *ilahi* (religious hymn) that describes how music is "food for the soul." Placing musicians' thoughts about the possible lessons learned by musicking this *ilahi* at the center, I argue that musicians' general assumptions about the relationship between "soul" and "music" illuminate how melancholy can be positioned as reparative; melancholy is a modality for mending, tending to, and repairing dis-ease.

I ground my claims about the social work that melancholy does in and through sonic practices by considering seriously the intersections of melancholy, music, and healing. I outline five centuries of Ottoman philosophers' writings in which melancholy was neither a stage to be moved beyond nor an illness that needed to be cured. This chapter includes discussions of music compositions that focus on healing accomplished through melancholy, with analyses of improvisations by a musician diagnosed with melancholy, depression, and other psychological dis-eases in his day.[2] I expose how present-day Turkish classical musicians, like the sheikh above, have resurrected Ottoman notions of the positive effects of melancholy after the medicalization of psychological states in the early years of the Turkish Republic. Today, musicians deem melancholy a position to dwell in because it is pleasurable and connects individuals to one another vis-à-vis religious discourses that validate, as the sheikh would tell us, the idea "*dert dermandır* [suffering is remedy itself]."

MELANCHOLY AS ILLNESS

For over five centuries, Ottoman physicians and philosophers were concerned with how the audition of music affected the spiritual, psychological, and physical states of individuals suffering from trauma, humeral imbalance, and mental illness. Parsing out how Ottoman music therapy programmers used melancholic music to heal melancholics—individuals suffering with the physical and physiological ailment of melancholy—is a challenging task due to the multiple terminologies used to describe melancholy as emotion or feeling versus melancholy as disease or disorder. Melancholic music materials—specifically, *makam*-s that were understood as housing sonic melancholy—were used for the methods of curing and coping. The healing that took place with melancholic music during the Ottoman era always happened in community (e.g., social, collective environments in hospitals) and not on an individual basis, demonstrating that melancholy was something Ottomans believed should be experienced in and with community.

Derived from the Greek *melan* ("dark" or "black") and *cholē* ("bile"), melancholy has been viewed by scholars, doctors, and philosophers of the Middle East since the Middle Ages as a humoral imbalance caused by an excess of black blood. The four humors of Hippocratic medicine were both physical and metaphysical manifestations reflecting these communities' understandings of the body, mind, soul, and the properties of the natural world. This philosophy maintained an understanding of the cosmos as composed of fours: four elements, four forces, four qualities, four humors, four temperaments. The humors themselves were cognitively mapped in relation to the elements and properties:

Blood—Air—Wet
Phlegm—Water—Cold
Yellow bile—Fire—Hot
Black bile—Earth—Dry

According to the medical and philosophical traditions of the Islamic Middle East, health and wellness were considered possible to sustain only when there was symmetry between the four humors. Symptoms of melancholy included an unbalanced mind and manic, depressive, and violent tempers. Yet melancholy was not just about physical bodies in humeral imbalance, and the variety of terms designed to articulate melancholic positions reflect the emphasis Ottomans placed on spiritual states.

Islamic philosophers believed that when deployed correctly, the audition of music (Ar. *sama'*) had the potential to purify the soul. Assumptions about the beneficial elements of sound or music, emotion, and healing generated in Ottoman, Turkish, and Islamic belief systems clearly draw on the writings of Plato and Aristotle. These classical philosophers argued that music possessed an ethical value and affected the morality of the listener. Music's importance in education for Ottomans reflected the Arab connection to Greek and Roman beliefs about sound and healing. Furthermore, significant portions of Arabic medicinal and philosophical treatises were adopted into the Latin curriculum (*quadrivium*) taught at Christian universities in the Middle Ages that educated students in astronomy, geometry, arithmetic, and music.

Having read key Islamic texts written by the philosophers al-Farabi (870–950), Zekeriya al-Razi (854–932) and Ibn Sina (980–1037), Ottoman philosophers such as Hekimbaşı Gevrekzâde (d. 1801) and Abbas Vesim (d. 1759 or 1760) argued that music must be included in Ottoman medical education, and that a competent physician and healer must be trained in music. The logic supporting music and healing practices depended on the assumption that human beings are part of a neo-platonic cosmologic "harmony of the spheres." Attaining harmony between body, spirit, and mind necessarily led to health and wellness of both the individual and of Ottoman society as a whole. The Ottomans understood sound itself as inherently spiritual, often looking to the sole primary source of Islam, the Qur'an, for supporting evidence. The divine character of sound was most cited by Ottoman philosophers in the verse "when God decrees a thing, God only says to it 'Be' and it is" (Qur'an 2: 117), who pointed out that the world was brought into existence by God in and through sound. The Muslim belief that sound forms and structures the natural and cosmological world played an important part in fostering Ottoman healing practices whose outcome was to reestablish the upset harmony of the patient with balancing, reparative sounds.

As previously mentioned, healing with music in Ottoman medicinal practices was always done in and with community. Ottoman writers offered historical accounts confirming that music therapy in Ottoman hospitals was not practiced in one-to-one settings but rather happened only when a group of patients actively listened to and sat with a group of musicians.[3] These written descriptions are verified through Ottoman miniature painters' artistic representations of music and healing.

One of the most popular sites for healing with music was the Ottoman hospital in Edirne (also known in this time as Adrianopole). The Darüşşifa, or "house of health," was commissioned by Sultan Beyazid II and functioned from its opening in 1488 until Edirne's occupation by the Russians in 1878. It was meticulously built approximately 235 kilometers northwest of Istanbul in a quiet, green location. Since 1997, it has been a popular museum known as the Edirne Health Museum (*Edirne Sağlık Müzesi*). The Darüşşifa hospital was constructed with great attention to acoustics, as the architectural walls of individual rooms included shafts that allowed patients to hear and experience the sound of music and flowing water during specific moments of the day. While individuals' sleeping quarters were often more private, communal spaces had built-in places for musicians to sit together with patients, again demonstrating that Ottoman practices of music and healing was necessarily a collective activity. Here again, the role of space and acoustics was considered in the construction of a high circular space for group music therapy, a space that was the center of healing practices for the institution. The Darüşşifa in Edirne is one of several Ottoman houses of healing that promoted and sustained the practice of collective music therapy.

MUSICAL MODES AS MUSIC THERAPY

Of course, pharmacy must not be mistaken for cookery,
and the objective of medicines is not to be tasty.
Music as food for the soul (following Sufis' formula) is one thing;
sound sequences [and *makam*] intended for endocrinal stimulation are something else.
—Jean During[4]

Ottoman manuscripts that outline and describe music therapy procedures, especially Evliya Çelebi's *The Book of Travels* (1664) and Şuurî's *The Adjustment of Temperaments* (1693), demonstrate the extent to which physicians thought of themselves as taking rational approaches to illness when utilizing music therapies. While sound was understood as inherently divine, considering a patient's soundscape as a form of healing was not seen as an attempt to cure through any intervention of the divine per se. Rather, prescriptions for healing based on knowledge of melodic modes, or *makam*, were used by Ottoman physicians empirically. The clearest link to understanding how particular sounds deemed melancholic were used in healing can be located in historical texts on *makam* (see especially Mehmed 1864 [1853] and Gevrekzâde 1794).

As patterns of perfectly organized sounds reflecting the perceived organization of the cosmos, intervals between and of *makam*-s were believed to induce specific effects on listeners, and thus had an important place in Ottoman healing practices from the fifteenth century on (Tucek 1997, Y. Çetinkaya 1995, Grebene 1978, Arel 1952). In Islamic medieval texts, which took Greek understandings of modes and further developed them, *makam*-s were mapped onto seasons and times of day, and classified as hot, cold, dry, or damp. Ottoman philosophers drew on Islamic texts, whose authors further associated the twelve fundamental *makam* with the twelve signs of the zodiac, which were themselves distributed among the four elements and four humors, and alternatively classified as male or female.

Hearing a particular *makam* had the potential to heal because the *makam* could reestablish a patient's equilibrium in body, mind, and spirit in one of two ways: first, a *makam* could be helpful in targeting specific illnesses an individual might have, and second, a *makam* could affect the emotions of individuals with certain temperaments, bringing out those emotions. Yet a given *makam* influenced listeners not because, for example, the *makam* itself was hot or dry, but rather the influence was believed to lie in the humor a *makam* aroused and affected. As one of the four central humors, black bile, or melancholy, was carefully considered by Ottoman musico-medical specialists, and, centuries before the founding of the Ottoman Empire, Islamic philosophers articulated the ways that various *makam*-s that were able to arouse that humor.

In accordance with related philosophies of the harmony of the spheres and the numerology and astrology linking cosmology to Hippocratic understandings of the four humors in the human body, twelve central *makam*-s laid the foundation of Islamic music therapies. Of the celebrated Islamic philosophers of the past most influencing debates, the *Kitab el-Musika el-Kebir* ("The Great Book of Music") manuscript by al-Farabi (872–950) held particular significance. In this text, al-Farabi set forth the mathematical relationship between sound, physics, and astronomy that was to be the basis for Ottoman music therapy practices as well as the musico-medicinal practices of early Europe (Sezer 2013, Gençel 2006, Altınölçek 1998, Güvenç 1993). Al-Farabi delineated the effects of *makam*-s on the soul in his work, classifying them as follows:

> Rast makamı: elicits comfort
> Saba makamı: elicits bravery

Hicaz makamı: elicits humility
Neva makamı: elicits contentment
Uşşak makamı: elicits laughter
Hüseyni makamı: elicits ease
Buselik makamı: elicits strength
Isfahan makamı: elicits security and the capacity to act
Rehavi makamı: elicits a feeling of eternity
Kuçek makamı: elicits sadness
Büzürk makamı: elicits fear
Zirgüle makamı: elicits sleepiness

While the specific melodic content of these *makam*-s are unknown today, *makam*-s with the same names were listed in Ottoman musico-medicinal treatises, and contemporary *makam*-s exist with the same names. Furthermore, *makam* itself is a system that determines tonal relations, indicates correct movement between microtonal intervals, and establishes key melodic patterns unique to a given *makam*. Many of the nuances of movement and melodic contour of the past may be lost and altered, while the names remain. Moreover, the assumption that particular musical modes influence our affective states, while not rigorously classified or followed in a centralized music therapy methodology, continues to prevail today.[5]

Another critical early Islamic scholar who wrote about extramusical qualities of *makam* that were foundational for Ottoman philosophers and physicians was Ibn Sina (980–1037), a scholar who evidently drew heavily from al-Farabi in his own work. Musicologist Pınar Somakçı argues that Ibn Sina clearly understood music therapy as palliative and preventative care, and writes that Ibn Sina saw playing music for a patient as the most effective treatment to strengthen the mental and spiritual fortitude of the patient and give him more courage to fight illness (2003). Ibn Sina's famous *El Kanun fi't-tıbbi* ("The Canon of Medicine") was translated into Ottoman in the eighteenth century by Hekimbaşı Gevrekzâde Hasan Efendi (see Gruner 1970).

Gevrekzâde is credited by Ottoman music therapy historians as solidifying Ottoman classifications designating which *makam*-s would be effective in the treatment of particular illnesses:

Rast makamı: useful for individuals suffering from paralysis
Hicaz makamı: useful for diseases of the urinary tract
Neva makamı: useful for sciatica
Uşşak makamı: useful for insomnia and foot pains
Hüseyni makamı: useful in the treatment of the liver, heart disease, seizures, and fevers
Buselik makamı: useful in the treatment of pain in the head and of eye diseases
Isfahan makamı: useful for preventative care against fevers

Rehavi makamı: useful for treating headaches, nosebleeds, and phlegmatic diseases

Büzürk makamı: useful for the treatment of cramps and fatigue

Zirefkend makamı: useful for the treatment of backaches and after strokes

Irak makamı: useful for the treatment of childhood meningitis

Zirgüle makamı: useful for the treatment of heart pain and heartburn

Many Ottoman physicians further believed that certain *makam*-s reflected an essentialist notion of particular ethnic groups as well:

Uşşak makamı: Turkic Ottomans

Hüseyni makamı: Arab Ottomans

Buselik makamı: Greek Ottomans

Irak makamı: Persians

Importantly, these extramusical meanings do not lie in a given *makam* itself, but in the effectiveness of a given *makam* to promote healing or another significant physical or psychological change in an individual of a certain ethnicity, having a certain illness, or having a certain personality. As a collection of microtonal intervals, as including specific melodic contours (which may have been heard as tension moving to release), and as having particular directional momentum (horizontal, vertical, ascending, descending), *makam*-s were understood as vibrational tools to activate the illness or problematic humor of a suffering patient. A patient's unique body would receive these vibrations and through having the patient's quality or illness being affected by these sounds, the patient would be "moved" toward healing. Ottoman physicians broadly believed that music's capacity to effect change—to affect an individual, to move one from illness to health—lay in the individual body's response to sonic vibrations, not in the sonic object itself.

When physicians considered particular music therapies for individuals with an excess of black blood—melancholics—they mindfully selected specific *makam*-s to stimulate a heightened melancholic response in patients. *Makam*-s such as *Bestenigar, Saba, Hüzzam*, and *Segah* ostensibly instilled feelings of melancholy in listeners that would decisively activate a patient's excess of black blood and move them toward a state of health, balance, and wellness (Yiğitbaş 1972). Ottoman physicians additionally used particular *makam*-s in music therapy regimens to positively produce particular states believed to positively alter the "moral" states of patients suffering with an excess of black bile:

Hicaz makamı: increases humility

Neva makamı: increases bravery

Hüseyni makamı: provokes appreciation of beauty

Irak makamı: increases pleasure

Ottoman physicians further believed that other *makam*-s could induce particular physical effects that would help balance melancholics:

Rehavi makamı: incites weeping

Uşşak makamı: incites laughter

Zirgüle makamı: induces sleep

Generally speaking, patients experiencing some sort of physical, mental, or psychological trauma were encouraged to listen to musical compositions and *makam*-s that helped them to *keder çekmek:* "pull grief" (*keder*). Pulling *keder* was a way to relive the event that caused imbalance and trauma through the safe, controlled and community-shared medium of live music listening in music therapy sessions. Melancholic patients whose melancholic state was not caused by a specific trauma were believed to be experiencing melancholy due to a physical excess of black bile, and their treatment included *makam*-s that activated or effectively caused vibratory movement of the black bile itself. Furthermore, music with *hüzün* (a "melancholy" different from the black bile "melankoli") was used as treatment because music sounding *hüzün* balanced the equilibrium between and among the four humors of the body.

Ottoman music therapy included the playing of specific *makam*-s prescribed by physicians—themselves trained in music—for patients with a variety of ailments and illnesses. As music therapy was necessarily communal, any individual patient was reportedly subjected to a variety of *makam*-s in any given music therapy session based on the prescriptions of the other individuals in the hospital. We do not know further particulars of how Ottoman music therapy sessions unfolded. We do know that the central goal of music therapy, with methods based in Greek and Islamic philosophy and grounded in Ottoman observations, was to treat illness by maintaining or reestablishing the humeral balance and overall harmony of the individual-in-community.

A healthy balance between body, mind, and soul was possibly for a listener whose body responded to the vibrations of particular *makam*-s that were to lead him/her to experience specific emotions, often vis-à-vis laughter and crying. While an excess of black bile produced the physical unbalance of the illness melancholy, Ottoman physicians crafted music therapy regimens that used particular *makam*-s that were heard as melancholic to promote equilibrium in a patient. By eliciting feelings that could heal and reestablish body-mind balance by vibrating—and therefore directly affecting—the particular humor or illnesses in question, Ottomans ultimately believed that balancing the mind and body would also bring about health for the soul.

MELANCHOLY AND HEALTH BETWEEN "EAST" AND "WEST"

From the tenth century on, special care for individuals suffering from emotional imbalance and psychological discomfort developed in the Islamic world earlier and in a more organized fashion than in the medieval west.[6] This development is testified by the existence of Ottoman asylums and medical texts written about patient care. The classification of mental diseases and their treatments was as rigorously categorized as that of physical diseases, and it is not surprising that we find the classifications of musical remedies for such diseases similarly rigorous (Burnett 2000: 90). We know that the west received classical Greek sources—philosophies put forth by the schools developed around Plato, Aristotle, Pythagoras, and others—directly from Arabic centers of learning in the medieval period, especially Damascus and Baghdad. Since medieval transcriptions of Greek philosophies were being translated into Latin often from Arabic, we can locate a number of shared assumptions about music and melancholy between medieval European and early Ottoman scholars. Particular cosmological ideas were shared across "east" and "west," while specific communities developed disparate forms of tuning and temperaments, such as the modal systems in use for contemporary Turkish classical music as well as the modal systems used by Jewish communities (Kligman 2009, Seroussi 1990).[7] Philosophers historically writing in Arabic, Hebrew, and Latin inherited and shared some common beliefs inherent in ancient Greek philosophy, one of which was the assumption that the sound and harmony of the spheres is representative of the relationship between human beings' bodies and souls (Shiloah 2000).

Before the founding of European universities in the thirteenth century, medical treatises and theories were primarily produced in the context of Christian monasteries. One of the most outstanding representatives of medicinal practices in the medieval period is Hildegard of Bingen (1098–1179). In her two medical treatises, Hildegard articulates the widespread belief that humors are a product of the human condition and fall from grace. She argues that blood is the only positive humor, representing the body in a state of purity as it was in Eden (Callahan 2000: 158). Melancholy, in particular, was first manifest in Adam as a result of original sin (Callahan: 159). What is important to note about these early theorizations in European medicinal treatises is that melancholy was seen as an illness or disease that was essentially spiritually derived. The belief that melancholy could ultimately be traced to man's fall from grace in the Garden of Eden pervaded western medical philosophy for centuries to come (Gouk 2000: 180). Hildegard and the philosophers that followed her believed that music could counter the effects of melancholy, as music was understood as a "manifestation of spiritual wholeness and a means by which to achieve it" (Callahan 2000: 160).[8] Assumptions about the nature and work of medicine, music, magic, and the cosmos were solidified in western medicinal texts by the fifteenth century, during the Renaissance period (Callahan: 152).

Robert Burton's multi-volume *The Anatomy of Melancholy*, first published in 1621, was the first major work in English to summarize and expand upon earlier writing on melancholy. Burton's groundbreaking text became an essential reference work on the subject for later medical and musical professionals and scholars. In his work, Burton identifies two kinds of melancholy. The first is *transitory* melancholy, a temporary state that can be experienced by any individual feeling sadness or loss. Burton is more interested, however, in understanding *settled* melancholy, a state resulting from an upset humor that becomes a chronic and fixed, habituated state.[9] Yet these melancholic varieties, for Burton, can ultimately be attributed to an excess of black bile, which negatively affects people's behavior. It is crucial to note that in Burton's work, melancholy is understood as either a disease of the body or as an imbalance between the body and the soul. Theorizations of melancholy proposed by Burton therefore maintain and recreate the belief that melancholy, while manifesting in the body, might be fundamentally caused by spiritual imbalance.

By the end of the sixteenth century in Europe, "melancholy" had come to stand for any non-specific disease characterized by gloominess or sorrow (Austern 2000a: 116). After this point, melancholy defied simple codification even within a single western era or location, and was simply understood as a condition of "infinite sadness" (Austern 2000b). Through time, melancholy maintained a reputation as being an elite disease of the visionary, solitary intellectual or artist. In her famous description of the disease, philosopher Julia Kristeva likens melancholy to a black sun whose lethargic rays strike the sufferer from a distant galaxy, causing

> [a] life that is unlivable, heavy with daily sorrows, tears held back or shed, a total despair, scorching at times, then wan and empty. In short, a devitalized existence . . . ready at any moment for a plunge into death . . . a living death . . . absorbed into sorrow. (Kristeva 1989: 4)

Throughout this history of contemplating melancholy in the west, music has been understood—and in some cases marketed—as "medication for the self-cure of whatever ails body and soul" (Austern 2000a: 113).

The short review of important western ontological and epistemological approaches to music and melancholy is not intended to imply that melancholy is a universal disease with similar symptoms, understandings, and treatments. Indeed, Ottoman practices and philosophies of melancholy and musical healing differed radically from the medicinal and musical thought and practices of western Europe during the same period. My intention in invoking such a comparison is to highlight two important considerations: first, Middle Eastern and European philosophers were drawing upon similar texts and assumptions to formulate their understanding of body systems as humeral, and second, these same philosophers believed that melancholy simultaneously manifested as mental, physical, and spiritual dis-ease.

Yet while the assumption that melancholy was related to an individual's spiritual state was shared between the European and Ottoman philosophers and physicians, European scholars did not adopt the in-depth Muslim texts on music therapy and spirituality, primarily due to the fact that Europeans' spiritual states were in the domain and concern of the Church. For example, one important thread that was maintained in translation from Greek to Arabic to Latin was the idea that particular *makam*-s expressed and affected the emotional and the ethical state of a listener. However, musical treatises on *makam*-s were not entirely translated into Latin. Arabic, Ottoman, and Persian musical modes were more numerous and meticulously classified than older Greek understandings. While Middle Eastern astrological theory was entirely adopted by western theorists, the distribution of musical modes amongst the planets or signs of the zodiac were not translated, nor were discussions of music therapy. One of the main reasons particular elements of Middle Eastern musico-medicinal texts remained untranslated was due to sections entitled "spiritual medicine" (Ar. *al-tibb al-ruhani*) on the passions of the mind (e.g., mental health). These sections went beyond discussing theory and philosophy, as they additionally considered practical knowledge and music therapy techniques for mental, psychological, and spiritual disease. It was precisely because the *al-tibb al-ruhani* texts reflected core Islamic tenets and Muslim belief structures that they largely remained untranslated into Latin.

The efficacy that Islamic philosophers placed on spiritual subjectivity in relation to musical modes and healing is perhaps the key reason we can historically understand the disjuncture of philosophies and practices of music therapy geographically between the constructed areas we today name as east and west. In Europe, melancholy increasingly became a disease associated with a stricken individual (often male) genius of the upper classes. By the time Jean-Martin Charcot (1825–1893) and Pierre Janet (1859–1947) established psychology as a legitimate scientific discipline, melancholy was firmly separated from humeral theory or any spiritual efficacy, and positioned as a disease of the mind. Sigmund Freud (1856–1939), one of Charcot's celebrated students, established the theories of melancholy that continue to pervade western assumptions today, and indicated the advent of the term "depression."

With the founding of the Republic of Turkey and the intense modernization efforts espoused by the government, western psychology was adopted by newly formed medical institutions in Turkey's largest cities. In these hospitals, biomedical assumptions about selfhood, mind-body dualisms, and secularism appropriated from western psychology shifted local perceptions about illness from spiritual discourse to biomedical discourse. Ottoman-Turkish classical musicians emerged as one particular contingent that maintained earlier Ottoman assumptions about the relationship between melancholy and healing. Indeed, contemporary Turkish classical musicians' narratives demonstrate the multiplicity of ways that experiencing melancholy-as-healing is memorialized and valorized as a richness of Ottoman tradition. The next three examples, featuring vignettes from my ethnographic fieldwork, illuminate how contemporary musicians today labor to render melancholy as a reparative, healing practice, demonstrating how musicians validate musicking melancholy through recourse to their understanding of Ottoman music therapy.

ICONIC MELANCHOLIC MUSICIANS: NEYZEN TEVFİK

While having tea in Istanbul with six professional Turkish classical musicians—all instrumentalists—after their state-sponsored ensemble rehearsal, one of the musicians asked me what clues (*ipucu*-s) about melancholy and music I was investigating at the moment. I explained my recent trip to the archives in the capitol, Ankara, and my investigation into music therapy (*müzik tedavisi*) of the Ottoman period. I explained that while I could find documentation of how melancholic dis-eases—*melankoli* and *kara sevda,* for example—were treated with special *makam*-s, I was interested in finding out if Ottoman musicians had ever been treated in the same way. I wondered to my companions out loud, "Does healing with *makam* have the same effect on musicians, who embody *makam* when they play? If one of you were suffering from some form of *melankoli* [the term indicating melancholy caused by physiological problems], would a particular *makam* help you?"

"Probably not," a young *tanbur* (long-necked lute) player answered. "In the Ottoman times hearing music was a special activity—now music blasts from every car, train station, and grocery store. So we are desensitized."

The *kanun* (trapezoidal zither) player interjected. "I think it would help me. I listen to recordings, old 78s [*taş plakları*] with specific *makam*—especially *Saba* and *Buselik*—that Ottomans believed balanced your emotions. Maybe I just believe the Ottomans and it's not in the *makam* itself, but I do feel better. Listening is good but playing them is better. Playing is like taking two pills instead of one."

There was a brief wave of laughter around the table. I decided to continue pursuing the topic.

"So playing *makam*-s that are melancholic, that's like taking a pill? You just feel better afterwards or does it take the melancholy away?"

The *kanun* player thought before responding.

"Melancholy does not go away. It comes and goes [*gelir ve geçer*]. But after all I'm not a melancholic. Not like the famous melancholics of the past at least."

The *ud* (short-necked lute) player jumped into the conversation.

"Yes, some of the best musicians of our past were melancholics. When I was a young musician I memorized what they did, thinking I was becoming a good musician, but I realize now I was just learning to become melancholic!"

Another bout of laughter was waved away by the *kanun* player. He spoke to his friend, saying, "Truly our loveliest music comes from musicians in the deepest pain. Music gets nutrition from pain [*musiki acıdan beslenir*]. One of our tasks as musicians is to sit with pain, you know? People today do rush and take pills [antidepressants] to stop feeling. We must feel to be musicians, even when listeners can't feel. Especially when they can't feel."

I took the *kanun* player's bold statement as invitation to push him further. "How do you feel pain with music?"

The *kanun* player shifted in his seat before offering a response.

"There is not one answer, but the best start is to listen to those great melancholics of the past. The ones who, when making *taksim* [instrumental improvisation], used shouting melodies [*feryad eden nağmeler*]. As our *udi* [ud-player] friend said a moment ago, we listen to what they did and replicate their intensity. And without poetic texts [*güfte*], what we rely on is melody [*nağme*]. Those melancholic musicians of the past, their *taksim*-s were melody after melody after melody. . . ."

Makam-s are collections of microtonal intervals that contain specific rules pertaining to melodic movement, or *seyir*. My own teacher's teacher, the celebrated *udi* and composer Cinuçen Tanrıkorur (1938–2000), taught that *makam* is mostly derived from the idiomatic melodic contours associated with any given mode. He actively wrote against a general trend to depict *makam* simply by pitches (*dizi*-s) (Tanrıkorur 2003a, 2003b). Tanrıkorur often used this particular equation to demonstrate his point that *makam* was more about moving through intervallic space in time than about pitch:

Dizi		*Seyir*		*Makam*
Pitch collection	+	Melodic movement	=	Melodic Mode
20%		80%		100%

For an overwhelming number of individual instrumentalists I interviewed, *seyir* emerged as the greatest indicator of a musician's competence. Memorizing the collection of pitches is easy, I was told: knowing how they go together is more challenging. Furthermore, musicians indicated that affective intensity itself lies in a musician's ability to create beautiful melodies (*nağme*-s) while doing *taksim* to such an extent that listeners would not think about the *seyir* of the *makam* but rather be tricked into hearing unfolding melodies in succession. One of the key ways contemporary Turkish classical musicians adopt these skills is by modeling their *taksim*-s after those of past musicians who were deemed particularly melancholic.

One of the greatest case studies of a musicking individual deemed melancholic was Neyzen Tevfik (1879–1953), a *neyzen* who was never was without his reed flute, *ney*, in hand (he ostensibly even bathed with his instrument). A virtuoso on the *ney*, Neyzen Tevfik was a prominent member of both Mevlevi and Bektaşi Sufi sects. His instrumental compositions, especially his *Suzinak*, *Şehnazbuselik*, and *Nihavent saz semaileri,* continue to be integral texts in the contemporary Turkish classical music canon and are played and memorized by contemporary musicians.

Tracing Neyzen Tevfik's engagement with medical institutions elucidates significant changes in approaches to mental health that occurred in Turkey during the *Tanizmat* reforms and in the years of the early nation-state. When the Ottoman Empire was formally dismantled and the Republic of Turkey was created in 1923, architects of the nation-state labored to create new identities for Turkish citizens that were distant from the powerful prevailing ideologies of the Ottoman Empire, moving away from patterns of thinking and organizing life according to Islamic belief practices. Medical institutions were recast to promote secular, westernized, biology-based ideologies that established individual patients as having autonomous bodies bifurcated from social communities, to be studied by instruments of objectivity. This process of medicalization is aptly illustrated in naming practices, as the Ottoman term for hospitals as "houses of healing" (*darüşşifa*-s or *şifahane*-s) was replaced with renaming hospitals as "houses of the sick" (*hastane*-s), a language practice that continues today.

Neyzen Tevfik's life demonstrates the challenges of shifting assumptions about the interrelationship between body-mind-spirit to a system focused on diseased bodies, disorders, and disabilities to be fixed. Diagnosed with melancholy (*melankoli*), epilepsy, and alcoholism, Neyzen Tevfik was in and out of the Bakırköy and Haydarpaşa hospitals in Istanbul and a frequent patient of Dr. Mazhar Osman (1884–1951), a key figure in introducing and developing western psychology in the republican era. In his own public statements, Neyzen Tevfik exhibited distaste for medical institutions whose aim was to "cure him." He claimed that the only benefit of being hospitalized was that he was able to sleep comfortably for a few days.

An incredibly prolific poet as well, Neyzen Tevfik created poems that were often found somewhat grotesque by audiences of his era. Today, Neyzen Tevfik is celebrated in Turkish public spaces as a musician but even more for his audacious poetry, which often used swear words and deplorable language to make deep philosophical claims about life. The numerous statues of Neyzen Tevfik constructed in the 1990s and early 2000s speak more to the visibility of memorializing Neyzen Tevfik as a poet than as a musician: while he is depicted in stone with his *ney*, his representation as a statue in the public realm is not a common practice for other Ottoman-Turkish classical musicians of his age. While a statue of Neyzen Tevfik in the municipal square of Kartal is extremely large and looming, his statue in Maçka (Figures 5.1 and 5.2) invites more intimate encounters. In Maçka, Neyzen Tevfik is life sized, and occupies part of a park bench. Across from him sits a round picnic table. Engaging with Neyzen

Figure 5.1 Life-sized statue of Neyzen Tevfik in Maçka, Istanbul (photograph by İpek Orhon).

Figure 5.2 An invitation to sit with Neyzen Tevfik (photograph by İpek Orhon).

Tevfik in Maçka is a kind of personal experience, one that many Turkish classical musicians celebrate.

Turkish classical musicians deeply revere Neyzen Tevfik as a musician and as a spiritual authority. Beyond naming him melancholic ("*Neyzen Tevfik melankoliktir*"), the musicians I work with further interpolate Neyzen Tevfik as a *meczup*, one of the Ottoman designations denoting "mad" or "insane." This position of madness, however, carries spiritual weight in local Islamic belief as the one that reaches a positive threshold on the road to God. The word *meczup* itself denotes an ecstatic attraction to God. *Meczup*-s hit a horizon where they lose themselves, ostensibly see beauty and God in everything, and cannot pass back into the realm of the mundane (or the sane).

Can one hear Neyzen Tevfik's melancholy in his music? Contemporary Turkish classical musicians argue that they can, although they believe that only those with a deep understanding of Ottoman-Turkish classical music and its associated listening habits can do so. The musicians I interviewed claimed that the most telling feature of melancholy in instrumentalists is how they render their *taksim*-s (solo improvisations). According to present-day musicians, individuals suffering with melancholy render *taksim* as melody after melody after melody, so much so that instead of hearing lines of exploration of a given *makam*, musicians claim they find themselves listening to fountains of compositions.[10] Sitting with musicians and listening together to Neyzen Tevfik's recordings, in a moment of bi-aurality, I came to develop ears that fixated on moments when a *taksim* sounded more composed than merely passing through particular intervals or idiomatic melodic patterns.[11]

Musicians thus articulate that the most significant moments in Neyzen Tevfik's *taksim*-s where they "hear melancholy" is in the melodies, the *nağme*-s, he comes up with in his improvisations. This first example of such a melody (Example 5.1) comes from a recording of Neyzen Tevfik improvising in *Nihavend makamı*:

Example 5.1 *Nağme* in Neyzen Tevfik's improvisation in *Nihavend makamı*.

Musicians agreed that in Neyzen Tevfik's *taksim* in *Rast makamı* (Example 5.2), he created iconic melodies that bore little resemblance to traditional renderings of the *makam*'s *seyir*. Musicians further explained that because of Neyzen Tevfik's influence on oral music transmission and the circulation of his recordings, this particular melody today is widely used in *taksim* in this *makam*, meaning that Neyzen Tevfik facilitated a change in present-day improvisation of *Rast* itself.

Example 5.2 *Nağme* in Neyzen Tevfik's improvisation in *Rast makamı*.

This final example (Example 5.3), Neyzen Tevfik's improvisation in *Saba makamı*, was also noted by the musicians who listened to recordings of his *taksim*-s with me. One *ney* player even said he took this very line and uses it regularly in his *taksim*-s. "Unfortunately," he tells me, "master-musicians immediately know that I stole this passage from Tevfik!"

Example 5.3 *Nağme* in Neyzen Tevfik's improvisation in *Saba makamı*.

Musicians with whom I spoke claim that when they listen to Neyzen Tevfik's improvisations, they find themselves "undone." These musicians explain that they are lost in these melodies and lose their attention to a given mode's progression; this "losing," while experienced at the level of an individual listener, is actually a product of years of music transmission and learning how to hear. Losing oneself in this way is ultimately about pleasure and satisfaction. These musicians articulate that generally, their extensive knowledge of music theory reduces their listening to hearing structure over melody. Neyzen Tevfik surfaces as a unique musician in their normative listening habits precisely because his *taksim* of melody upon melody upon melody disrupts the structures they use to understand *seyir* and intervallic movement in *makam*. As a musician with apparent psychological and physiological dis-ease, Neyzen Tevfik and his melancholic musicking set him in a different category than that of musicians who made melancholic music due to trauma. In contrast to the example of Neyzen Tevfik, when written Ottoman music emerged from a composer crafting musics after experiencing a specific pain (*acı*) or traumatic incident, present-day musicians are tasked with remembering that pain and rendering it audible for contemporary audiences.

The listening structures my consultants engage when hearing melancholy in Neyzen Tevfik's improvisations further elicit the tension between the nature of authorship and musical virtuosity (*virtüöz*). Tevfik himself recorded during the period of national transformation that witnessed the rise in recording technology, the expansion of discourses of musical virtuosity, and the invention of the concept of the autonomous individual (*birey*). Musicians today position him as a liminal artisan in every way—between the sane and insane, between Sufi order involvement and his recording work for the (secular) state radio, between a solo artist and a sonic representation of communal musicking. Neyzen Tefik as a musician—and as an imagined, remembered, historicized icon—demonstrates the rhizomatic complexity within which ideas of authorship, virtuosity, individual autonomy, and mental health emerge in the ways present-day musicians listen to his improvisations.

Neyzen Tefik melancholic taksim (improv) displays this

MELANCHOLIC MUSICKING: "THERE IS NO MEDICINE"

"You know the expression, Denise. Music gets nutrition from pain [*musiki acıdan beslenir*]."

"Yes, *Hocam*." I continue taking notes during my interview with the sheikh who ostensibly heals depression and bipolar disorders with sound.

"The root cause of pain and suffering is ignorance. We think that suffering is a bad thing. But it is not. You could not suffer if you did not have much love for or pleasure from something."

I nodded.

"You see, the only true pain in life comes from that which we love. So pain in music can really only come from two places: separation [*ayrılık*] or death [*ölüm*]. We love someone or something and are separated from them. We love life and die, or a loved one dies and leaves us here in the world. So on the surface pain seems to be a bad thing. But if you really understand suffering and pain, you know that they come from love. For those of us on the straight path [e.g., Islam], we understand death as a kind of antidote to separation as we are reunified with the divine."

In my notes, I write (in English): life = pain = separation.

The sheikh falls silent and looks out the window. I take it as my cue to ask a question.

"So *Hocam*, if suffering is remedy itself [*dert derman ise*], what shape does the remedy take? What is the final product of suffering-as-remedy?"

He smiled.

"A good question. The goal is to consume suffering and pain into yourself. Suffering tells you where you are on the path. Suffering requires you to die into it and give up the image you hold dear about yourself. You give yourself up to be made anew. Do you know what our Prophet says about dying?"

He was quizzing me.

"Die before dying [*'ölmeden önce ölün'*]."

"Very good. 'Die before dying.' A great lesson for us all. Give yourself up, embrace suffering, and come out of it anew. The final product of suffering-as-remedy, as you ask, is a feeling of wholeness. As illness is a test, those who pass the test understand themselves as constituents of God."

"And so healing is . . ." I started.

He interjected and finished my thought: "knowing your wholeness as dependent on God. Knowing this is experienced as a feeling [duygu]. You feel whole in your suffering."

He smiled, and gave me his final thoughts.

"You see, what I do is healing. Not medicine. There is no medicine for suffering. The people I am called to help know that there is no medicine for suffering. I help them live with suffering. Some tell me I cure them. I say there is no 'I.' My duty is to remind them of that which we all inherently should know: suffering comes from divine love. Living with this knowledge is 'dying before you die.'"

When the sheikh claimed "there is no medicine for suffering," he deployed the title of a well-known Ottoman-Turkish classical song from the nineteenth century of the same name, "Olmaz İlaç" ("There is No Medicine"). The lyrics of the song were written by Ottoman poet Nâmık Kemâl (1840–1888). Ottoman court composer Hacı Arif Bey (1831–1885) put this poem into a song in the makam of Segâh and the rhythmic mode (usûl) of curcuna (Example 5.4):

> Olmaz ilâç sine-i sad pareme
> Çare bulunmaz bilirim yareme
> Baksa tabiban-i cihan çareme
> Çare bulunmaz bilirim yareme
>
> Kastediyor tir-i müjen canıma
> Gözleri en son girecek kanıma
> Şerhedemem halimi cananıma
> Çare bulunmaz bilirim yareme

> There is no medicine for my breast [that has] shattered
>   into a thousand pieces
> I know there is no cure for my wound
> If all doctors in the world sought a cure for me
> I know there is no cure for my wound
>
> The arrows of [my love's] eyelashes loom over my life
> In the end those eyes will shed my blood
> I cannot reveal my situation to my beloved
> I know there is no cure for my wound

Example 5.4 Transcription of the piece "*Olmaz İlaç*" by Hacı Arif Bey (1831–1885).

For twenty-first century listeners, contemporary musicians should ideally (and convincingly) perform melancholy in their rendition of this famous song. While there are many versions to discuss, one prominent rendition comes from singer Kani Karaca (1930–2004). Audiences today hear Kani Karaca's performance as particularly affecting because of the scarcity of accompanying musicians and solo singer, practices that undoubtedly reflect the way the composer Hacı Arif Bey performed this piece in the nineteenth century Ottoman court. They further locate a successful performance of melancholy in Karaca's use of *goygoy*—a guttural, chest-voice ornamentation used highly by individuals trained in Qur'anic recitation.

Melancholy needs to be present, musicians argue, because this song is itself about one particularly harsh manifestation of melancholy in the form of psychological disorder *kara sevda*, or "black love." The lyricist, Nâmık Kemâl, was an Ottoman author and poet who dedicated his pen to supporting the Young Turk political movement and criticized the rule of the sultanate. Kemâl wrote this poem when suffering in *kara sevda* due to the trauma he experienced when the Sultan had deported him from the city of Istanbul as punishment for his political efforts. The well-known Ottoman composer and palace musician, Hacı Arif Bey, put the poem to music when suffering from *kara sevda* after the death of his wife. Contemporary musicians do not put his suffering only on the loss of his beloved wife. "Arif Bey had many losses [*kayıp*]," claimed one musician. "Equally significant to the death of and separation from his wife was the change of his circle ... it was the *Tanzimat* [reforms] and westernization of the Ottoman court that really ended him."

These narratives and associated feelings of loss, estrangement, and melancholy must be present in contemporary performances. One of the reasons Kani Karaca is believed to render a melancholic performance is because of his work as a *hafiz*, a person who has memorized and recites the Qur'an. Listeners claim that Kani Karaca's voice captures a weeping quality that activates a sense of pain, loss, and melancholy because his voice was an Islamic voice. An eighteen-year-old conservatory student studying voice told me that Karaca's version was unrivaled simply because Karaca was differently abled—he lacked sight—as Hacı Arif Bey suffered from his wife's death and Nâmık Kemâl suffered from his exile from Istanbul. When Kani Karaca himself died in 2004, musicians immediately began to cite his death as further evidence of the death of Turkish classical music. We thus see in this example how narratives of loss and historical memory intersect and reemerge in contemporary Turkish music practices to render performances melancholic.

Yet there is more beyond simply connecting this melancholic song to the social and political contexts of its day or the ideologies of hearing Qur'anic timbres as particularly suited to melancholic music production. Some of the musicians I interviewed espoused a narrative about the piece akin to the sheikh's interpretation of suffering. These musicians read into the claims of the text, arguing that in saying "there is no remedy" and "there is no medicine" that listeners are invited to struggle—as Hacı Arif Bey did—with how to continue living when there is no cure for your pain.

"You see, Denise," a singer explained to me in an interview, "I have not lost my spouse and I have a nice salary as a musician, so it would seem that I have little in common with Hacı Arif Bey."

She continued, "But that is not the point, I think, of the song. You see, we love singing this song. We can sing this song with a smile on our faces, even though the song is about pain and suffering. But we smile because through singing about this pain we embrace this pain.

"We live with this pain. It helps us deal with other kinds of pain. It is relieving to sing, almost like singing itself is the solution.

"Writing music was probably how Hacı Arif Bey himself must have coped with *kara sevda*. Yes, there is no medicine [repeating the first line of the text, *olmaz ilaç*] but writing and doing music must have been for him what it is for me . . . a way to live suffering and even make something beautiful out of suffering. Have you ever heard the expression that some Sufi-oriented Turks use, 'suffering is a remedy itself [*dert dermandır*]'?"

"Yes," I responded. "I have heard that."

MUSICKING AS FOOD FOR THE (MELANCHOLIC) SOUL

During an afternoon of playing with four prominent male Turkish classical musicians, our post-musicking conversations over tea turned, because of my line of inquiry, to the relationship between music and healing.

An *ud* player spoke first: "Turks today may mix up the word *melankoli* with depression [*depresyon*]. The word *depresyon* is not a Turkish word. That did not come from us, and I would even believe that as a nation [*millet*] we had no depression before it was imported by the west. Probably to sell their medicines and get fat [e.g., get rich] out of suffering."

A *tanbur* player changed the tone of the discussion, waving the *ud* player away with his hand. He said, "I cannot speak about pharmaceutical issues, but we all know Ottoman music therapy was incredibly successful and that we still benefit from that history as musicians."

"How so?" I asked.

The *tanbur* player continued, "Well, even if we all do not remember the details of healing in *makam*, we remember some fundamental lessons that Ottomans passed down. Making music is a way to keep living despite suffering, whether a person is in bodily or psychological or spiritual pain. I think people in the west think that music helps them forget their problems. That is not how we experience music in Turkey. Making music about suffering is a way to live *with* our problems. We can cope."

The *ney* player joined the conversation.

"Denise, you will hear people in Turkey always saying, '*musiki ruhun gıdasıdır*.' You also have the same expression in English, yes? [*switching to speaking English*] 'The music is the food for the soul' [*switching back to Turkish*] or something like that."

I nodded and said the expression in English.

He went on. "Well you see most Turks do not know that the expression 'music is food for the soul' comes from *Mevlid-i şerif*, some of our most important religious Islamic music. You see, 'music is food for the soul' has two meanings: one clear to most of us and one known only to those of us who ascend [*erenler*, e.g., ones following a religious, generally Sufi, path].

"The first meaning of 'music is food for the soul' is that whatever exists in a person's soul, music will bring it out."

The *kemençe* (short pear-shaped fiddle) player joined in, also speaking directly to me:

"So if a person's soul is happy, music makes him/her feel happy. If a person's soul is joyful, playing music or hearing music will increase his/her joy. If a person suffers from [lit.] 'soul sickness' [*ruh hastası*], the music will bring out more sickness."

"And what about melancholy?" I asked.

The *kemençe* player answered quickly. "If the soul is melancholic, then playing or hearing music will be experienced as melancholy. So you see, not all of our music is melancholy, as you know. It's just that so often people making or listening to music are melancholic. Because it's *in the people*, the music is melancholy. Do you understand?"

I nodded.

The *tanbur* player joined the conversation:

"It's true that if a man is melancholic, especially if he keeps his feeling hidden inside, when I make *taksim* I often can hit a melody [*nağme*] just right to make him cry. This is a good thing. I might not be feeling melancholy in that moment but he is. My music makes him cry. He cries, empties [himself], and feels relaxed. Because he is now relaxed he will become well. Because his soul is now more relaxed his body will start working normally again. My music helped his health, and helped him feel balanced."

The *kanun* player interjected.

"This of course is one possibility. Often 'music is food for the soul' because we musicians are suffering. In that case, the playing of music, putting ourselves into music, nourishes our pain. So sometimes music's meaning can also be really in us. But yes, 'music is food for the soul' is also about listeners. They experience in our music what they bring to our music. I might think my music is about one thing, they have a different experience."

The *kemençe* player joined again:

"That is why music can be a food for all souls in different ways. We could be listening to the same thing. You would get melancholic, I would not, the person listening would get up and start dancing [*göbek attar*]. . . ."

Laughter ensued.

In this insightful conversation, I record the complicated nexus that is musical meaning itself—intersections of musicians' intent, context, listeners' expectations, past histories, spiritual philosophies, ideas of authorship, uncovering the deep instrumentality of music . . .

"But 'music is food for the soul' has a second interpretation we must think about," the *ney* player said as he centered the conversation again on the relationship between music and the soul.

"You see our souls need developing. After all, the Islamic concept *sama'* [listening] is all about using music to develop your soul. And you know, Denise, happiness and laughter and good feelings do not develop the soul. Developing the soul can only come through tests and trials. This is why musicians, especially those of us who understand music as a way to connect to God, will see the music as a kind of suffering. 'Music is food for the soul' could, for me, also be the expression 'suffering is food for the soul.'"

The *ud* player directed his question to the *ney* player:

"But brother [*ağabey*], do not scare Denise. The suffering [*dert*] you talk about in music can also be about happiness and laughter and peace, is it not so?"

The *ney* player responded:

"Why of course. You see, it's all about perspective. Suffering is a good thing. It is a blessing [*nimet*]. It can feel good. It might not feel good to everybody, but it feels good for us. We share that suffering as a community of musicians and it helps us deal with other parts of life."

"Yes, making music is preventative care [*musiki yapmak 'preventative care'dir*]," the *kanun* player added, conjuring a half-Turkish, half-English sentence.

After a few moments of silence, the *ney* player continued:

"You know it is true, most people hear our music in Turkey as melancholic. But that is because they lump in Turkish classical music with folk music and with *arabesk* [lit., "in the style of the Arabs," a popular and controversial urban popular music genre {Stokes 1992}]. The problem with music and melancholy becomes this: it feels so good sometimes that we forget that suffering is supposed to be in balance. You know my son, Denise?"

I nodded.

"Well, he is a teenager [*delikanlı*, lit., 'hot-blooded']. And you know he listens to a lot of your [North American] popular music. Sometimes it is heavy metal. Last week he was telling me about a genre called 'emo.' 'It's all about suffering, Dad,' he told me."

He paused to sip his tea.

"Well, teenagers develop through the suffering of becoming an adult. It makes sense that his music tastes will be about suffering and pain. But the reason I bring up my son is to remind us that not all musical suffering is the same. You know, the kinds of emotions that arise in Turkish classical music should not always be compared. We do not shout or scream or cry in our music. We transform shouting, screaming, crying into beauty."

"You are right, brother. *Elhamdülillah* [praise be to God]," the *ud* player responded.

The *ney* musician smiled, and spoke:

"These are not my ideas. What did Sultan Veled [son of Mevlana Celaluddin Rumi and founder of the Mevlevi Sufi order] write? *Dinle sözümü sana direm özge edadır* [listen to my words, money is a strange manner for you]."

The *kanun* player smiled and continued, speaking:

"*Derviş olana lazım olan aşk-ı hüdadır* [For a *derviş*—Sufi—needs the love of God]. . . ."

And the *ud* player, who had put his tea down, began to pick out the melody as he spoke:

"*Aşıkın nesi var ise maşuka fedadır* [Whatever the lover has is worthy for the Beloved]. Even when all we are given is suffering!"

By the time the *ud* player got to the refrain of the text to this well-known *ilahi*, or religious hymn, we had all gathered our instruments in our hands and sang together:

"*Sema Sefa Cana Şifa Ruha Gıdadır! Sema Sefa Cana Şifa Ruha Gıdadır* [lit., *Sema*—the Mevlevi ecstatic turning ritual—induces *can*—light—into health—*şifa*—which feeds *ruh*, the soul]."

All together, we continued musicking the second part of the song (Example 5.5).

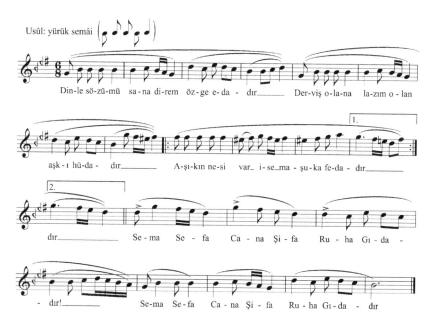

Example 5.5 Transcription of the *ilahi* (religious hymn) "*Dinle Sözümü*" penned by Sultan Veled, son of Mevlana Celaluddin Rumi.

> *Ey sofu bizim sohbetimiz cana şifadır*
> *Bir curamızı nuşedegör derde devadır*
> *Hak ile ezel ettiğimiz ahde vefadır*

Sema Sefa Cana Şifa Ruha Gıdadır
Sema Sefa Cana Şifa Ruha Gıdadır

O devoted one, our conversation feeds [your] life
See our instrument in ecstasy which is the cure
And this [e.g., "our cure is our pain/suffering/grievance"] is our imme-
morial pledge to God

Inducing turning [the *sema* ritual], health in life, and food for the soul
Inducing turning is health in life and food for the soul

By the time we ended the song, the *ney* player shared a final thought before
we packed our instruments and left for the afternoon. "Yes, our cure is our
pain. For is it not good to feel weak when confronted with God? And is it not
pleasurable and beautiful to experience that weakness in music?"

SUFFERING AS REMEDY: WHAT TO TAKE AWAY
FROM MELANCHOLIC MUSICKING

What can we learn from Turkish classical musicians who engage their established terms, ideas, and musicking of melancholy for ostensibly therapeutic
ends? Ottoman physicians crafted music therapy practices over five centuries, believing that hearing music and experiencing vibrations from *makam*
may be positively affect specific illnesses. If we take seriously the statement
dert dermandır ("suffering is remedy"), as many of the musicians I worked
with did, what is the remedy in suffering? In these unique linguistic frames,
suffering and pain and grievance surface as *dert* and reparation and healing
and antidote materialize as *derman*. "Pain and remedy [*dert ve derman*] are
like two faces of a coin," a famous violinist explained to me. "The antidote
comes attached to your grievance [*derdiniz kendi dermanı ile gelirdir*]. The work
is this: you must understand the message that the pain gives you to discover
the remedy."

Musico-medical practices in Turkey ultimately validate melancholy as a
reparative position to be endured. The concept of "positions" from Kleinian
object-relations psychological theory maintains that these states are not
stages that must or should be moved beyond. As a kind of interjection, melancholy is a position to be lived in as a site of potentiality. Considering melancholy as a position to be inhabited is reparative in that it recognizes how
musicians may strive for senses of belonging that do not ignore the hardships
or obstacles in life. The position of melancholy is itself a tolerance of the loss
that underlies musicians' sense experiences, forms of self-fashioning, and the
structuring and monitoring of their communal boundaries.

Contemporary musicians' articulations of melancholy tell us a story about inhabiting the boundary between ease and dis-ease and accounting for loss. At the philosophical center, Islam validates these positions and offers individuals ideological and musical tools to endure and inhabit their world in this way. The sheikh quoted at the beginning of this chapter contended that dis-ease is given by God. I suggest that one of the central reasons this sheikh's healing practices may "work" is because he positions illness or dis-ease as *nimet*, or blessings, that will cleanse you of your ego and raise your spiritual state (*manevi makamı*). The individuals and communities this sheikh serves believe that if God loves you, God will provide you with suffering. We can recall the *hadith* or discourse of the Prophet Muhammed that states, "whoever knows his/her Soul knows God." Suffering souls know God, they feel their separation from God, and these feelings locate them as knowledge-bearers. In such a community, melancholy may be a condition for dialogue with God. I suggest that this dialogue can be heard if we listen in. The revered Ottoman poet Niyazî Mısrî (1618–1694) perhaps expressed it best when he wrote:

> *Derman aradım derdime*
> *Derdim bana derman imiş*
>
> I searched for a cure for my suffering
> When [in reality] my pain was the cure

Conclusion

THEORIZING AFFECT IN MUSICS AND BEYOND

In our focus on music practices and our investment in ethnographic method-ologies, ethnomusicologists are uniquely situated to analyze how socialization emerges as processes of learning how to feel and express that feeling in sound. The question "who am I?" already alludes to a belief that specific collections of feelings should be had and that some affective modalities are understood, articulated, and lived as the correct way to inhabit the world. Studying feelings that are meant to be had is a central theme of this book, where melancholy emerges as reparative, healing, pleasurable, community making, and spiritu-ally rewarding for present-day Turkish classical musicians. In this conclusion, I share thoughts about what ethnomusicologists in particular can contribute to transdisciplinary debates about affect, and lay out a number of concerns that emerged in my own endeavor to engage ethnographic ways of knowing to speak with and against theories of affect and emotion.

While we are beyond the so-called "affective turn" in the humanities that emerged in the early 1980s, the literature today we canonize in the linguistic utterance "affect theory" continues to offer much to music and sound stud-ies. In engaging reworkings, destabilizations, and co-assemblings based on the work of Spinoza (see Ruddick 2010, Gregg and Seigworth 2010), Tomkins (1962), Sedgwick (2003 and 2007), Thrift (2000, 2004, 2008), Massumi (1996 and 2002), Bergson (see Saji 2004 and Watson 2003), and Deleuze and Guattari (1987 [1980]), we are presented with theories that describe a realm of experiencing that is preverbal and preconscious. *Intensification* is a key word in affect theory, as bodies and objects circulate in space and induce felt sensa-tions that escape immediate perception. Affect theory trades explanatory tools for description—and thus may be why ethnomusicologists are so inspired to grapple with affective entanglements: affect theorists study objects that are reportedly preverbal, making it seem an immediately useful applicable theory to account for sound, musics, and musical practices.

Affect theory is, in part, about destabilizing the discursive domains that divide disciplines, an aspect that proves challenging when we delve beyond terminology and investigate the *assumptions* that underlie different theories. Affect theory is one—but only one—important path for studying messy fields of feeling that are simultaneously central to sense experience yet inaudible in many methodologies. Other theories, from psychology, anthropology, neuroscience, and cognitive studies to philosophy, gender studies, cultural studies, sociology, political science, and music studies, offer distinct approaches to the study of affect and emotion. In my own experiences mapping out these different theoretical trajectories, I have struggled with the taxonomies and literatures that tend to treat affects, moods (especially Heidegger's concept of *Stimmung*), sentiments, feelings, and emotions as interchangeable and overlapping. Every scholar—and I include myself in this critique—seems to need to reinvent the wheel because of this messiness, a response that is productive for creating new ways of asking questions but not always as useful for engaging beneficial methodological tools that already exist.

Let us examine relevant works by historians and literary scholars as an example of this working and reworking—considering Stearns and Stearns's work on "emotionology" (1985), studied by Harré as "emotives" (1986), renamed as "emotional regimes" by Reddy (2001), and most recently revised by Flatley as "affective mapping" (2008). These taxonomies all indicate that particular feelings are constructs experienced by specific communities in different linguistic regions or historic eras in response to particular political and social contexts.

Social constructionist scholars from anthropology and gender studies have considered situated "feeling rules" (Hochschild 1983) and "affective discourses" (Abu-Lughod and Lutz 1990, Lupton 1998) that shape what kinds of affects and emotions are representative of what Rosenwein names "emotional communities" (2006) or what Walkerdine brands "affective communities" (2009 and 2010). Utilizing a wide array of methodologies, these scholars argue that emotions *are themselves* that which binds a collective together (exemplary works here are Abu-Lughod 1986 and 2005, Berlant 2008 and 2011, Lutz 1998, and Rosaldo 1984). These perspectives have solidified a foundational frame that early articulations of affect theory cannot fully account for—namely, how affect is *primarily about othering* and boundary making. In identifying how dominant hegemonic social forms and norms work through repetition, we come to understand that is through coercion and domestication that worlds materialize and boundaries are produced. Affect, in other words, connects us to conditions of subordination.

The perspectives outlined thus far—affect theory and social constructivist and historical perspectives—do coalesce, with some shared roots in Marxist theory, in assuming affect as an object and the body as object, and focusing on the circulation and often the stickiness of objects in collision with other objects. Music making of course includes objects—instruments, bodies, texts, recordings, and other sonic commodities—that "involve the transformation of others into objects of feeling" (S. Ahmed 2004: 11). Yet throughout this book I have argued against a perspective that would psychologize or individualize emotions as something "we have" or that moves from "outside in." Rather, emotions differentiate the boundary between the "I" and other objects in our social worlds. I have utilized the brilliant work of Sara Ahmed and her model of the "sociality of emotions"; Ahmed suggests that emotions are crucial to the very constitution of the psychic and the social as objects, a process that suggests that the "objectivity" of the psychic and social is an effect rather than a cause (S. Ahmed 2004: 10). Yet Ahmed's model—rooted in the importance of the bodily boundary and border—is not necessarily applicable to ethnography, because of her focus on emotion as a disembodied force that circulates in texts, not located in the practices of specific social actors, and not necessarily rooted in diverse bodily experiences in performance. Furthermore, my work has resisted tendencies in scholarship—of affect/emotion and of Islamic communities—that reify notions of individuality and assume autonomy.

Beyond the issues of authors defining "affect" and "emotion" in diverse genealogical ways, these few perspectives I have thus far underscored also issue the fundamental problem for music and sound studies scholars who may be tempted to adopt multiple approaches. Even as these theories share a focus on becoming and object-ness, they do not share the same assumptions about the importance of power or difference. Please note that I believe that combining theories that have different assumptions about affect/emotion/feeling, the body, the idea of individual and collective (self-)fashionings, object-ness, and interaction is *interestingly syncretistic, not necessarily contradictory*. But we need to take care. We need to know that we are dancing through different terrains not just in terms of topic, method, and approach, but in terms of basic assumptions and research goals. Let me briefly outline five of the concerns I have focused on in shaping my own research on affective practice in a unique community of highly nostalgic, intensely idiosyncratic, and diverse musicians in Turkey. In parsing out and combining various approaches to affect and emotion, I take care to avoid the following "wrong turns" (Wetherell 2012) that I believe may be inherent in the very utterance of "affect" and "emotion" itself in scholarship on music and sound.

First, the faulty division between the biological and the cultural or the psychological and the social is a bifurcation that ethnomusicologist Judith Becker's work on trance and trancing in diverse cultural and historical contexts has complicated and challenged (2004). On the empiric end, scholars engaging Darwin's physiological accounts and the James-Lange theory (which outlines emotions as resulting from physiological reactions to events) frame emotional objects and affective processes in terms of the basic emotions that dictate that bodily responses give rise to affective states. On the cultural or social end, scholars may tend to neglect critical bodily responses that are generative to the experience, expression, and voicing of emotion.

We may all agree that we must reintroduce the energetic, the sensual, and the physical in humanities and social sciences research, a task that brings me to my second concern: in an attempt to account for the transmission (Brennan 2004) or contagion (Reicher 2001) of affect in group settings, the physical and diverse instantiations of difference in bodies and what those differences might index are absent. Assumptions about human universality may be uncritically presented. Diversities in gender, able-bodiedness, age, race, ethnicity, and class are erased. Of course, embodiment is central in structuring and validating musicians' and audiences' affective attachments. Individuals' bodies become customized through inculcated cultural processes in a kind of growing or "pruning" process (Rose 2004). Yet as ethnographers of musicians and listeners and dancers, I argue we should not uphold the sameness in the utterance of "body" used by theorists of affect and emotion. While the study of autonomic and central nervous systems provide us with significant normative insight into general neurological human responses of arousal, we are also deeply observant of difference in diverse individuals' sense experiences. We can challenge scholarship that ignores neurodiversity and the experiences of differently-abled individuals, that prioritizes and normalizes able-bodiedness, or that validates specific ethnocentric perspectives of embodiment. Here, ethnomusicologists can intervene by resisting the collapsing of difference in bodies and in listening through ethnography.

A third wrong turn in flattening diverse theories of affect and emotion is the elision between approaching affect *as an object* and affect *as a process*. Meshing social constructivist and philosophical works on affect, which consider affect as a becoming, potential, and virtual (Massumi 1996, Clough 2009, Thrift 2008), is a significant challenge. It is easy to lose track of *how* these affective objects and processes function—or what these processes sound like—in terms of power, institutions, and the struggles of real agents in specific contexts. Ethnomusicologists intimately know that ontological concerns are not outside of violence, domestication, resistance, negotiation, and coercion.

Furthermore, we cannot collapse theories that situate affect-as-object with affect-as-process without detailed consideration of phenomenology. Here I turn to Harry Berger's excellent work, which lays out a method to approach emotion as practice and understand how individuals can take a "stance" in expressive culture (2009), and Tony Perman's important work with Peircean semiotics that can pinpoint how emotion can go wrong in performance (2010).

We should also venture issues of reception, potentially alongside the work of scholars in music cognition such as David Huron (2006, 2010, 2011). Yet as ethnomusicologists, we know that musicians can *appeal* to emotions through their performances *without necessarily producing them* in individual listeners. In this book, I strongly advocate a practice-oriented approach to the study of affect, wherein we explicitly interrogate how particular people claim that they actively recruit and deploy distinct sounds or musical patterns to make themselves, and potentially their listeners, "feel." It is possible to oscillate, on the one hand, between considering how musicians speak about music as a thing "to act" on us (*afficere*, whence affect) or "to move" us (*emovere*, whence emotion) and, on the other hand, to devoting sustained attention to affect as a practice—as something musicians "do" (see my oscillations between sonic melancholy as object and as practice in chapters 4 and 5). Yet instead of prioritizing the question "what is affect?" we must first ask "what is affect *for*?" Ethnomusicologists are poised to productively argue against sonicist perspectives that ascribe agency to music and portray sound or aesthetics as sentient beings in anthropomorphic terms. Hence the need for future work to shift focus to the original agent, the persons and peoples who sense, enact, transmit, perform, and repetitively practice affect.

A potential fourth area of caution for the study of affect and emotion in music is our tendency to assume the individual and autonomous selfhood. In chapter 3, I focus on the specific decades in Ottoman Turkey when the term *virtüöz* was adopted from the French *virtuosité*, an appropriation that coincided with the birth of the idea of the autonomous individual, or (Tr.) *birey*. Before this point in the mid-twentieth century, Turks had not fully conceptualized selfhood in terms of autonomy per se. If a music scholar investigating affect for Turkish musicians in and around these historical areas is to make a significant contribution, she must check her assumptions about individual selfhood and seek other epistemological terrains. In the case of contemporary Turkish classical musicians, autonomous individuality falls away with an understanding of the importance of the dyadic master-apprentice relationship and one's place in the musicians' music lineage. Rhizomatic genealogies and communal selfhood surface as the primary means of identification over individual autonomy. What understandings about selfhood and subjectivity might the study of affective practice in other musical communities yield?

That question brings me to my fifth concern about broadly studying affect and emotion in the humanities: I believe we as ethnomusicologists can significantly intervene in theoretical slippages by utilizing our ethnographic tools in the realm of language, naming, and translation. Consider this: as affect theorists seek to describe the preverbal and preconscious somatic realm of experiencing, they choose musical metaphors to describe the workings of affect. Not so different from biomedical textbooks and publications that talk about body systems needing to be "in harmony," affect theory abounds with terminology such as "attunement," "enactment," "sympathetic," "consonance," and "vibration." While it is easy to cut and paste these approaches in a study of music and musicians simply because affect theorists use sonic metaphors, we must resist this impulse and first question the frameworks generating the metaphor. So often scholars gravitate toward such metaphors in explaining terminology because they assume sonic metaphors—like "music"—exist in an immaterial, ethereal, or alternate space of aesthetics. Ethnomusicologists would not necessarily agree that musics or sounds themselves convey a preconscious, intermediary space, and we should loudly amplify this critique in the humanities.

Yet my intervention here about language and naming in English-language academic debates is more far-reaching. I encourage all of us to take care with our valuation of theories of affect, emotion, and feeling in English, German, and French at the expense of local epistemological and ontological structures and discourses. Ethnomusicologists already have extensive methods for studying musical meaning. We take care when translating texts and contexts, and when we modify cosmological ontologies for normative secular academic discourses. We specialize in calling assumptions about feelings and emotions into question in and through listening.

And we have excellent ethnomusicological works to draw on for inspiration. In her exceptional book *Fado Resounding: Affective Politics and Urban Life* (2013), Lila Ellen Gray analyzes the way *fado amador*, a Portuguese music genre and amateur music practice, circulates and transforms affect to render history and "soulfulness" public. Through an "ethnography of the sonorous" and with careful attention to the dialectic between listing and voicing, Gray traces the counters of genre and feeling, place-making, and memory. Ethnomusicologists interested in emotion and affect must also look to one of the foundational texts of our field, Steven Feld's *Sound and Sentiment: Birds, Weeping, Poetics, and Song in Kaluli Expression* (first published in 1982). Feld explores the relationship between the cultural system of the Kaluli community in Papua New Guinea as inextricably linked to and informed by the meaningful sounds that surround them (poetics, song, weeping, birds). Feld offers us an exemplary model of how "expressive modalities are culturally constituted by performance codes that both actively communicate deeply felt sentiments and reconfirm mythic principles" (1990 [1982]: 14).

In my own work, my insistence on evaluating the melancholies purposefully cultivated by Turkish classical musicians as affective practice and as a modality (in the quintessential definition of modality as a path and process) is not drawn from western scholarship on affect/emotion/feeling but rather from music ethnography itself. Despite my wide reading across many fields, prioritizing people and experience-centered ethnography required a necessary decentering the assumptions generated by western epistemological frameworks. Of course, I engage these well-known theoretical understandings of affect/emotion/feeling to help me translate musicians' melancholic musicking in the normative linguistic frameworks available to me as a native English-speaking academic. Nor do I suggest that contemporary Sufi-influenced onto-logical frameworks sedimented in urban centers of Turkey offer an alternative to the epistemologies generated in "western" frameworks and debates. That would be the wrong turn of essentialism and orientalism. However, I do suggest that our commonly-used theoretical structures and ontological assumptions are themselves not expansive enough to provide the critical explanatory or descriptive power we currently need to understand diverse affective practices. By provincializing normative theoretical frameworks on affect and emotion and by prioritizing our ethnographic evidence, ethnomusicologists can insightfully attend to multi-sensorial experiences that have yet to meet with a theoretical becoming, and attune to vibrations not yet sensed in the diverse scholastic terrains within which we wander.

BRINGING THE RHIZOMES OF TURKISH CLASSICAL
MUSICIANS TO BEAR BEYOND THE ACADEMY

Let us return to the farewell greeting some Turkish classical musicians say in parting that opened this book: *Allah derdini arttırsın,* "May God increase your pain/suffering." In the interviews that formed the content of this book on melancholic modalities, a few Turkish classical musicians ended our discussions with a famous line from the Qur'an, "He increases in His creatures that which He wills" (35:1). In referencing God as the ultimate cause of melancholy—and in voicing the Qur'an as the conclusory archival source in an interview postlude—these Turkish classical musicians rhizomatically root their affective practice in spiritual discourse. Why are the tenets and practices of Islam such present rhizomes in musicians' melancholic modalities?

The Arabic word for divinity (*ilah*)—the root of *Allah* (lit., "the divine")—may itself come from the Arabic root w-l-h, which connotes sadness, melancholy, and sighing. Multiple *hadith*-s of the Prophet Muhammed and verses of the Qur'an instruct believers that God created humans in order to be known by them. Since the thirteenth century, Islamic philosophers like Ibn al-'Arabi have written about "a God whose secret is sadness, melancholy, and nostalgia that arises from God's aspiration to know himself in the beings who manifest God's being" (Corbin 1969: 94; see also Almond 2003). If God's secret is melancholy that results from God's desire to be known, the secret that manifests among Turkish classical musicians is that their melancholic musicking is itself an endeavor to know God.

This book tells a story of artists—in a particular national context and situated period of time—who engage local Sunni and Sufi Islamic discourses and leverage experiences of pain and suffering into creative power, deploy loss as a kind of musical meaning itself, and render melancholic musicking as cathartis and as pleasurable. I pull apart the constitutive elements of present-day

Turkish classical musicians' melancholic affective practice: loss narratives that highlight musicians' celebration and fabrication of an idyllic Ottoman past and the mourning of an impossibility of return (chapter 1), spiritual ideologies of melancholy as a necessary effect of separation from the divine (chapter 2), individual self and collective understandings gained in the emotional and musical transmission practices of master to apprentice in specific musical lineages (chapter 3), embodied performances, tearful experiences, and gendered practices that Turkish classical musicians articulate as specific to their genre (chapter 4), and musicians' present-day reparative practices that draw on Ottoman musico-medicinal beliefs that melancholic sounds ultimately heal (chapter 5). This book is about coming to grips with Turkish classical musicians' philosophy of how one should experience suffering with sound.

These stories about melancholic affective practices from a unique musical community in Turkey may invite some readers to consider expanding the affective modalities that our own diverse social lives engender. As I complete this book, deeply aware and critical of my multiple intersecting racial, linguistic, employment, citizenship, and class privileges, it is hard not to link the stories I tell with what scholars observe as a problematic, sustained investment in "happiness" in neoliberalism (Berlant 2011, S. Ahmed 2010, Ehrenreich 2010). Meditating on these different approaches to value—which I feel press on me intimately as an ethnographer of Turkish musics who has an eagle on her passport—I think critically about my own national community's invested insistence on feeling good and searching for happiness. Perhaps rather than "how can I be happy?" we might gain insight from Turkish classical musicians' valuing of melancholy and consider asking, instead, "what kinds of suffering am I willing to invite in and sustain for what I value and give importance to in life?"

For even if we maintain that happiness is our ultimate goal, any search for happiness is not without hardship, struggle, and pain. Turkish classical musicians are incredibly articulate about the mobile oscillation between happiness and sadness, pleasure and pain. My field notes are covered with statements from musicians pointing to this dialectic, such as, "for us, even entertainment has melancholy and grief [*bizde eğlencede bile bir hüzün ve keder vardır*]."

Melancholy is possible only in the presence of love, which confers meaning to loss, pain, and suffering. Turkish classical musicians do not "feel melancholy" all of the time. Yet they have the multiple names and terms for "melancholy." Melancholies are richly, diversely, numerously named in Turkish and in Ottoman because of their uniqueness inside the full spectrum of emotional life. Thus in the larger emotional fabric of musicians' experiences, melancholy surfaces as an affective practice that is sustained in forms of joy and happiness.

As a whole, this book centers on what Turkish classical musicians claim melancholy does for them, focusing on how they enact iterations of melancholy in musicking and listening, and how their melancholic affective practices shape and reflect their understandings of themselves in contemporary political life. Music making produces sound in acoustic space, supported by social quieting. Musics frame a shared social space in which musicians communally make melancholy an external object to deal with in and through sound. Making melancholy musically is safe—you feel sad and, through musical turns, tensions, releases, and conclusions, you find in musical melancholy not just a metaphor but also a tool to cope with the world. Sounding melancholy, for musicians, happens a temporally unique and liminal space that allows for a moving forward and working through in *makam* modulations and momentum. Melancholic modalities not only teach musicians how to deal with suffering in life, but also render that life spiritually rich.

Modality denotes an approach, a way of grappling with difficult things. My focus on melancholic modalities offers music scholars the theoretical modalities of rhizomatic analysis and bi-aurality. I have discovered that the only meaningful way to understand affect in the lives of Turkish classical musicians is by accepting the rhizomatic nature of affective practices themselves. In this book, I seized on one prominent offshoot of musical meaning for musicians—that of melancholy—and attempted to lead readers through a nest of settled worldviews and life paths that allow me to explain why and how melancholy comes into meaning in sound and in life. It is critical that you know that there are other shoots I could have grabbed for.

Yet is also imperative to view the book itself as a rhizome: it conceals as much of the rhizomatic nature of melancholic modalities as it uncovers. The book is also a commodity: like the rhizomatic reeds that are cut, transported, crafted into *ney*-s, and sold, the text in your hands (and its author) have been rendered objects of circulation and commodification. As the author of this rhizomatic book, I acknowledge the inherent danger in my focus on melancholic modalities: ethnomusicologists and musicians alike may be surprised or offended by my insistent focus on melancholy and believe that I problematically compact the rich affective geographies of all Turkish classical musicians into a singular category. That would be an unfortunate reading of this book. I instead hope readers find that this book maintains a focused approach on melancholic modalities to ultimately unweave and follow the deeply embedded assumptions about sound, separation, piety, ethics, and humanity that inform musicians' practices.

I also acknowledge that some readers may hear in this book a prescription for acknowledging and working with suffering in our own lives. While I myself have found some of the selected stories I share to be reparative and generative, I do not view myself as a comfortable or confident advocate of melancholic modalities as a path, if it could be interpreted in that way. Perhaps this is because I am highly attuned to my commitment to equity and to the weight of genuinely representing others' voices, listening habits, and beliefs. I believe that readers acknowledge my primary appreciation of melancholic modalities as themselves a practice of beauty and as a particularly artistic life path. I acknowledge that I made particular decisions in the writing of this book that you, as readers, will take and make yours in a myriad of positive, negative, and neutral ways. Recognizing this two-way street offers me a chance to celebrate vulnerability: the exposed openness of the musicians with whom I work as well as my own.

For indeed, selves can be rhizomatic, too. Parts of selfhood may be exposed beyond the surface of the water, while the rich weaving of breadth, movement, and growth continues in unforeseen directions beyond immediate view. That is certainly the case with *arundo donax,* the scientific term for the giant cane *kamış* (reed) that, after being cut, bent, burned, and shaped by a master's hands, will become the *ney* reed flute (see chapter 2).

I once traveled to the Antep region of southern Turkey specifically to watch the process of gathering *arundo donax.* I waded deep in muck through freshwater marshes where my companion and guide selected and cut reeds to sell to *ney* makers in Istanbul. Watching the process of the *ney*'s first separation from the reed bed, I realized I had traveled two days on a bus with the belief that I would myself gather some deep insight when my skin hit the bottom of the reed bed. I expected a transformational experience, and instead just experienced. The reeds we gathered to be made into *ney*-s did not alter my appreciation of the rhizomatic as much as the immensity of the reeds that were left behind did. Every *ney* I heard after my experience in the wetlands brought the sense memory of standing within rhizomes and knowing that anything that is cut can bear witness only to a part of what it once was.

While this book may be a material object representing a kind of melancholy in and of itself, I have publicly performed melancholic modalities in other ways. I acknowledge especially my relationship with my teachers and their families and lineages: in interviews with other musicians I was aware of how my knowledge was tested and how my questions were evaluated as representative of larger—and often opposing—musical worldviews. There is much in the realm of affective practices that I was subjected to that I could not take in and make my own. This reaction is understandable, of course: almost all ethnographers, and almost all students, may find particular observations or lessons contrary to their own instincts. These moments allow us to both question the lesson and interrogate the disjuncture of opposing assumptions clashing: we see in discord the boundaries of diverse ontological domains.

Let us remember Mevlana's poignant metaphor that "the wound is the place where light enters you." This is not a book about music per se; it is a book that prioritizes musicians' lives, beliefs, narratives, music making, and experiences. The regarded composer and musician Mesud Cemil (1902–1963) described his father, master *tanbur* (long-necked lute) musician and composer

Tanburi Cemil Bey (1873–1916) in terms that privileged his humanity and character over his virtuosic musicking. Mesud Cemil said, "My father's moral code was superior to his music [*babamın ahlakı musikisinden üstündü*]." During my fieldwork, I observed the esteemed *neyzen* (reed-flute master) Niyazi Sayın (b. 1927) refer to his renowned teacher Halil Dikmen (1906–1964) in the same terms ("*hocamın ahlakı musikisinden üstündü*").

Throughout this book, I have considered the question "what is melancholy *for?*" in terms of a model of the sociality of emotion, neoliberal political life in present-day Turkey, spiritual labor, genealogies of history, bi-aurality, processes of embodiment, and in the reparative practice and maintenance of psychological health. However, many musicians' investment in *ahlak*—moral code and ethics—over musical endeavors points to another critical interpretation of the social work of melancholies in music. Musicians' melancholic affective practice is an integral part of their moral character from which they produce and make sense of sound.

In melancholy—and in loss, suffering, pain, separation, joy, and ecstasy—our bodily boundaries are made porous and opened to others (again, "the wound is the place where light enters you"). Melancholy softens us, exposes us, and allows us the opportunity to be together with, respond to, and witness others' vulnerabilities. In musicking melancholy and cultivating melancholic modalities as artists, musicians offer a sonic experience wherein they and their listeners safely and openly respond with empathy and with sympathy to others through the sound worlds of music and musicking. As pain, suffering, and loss require labors that Turkish classical musicians believe they must sustain throughout life, melancholy surfaces as a condition for dialogue between musicians making music. A *neyzen* once chuckled and told me, "One thing I know in this life is that the best musicians are also the best human beings. We already have holes in our hearts and are full of empathy. It's a gift to make suffering into something beautiful in sound."

A gift it is, indeed.

NOTES

INTRODUCTION

1. At a practical musical level, I further justify my focus on Turkish classical musicians' melancholic modalities in part through an understanding that the musicians making Turkish classical music are often involved with crafting other genres. Most of my consultants have had musical lives outside of the genre of Turkish classical music. Here are three short examples from some of my close consultants: one Turkish classical musician performed folk music in his youth on a different instrument from his current primary instrument; another played light art music at *gazino* entertainment spaces and at state-sponsored brothel houses; another still performed Turkish classical music while composing popular music sung by pop artists such as Bülent Ersoy, Yıldız Tilbe, and Ajda Pekkan. These musicians often do not parade these other musical associations publically, since performing Turkish classical music comes with a particular prestige and cultural capital. Musically speaking, because of their deep knowledge of *makam* (melodic modal systems), Turkish music theory, and their fluid ability to improvise (*taksim etmek*) on the spot and produce new musical ideas, I suggest that modern Turkish classical musicians may occupy a particularly privileged musical position from which they easily transfer their skills and knowledge into other musical genres and discursive realms. Of course, this example also proves the fluidity between music genres we tend to present as fixed and disparate (see my article on transmission, Gill-Gürtan 2011, for a case study).

2. One exceptional example is anthropologist Yael Navaro-Yashin's study of melancholic geographies in postwar Cyprus (2012). She studies Turkish-Cypriot dialect and usage of the term *maraz*, which refers to "a state of depression, deep and inescapable sadness and unease" (2012: 160). In the specific local and context of Northern Cyprus, Turkish residents experience *maraz* as the unrecognizable grief in the impossibility of naming the "lost" people of their community, Greek Cypriots positioned as the other so-called enemy. For the community in Northern Cyprus with which Navaro-Yashin works, melancholy is experienced through the geography of ruins and ruination—the lingering presence of the abandoned houses and discarded objects of the Greeks—as "a loss of a sense of moral integrity" (Navaro-Yashin 2012: 174).

   Importantly, *maraz* was not a term that surfaced in my ethnography, precisely because the melancholies circulating in Turkish classical musicians' discourses are seen as reparative and carry a sense of hope, unlike *maraz* which expresses multisensorial states of non-reparative anxiety and discomfort.

3. European language texts on melancholy over many centuries oscillate between the terms *melancholy, melancholia,* and *melancholic state.* Broadly speaking, *melancholy* in the long history of European works emerged as a vernacular term denoting "sadness." *Melancholia,* on the other hand, referred to the structural identification predicated on the loss of self. Freud's 1917 "Mourning and Melancholia" marks the watershed moment in western history, philosophy, and psychoanalysis that scholars today consider the break between previous understandings of melancholy and the modern birth of a psychologized discourse that would be eventually reworked and named clinical depression. For English-language works on the rich and distinct pre-Freudian (western) history of melancholy, please see Feld (2011), Radden (2000), Flatley (2008), Bowring (2008), and Horwitz and Wakefield (2007). See chapter 5 for a more thorough discussion of the developments and treatments of melancholy with music in western European, early Arab, and Ottoman practices.

4. Of course, there is an enormous diversity of understandings, practices, and beliefs about the role of melancholy or its effect in western epistemological history, topics that I do not cover here.

5. Archeological analysis can be seen as a historically based study of what the discourses within the archive allow to be stated authoritatively. The archive is the system that "governs the appearance of statements as unique events" (Foucault 1972 [1969]: 129). Archeology is the analysis of this system of unwritten rules that produces, organizes, and distributes the *statement* (authorized utterance) as it occurs in an *archive* (an organized body of statements). Archeology helps us to explore the networks of what is said, and what can be seen in a set of social arrangements: in the conduct of an archeology, one finds out something about the visible in "opening up" statements and something about the statement in the "opening up visibilities" (Foucault 1972 [1969]: 91–92). Archeology is thus Foucault's metaphor for his approach to analyzing knowledge itself, a sort of critical epistemology of epistemologies.

6. In his 1927 *Being and Time* (*Sein und Zeit*), Martin Heidegger argues for consideration of being in terms of *Dasein* ("existence," "being-there") and *in-der-Welt-sein* ("being-in-the-world"). Heidegger's formulation of being in terms of "being-in-the-world" places the observer in the realm of that which is observed, which added great insight to the legacy of philosophic inquiry of ontology and epistemology. Heidegger, in short, shows that ontology itself is inextricably linked with understanding. Linking a study of affect/emotion to these philosophical trajectories makes most sense in considering Heidegger's concept *Stimmung,* which can mean "mood" but also "attunement" (see also Rice 1996).

Following a tradition of inquiry inspired by Heidegger's concept of *Dasein,* Hans-Georg Gadamer claims that the field of philosophical hermeneutics should not be defined by textual interpretation but instead by a focus on the deeper processes involved in understanding itself (1992). Gadamer argues for a dialogic view of understanding, highlighting that understanding is a relational way of being.

For my purposes, there are a number of key concepts in Gadamer's philosophical reflections on dialectic understanding that are useful. First and foremost is Gadamer's idea of play in dialogic understanding, a dialogic play between self and other, tradition and future, question and supposition. Such play opens up the possibility for the productive interplay of subjectivities that ultimately create new types of understanding. At the same time, following Heidegger, Gadamer maintains that understanding necessarily includes self-understanding, through the form of encounter. Such dialectic understanding, rooted in self-understanding, allows us to potentially come to understand the other. Gadamer claims that understanding "is not an act of subjectivity, but proceeds from the commonality that binds us to a tradition" (1992: 293). See chapter 3 for the challenges my work poses to scholarship that assumes individual selfhood and autonomy.

7. The Latin *affectus* is the past participle of *afficere*, to act upon. From *ad* ("to") and *facere* ("to do").

8. Darwin's understanding of emotions as evolutionary is a key perspective in this regard, as the belief that being emotional signals an unreasonable state (i.e., weak and often femininized) tends to be an idea that still circulates today. For Darwin, emotions are narrated as a lingering aspect of human primitiveness, and understood as less important than reason and thought (1904). Affect and emotions are therefore bound up with the securing of social hierarchy. René Descartes, David Hume, and William James continued with theorizing emotions as tied primarily to bodily sensations, whereby emotions are understood as the feeling of bodily change. Descartes' work in particular illuminates how feelings take the shape of contact we have with objects (1985). Hume's work showcases how emotions impress us and upon us: experiencing emotions is also an experiencing of surfaces (1964: 75). Another trajectory in the scholarship on affect and emotion is based on the ideas of Aristotle as refashioned by Sartre. This view holds that emotions are tied primarily to cognition. Thus emotions are not reducible to bodily sensations, as they involve appraisals, judgments, and attitudes (Sartre 1962: 9).

   Increasingly since the 1990s, poststructural and social constructivist analyses of emotion draw significantly on Marxism. Marx furthers our understanding that the circulation of objects of emotion involves the transformation of others into objects of feeling. Marx's work shows that emotions work as a form of affective value that can accumulate over time: feelings become fetishes, qualities that seem to reside in objects only through an erasure of the history of their production and circulation (1976: 248–254). Emotion does not reside *in* an object or a sign, but is an *effect* of the circulation between objects and signs. In the context of Turkey, particular affective circuits initiate emotional responses in part because of extreme social coherence and histories of articulation (as argued in this book and Stokes 2010).

9. While some scholars work from modified "basic emotions" approaches, it is increasingly more common to see scholars working from different conceptions (e.g., the "arousal-valence" theory, whereby different emotions are thought to be characterized by different combinations of intensity ["arousal"] and pleasantness ["valence"]). For an overview of various approaches to basic emotion in music, see Juslin and Sloboda (2011).

10. For key works that demonstrate how affect and emotion attach us to conditions of subordination, see especially Judith Butler (1997), Wendy Brown (2001), and Lauren Berlant (1998, 2008).

11. Foucault's conceptualization of discourse and development of discourse analysis illuminate the workings of power. Instead of considering that language simply reflects an underlying reality, in *The Archeology of Knowledge* (1972), Foucault asserts that discourse determines the reality that we perceive. For Foucault, discourse is the site where these struggles are acted out. He claims that "as history constantly teaches us, discourse is not simply that which translates struggles or systems of domination, but is the thing for which and by which there is a struggle" (Foucault 1981: 52–53). Agents enact discourses and participate in their circulation.

Discourse is not simply a set of statements that have some coherence. Foucault calls us to understand discourse as the exercise of power, claiming that discourses proliferate as agents and institutions attempt to gain or evade power (1981). Not everyone is able to make or circulate statements, or have his or her statements taken seriously by others. Some statements are more authorized than others, in that they are more associated with those in positions of power or with institutions.

Foucault sees power as a set or web of relations and strategies dispersed and circulated throughout society and enacted at every moment of interaction (1978). It therefore becomes necessary to analyze the way that institutions operate and the way that they are constrained by the demands and resistance of individuals within the organization as well as individuals and groups outside it. As Foucault's notion of discourse concerns realms of knowledge creation and production, knowledge is inextricably linked with power. Discourse is essentially deployed in the struggle for power.

12. I do not focus attention in this book at audience reception except in areas where musicians articulate the ways they attempt to elicit melancholic responses in listeners (see chapter 4 for musicians' explanations of how they appeal to the emotions of listeners in singing). Focusing on musical or acoustic cues that evoke melancholy in listeners would require extensive cognitive assessments of the stimulus and music object used on one hand, and in-depth sociocultural analysis of diverse modes of listening on the other (see Huron 2006, 2010, and 2011; Crowder et al. 1991 and Crowder 1985; Balkwill et al. 2004; Davies 1997; Juslin and Laukka 2004). Above all, a dissection of sonic material to interrogate particular ("universal") responses would, in my view, problematically reify music objects, locating that which produces emotion in sound, and assume able-bodied structures of acoustic distribution.

13. Pierre Bourdieu's examination of the relationship between social institutions, systems of thought, and formations of material and symbolic power illuminates the workings of diverse types of capital uncovered in structuration (1993). Bourdieu's frameworks have come to be known as practice theory, as his work provides a productive theory for the social analysis of cultural practices. He examines the way in which unequal power relations, which remain unrecognized and therefore are considered legitimate, are embedded in everyday life in and through cultural practices (2002 [1979]).

Practice theory, as a critique, accounts for asymmetrical power relations, as it explicates the hegemonic constraints and effects of institutional violence on individuals and their cultural practices. Important here is Bourdieu's conceptualization of agency, understood as the capacity for human beings to act through their goals and interests. Through musical practices, for example, agents continually negotiate and renegotiate power and social relations that organize and structure their society and community.

Of central concern to ethnomusicologists is Bourdieu's theoretical conception of *habitus*, which can be defined as normative aspects of behavior, or collective habits or dispositions, that generate practices and perceptions. Habitus not only recreates "common sense" behaviors; it is a product of history as well and also produces history through individual and collective practices (Bourdieu 1990 [1980]: 52–65). As Bourdieu sees habitus as the result of a long process of inculcation, cultural and symbolic practices can be understood as vehicles for the production and reproduction of specific social and power relations (for examples from ethnomusicology, see Becker 2004, Buchanan 2006, and Turino 2000).

14. A few of these musicians, excited about the project, took it upon themselves to outline the organization and structure of this very book. Some musicians insisted that my book must focus on the importance of how they make listeners hear in music. Other musicians would agree with my Turkish translations of "affective practice" when describing melancholy, but would prefer if I organized my book around melancholy in the Ottoman poetry that makes up the bulk of lyrics in Turkish classical vocal music. A third camp of consultants believed my entire introduction should just be a careful exegesis of the Qur'anic mentions of melancholy, grief, suffering, and sadness, as the Qur'an is the only primary text in Islam. A final collection of consultants urged me to shift my focus away from melancholy and onto love and lovers, arguing that melancholy can happen only when someone or something is lost and the lover and beloved are separated. I have invited and valued these perspectives throughout the internal chapters of this book.

15. Some key ethnomusicological studies of music and emotion offer us insight into understanding how music and sound evoke and instill national sentiment (Buchanan 2006, Turino 2008, Stokes 2010); the relationship between music, emotion, social life, and the sounding environment (Feld 1990 [1982]); how emotion becomes an elemental aspect of ritual through music (Wolf 2001); how emotion acts as a discursive space for negotiating the self in society through music (Henderson 1996); how emotion intersects with musical style (Berger 2009); how sound creates a way for individuals and communities to experience emotional release (Roseman 1991); and how emotive responses engendered by music and dance performance can themselves be instantiations of political and social community and opportunities for commentary on the same (Perman 2010, Turino 2008).

16. This book additionally contributes to a rich body of previous ethnomusicological scholarship in the related geographical areas of Turkey, the Middle East, and Southeastern Europe that considers some of the affective work accomplished in musical practices, evidenced especially by the work of Ali Jihad Racy (2003), Deborah Kapchan (2008 and 2009), Jonathan Shannon (2006), Jane Sugarman (1997), Donna Buchanan (2006), Jane K. Cowan (1990), Sonia Tamar Seeman (2006), and Martin Stokes (2010).

17. Previous formative studies have focused on surveying specific features of the genre of Turkish classical, art, or *alaturka* musics and its poetic traditions (Reinhard and Reinhard 1984, Signell 1977, Ederer 2011, Abacı 2000) and Ottoman music history (Behar 1993 and 2003 [1998], Feldman 1996, Tanrıkorur 2003, Wright 1992 and 2000, Aksoy 1994, Greve 1995), tracing the relationship between national discourses and institutions (O'Connell 2000, 2003, and 2005; Stokes 1995; Popescu-Judetz 1996) or performance sites (Beken 2003), interrogating the repertoire brought in to make up the canon (Feldman 1990–1991 and 1996; Hall 1989), or examining the formation of the genre in terms of style and the commodification of taste (O'Connell 1996 and 2013). Rich ethnographic accounts of Turkish contemporary music life exist (Bates 2010), especially for popular music (Stokes 1992 and 2010) and music making of minority communities (Jackson 2013, Markoff 1986, Seeman forthcoming). This book is most deeply indebted to the work of John Morgan O'Connell and Martin Stokes.

In *Alaturka: Style in Turkish Music (1923–1938)* (2013), O'Connell outlines the commodification of style during an important period of transformation in the early years of the Turkish republic. A tremendous historical ethnography focusing on the life and works of Münir Nurettin Selçuk (1899–1981), O'Connell's book elucidates the way "Turkish classical music" was simultaneously national ("Turkish") and respectable ("classical," linking the genre to the privileged discourses of western classical music).

When we turn to Turkish popular music and the theoretical framework of cultural intimacy (Berlant and Warner 1998, Herzfeld 1997), in *The Republic of Love: Cultural Intimacy in Turkish Popular Music* (2010) Martin Stokes interrogates the workings of sentiment by focusing on political anxieties about love in the contemporary Turkish public sphere. This insightful and compelling text weaves together popular song and the voices of three icons—singers Zeki Müren, Orhan Gencebay, and Sezen Aksu—to form a cultural history of Turkey since the 1950s. Stokes demonstrates that popular musicians have been central to the development of discourses about Turkish citizenry as subjects and as objects interwoven with structural reforms and upheavals, aggressive neoliberalism, and political violence. As authors of public narratives on the nation, these Turkish popular musicians have helped constitute an intimate space—layered in, alongside, and against official discourses—in which critical sensibilities about citizenship and civility have taken shape and been made meaningful in everyday experience for Turkish audiences.

18. The musical notation I provide does not—indeed, cannot—provide what would be necessary for aptly describing or reexperiencing these musickings in context. My brief transcriptions beckon toward an absent performance, one that may speak only to some specialized scholars or performers of Turkish musics. I hope that they prove useful to other readers, who might have an interest in Turkish classical music and have found themselves ill at ease with accessing the common Turkish use of notation; with this readership in mind I have transcribed examples to playing pitch. See the Conventions section for an explanation of Turkish *makam* and *usul* in relation to my transcription practices.

What are the implications of the readerly demand for this notation? Like the diverse untranslatable terms denoting "melancholy," much of the valuable musical material of these musicking moments is fundamentally untranscribable. My transcriptions represent a kind of metaphoric call and response (in Turkish, this musical patterning is named after the cormorant, an aquatic bird that dives in and out of water: *karabatak*). These transcriptions are an invitation to a performance that is ultimately absent in this book itself. I have offered a selected discography at the end of the book to help you project, transfer, and imagine the sonic experience of these moments of musicking.

19. I have also written this book's chapters rhizomatically to aid in ethnomusicological teaching as well. For example, chapter 1 could be assigned to broaden understandings of the musical transitions that accompanied and supported the shift from the Ottoman Empire to the Republic of Turkey. Chapter 2 would be especially useful in the context of discussions about music, cosmology, organology, spirituality, and Sufism. Chapter 3 brings in case studies of musical genealogy outside of Turkey, and is uniquely suited to cater to issues of pedagogy, music transmission, and historical memory. Chapter 3 also introduces the method of bi-aurality in hearing how particular pasts are manifest in the present. In chapter 4, students may find useful case studies of embodiment, especially in relation to gender and movement (*sema* turning ritual). The fifth chapter of this book is suited for classes on music and healing, health reforms, musical modes and extramusical meaning, and improvisation.

CHAPTER 1

1. Necati Çelik (b. 1955, Konya) is one of the most prominent *ud* (short-necked lute) players in Turkey today, and a long-time member of the Istanbul state chorus (*İstanbul Devlet Türk Müziği Korosu*). I have had the privilege of studying Turkish classical music with Necati Hoca in a master-student/apprentice relationship since 2004 (see Bates 2010: 37–38 for another ethnomusicologist's discussion of working with Necati Çelik). I refer to Necati Çelik as "Necati Hoca" (lit., "Necati teacher") in this book, deploying this common and appropriate naming practice with other teachers to replicate the language practices used by the individuals and communities I engage with and re-present. When talking to Necati Hoca in person, I refer to him as "Hocam" (lit., "my teacher").

2. *Abla* means "older sister." Ayşe Çelik (b. 1958, Konya) is the wife of Necati Çelik. She is actively involved and supportive of her husband's music studio (*atölye*) and biannually hosts large gatherings of his students. An amazing cook and conversationalist whose wit is matched only by the veracity of her laugh, Ayşe Abla is a strong mentor and role model for me and many of Necati Hoca's other students.

3. The Ottoman and Arabic associations of *makam* with emotions, times of the day, the zodiac, and the bodily humors of Hippocratic medicine are discussed in chapter 5.

4. For ease in reading, I have transcribed select portions of Necati Hoca's *taksim* in this exchange to a tonic on A. While musicians can *Uşşak makamı* on any tonic, particular tunings are common for playing collectively with others. These tuning systems are generally set by common types of *ney*, which come in different sizes with different tonic pitches (e.g., *mansur*), or by a singer, who chooses the tonic "key" on the basis of his or her vocal range. I have changed Necati Hoca's *taksim* from a B tonic to A to standardize the transcription with normative notational practices for *Uşşak makamı*, which generally present compositions on an A tonic.

5. The idea of a "beautiful modulation" in this example, for my teacher, is based on the idea that an informed listener will still think s/he is hearing *Uşşak makamı* and not immediately notice the modulation to *Eviç*. A seamless modulation that does not move from *makam* to *makam* in a way that segments or divides a listener's experience is an aesthetic mark of "beauty."

6. The direct translation to English of this genre is "classical Turkish music." I have chosen to maintain the use of "Turkish classical music" in naming this genre for two reasons. First, many previous scholars, including native Turkish speakers who have published in English, have named this genre Turkish classical music to easily differentiate it from Turkish folk music, Turkish art music, and other genres (Behar 1993 and 1987). Second, while all of my interviews were conducted in Turkish, two Turkish musicians who preferred to converse in English also chose to oscillate between saying "classical music" and "Turkish classical music" when referring to this genre.

7. The primary and most longstanding instruments of the Ottoman court include the *ney* (the end-blown reed flute discussed in depth in chapter 2), the *tanbur* (long-necked lute), and the *kudüm* (double kettle drum). Many other variations of instruments came in and out of the court traditions during various epochs; for more on this rich history in English, see the work of Walter Feldman (1996) and John Morgan O'Connell (1996).

8. Paradoxically, the *mehterhane*, which was the ensemble providing the sonic symbol of Ottoman military power, performs regularly today at the Military Museum in Istanbul, and is often sent out on international tours that are sponsored by the

Turkish government. The Ottoman military band was revived by the Republic of Turkey in 1952 after 126 years of inactivity, and is supposed to sonically archive and represent the heroic history of Turks (Signell 1967).

9. This particular historical record therefore indicates that the visible, funded existence of the women's harem orchestra was itself seen as a form of westernization, even though women musicians were great performers and composers in a variety of Ottoman musical forms.

10. See chapter 2 for an *ilahi* composed by Zekai Dede Efendi.

11. The suppression of the Kurds in 1925 was ostensibly part of the drive to secularize because they may have been the main constituents that collapsed ethnicity and language with religion. The problematic assumed homogeneity between language, ethnicity, and religion also led to the devastation and violent population exchanges of Armenian and Greek communities of Anatolia in the preceding years. Religion took the place of national belonging, as Muslims in Greece were rendered "Turks" and Christians in Anatolia were rendered "non-Turks."

12. We must note, however, that many educated Ottoman Turks had come to identify themselves as Turkish already in the nineteenth century. In 1896, a contributor for the daily newspaper *İkdam* wrote, "[b]y our social order, we are Ottoman, by our religion [we are] Muslims, and by our ethnic nationality (*kavmiyet*) we are Turks" (in Kushner 1997: 221).

13. For a discussion of the assimilation of musicians of different ethnic and religious groups within the Ottoman court, see Bülent Aksoy's essay entitled "The Contributions of Multi-Nationality to Classical Ottoman Music" (2002).

14. For example, Donizetti's Imperial Band was renamed the Presidential Orchestra and moved from Istanbul to the new capital, Ankara, in 1924 (And 1984: 220).

15. The musical traditions of the Mevlevi essentially went underground at that time and have only begun to cautiously surface since the 1950s. Currently, there are public ceremonies, most notably the annual Mevlana Festival held in Konya during the two weeks preceding December 17 (*Şeb-i Arus*, Mevlana's "wedding night"). However, these ceremonies are marked as tourist attractions and historical reproductions, and while they might be experienced as sacred by the participants, they are not official religious ceremonies.

16. It is not surprising that the founder and current leader of the AKP (Justice and Development Party) in Turkey, Recep Tayyip Erdoğan (b. 1954), has been also deeply inspired by the writings of Ziya Gökalp. White has documented that the complicated AKP view of Turkey taking a leadership role in the Muslim world globally is directly related to two of Gökalp's foundational ideas: (1) Turkish culture and Turkish Islam are central to national identity, if they are appropriately separated and cleansed of Arab cultural influences, and (2) post-Ottoman Turkish civilization is superior and therefore justifies this leadership role in the Muslim world (J. White 2014: 48).

17. The emergence and naming of a discourse on "folk" music follows similar routes. While clearly drawing from western—and importantly, German—conceptions of the rural individual as embodying the tenets of national civility, it is surprising that the word *Volk* was not simultaneously introduced into the Turkish language. Instead, individuals shaping and naming a genre of "folk music" utilized the Turkish world *halk*, which, while it translates to "people," comes from the Arabic *halqa*, denoting a circle of individuals coming together. While we currently translate the term *halk* as "folk," it is interesting that the naming of this genre was not an import from western discourse but rather a product of local Turkish and

Ottoman language practices that had been overlooked in the language-cleansing policies of the early nation-state that sought to rid Turkish language practices of non-Turkish vocabulary.

18. The full text from Gökalp reads, "Before the introduction of European music, there were two kinds of music in Turkey: one was Eastern music, which Farabi took from the Byzantines, the other was folk music, which was a continuation of ancient Turkish music. Eastern music, like Western music, was derived from that of the ancient Greeks. The ancient Greeks, finding insufficient the full and half tones that existed in folk music, added quarter, eighth, and sixteenth tones and called them quarter tones. Quarter tones were not natural but artificial. For this reason, they do not exist in the folk music of any nation. Therefore, Greek music was an artificial music based on unnatural tones. Furthermore, there was in this music a boring monotony due to the repetition of the same tones, which again is something unnatural. Opera, which originated in Europe in the Middle Ages, eliminated these two shortcomings of Greek music. Quarter tones were not suitable for opera. Composers and singers were from the people; thus, they were unable to understand quarter tones. Under these conditions, opera eliminated quarter tones from Western music. Furthermore, as opera was a representation of a succession of human feelings, emotions, and passions, it adopted [polyphonic] harmony and saved Western music from monophony. These two innovations prepared the way for the rise of a more fully developed Western music. Eastern music, on the other hand, remained in its previous state. It preserved the quarter tones on the one hand, and remained foreign to harmony on the other. This morbid music, after being transmitted by Farabi to the Arabs, passed to the Persians and Ottomans chiefly because of the esteem in which it was held at the course. The Greek Orthodox, Armenian, Chalean, and Syrian churches and Jewish synagogues also accepted the same music from Byzantium. In the Ottoman lands this music was the only institution common to all Ottoman ethnic and religious communities, and for this reason we may properly call it the music of the Ottoman peoples. Today we are faced with three kinds of music: Eastern music, Western music, folk music. Which one of them is ours? Eastern music is a morbid music and non-rational. Folk music represents our culture. Western music is the music of our new civilization. Thus, neither should be foreign to us. Our national music, therefore, is to be born from a synthesis of our folk music and Western music. Our folk music provides us with a rich treasure of melodies. By collecting and arranging them on the basis of the Western musical techniques, we shall have both a national and a modern music. This will be the program of Turkish music. It is the task of our composers to bring this aim to fruition" (Gökalp in Berkes 1959: 299–301).

19. We should note that Gökalp did not create these discourses, but instead shaped and reformulated ideas about Turkish folk music already in play. When Riza Nur became the Minister of Education in 1920, for example, he set up a Bureau of Culture (Hars Dairesi) that collected folk songs on rural field trips to Anatolia. By 1926, musicians such as Adnan Saygun, Ulvi Cemal Erkin, and Halil Bedii Yonetken were trained to collect folk tunes from villages and return to Istanbul and Ankara to present them (Aksoy 1985 and 1994, And 1984).

20. At this time, the authority to broadcast was reserved to the PTT, the state-owned Post, Telephone, and Telegraph Service. In 1940, the responsibility to broadcast was given to the General Directory of Press and Broadcasting, a government institution that also oversaw newspapers and tourism (Öngören 1986: 185). The

national monopoly over radio and television did not end until privatization in 1992 (see Algan 2003 and Şahin and Aksoy 1993).

21. It is curious to consider Mustafa Kemal's official legislation against Turkish classical music in light of the fact that he himself was an avid supporter of the genre in his private life. Many times, Atatürk had the Turkish classical music singers Münir Nurettin Selçuk and Safiye Ayla and the synagogue cantor İsak Algazi perform privately for him at Yıldız Palace. See O'Connell 2013 and Tanrıkorur 2004.

22. The first official TV telecasting aired in Turkey on January 31, 1968, under state control through TRT (Öngören 1986).

23. For example, consider the TRT chorus and radio program called *Yurttan Sesler* ("Voices from the Homeland"), founded by Mustafa Sarısözen in 1948 (Stokes 1992: 40–41 and Seeman: forthcoming).

24. O'Connell emphasizes that this control was not simply discursive. The nation-state and the republican elite were able, for example, to maintain control through economic isolation and institutional restructuring (O'Connell 2000: 136).

25. Münir Nurettin Beken claims that İTÜ was founded because the right wing obtained enough power to allocate resources toward the preservation and maintenance of Turkish classical music: "Until the 1970's the decision-making process on social, political and cultural issues accommodated only left wing intellectuals" (Beken 1998: 25, n22). This particular political moment may lead one to believe that Turkish classical music is appreciated only by those on the political right, when in fact, alliances are not this clean.

26. Currently, hybridized pedagogical practices can be observed in individual music lessons at conservatories throughout Turkey, including learning pieces while beating the rhythm (*usûl*) on the knees while reciting *solfej*, which itself was a practice used in the Ottoman court in the nineteenth century.

27. See White's description of the Fatih Book Fair before the specific changes I describe, and her analysis of this kind of consumerism as a "desacralization of religious practices" (J. White 2014: 124–125).

CHAPTER 2

1. "Rumi" was a term first adopted by Byzantines referring to themselves, a naming practice that was later taken up by the Ottomans (Kafadar 1995).

2. While Figure 2.1 offers the opening couplet of Mevlana's *Mesnevi* in its original Farsi script, the in-text transliteration I offer is the Ottoman (Os.) transliteration most circulated by musicians today.

3. Konya is a city with a current population of around one million residents in the central Anatolian region of the Republic of Turkey. It was historically the capital of the Seljuk Sultanate and hosts a Neolithic settlement (Çatalhöyük) that is a UNESCO World Heritage Site.

4. For an excellent study of the musical concept and expression of "burning" in Turkish musics, see the work of Ayhan Erol (2007). Erol examines the diverse interpretations of the vocal quality *yanık*, a bittersweet quality of burning associated with being inflamed with love.

5. The word *Sufi* comes from the Arabic *sufiyya*, the one who wears woolen clothes (*suf*), the rough garb of mystics. This term was not used to designate Sufis until the eighth century (AH second century).

6. Following Foucault, Navaro-Yashin writes against analytical categories such as "public culture," "the state," and "the public sphere" in an effort to see the political in each and every domain (Navaro-Yashin 2002a: 2–3). She argues that the terms

"society" and "public" and "the people" do not have singular or essential qualities but are contingent and bound by context; she claims that "[t]he political is generated in their construction" (Navaro-Yashin 2002a: 153).

7. In speaking of Islamism, I differentiate between Muslim, which expresses religious identity, and Islamist, which refers to social movements through which specific collectives of individuals and communities appropriate Muslim identity as a basis for an alternative political project or movement. In speaking of Kemalists, I identify supporters of Mustafa Kemal's emphasis on laicist reforms. Kemalism refers to the social movement that labors to ensure a secular nation-state and society through the government, military, judiciary, and educational systems. State-enforced secularism (Tr. *laiklik*) was a policy first put into practice by the Young Turks at the end of the Ottoman Empire, who had been highly influenced by the French Revolution and adopted the Jacobian concept of *laïcité*.

8. One important observation in the visual art realm that also continues and reifies a bifurcation between the Ottoman past and the nation-state and, more generally, religious and secular artifacts lies in the common ways these Ottoman artistic practices are named in present-day Turkish. Visual art that is assumed to have generated in the west—sculpture, painting, photography—is referred to as *sanat*, or "art." Material objects and visual art that are marked as Ottoman or Islamic (and found in similar practices in Iranian and Arab regions)—Islamic calligraphy, *ebru* water marbling, miniatures, the intricate carving of *tesbih* prayer beads—are generally referred to by words that translate as "craft," such as *el işi, beceri, hüner*, or *zanaat*. This discursive bifurcation does not simply work to separate two kinds of artistic material objects: these language differences also function to validate and promote one over the other.

9. I replicate Turkish language practices here as I translate the genderless third person singular and plural pronoun ("o") as it or as s/he. Many of the Turkish musicians I work with are quick to discuss the genderlessness of God and the way that the Turkish language reflects this important aspect of God's being in the language of the everyday.

10. Al-Hallaj's statement (*ana al-Haqq*) used the term "Truth" (Ar. *Haqq*, Os. *Hakk*), one of the ninety-nine attributes or names of God.

11. See Ayfer Karakaya-Stump's *Rethinking Alevi-Bektashi History: Sources and Historiography* for more on the nuances and intersections of Alevism and Bektasism (2015).

12. Bektaşi orders were forbidden in 1825 (along with the *yeni çeri*, or Ottoman military class) but reconstituted themselves afterward in Izmir, Istanbul, and Salonika. Bektaşi-s in Anatolia were progressively absorbed by the Alevi-s, and espoused the movement for reform against Sultan Abdülhamit II (1942–1918). Alevi and Bektaşi resistance to the sultanate, coupled with their ostensible valuing of the laws of their *tarikat*-s (brotherhoods) over the laws of the Ottoman Empire, created hostility between Ottoman governing bodies and these orders.

Another prominent Sufi order, the Nakşbandi, enjoyed popularity and visibility at the beginning of the nineteenth century in the Ottoman Empire, especially amongst the Kurds of the Empire's eastern provinces. The Nakşbandi supported the Ottoman sultanate, and had members in the palace staff. After the 1908 revolution, many Nakşbandi-s participated in the Young Turk movement.

13. While facing violent persecution in Turkish public life generally, Alevi doctrines were favored by the Kemalist regime, as Alevi-s historically had resisted and openly protested Ottoman rule. The Alevi-s reciprocated with revering Kemalism

in their poetic texts and song lyrics, often referring to Mustafa Kemal (Atatürk) as *mahdi* ("messiah") (Dressler 2003: 121–125).

14. Some of the musicians most reputed as knowledge-bearers of Mevlevi practices are quite emphatic that Mevlevism (Tr. *Mevlevilik*) no longer exists. They argue that musicians who call calling themselves "Mevlevi" are misguided. These musicians mourn the loss of the Mevlevi order, which they believed to have "died" at the hands of the nation-state.

15. "*Hu*: 1. Hey, there; 2. *Mystical orders, greeting formula*; 3. He (i.e., God)" (Redhouse 1997: 491).

16. It is important to note that *Hû* does manifest in Arab and Persian communities, existing as a name of God and in diverse practices of *dhikr*. However, the case study of *Hû* I offer here is situated in Turkey, especially Istanbul, and emerges as particularly unique in the larger region to Turkish *ney* instrumental technique.

17. This *ilahi* engages a kind of double reading or wordplay, as to be expected in most Ottoman-Turkish poetic texts. For example, the text "*Hû ismi azam*" simultaneously translates to "the name *Hû* is the greatest" and "The name *Hû* is the name of God," as *Azam* is another one of the ninety-nine attributes of God, denoting "greatest" and "largest."

18. See http://www.gavsulazam.de/turk/tasavvuf/hu.htm, which discusses one blogger's exegesis of *Hû* in Turkish. The same blogger drew on another important trope by claiming that *Hû* occurs in every human breath. He argued that if in the twenty-four-hour day any given person takes 24,000 breaths, we each sound out *Hû* 24,000 times a day and effectively call God into being in our bodies through *zikir* 24,000 times a day.

19. The words *Hay* ("everlasting life") and *Hakk* ("truth") could also have been the focus of this chapter, as they are also names and attributes of God that have a rich legacy in music, poetry, and philosophical discourse. The crucial difference is that *Hû* as sound is concretely embedded in music training and in the philosophies of the breath and breathing, so much so that one would be hard pressed to find a "secular" Turkish *ney* player who will not connect what s/he does musically with the spiritual world from which Turkish musicians historically drew inspiration.

20. Viewing the body as a process and not as a natural, fixed object is a theoretical position generated by feminist scholarship. See Butler 2004: 29 and Scheper-Hughes 1992: 184–185.

21. One calligrapher I interviewed said that this expression primarily circulated during the Ottoman Empire in the Persian form *in nist begzerad*, without the *Hû*, meaning "this cannot be permanent." The first Ottoman calligrapher to write this expression in Persian was Aziz Rufaî Efendi (1871–1934), a sheikh of the Rufai Sufi order. Necmeddin Okyay was the first to write it in Ottoman-Turkish, raising issues about the shifts in language that were already occurring at the time of the fall of the Ottoman Empire even in the artistic practices of Islamic calligraphy. It is not clear when or how the *Hû* was added to the Turkish-language manifestation of this expression, although all of the people I asked about this expression claim that it is unheard of to use the expression without the "*ya Hû*" in Turkey today.

CHAPTER 3

1. One potential exception to the story that there cannot be a child prodigy in Turkish classical music is the celebrated composer and virtuoso Tanburi Cemil Bey (1876–1916), who achieved notoriety relatively early in his twenties. While some musicians will note Cemil Bey as an exception to the child prodigy narrative,

it must be pointed out that Cemil Bey became proficient in his teenage years and not as a young child per se.

2. This master-teacher's narrative is a veiled reference to a passage in the Qur'an:

> And your Lord took the offspring of the children of Adam from their backs, and made them bear witness upon themselves saying: "Am I not your Lord?" They said: "Yes indeed, and we bear witness [to your being]." So that on the day of resurrection you may not say "we were unaware of this" (Qur'an 7:172).

This musician is instinctively recreating music history through narration of religious belief.

3. This master-teacher espouses a particular Turkish discourse first introduced in the early republican era. He perceives the Turks as constantly "homeless," wanderers who trace their lineage back to Mongolia. This voicing of homelessness is further related to national anxieties and some situated understandings of how Turks are perceived as unappreciated in current historical and political debates globally.

4. Öztürk 1997: 180.

5. See chapter 5 for an investigation of suffering as nutrition for the soul.

6. Tanrıkorur 2003: 208.

7. Importantly, theorizing modulations and movement within improvisation in terms of moving between tetrachords is a concept that can be traced to Suphi Ezgi (1869–1962), an important author and codifier of *makam* theory and practice during the early years of the republic.

8. This statement raises interesting questions about the nature of the *sama'* polemic in context of contemporary Turkish classical music practices (see especially Kusić 1997). While historical and contemporary debates about audition and listening to music (Ar. *sama'*) arise to elucidate the separation between the human and the divine, most of the musicians I work with in Turkey instead see a need to deliberately connect the human with the divine, a labor against the secular normativity within which their musicking occurs.

9. Similar practices take place in contemporary Egypt. For example, Scott Marcus writes about moments when his *'ud* teacher, George Michel, "grab[ed] a pen and produce[d] a new transcription from memory" (2002: 45).

10. Cantemir collected and notated almost 350 instrumental pieces during his lifetime, thirty-six of which are reportedly his own compositions (Signell 1977: 5).

11. See Maureen Jackson (2010 and 2013) for rich analyses on interreligious collaboration between Jewish and Muslim musicians in Turkey.

12. For a detailed study of Ali Ufki's manuscripts and transcriptions, see Cem Behar's *Ali Ufki ve Mezmurlar* (1990).

13. Raûf Yektâ deserves special attention, as he was one of only three employees retained at Darül'elhan Institute in music during the early days of the Republic of Turkey. While he had been trained in *meşk* as a musician and also in a Mevlevi Sufi order, Yektâ was directed to shape and secure a secular framing of Ottoman court and *tekke* musics. As such, he had the primary duty of documenting and recording the repertoire that would be codified as "Turkish" (at a time when the nation-state was only starting to exist) and as "classical" (in an era when looking to western models of elite music production was central to the production of national arts culture). Feldman explains that "[i]n terms of the repertoire Raûf Yektâ understood that his primary task was to notate the core classical repertoire (essentially vocal) from the most authoritative living traditional sources. He realized that the traditional oral method of instruction [*meşk*] as the primary method

of transmission of repertoire would not survive long into the next century, so that establishing authoritative versions of the classical repertoire was absolutely essential for the survival of Turkish music" (Feldman 1990–1991: 96).

A government official, Yektâ was fluent in Turkish, French, Arabic, and Persian, and had been a participant in conferences about the relationship between music, nationalism, and folklore in Europe and the Middle East (notably, the 1932 Cairo Conference of Arab Music). His lengthy article in the French Lavignac encyclopedia, still considered to be one of the most authoritative sources on Turkish classical music in a European language, contains analysis of Turkish melodic and rhythmic modes (*makam* and *usul*, respectively), as well as a description of intervals and *koma*-s and over seventy musical examples (Yektâ 1922). In his role as chairman of the *İlmi Heyet* (Scientific Investigations Committee), he oversaw the codification and publication of over 180 compositions of "Turkish classical music" in the *Darülelhan Külliyati* and forty-one ritual compositions (*ayin*) of the Mevlevi *sema* ceremony. Ultimately, contemporary Turkish music theory and notation practices are the result of Yektâ and his collaborators, Ezgi and Arel.

14. A *koma* is one of nine divided parts between two consecutive whole tones.
15. During the time of the final manuscript preparation for this book, a number of musicians in one of the primary *ney silsilesi* of *neyzen* Niyazi Sayin established a website to document their lineage. See www.neysilsilesi.com.
16. Many musicians I interviewed argue that Raûf Yektâ's own transcriptions disclose his *silsile*'s practices in a codified way, which is why they take the official notation housed in the archives of Turkish Radio and Television and reinscribe it with different accidentals (to identify passages they hear should be rendered in an alternate *makam*), different phrasing, and unique idiomatic ornamentation.

CHAPTER 4

1. In this way, *eser* as "work" may be brought into a dialogue with the "work concept" of western classical/art musics (e.g., Beethoven's Fifth Symphony as "a work"). However, the term *eser*, indicating work and labor, is not an import from the west or a response to debates about hierarchical value systems in western canons.
2. For more on the neurological changes affected by repetitive practices like musicking, see Panksepp and Bernatzky 2002, Magee and Davidson 2002, and Doidge 2007 for summaries of psychobiological research on the plasticity of the brain and the central neural circuitry of emotion.
3. Master-apprentice relations, discussed in chapter 3, were often gender segregated. The few famous female composers and musicians we know about were all members of the imperial *harem*, and were trained within a master-apprentice system that was separate from the one associated with the Ottoman court and Sufi lodges. The practice of women teaching women seemed to dissipate with the *Tanzimat* (reforms) of the late Ottoman period, as male musicians visited women's spaces for the purpose of providing musical education to women. Today, women musicians gain musical education from men and vice versa. See Feldman (1996), especially chapter 1, "Professionalism and the Music of the Ottoman Court," for an English-language discussion of the organization of musicians in the court tradition.
4. Turkish third person pronoun (singular *o* and plural *onlar*) are gender neutral.
5. In interviews with many vocalists, a few even offered a particularly gutteral vocal ornament akin to sobbing that they variously called *hıçkırık* or *ağlama*, terms that

bring a weeping vocal quality into a musical line. Sitting on consonants is also a practice of Qur'anic recitation, and many Turkish classical vocalists will listen to and replicate the ornamentation of important previous Qur'anic reciters (*hafiz-s*) such as Hafız Sami (1874–1943).

6. For an anecdotal example, I once saw a performance of Kevser Hanım's *Nihavent Longa* by a Romanian ensemble touring the United States who claimed it was a Bulgarian folk tune. Two local Arab musicians (one Syrian and one Lebanese) I currently make music with in the midwest United States both accept that while they thought it was Egyptian, it could be a tune left over from Ottoman imperialism (I needed to show archival evidence, however, to convince them that it could possibly be written by a woman). Like Buchanan's impeccable study of the tune "*Üsküdar'a Gider İken*" ("On my Way to Üsküdar"), this instrumental *longa* has traveled with individuals and communities as they move through currently demarcated borders of language, culture, religion, and nation, offering an example of a shared tradition despite vehement claims of ownership (2007). For more on women composers and performers in this region, see Woodard 2011, Jackson 2010, Naroditskaya 2000, and Menemencioğlu 1983.

7. See chapter 3. Scholars before me have noted similar gendered musical attributes (see especially O'Connell 2013).

8. This process raises critical questions about the challenges and consequences that arise when men teach women how to sound out femininity, and when sonic femininities are sounded out by men, topics that I do not investigate here.

9. The composition of tears produced in what biomedical narratives describe as "emotional crying" contains greater quantities of potassium, manganese, the prolactin leu-enkephalin, and adrenocorticotropic hormone.

10. See Nelson (1985) chapter 3, for more on *sama'*.

11. As S. Marcus (2007), Nelson (1985), and Rasmussen (2010) have demonstrated, diverse Muslim communities globally have deployed the term *sama'* and considered music's efficacy and place. As previously mentioned, Nelson dubbed the debate over if music is lawful (*helal*) or unlawful (*haram*) "the *sama'* polemic" (1985).

12. From a linguistic perspective, the Arabic *sama'* was eradicated and replaced with the present-day Turkish term *sema* during the language and alphabet reforms of the early Republic, explained in chapter 1.

CHAPTER 5

1. Another obvious example of a melancholic—besides Neyzen Tevfik and Hacı Arif Bey—is the virtuosic composer Tanburi Cemil Bey (1873–1916). Yet while the ethnographic evidence from contemporary musicians who "hear melancholy" in Cemil Bey's improvisations is extensive, I found that because of the important and central status of Cemil Bey in Turkish classical music, musicians were quick to contest or defend a variety of contradictory perspectives about him in relation to his improvisations and his ostensible melancholy. Investigating the power relations at work in vying claims about affective practice, music listening, and memorialization is rich terrain for future research.

2. My tendency to speak in terms of psychological "dis-ease" (out of ease) instead of "disease" (ill or sick) reflects my understanding that for many individuals and communities, particular psychological states that we may tend to classify today as illnesses or disorders to be cured would more appropriately be analyzed as spiritual, psychological, physical, and social positions to be inhabited.

3. For more on Ottoman music therapy practices, see the archival manuscripts that informed this section: the *Edvar-i 'ilmü'l mûsiki* at the Istanbul University Library, Gevrekzâde's *Neticetü'l fikriyye ve Tedbir-i velâdetü'l bikriyye* at the Topkapi Palace Library, Kantemiroğlu's *Kitâbu 'ilmi'l-mûsiki 'alâ vechi'l- hurûfât* at the Türkiyat Institute, Haşim Bey's *Musiki Mecmuasi* available in the archives listed above, and Şuurî's *Tadilü'l Emzice* at the Medical History Dept. Library archives in Cerrahpaşa Medical School.

4. During 2008: 371.

5. For a discussion of extramusical associations for *maqam* in the modern period of Arab (Egyptian) musical theory and practice, see S. L. Marcus 1989: 747–753.

6. I do not imply that the transportation and circulation of manuscripts and various translations at this time shared within a region that was united as "Europe." Rather, I use the category "western European" to simply indicate the geographical movement of texts from Damascus and Baghdad to the Latin world and to demonstrate that these texts eventually solidified European medical practices to the extent that by the late nineteenth century, some of these assumptions were considered "western."

7. For more on modal structures in Jewish musics, see Bahat 1980, Idelson 1992, Jackson 2013, Kligman 2009, O'Connell 2015, and Summit 2016. For more on modal structures as they developed in Balkan musical practices see Pennanen 2004 and Petrović 1988.

8. For further information on humoral theories of healing in relationship with western European art music traditions and melancholy, see Austern 2000a and 2000b, Gouk 2000, Jackson 1986, and Schleiner 1991.

9. See Gouk 2000: 179–182 for an excellent summary and discussion of settled versus transitory melancholy in regards to music.

10. A similar practice of improvisation—and perceiving successful improvisations as phrase-length compositions in succession—also exists in Persian classical music. See Nooshin 1996, 1998, and 2003.

11. See S. L. Marcus 1989 for detailed examples in the Arab art musical practices of Egypt.

BIBLIOGRAPHY

Abacı, Tahir. 2000. *Yahya Kemal ve Ahmet Hamdi Tanpınar'da Müzik*. İstanbul: İkaros Yayınları.

———. 2013. *Türk Müziğinde Bestelenmiş Şiirler*. İstanbul: İkaros Yayınları.

Abrahamov, Binjamin. 2003. *Divine Love in Islamic Mysticism: The Teachings of Al-Ghazâlî and Al-Dabbâgh*. London: Routledge Curzon.

Abu-Lughod, Lila. 1986. *Veiled Sentiments: Honor and Poetry in a Bedouin Society*. Berkeley, CA: University of California Press.

———. 1993a. "Islam and the Gendered Discourses of Death." *International Journal of Middle East Studies* 25, no. 2: 187–205.

———. 1993b. *Writing Women's Worlds: Bedouin Stories*. Berkeley, CA: University of California Press.

———. 2005. *Dramas of Nationhood: The Politics of Television in Egypt*. Chicago, IL: University of Chicago Press.

Abu-Lughod, Lila, and Catherine A. Lutz. 1990. "Introduction: Emotion, Discourse, and the Politics of Everday Life." In *Language and the Politics of Emotion*, edited by Catherine A. Lutz and Lila Abu-Lughod, 1–23. Cambridge, UK: Cambridge University Press.

Afary, Janet. 2009. *Sexual Politics in Modern Iran*. Cambridge, UK: Cambridge University Press.

Aflākī, Shams al-Dīn Aḥmad-e. 2002. *Manāqeb al-'Ārefīn [Feats of the Knowers of God]*. Translated by John O'Kane. Leiden, The Netherlands: Brill.

Ahmad, Feroz. 1993. *The Making of Modern Turkey*. London, UK: Routledge.

Ahmed, Leila. 2000. *A Border Passage: From Cairo to America—A Woman's Journey*. New York: Penguin.

Ahmed, Sara. 2004. *The Cultural Politics of Emotion*. London: Routledge.

———. 2006. *Queer Phenomenology: Orientations, Objects, Others*. Durham, NC, and London: Duke University Press.

———. 2010. *The Promise of Happiness*. Durham, NC, and London: Duke University Press.

Ak, Ahmet Şahin. n.d. *Türk Musikisi Tarihi*. İstanbul: Akçağ Yayınları.

Akcan, Esra. 2005. "Melancholy and the 'Other'" *Eurozine*, 25 August. http://www.eurozine.com/articles/2005-08-25-akcan-en.html

Aksoy, Bülent. 1985. "Tanzimat'tan Cumhuriyet'e Musiki ve Batılılaşma." In *Cumhuriyet Dönemi Türkiye Ansiklopedesi* 5, 1212–1236. İstanbul: İletişim.

———. 1994. *Avrupalı Gezginlerin Gözüyle Osmanlılarda Musiki*. İstanbul: Pan Yayıncılık.

———. 2002. "The Contributions of Multi-Nationality to Classical Ottoman Music." *Golden Horn Records*. Golden Horn Productions, accessed September 7, 2015. http://www.goldenhorn.com/

Aksoy, Ozan. 2006. "The Politicization of Kurdish Folk Songs in Turkey in the 1990s." *Music and Anthropology Journal of Musical Anthropology of the Mediterranean* 11.

Aktürk, Şener. 2007. "Incompatible Visions of Supra-Nationalism: National Identity in Turkey and the European Union." *European Journal of Sociology* 48, no. 2: 347–372.

Alarcón, Norma. 1996. "Conjugating Subjects in the Age of Multiculturalism." In *Mapping Multiculturalism*, edited by Avery F. Gordon and Christopher Newfiel, 127–148. Minneapolis: University of Minnesota Press.

Alexander, M. Jacqui. 2005. *Pedagogies of Crossing: Meditations on Feminism, Sexual Politics, Memory, and the Sacred*. Durham, NC, and London: Duke University Press.

Algan, Ece. 2003. "Privatization of Radio and Media Hegemony in Turkey." In *The Globalization of Corporate Media Hegemony*, edited by Lee Artz and Yahya R. Kamlalipour, 169–195. Albany: State University of New York Press.

Ali, Filiz. 1983. "Türkiye Cumhuriyeti'nde Konservatuvarlar." In *Cumhuriyet Dönemi Türkiye Ansiklopedisi*, 1531–1534. İstanbul: İletişim.

Almond, Ian. 2003. "Islam, Melancholy, and Sad, Concrete Minarets: The Futility of Narratives in Orhan Pamuk's *The Black Book*." *New Literary History* 34, no. 1: 75–90.

Altınay, Rüştem Ertuğ. 2008. "Reconstructing the Transgendered Self as a Muslim, Nationalist, Upper-Class Woman: The Case of Bülent Ersoy." *Women's Studies Quarterly* 36, nos. 3–4: 210–229.

Altınölçek, Haşmet. 1998. "Bir iletişim aracı olarak müzik ve müzikle tedavi yöntemleri." Ph.D. dissertation, Anadolu Üniversitesi.

Altun, Ahmet. 2011. *Hz. Peygamber Sünnetinde: Sağlık Mucizeleri*. İstanbul: Ensar.

And, Metin. 1977. "The Mevlana Ceremony." *Drama Reviews: TDR* 21, no. 3: 83–94.

———. 1984. "Atatürk and the Arts, with Special Reference to Music and Theater." In *Atatürk and the Modernization of Turkey*, edited by Jacob M. Landau and E. J. Brill, 215–232. Boulder, CO: Westview Press.

Anderson, Benedict. 1983. *Imagined Communities: Reflections on the Origin and Spread of Nationalism*. London, UK: Verso.

Andrews, Peter Alford, ed. 1989. *Ethnic Groups in the Republic of Turkey*. Wiesbaden, Germany: Dr. Ludwig Reichert Verlag.

Andrews, Walter. 1984. *Poetry's Voice, Society's Song: Ottoman Lyric Poetry*. Seattle, WA: University of Washington Press.

Andrews, Walter, and Mehmet Kalpaklı. 2005. *The Age of Beloveds: Love and the Beloved in Early Modern Ottoman and European Culture and Society*. Durham, NC: Duke University Press.

Ansari, Abdul Haq. 1999. "Ibn 'Arabi: The Doctrine of Wahdat al-wujud." *Islamic Studies* 38: 149–192.

'Arabi, al-, Ibn. 1978. *Tarjumán al-ashwáq: A Collection of Mystical Odes*. Translated by Reynold A. Nicholson. London, UK: Theosophical Publishing House.

———. 1980. *The Bezels of Wisdom*. Translated by R. W. J. Austin. New York: Paulist.

Aracı, Emre. 2006. *Donizetti Paşa: Osmanlı Sarayının İtalyan Maestrosu*. İstanbul: Yapı Kredi Kültür Sanat Yayınları.

Arango, Tim. 2016. "In Istanbul, Optimism Fades to a Familiar Melancholy." *New York Times*, July 18, 2016. Accessed 19 August, 2016. http://www.nytimes.com/2016/07/19/world/europe/istanbul-turkey-coup.html?_r=0

Arat, Yeşim. 1985. "Obstacles to Political Careers: Perceptions of Turkish Women." *International Political Science Review* 6, no. 3: 355–366.

———. 1996. "On Gender and Citizenship in Turkey." *Middle East Report* 198: 28–31.

———. 1997. "The Project of Modernity and Women in Turkey." In *Rethinking Modernity and National Identity in Turkey*, edited by Sibel Bozdogan and Resat Kasaba, 95–112. Seattle: University of Washington Press.

———. 1998. "Feminists, Islamists, and Political Change in Turkey." *Political Psychology* 19, no. 10: 117–131.

Arel, Hüseyin Sadettin. 1952. "Makamlardaki Duygu Unsuru." *Musiki Mecmuasi* 48: 46–55.

———. 1969. *Türk Musikisi Kimindir?* İstanbul: Milli Eğtim Basımevi.

Arif Bey, Hacı. 1873. *Mecmua-i Arîfi.* İstanbul: İbrahim Sırrı Efendi Matbaası.

Armbrust, Walter. 1996. *Mass Culture and Modernism in Egypt.* Cambridge, UK: Cambridge University Press.

Asad, Talal. 2003. *Formations of the Secular: Christianity, Islam, Modernity.* Stanford, CA: Stanford University Press.

Ataman, Sadi Y. 1991. *Atatürk ve Türk Musıkisi.* Ankara, Turkey: Kültür Bakanlığı.

Atatürk, Mustafa K. 1961. *Atatürk'ün Söylev ve Demeçleri.* 3 vols, edited by Nimet Arsan. Ankara, Turkey: Türk Tarihi Kurumu.

Attar, Farid al-Din. 1966. *Muslim Saints and Mystics: Episodes from the Tadhkirat al-awliya' of Farid al-Din 'Attar.* Chicago, IL: University of Chicago Press.

Austern, Linda Phyllis. 2000a. "Musical Treatments for Lovesickness: The Early Modern Heritage." In *Music as Medicine: The History of Music Therapy since Antiquity*, edited by Peregrine Horden, 213–245. Aldershot, UK: Ashgate.

———. 2000b. "'No Pill's Gonna Cure My Ill': Gender, Erotic Melancholy and Traditions of Musical Healing in the Modern West." In *Musical Healing in Cultural Contexts*, edited by Penelope Gouk, 113–136. Aldershot, UK: Ashgate.

Austin, J. L. 1962. *How to Do Things with Words.* Cambridge, MA: Harvard University Press.

Aydemir, Murat. 2010. *Turkish Music Makam Guide.* Edited and translated by Erman Dirikcan. İstanbul: Pan Yayıncılık.

Aydemir, Şevket. 1992. *Tek Adam: Mustafa Kemal 1881–1919.* 3 vols. İstanbul: Rezmi Kitabevi.

Aydüz, Davut. 2011. *Kur'ân-i Kerîm'de Besinler ve Şifa.* İstanbul: Işik Yayınları.

Ayvazoğlu, Beşir, Cem Behar, İskender Savaşır, and Semih Sökmen. 1994. "Müzik ve Cumhuriyet." *Defter* 7, no. 22: 7–27.

Bahat, Avner. 1980. "The Musical Traditions of the Oriental Jews: Orient and Occident." *World of Music* 22, no. 2: 46–58.

Bakhle, Janaki. 2005. *Two Men and Music: Nationalism in the Making of an Indian Classical Tradition.* Oxford, UK: Oxford University Press.

Balakrishnan, Rajagopal. 2003. *International Law from Below: Development, Social Movements, and Third World Resistance.* Cambridge, UK: Cambridge University Press.

Balkwill, Laura-Lee, William Forde Thompson, and Rie Matsunaga. 2004. "Recognition of Emotion in Japanese, Western, and Hindustani Music by Japanese Listeners." *Japanese Psychological Research* 46, no. 4: 337–349.

Bartók, Béla. 1976. *Turkish Folk Music from Asia Minor*, edited by Benjamin Suchoff. Princeton, NJ: Princeton University Press.

Bates, Eliot. 2010. *Music in Turkey: Experiencing Music, Expressing Culture.* Oxford and New York: Oxford University Press.

————. 2016. *Digital Tradition: Arrangement and Labor in Istanbul's Recording Studio Culture*. Oxford and New York: Oxford University Press.

Baydar, Evren K. 2010. *Osmanlı'nın Avrupalı Müzisyenleri*. İstanbul: Kapı Yayınları.

Bayzan, Ali Riza. 2013. *Sûfî ile Terapist*. İstanbul: Etkileşim.

Becker, Judith. 2004. *Deep Listeners: Music, Emotion, and Trancing*. Bloomington: Indiana University Press.

————. 2009. "Ethnomusicology and Empiricism in the Twenty-First Century." *Ethnomusicology* 53, no. 3: 478–501.

Behar, Cem. 1987. *Klasik Türk Mûsıkisi Üzerine Denemeler*. İstanbul: Bağlam Yayınları.

————. 1990. *Ali Ufki ve Mezmurlar*. İstanbul: Pan Yayıncılık.

————. 1993. *Zaman, Mekan, Müzik: Klasik Türk Musikisinde Eğitim (Meşk), İcra ve Aktarım*. İstanbul: AFA Yayınları.

————. 2003 [1998]. *Aşk Olmayınca Meşk Olmaz: Geleneksel Osmanlı/Türk Müziğinde Öğretim ve İntikal*. İstanbul: Yapı Kredi Yayınları.

————. 2004. *Musıkiden Müziğe: Osmanlı/Türk Müiği: Gelenk ve Modernlik*. İstanbul: Yapı Kredi Yayınları.

————. 2006. "The Rise and Development of an Ottoman Musical Tradition in the Sixteenth and Seventeenth Centuries." In *20. Yil Pan'a Armağan*, edited by Işik Gençer and Ferruh Gençer, 52–66. İstanbul: Pan Yayıncılık.

Beken, Münir Nurettin. 1998. "Musicians, Audience and Power: The Changing Aesthetics in Music at the Maksim Gazino of Istanbul (Turkey)." Ph.D. dissertation, University of Maryland.

————. 2003. "Aesthetics and Artistic Criticism at the Turkish *Gazino*." *Journal of Musical Anthropology of the Mediterranean* 8. http://www.umbc.edu/MA/index/number8/gazino/bek_00.htm

Beken, Münir Nurettin, and Karl Signell. 2006. "The Problematic Nature of Defining a Turkish Makam." In *Maqam Traditions of Turkic Peoples*, edited by Jürgen Elsner, Gisa Jähnichen, Thomas Ogger, and Ildar Kharissov, 204–215. Berlin: Trafo Verlag.

Bell, Michael. 2000. *Sentimentalism, Ethics and the Culture of Feeling*. Houndmills, UK: Palgrave.

Berger, Harris M. 2009. *Stance: Ideas about Emotion, Style, and Meaning for the Study of Expressive Culture*. Middletown, CT: Wesleyan University Press.

Berkes, Niyazi, editor and translator. 1959. *Turkish Nationalism and Western Civilization: Selected Essays of Ziya Gökalp*. London, UK: Allen and Unwin Press.

————. 1964. *The Development of Secularism in Turkey*. Montreal: McGill University Press.

————. 1965. *Batıcılık, Ulusçuluk ve Toplumsal Devrimler*. İstanbul: Yön Yayınlar.

Berlant, Lauren. 1998. "Intimacy: A Special Issue." In *Intimacy*, edited by Laura Berlant. Special issue, *Critical Inquiry* 24, no. 2: 281–288.

————. 2008. *The Female Complaint: The Unfinished Business of Sentimentality in American Culture*. Durham, NC, and London: Duke University Press.

————. 2011. *Cruel Optimism*. Durham, NC, and London: Duke University Press.

Berlant, Lauren, and Michael Warner. 1998. "Sex in Public." *Critical Inquiry* 24: 547–566.

Beyatlı, Yayhâ Kemal. 1995. *Kendi Gök Kubbemiz*. İstanbul: İstanbul Fetih Cemiyeti.

Beşiroğlu, Şefika Şehvar. 1998. "Methods of Traditional Musical Education: A Turkish Case Study." *Islamic Culture* 72, no. 2: 75–79.

Bhabha, Homi. 2004. *The Location of Culture*. London, UK: Routledge.

Bleicher, Josef. 1980. *Contemporary Hermeneutics: Hermeneutics as Method, Philosophy and Critique*. London, UK: Routledge.

Bohlman, Philip V. 1997. "World Musics and World Religions: Whose World?" In *Enchanting Powers: Music in the World's Religions*, edited by Lawrence Sullivan, 61–71. Cambridge, MA: Harvard Center for the Study of World Religions.

———. 1999. "Ontologies of Music." In *Rethinking Music*, edited by Nicholas Cook and Mark Everist, 17–34. Oxford and New York: Oxford University Press.

———. 2002. "World Music at the End of History." *Ethnomusicology* 46, no. 1: 1–32.

Bolak, Hale Cihan. 1997. "When Wives Are Major Providers: Culture, Gender, and Family Work." *Gender and Society* 11, no. 4: 409–433.

Boltanski, Luc. 1999. *Distant Suffering: Morality, Media and Politics*. Cambridge, UK: Cambridge University Press.

Born, Georgina. 1998. "Anthropology, Kleinian Analysis, and the Subject in Culture." *American Anthropologist* 100, no. 2: 373–386.

———. 2005. "On Musical Mediation: Ontology, Technology and Creativity." *Twentieth-Century Music* 2, no. 1: 7–36.

Bourdieu, Pierre. 1990 [1980]. *The Logic of Practice*. Stanford, CA: Stanford University Press.

———. 1993. *The Field of Cultural Production: Essays on Art and Literature*, edited by Randal Johnson. New York: Columbia University Press.

———. 2001 [1998]. *Masculine Domination*. Translated by Richard Nice. Stanford, CA: Stanford University Press.

———. 2002 [1979]. *Distinction: A Social Critique of the Judgment of Taste*. Translated by Richard Nice. Cambridge, MA: Harvard University Press.

———. 2005. "Habitus." *Habitus: A Sense of Place* 2: 43–49.

Bowen, Donna Lee, and Evelyn A. Early, eds. 2002. *Everyday Life in the Muslim Middle East*. Bloomington: Indiana University Press.

Bowen, John R. 2012. *The New Anthropology of Islam*. Cambridge, UK: Cambridge University Press.

Bowring, Jacky. 2008. *A Field Guide to Melancholy*. Harpenden, UK: Oldcastle Books.

Bozdoğan, Sibel and Reşat Kasaba, eds. 1997. *Rethinking Modernity and National Identity in Turkey*. Seattle, WA: University of Washington Press.

Bozkurt, Barış, Ozan Yarman, M. Kemal Karaosmanoğlu, and Can Akkoç. 2009. "Weighing Diverse Theoretical Models on Turkish Maqam Music against Pitch Measurements: A Comparison of Peaks Automatically Derived from Frequency Histograms with Proposed Scale Tones." *Journal of New Music Research* 38, no. 1: 45–70.

Brennan, Teresa. 2004. *The Transmission of Affect*. Ithaca, NY: Cornell University Press.

Brophy, Sarah. 2002. "Angels in Antigua: The Diasporic of Melancholy in Jamaica Kincaid's 'My Brother.'" *Publications of the Modern Language Association of America* 117, no. 2: 265–277.

Brown, Wendy. 2001. *Politics out of History*. Princeton, NJ: Princeton University Press.

Bryant, Rebecca. 2005. "The Soul Danced into the Body: Nation and Improvisation in Istanbul." *Journal of the American Ethnological Society* 32, no. 2: 222–238.

Buchanan, Donna A. 1995. "Metaphors of Power, Metaphors of Truth: The Politics of Music Professionalism in Bulgarian Folk Orchestras." *Ethnomusicology* 39, no. 3: 381–416.

———. 2000. "Bartók's Bulgaria: Folk Music Collecting and Balkan Social History." *International Journal of Musicology* 9: 55–91.

———. 2006. *Performing Democracy: Bulgarian Music and Musicians in Transition*. Chicago, IL: University of Chicago Press.

———. 2007. "'Oh Those Turks!' Music, Politics, and Interculturality in the Balkans and Beyond." In *Balkan Popular Culture and the Ottoman Ecumene: Music, Image, and Regional Political Discourse*, edited by Donna A. Buchanan, 3–55. Lanham, MD: Scarecrow Press.

———. 2010. "Sonic Nostalgia: Music, Memory and Mythology in Bulgaria, 1990–2005." In *Post-Communist Nostalgia*, edited by Maria Todorova and Zsuzsa Gille, 129–154. Oxford and New York: Berghahn.

Burnett, Charles. 2000. "Spiritual Medicine: Music and Healing in Islam and Its Influence in Western Medicine." In *Musical Healing in Cultural Contexts*, edited by Penelope Gouk, 85–91. Aldershot, UK: Ashgate.

Burney Abbas, Shemeem. 2002. *The Female Voice in Sufi Ritual: Devotional Practices of Pakistan and India*. Austin: University of Texas Press.

Burton, Robert. 1857 [1621]. *Anatomy of Melancholy, What It Is; With All the Kindes, Causes, Symptomes, Prognostickes and Several Cures of It: In Three Maine Partitions with Their Several Sections, Members, and Subsections, Philosophically, Medicinally, Historically Opened and Cut Up, by Democritus Junior*. Philadelphia: J. W Moore.

Butler, Judith. 1988. "Performative Acts and Gender Constitution: An Essay in Phenomenology and Feminist Theory." *Theatre Journal* 49, no. 1: 519–592.

———. 1993 *Bodies That Matter: On the Discursive Limits of 'Sex.'* London, UK: Routledge.

———. 1997. *The Psychic Life of Power: Theories in Subjection*. Stanford, CA: Stanford University Press.

———. 2004. *Undoing Gender*. London, UK: Routledge.

Butler, Judith, Jürgen Habermas, Charles Taylor, and Cornel West. 1988. *The Power of Religion in the Public Sphere*, edited by Eduardo Mendieta and Jonathan Venantwerpen. New York: Columbia University Press.

Butler Schofield, Katherine. 2010. "Reviving the Golden Age Again: 'Classicization,' Hindustani Music, and the Mughals." *Ethnomusicology* 54, no. 3: 484–517.

Callahan, Christopher. 2000. "Music in Medieval Medical Practice: Speculations and Certainties." *College Music Symposium* 40: 151–164.

Can, Şefik. 2008. *Fundamentals of Rumi's Thought: A Mevlevi Sufi Perspective*. Somerset, NJ: Tughra Books.

Çayır, Kenan. 2006. "Islamic Novels: A Path to New Muslim Subjectivities." In *Islam in Public: Turkey, Iran, and Europe*, edited by Nilüfer Göle and Ludwig Ammann, 191–225. İstanbul: Bilgi University Press.

Çelebi, Kâtip. 1957. *The Balance of Truth*, edited by Geoffrey Lewis. London, CA: Allen and Unwin.

Çelik, Zeynep. 1986. *The Remaking of Istanbul: Portrait of an Ottoman City in the Nineteenth Century*. Seattle, WA: University of Washington Press.

Cemil Bey, Tanburi. 1989 [1913]. *Rehber-i Musiki*, edited by M. Hakan Cevher. İzmir, Turkey: Ege Üniversitesi Basımevi.

Çetinkaya, Bayram Ali. 2006. "Mevlana Öğretisinde Müzik ve Ney." In *Uluslararası Düşünce ve Sanatta Mevlana*, 679–699. Konya, Turkey: Rumi Yayınları.

Çetinkaya, Yalçın. 1995. *İhvân-i Safâ'da Müzik Düşüncesi*. İstanbul: İnsan Yayınları.

Cevziyye, el-, Ibn 'ül-kayyim. 2005. *Sevenlerin Bahçesi: Aska ve Âsiklara Dair*. İstanbul: Ahsen Yayınları.

Cheng, Anne Anlin. 2000. *The Melancholy of Race: Psychoanalysis, Assimilation, and Hidden Grief*. Oxford and New York: Oxford University Press.

Chittick, William. 1998. *The Self-Disclosure of God: Principles of Ibn al-'Arabi's Cosmology*. Albany: State University of New York Press.

Çınar, Alev. 2001. "National History as a Contested Site: The Conquest of Istanbul and Islamist Negotiations of the Nation." *Comparative Studies in Society and History* 43, no. 2: 364–391.

———. 2005. *Modernity, Islam, and Secularism in Turkey: Bodies, Places, and Time.* Minneapolis: University of Minnesota Press.

Çiştî, Muînüddïn. 2011. *Sûfi Tıbbı.* İstanbul: İnsan Yayınları.

Çıtlak, Fatih M. and Hüseyin Bingül. 2007. *Rumi and His Sufi Path of Love.* New Jersey: The Light.

Chakrabarty, Dipesh. 2000. *Provincializing Europe: Postcolonial Thought and Historical Difference.* Berkeley, CA: University of California Press.

Chapman, Mary and Glenn Hendler, eds. 1999. *Sentimental Men: Masculinity and the Politics of Affect in American Culture.* Berkeley, CA: University of California Press.

Clifford, James. 1997. *Routes: Travel and Translation in the Late Twentieth Century.* Cambridge, MA: Harvard University Press.

Clough, Patricia Ticineto. 2003. "Affect and Control: Rethinking the Body 'Beyond Sex and Gender.'" *Feminist Theory* 4, no. 3: 359–364.

———. 2009. "The New Empiricism Affect and Sociological Method." *European Journal of Social Theory* 12, no. 1: 43–61.

Çoban, Adnan. 2005. *Müzikterapi: Cana Şifa Ruha Gıda.* İstanbul: Timaş Yayınları.

———. 2009. *Şizofreni: Bin Parça Akıl.* İstanbul: Timaş Yayınları.

Collins, Patricia Hill. 2000. "Gender, Black Feminism, and Black Political Economy." *Annals of the American Academy of Political and Social Science* 568: 41–53.

Connell, R. W. 1995. *Masculinities.* Cambridge, UK: Polity Press.

Contandini, Anna. 2013. "Sharing a Taste? Material Culture and Intellectual Curiosity around the Mediterranean, from the Eleventh to the Sixteenth Century." In *The Renaissance and the Ottoman World,* edited by Anna Contadini and Claire Norton, 23–61. Surrey, UK: Ashgate.

Cooley, Timothy J. 1997. "Casting Shadows in the Field: An Introduction." In *Shadows in the Field: New Perspectives for Fieldwork in Ethnomusicology,* edited by Gregory F. Barz and Timothy J. Cooley, 3–22. Oxford and New York: Oxford University Press.

Corbin, Henry. 1969. *Creative Imagination in the Sufism of Ibn 'Arabi.* Translated by Ralph Manheim. Princeton, NJ: Princeton University Press.

Cowan, Jane K. 1990. *Dance and the Body Politic in Northern Greece.* Princeton, NJ: Princeton University Press.

Crenshaw, Kimberlé Williams. 1991. "Mapping the Margins: Intersectionality, Identity Politics, and Violence against Women of Color." *Stanford Law Review* 43, no. 6: 1241–1299.

Crowder, Robert. 1985. "Perception of the Major/Minor Distinction: II. Experimental Investigations." *Psychomusicology* 5: 3–24.

Crowder, Robert, J. Steven Reznick, and Stacey L. Rosenkrantz. 1991. "Perception of the Major/Minor Distinction: V. Preferences among Infants." *Bulletin of the Psychonomic Society* 29: 187–188.

Cvetkovich, Ann. 2012. *Depression: A Public Feeling.* Durham, NC, and London: Duke University Press.

Damasio, Antonia R. 2003. *Looking for Spinoza: Joy, Sorrow, and the Feeling Brain.* New York: Harcourt.

Darwin, Charles. 1904. *The Expression of the Emotions in Man and Animals.* London, UK: John Murray.

Davies, Stephen. 1997. "Why Listen to Sad Music if It Makes One Feel Sad?" in *Music and Meaning*, edited by Jenefer Robinson, 242–253. Ithaca, NY: Cornell University Press.

Deeb, Lara. 2006. *An Enchanted Modern: Gender and Public Piety in Shi'i Lebanon*. Princeton, NJ: Princeton University Press.

Degirmenci, Koray. 2013. *Creating Global Music in Turkey*. Lanham, MD: Lexington Books.

Delaney, Carol. 1991. *The Seed and the Soil: Gender and Cosmology in Turkish Village Society*. Berkeley, CA: University of California Press.

Deleuze, Gilles. 1993. *The Deleuze Reader*, edited by Constantin V. Boundas. New York: Columbia University Press.

Deleuze, Gilles, and Félix Guattari. 1987 [1980]. *A Thousand Plateaus: Capitalism and Schizophrenia*. Translation and forward by Brain Massumi. Minneapolis and London: University of Minnesota Press. .

Dent, Alexander. 2009. *River of Tears: Country Music, Memory, and Modernity in Brazil*. Durham, NC, and London: Duke University Press.

Derrida, Jacques. 2001. *The Work of Mourning*, edited by Pascale-Anne Brault and Michael Naas. Chicago, IL: University of Chicago Press.

Descartes, René. 1985. *The Philosophical Writings of Descartes*. Translated by Cottingham, Stoothoff, and Murdoch. Cambridge, UK: Cambridge University Press.

Devellioğlu, Ferit. 1980. *Osmanlıca-Türkçe Ansiklopedik*. Ankara, Turkey: Lugat.

Dewey, John. 1894. "The Theory of Emotion: (I.) Emotional Attitudes." *Psychological Review* 1, no. 6: 553–569.

———. 1895. "The Theory of Emotion: (II.) The Significance of Emotions." *Psychological Review* 2: 13–32.

Dinç, Ayhan, Özden Çankaya and Nail Ekici, eds. 2000. *İstanbul Radyosu: Anılar, Yaşantılar*. İstanbul: Yapı Kredi Kültür Yayıncılık.

Doidge, Norman. 2007. *The Brain That Changes Itself: Stories of Personal Triumph from the Frontiers of Brain Science*. London, UK: Penguin Books.

Dole, Christopher. 2012. *Healing Secular Life: Loss and Devotion in Modern Turkey*. Philadelphia: University of Pennsylvania Press.

Doumani, Beshara. 1995. *Rediscovering Palestine: Merchants and Peasants in Jabal Nablus, 1700–1900*. Berkeley, CA: University of California Press.

Doyle, Jennifer. 2005. "Critical Tears: Melodrama and Museums." In *Getting Emotional*, edited by Nicholas Baume, 42–53. Boston, MA: Institute of Contemporary Art.

Dressler, Markus. 2003. "Turkish Alevi Poetry in the Twentieth Century: The Fusion of Political and Religious Identities." *Alif: Journal of Comparative Poetics* 23: 109–154.

During, Jean. 1995. *Quelque chose se passe: Le sens de la tradition dans l'Orient musical*. Lagrasse, France: Éditions Verdier.

———. 2008. "Therapeutic Dimensions of Music in Islamic Culture." In *The Oxford Handbook of Medical Ethnomusicology*, edited by Benjamin Koen, with Jacqueline Lloyd, Gregory Barz, and Karen Brummel-Smith, 361–392. Oxford and New York: Oxford University Press.

Ederer, Eric. 2011. "The Theory and Praxis of *Makam* in Classical Turkish Music, 1910–2010." Ph.D. dissertation, University of California, Santa Barbara.

———. 2015. *Makam and Beyond: A Progressive Approach to Near Eastern Music Theory*. Santa Barbara, CA: Plum Loco Publishing.

Edvar-i 'ilmü'l mûsiki. Istanbul University Library, No. 5636.

Ehrenreich, Barbara. 2010. *Bright-Sided: How Positive Thinking Is Undermining America*. New York: Picador.

Eickelman, Dale. 1989. *The Middle East and Central Asia: An Anthropological Approach.* Upper Saddle River, NJ: Prentice Hall.

Elçin, Şükrü. 1976. *Ali Ufki: Hayatı, Eserleri ve Mecmua-i Saz ü Söz.* İstanbul: Millî Eğitim Basımevi.

Eligür, Banu. 2010. *The Mobilization of Political Islam in Turkey.* Cambridge: Cambridge University Press.

Elias, Jamal J. 1995. "Mawlawiah." In *The Oxford Encyclopedia of the Modern Islamic World*, vol. 3, edited by John L. Esposito, 77–78. Oxford, UK: Oxford University Press.

Erdener, Yıldıray. 1995. *The Song Contests of Turkish Minstrels: Improvised Poetry Sung to Traditional Music.* New York: Garland.

Ergün, Sadeddin Nuzhet. 1944. *Bektaşi Şairleri ve Nefesleri.* İstanbul: Maarif Kitaphanesi.

Erguner, Süleyman. 2003. *Raûf Yektâ Bey: Neyzen—Müzikolog—Bestekâr.* İstanbul: Kitabevi.

Eriş, Metin, ed. 1997. *50. Sanat Yılında: Selâhattin İçli ve Besteleri.* İstanbul: Türk Kültürüne Hizmet Vakfı.

Erlmann, Veit. 1999. *Music, Modernity and the Global Imagination: South Africa and the West.* Oxford and New York: Oxford University Press.

Erman, Tahire. 1998. "The Impact of Migration on Turkish Rural Women: Four Emergent Patterns." *Gender and Society* 12, no. 2: 146–167.

Erol, Ayhan. 2007. "Associative Structure in the Perception of Music: The Case of Turkish 'Yanık' (Scorched)." *Journal of Interdisciplinary Music Studies* 1, no. 1: 86–96.

Esposito, John L. 1998. *Islam: The Straight Path.* Oxford and New York: Oxford University Press.

Evans-Pritchard, Edward E. 1940. *The Nuer.* Vol. 940. Oxford, UK: Clarendon Press.

———. 1949. "Luo Tribes and Clans." *Rhodes-Livingstone Journal* 7: 24–40.

Ezgi, Suphi. 1953. *Nazari ve Ameli Türk Müsikisi* İstanbul: Hüsütabiat.

Farrell, Gerry. 1997. *Indian Music and the West.* Oxford, UK: Clarendon Press.

Faruqi, al-, Lois I. 1986. "Handasah al Sawt or the Art of Sound." In *The Cultural Atlas of Islam*, 441–479. New York: Macmillan Publishing.

Feld, Alina N. 2011. *Melancholy and the Otherness of God: A Study of the Hermeneutics of Depression.* Lanham, MD: Lexington Books.

Feld, Steven. 1990 [1982]. *Sound and Sentiment: Birds, Weeping, Poetics, and Song in Kaluli Expression.* Philadelphia: University of Pennsylvania Press.

Feld, Steven, Aaron A. Fox, Thomas Porcello, and David Samuels. 2004. "Vocal Anthropology: From the Music of Language to the Language of Song." In *A Companion to Linguistic Anthropology*, edited by Alessandro Duranti, 321–345. Maiden, MA: Blackwell Pub.

Feldman, Walter. 1990–1991. "Cultural Authority and Authenticity in the Turkish Repertoire." *Asian Music* 22, no. 1: 73–111.

———. 1993. "Mysticism, Didacticism and Authority in the Liturgical Poetry of the Halvetî Dervishes of Istanbul." *Edebiyât* 4: 243–265.

———. 1996. *Music of the Ottoman Court: Makam, Composition, and the Early Ottoman Instrumental Repertoire.* Intercultural Music Studies 10, edited by Max Peter Baumann. Berlin: Verlag für Wissenschaft und Bildung.

———. 2000. "Music in Performance: Who Are the Whirling Dervishes?" In *Garland Encyclopedia of World Music* 6: The Middle East, 107–111. New York: Garland.

Fernea, Elizabeth W., and Robert Fernea. 1972. "Variation in Religious Observance among Islamic Women." In *Scholars, Saints, and Sufis: Muslim Religious Institutions in the Middle East since 1500*, edited by Nikki R. Keddie. Berkeley, CA: University of California Press.

Flatley, Jonathan. 2008. *Affective Mapping: Melancholia and the Politics of Modernism*. Cambridge, MA: Harvard University Press.

Fonton, Charles. 1751. "Essai sur la musique orientale comparée avec la musique europée[n]ne." Paris: Bibliothèque Nationale (ms. Fr. Nouv. Acq. 4023).

Foucault, Michel. 1972 [1954]. *Madness: The Invention of an Idea* [*Maladie mentale et personalité*], translated by Alan Sheridan. New York: Harper Perennial.

———. 1972 [1969]. *The Archeology of Knowledge*, translated by Sheridan Smith. London, UK: A. M. Tavistock.

———. 1977. *Discipline and Punish: The Birth of the Prison*. New York: Vintage Books.

———. 1978. "Nietzsche, Genealogy, History." *Semiotexte* 3, no. 1: 78–94.

———. 1981. "The Order of Discourse." In *Untying the Text: A Poststructuralist Reader*, edited by Robert Young, 51–78. London, UK: Routledge, Keagan Paul.

———. 1992 [1984]. *The Uses of Pleasure: The History of Sexuality* 2. London, UK: Penguin.

———. 1997. "What Is Critique?" In *The Politics of Truth*, edited by Sylvere Lotringer and Lysa Hochroth, 41–83. New York: Semiotext(e).

Fox, Aaron A. 2004. *Real Country: Music and Language in Working-Class Culture*. Durham, NC, and London: Duke University Press.

Freud, Sigmund. 1922. "Mourning and Melancholia." *Journal of Nervous and Mental Disease* 56, no. 5: 543–545.

Friedlander, Ira and Nezih Uzel. 1975. *The Whirling Dervishes: Being an Account of the Sufi Order Known as the Mevlevis and Its Founder the Poet and Mystic Mevlana Jalalu-ddin Rumi*. New York: Macmillian.

Frishkopf, Michael. 2003. "Authorship in Sufi Poetry." *Alif: Journal of Comparative Poetics* 23: 78–108.

———. 2010. *Music and Media in the Arab World*, edited by Michael Frishkopf. Cairo, Egypt: American University in Cairo Press.

———. 2012. "Tradition and Modernity: The Globalization of Sufi Music in Egypt." In *Popular Culture in the Middle East and North Africa: A Postcolonial Outlook*, edited by Walid El Hamamsy and Mounira Soliman, 162–183. London, UK: Routledge.

Gadamer, Hans-Georg. 1976 [1964]. "Aesthetics and Hermeneutics." In *Philosophical Hermeneutics*, edited and translated by David E. Linge, 95–105. Berkeley, CA: University of California Press.

———. 1992. *Truth and Method*. 2nd rev. ed. Translated by Joel Weinsheimer and Donald G. Marshall. New York: Crossroad.

Garfias, Robert. 1981. "Survivals of Turkish Characteristics in Romanian Musica Lautareasca." *Yearbook for Traditional Music* 13: 97–107.

———. 2015. "The *Saz Semaisi* in *Evcara* by Dilhayat Kalfa and the Turkish Makam after the Ottoman Golden Age." In *This Thing Called Music: Essays in Honor of Bruno Nettl*, edited by Victoria Lindsay Levine and Philip V. Bohlman, 180–195. Lanham, MD: Rowman & Littlefield.

Gazimihal, Mahmut R. 1924. "Musik'de İnkılâp." *Millî Mecmua* 17, 262–264, 281–284.

———. 1928. *Anadolu Türküleri ve Musiki İstikbalimiz*. İstanbul: Maarif Matbaası.

———. 1936. *Türk Halk Müziklerinin Kökeni Meselesi*. İstanbul: Akşam Matbaası.

———. 1961. *Musiki Sözlüğü*. İstanbul: Milli Eğitim Basımevi.

Geertz, Clifford. 1973. *The Interpretation of Cultures: Select Essays by Clifford Geertz*. New York: Basic Books.

Gellner, Ernest. 1969. *Saints of the Atlas*. London, UK: Weidenfeld & Nicolson.

———. 1981. *Muslim Society*. Cambridge, UK: Cambridge University Press.

Gençel, Özge. 2006. "Müzikle Tedavi." *Kastamonu Eğitim Dergisi* 14, no. 2: 697–706.

Gevrekzâde, Hasan. 1794. *Neticetü'l fikriyye ve Tedbir-i velâdetü'l bikriyye*. Topkapi Palace Library. Istanbul, Turkey.

Ghazali, al-. 1995. *Al-Maqṣad al-asnā fī sḥarḥ asmā Allāh al-ḥusnā [The Ninety-Nine Beautiful Names of God]*. Translated by David B. Burrell and Nazih Daher. Cambridge, UK: Islamic Texts Society.

———. 2002. *Al-Ghazzali on Listening to Music*. Translated by Muhammad Nur Abdus Salam. Chicago, IL: Kazi Publications.

Ghoussoub, Mai, and Emma Sinclair-Webb, eds. 2000. *Imagined Masculinities: Male Identity and Culture in the Modern Middle East*. London: Saqi.

Giddens, Anthony. 1990. *The Consequences of Modernity*. Stanford, CA: Stanford University Press.

———. 1992. *The Transformation of Intimacy: Sexuality, Love, and Eroticism in Modern Societies*. Stanford, CA: Stanford University Press.

———. 1993. *The Giddens Reader*, edited by Philip Cassell. Stanford, CA: Stanford University Press.

Gilroy, Paul. 2005. *Postcolonial Melancholia*. New York: Columbia University Press.

Gill, Denise. 2016. "Turkey's Coup and the Call to Prayer: Sounds of Violence Meet Islamic Devotionals." *The Conversation*, August 10, 2016. https://theconversation.com/turkeys-coup-and-the-call-to-prayer-sounds-of-violence-meet-islamic-devotionals-63746

———. 2011. "Performing *Meşk*, Narrating History: Legacies of Transmission in Contemporary Turkish Musical Practices." *Comparative Studies in South Asia, Africa and the Middle East* 31, no. 3: 615–630.

Glasser, Jonathan. 2012. "Edmond Yafil and Andalusi Musical Revival in Early 20th-Century Algeria." *International Journal of Middle East Studies* 44, no. 4: 671–692.

———. 2016. *The Lost Paradise: Andalusi Music in Urban North Africa*. Chicago, IL: University of Chicago Press.

Göçek, Müge. 1987. *East Encounters West: France and the Ottoman Empire in the Eighteenth Century*. Oxford, UK: Oxford University Press.

Gökalp, Ziya. 1923. *Türkçülüğün Esasları*. Ankara, Turkey: Matbuat ve İstihbarat Matbaası.

Göle, Nilüfer. 1997. "The Quest for the Islamic Self within the Context of Modernity." In *Rethinking Modernity and National Identity in Turkey*, edited by Sibel Bozdoğan and Reşat Kasaba, 81–94. Seattle, WA: University of Washington Press.

———. 2002. "Islam in Public: New Visibilities and New Imaginaries." *Public Culture* 14, no. 1: 173–190.

———. 2003. "The Voluntary Adoption of Islamic Stigma Symbols." *Social Research* 70, no. 3: 809–828.

———. 2005. *Interpénétrations: L'Islam et l'Europe*. Paris: Galaade Editions.

Gordon, Avery F. 2004. *Keeping Good Time: Reflections on Knowledge, Power, and People*. Boulder, CO: Paradigm.

Gouk, Penelope. 2000. "Music, Melancholy, and Medical Spirits in Early Modern Thought." In *Music as Medicine: The History of Music Therapy since Antiquity*, edited by Peregrine Horden, 173–194. Aldershot, UK: Ashgate.

———. 2002. "The Role of Harmonics in the Scientific Revolution." In *The Cambridge History of Western Music Theory*, edited by Thomas Christensen, 223–245. Cambridge, UK: Cambridge University Press.

Gray, Lila Ellen. 2013. *Fado Resounding: Affective Politics and Urban Life*. Durham, NC, and London: Duke University Press.

Grebene, B. 1978. *Müzikle Tedavi*. Ankara, Turkey: Güven Publishing House.

Gregg, Melissa and Gregory J. Seigworth, eds. 2010. *The Affect Theory Reader*. Durham, NC, and London: Duke University Press.

Greve, Martin. 1995. *Die Europäisierung orientalischer Kunstmusik in der Türkei*. Berlin: Europäischer Verlag der Wissenschaften.

Grewal, Nitasha. 2014. "Black Aesthetic Theory: A Perspective." *International Journal of Research in Economics and Social Sciences* 4, no. 1: 51–57.

Grondin, Jean. 1994. *Introduction to Philosophical Hermeneutics*. Translated by Joel Weinsheimer. New Haven, CT: Yale University Press.

Gruner, Oskar Cameron. 1970. *The Canon of Medicine of Avicenna: Incorporating a Translation of the First Book*. Birmingham, AL: Gryphon Press.

Güneş, Abdulbaki, and Mehmet Yolcu. 2006. *Müfredât: Kur'ân Istilahlari Sözlüğü Rağib el-İsfâhani*. İstanbul: Çira Yayınları.

Güngör, Nazife. 1990. *Arabesk: Sosyokültürel Açıdan Arabesk Müzik*. Ankara, Turkey: Bilgi University Press.

Güvenç, Rahmi Oruç. 1993. *Türk Musikisi Tarihi ve Türk Tedavi Musikisi*. İstanbul: Metinler Matbaa.

Haberstam, Judith. 2005. *In a Queer Time and Place: Transgender Bodies, Subcultural Lives*. New York: New York University Press.

Hahn, Tomie. 2007. *Sensational Knowledge: Embodying Culture through Japanese Dance*. Middletown, CT: Wesleyan University Press.

Hall, Leslie. 1989. "The Turkish Fasıl: Selected Repertoire." Ph.D. dissertation, University of Toronto.

Halman, Talat Sait. 1983. "Love Is All: Mevlana's Poetry and Philosophy." In *Mevlana Celaleddin Rumi and the Whirling Dervishes*, edited by Metin And and Talat Sait Halman, 13–46. İstanbul: Dost.

Harré, Rom. 1986. *Varieties of Realism: A Rationale for the Natural Sciences*. Oxford, UK: Basil Blackwell.

Hashemi, Nader. 2009. *Islam, Secularism and Liberal Democracy: Toward a Democratic Theory for Muslim Societies*. Oxford, UK: Oxford University Press.

Hatfield, Elaine, J. T. Cacioppo, and R. L. Rapson. 1993. "Emotional Contagion: Current Directions." *Psychological Science* 2: 96–99.

Hebdige, Dick. 1979. *Subculture: The Meaning of Style*. London, UK: Methuen Publishing.

Heidegger, Martin. 1962 [1927]. *Being and Time*. Translated by John Macquarie and Edward Robinson. New York: Harper & Row, Publishers.

Helminski, Kabir, ed. 2000. *The Rumi Collection: An Anthology of Translations of Mevlana Jalaluddin Rumi*. Boston, MA: Shambhala.

Helvacıoğlu, Banu. 2006. "The Smile of Death and the Solemncholy of Masculinity." In *Islamic Masculinities*, edited by Lahoucine Ouzgane, 35–56. London, UK: Zed.

Henderson, David. 1996. "Emotion and Devotion, Lingering and Longing in Some Nepali Songs." *Ethnomusicology* 40, no. 3: 440–463.

Herzfeld, Michael. 1985. *The Poetics of Manhood: Contest and Identity in a Cretan Mountain Village*. Princeton, NJ: Princeton University Press.

———. 1997. *Cultural Intimacy: Social Poetics in the Nation-State*. London, UK: Routledge.

Hirshbein, Laura D. 2009. *American Melancholy: Constructions of Depression in the Twentieth Century*. New Brunswick, NJ: Rutgers University Press.

Hirschkind, Charles. 2006. *The Ethical Soundscape: Cassette Sermons and Islamic Counterpublics*. New York: Columbia University Press.

Hızır, İlyas Ağa. 1857. *Tarihi-i Enderun*. İstanbul: Matbaa-yı Âmire.

Ho, Engseng. 2006. *The Graves of Tarim: Genealogy and Mobility across the Indian Ocean*. Berkeley, CA: University of California Press.

Hochschild, Arlie. 1983. *The Managed Heart: The Commercialization of Human Feeling*. Berkeley, CA: University of California Press.

Holbrook, Victoria. 1994. *The Unreadable Shores of Love: Turkish Modernity and Mystic Romance*. Austin, TX: University of Texas Press.

Horwitz, Allan V., and Jerome C. Wakefield. 2007. *The Loss of Sadness: How Psychiatry Transformed Normal Sorrow into Depressive Disorder*. Oxford and New York: Oxford University Press.

Hood, Mantle. 1960. "The Challenge of Bi-musicality." *Ethnomusicology* 4, no. 2: 55–59.

Hooks, Bell. 1994. *Teaching to Transgress: Education as the Practice of Freedom*. London, UK: Routledge.

Hume, David. 1964. *The Philosophical Works: A Treatise of Human Nature and Dialogues Concerning Natural Religion*. Vol. 2. London, UK: Scientia Verlag Aalen.

Hurmalı, Gönül. 2013. *Kur'ân ve Şan Tekniği Hû*. İstanbul: Işık Yayınları.

Huron, David. 2006. *Sweet Anticipation: Music and the Psychology of Expectation*. Cambridge, MA: MIT Press.

———. 2010. "A Theory of Music and Sadness: A Role for Prolactin?" In *Proceedings of the 11th International Conference on Music Perception and Cognition*, edited by Steven M. Demorest, Steven J. Morrison, and Patricia Shehan Campbell, 5–8. Seattle, WA: Causal Productions.

———. 2011. "Why Is Sad Music Pleasurable? A Possible Role for Prolactin." *Music Scientiae* 15, no. 2: 146–158.

Ibn 'Arabi, Muhyiddin. 1989. *Journey to the Lord of Power: A Sufi Manual on Retreat*. Translated by Rabia Terri Harris. Rochester, VT: Inner Traditions International.

———. 2008. *The Four Pillars of Spiritual Transformation*. Translated by Stephen Hirtenstein. Oxford, UK: Anqa Publishing.

Idelson, Abraham Z. 1992. *Jewish Music: Its Historical Development*. Mineola, NY: Dover Publications.

İnal, İbnülemin M. 1955. *Son Hattatlar*. İstanbul: Maarif Basımevi.

———. 1958. *Hoş sâdâ: Son asır Türk musikişinasları*. No. 10. Istanbul: Maarif Basımevi.

Inalcık, Halil. 1964. "The Nature of Traditional Society: Turkey." In *Political Modernization in Japan and Turkey*, edited by Robert E. Ward and Dankward A. Rustow. Princeton, NJ: Princeton University Press.

Inalcık, Halil, and Donald Quataert, eds. 1994. *An Economic and Social History of the Ottoman Empire, 1300–1914*. Cambridge, UK: Cambridge University Press.

Ioanide, Paula. 2015. *The Emotional Politics of Racism: How Feelings Trump Facts in an Era of Colorblindness*. Stanford, CA: Stanford University Press.

Itzkowitz, Norman. 2008. *Ottoman Empire and Islamic Tradition*. Chicago, IL: University of Chicago Press.

Jackson, Maureen B. 2010. "The Girl in the Tree: Gender, Istanbul Soundscapes, and Synagogue Song." *Jewish Social Studies* 17, no. 1: 31–66.

———. 2013. *Mixing Musics: Turkish Jewry and the Urban Landscape of a Sacred Song*. Stanford, CA: Stanford University Press.

Jackson, Peter. 1991. "The Cultural Politics of Masculinity: Towards a Social Geography." *Transactions of the Institute of British Geographers* 16, no. 2: 99–213.

———. 1994. *Maps of Meaning: An Introduction to Cultural Geography*. London, UK: Routledge.

Jackson, Stanley. 1986. *Melancholia and Depression from Hippocratic Times to Modern Times*. New Haven, CT: Yale University Press.

Jäger, Ralf. 1996a. *Katalog der hamparsum-notası-Manuscripte im Archiv des Konservatoriums der Universität Istanbul*. Schriften zur Musikwissenschaft aus Münster 7. Eisenach, Germany: Karl Dieter Wagner

———. 1996b. *Türkische Kunstmusik und ihre handschriftlichen Quellen aus dem 19. Jahrhundert*. Schriften zur Musikwissenschaft aus Münster 8. Eisenach, Germany: Karl Dieter Wagner.

James, Robin. 2015. *Resilience and Melancholy: Pop Music, Feminism, Neoliberalism*. Winchester, UK: Zero Books.

Juslin, Patrik N., and Petri Laukka. 2004. "Expression, Perception, and Induction of Musical Emotions: A Review and a Questionnaire Study of Everyday Listening." *Journal of New Music Research* 33: 217–238.

Juslin, Patrik N., and John Sloboda, eds. 2011. *Handbook of Music and Emotion: Theory, Research, Applications*. Oxford and New York: Oxford University Press.

Kafadar, Osman. 1995. "Türk eğitim sisteminde pragmatik yönelişler ve Mehmet Emin Erişirgil." *Yüzüncü Yıl Ünv. Türkiye I. Eğitim Felsefesi Kongresi* 5, no. 8: 173–186.

Kağıtçıbaşı, Çiğdem. 1986. "Status of Women in Turkey: Cross-Cultural Perspectives." *International Journal of Middle East Studies* 18, no. 4: 485–499.

Kalaycıoğlu, Rahmi, ed. 1962. *Türk Musikisi Bestekârları Külliyatı*. İstanbul: Türk Musikisi Bestekârları Külliyatı Yayınları.

Kandiyoti, Deniz. 1987. "Emancipated but Unliberated? Reflections on the Turkish Case." *Feminist Studies* 13, no. 2: 317–338.

———. 1988. "Bargaining with Patriarchy." *Gender and Society* 2, no. 3: 274–290.

———, ed. 1991. *Women, Islam and the State*. London, UK: Macmillian.

———. 1997a. "Gendering the Modern: On Missing Dimensions in the Study of Turkish Modernity." In *Rethinking Modernity and National Identity in Turkey*, edited by Sibel Bozdogan and Resat Kasaba, 113–132. Seattle, WA: University of Washington Press.

———. 1997b. "The Paradoxes of Masculinity: Some Thoughts on Segregated Societies." In *Dislocating Masculinity: Comparative Ethnographies*, edited by Andrea Cornwall and Nancy Lindisfame, 197–213. London, UK: Routledge.

Kandiyoti, Deniz, and Ayşe Saktanber. 2002. *Fragments of Culture: The Everyday of Modern Turkey*. New Brunswick, NJ: Rutgers University Press.

Kantemiroğlu, Dimitri. 2001. *Kitâbu 'ilmi'l-mûsiki 'alâ vechi'l-hurûfât*, edited by Yalçın Tura. İstanbul: Yapı Kredi Yayınları.

Kapchan, Deborah A. 2007. *Traveling Spirit Masters: Moroccan Gnawa Trance and Music in the Global Marketplace*. Middletown, CT: Wesleyan University Press.

———. 2008. "The Promise of Sonic Translation: Performing the Festive Sacred in Morocco." *American Anthropologist* 110, no. 4: 467–483.

———. 2009. "Learning to Listen: The Sound of Sufism in France." *World of Music* 51, no. 2: 65–89.

Karadeniz, M. Ekrem. n.d. *Türk Musikinin Nazariye ve Esasları*. Ankara, Turkey: Türkiye İş Bankası Kültür Yayınları.

Karahasanoğlu, Songül. 2008. "A Comparative View of the Mey, Balaban and Duduk as Organological Phenomena." *The Journal of Academic Studies in Sociological Abstracts* 37: 437–446.

———. 2009. "Türk Müziğinde Uygulama-Kuram Sorunları ve Çözümleri Uluslar arası Çağrılı Kongresi." Final Report, İstanbul İTÜ Maçka Campus, Istanbul Technical University. İstanbul: İstanbul Büyük Şehir Belediyesi Yayınları.

———. 2012. "Anatolian Folk Songs for Soldiers who Died in Yemen." *Cuademos de Etnomusicologia* 2: 249–268.

Karakaya-Stump, Ayfer. 2015. *Rethinking Alevi-Bektashi History: Sources and Historiography*. Istanbul: Bilgi University Press.

Karakoyunlu, Yılmaz. 1998. *Yahya Kemâl Şarkıları*. İstanbul: Türk Musıkisi Vakfı Yayınları.

Karpat, Kemal. 1963. "The People's Houses in Turkey: Establishment and Growth." *Middle East Journal* 17, nos. 1–2: 55–67.

Kasaba, Reşat. 1997. "Kemalist Certainties and Modern Ambiguities." In *Rethinking Modernity and National Identity in Turkey*, edited by Sibel Bozdoğan and Reşat Kasaba, 15–36. Seattle, WA: University of Washington Press.

Katz, Max. Forthcoming. *Lineage of Loss: Counternarratives of North Indian Music*. Middletown, CT: Wesleyan University Press.

Kaygısız, Mehmet. 2000. *Türklerde Müzik*. İstanbul: Kaynak Yayınları.

Kayhan, Hacı Ahmet. 2011. *Sohbetler*. İstanbul: Birinci Basımevi.

Keil, Charles. 1966. "Motion and Feeling in Music." *Journal of Aesthetics and Art Criticism* (Spring): 337–349.

Keyder, Çağlar, ed. 1999. *Istanbul: Between the Global and the Local*. Lanham, MD: Rowman and Littlefield.

Klaser, Rajna. 2001. "From an Imagined Paradise to an Imagined Nation: Interpreting Şarkı as Cultural Play." Ph.D. dissertation, University of California at Berkeley.

Klein, Melanie. 1940. "Mourning and Its Relation to Manic-Depressive States." *International Journal of Psychoanalysis* 21: 125–153.

———. 1986. *The Selected Melanie Klein*, edited by Juliet Mitchell. New York: Free Press.

Kligman, Mark L. 2009. *Maqam and Liturgy: Ritual, Music, and Aesthetics of Syrian Jews in Brooklyn*. Detroit, MI: Wayne State University Press.

Koen, Benjamin D. 2008. "Music-Prayer-Meditation Dynamics in Healing." In *The Oxford Handbook of Medical Ethnomusicology*, edited by Benjamin Koen, with Jacqueline Lloyd, Gregory Barz, and Karen Brummel-Smith, 93–120. Oxford and New York: Oxford University Press.

Knapp, Steven. 1989. "Collective Memory and the Actual Past." *Representations* 26: 123–149.

Knight, Nick. 2014. "Why Do We Cry? The Science of Tears." *Independent* 18 (September, 2014). Accessed 17 September, 2015. http://www.independent.co.uk/life-style/health-and-families/features/why-do-we-cry-the-science-of-tears-9741287.html

Kocabaşoğlu, Uygur. 1980. *Şirket Tesizden Devlet Radyosuna*. Ankara, Turkey: SBF Yayınları.

Kocatürk, Utkan. 1988. *Atatürk ve Türkiye Cumhuriyeti Tarihi Kronolojisi, 1918–1938*. Ankara, Turkey: Türk Tarihi Kurumu Basımevi.

Konur, Himmet. 2007. *Sufi Ahlakı: Din, Ahlak ve Tasavvuf*. İstanbul: Ensar Nesriyat.

Koskoff, Ellen. 2001. *Music in Lubavicher Life*. Urbana and Chicago, IL: University of Illinois Press.

Kozanoğlu, Cevdet. 1988. *Radyo Hatırlarım*. Ankara, Turkey: TRT Yayınları.

Kristeva, Julia. 1987. *Soleil noir: Dépression et mélancolie*. Paris: Éditions Gallimard.

———. 1989. *Black Sun: Depression and Melancholia*. Translated by Léon Roudiez. New York: Columbia University Press.

———. 2004. *Melanie Klein*. Translated by Ross Guberman. New York: Columbia University Press.

─────. 2014. "On the Melancholic Imaginary." In *Discourse in Psychoanalysis and Literature*. Translated by Shlomoth Rimmon-Kenan, 104–123. New York: Methuen.

Kuşeyri, Abdu'l Kerim, el-. 1966. *Risale I.* İstanbul: Millî Eğitim Basımevi.

Kushner, David. 1997. "Self-Perception and Identity in Contemporary Turkey." *Journal of Contemporary History* 32, no. 2: 219–233.

Kusić, Dane. 1997. "Positivity of Music and Religion in Turkey." *Narodna Umjetnost* 34, no. 1: 147–178.

Kuyucu, Michael. 2005. *Pop Infilakı.* İstanbul: Kar Yayınları.

Langer, Robert. 2011. "Transfer Processes within Sufi Rituals: An Example from Istanbul." *European Journal of Turkish Studies* 13: 2–15.

Latour, Bruno. 2004. "How to Talk about the Body? The Normative Dimension of Science Studies." *Body & Society* 10, nos. 2–3: 205–229.

Lewis, Bernard. 1969 [1961]. *The Emergence of Modern Turkey.* 2nd ed. Oxford and New York: Oxford University Press.

Lupton, Deborah. 1998. *The Emotional Self: A Sociocultural Exploration.* London, UK: SAGE.

Lutz, Catherine A. 1988. *Unnatural Emotions: Everyday Sentiments on a Micronesian Atoll and Their Challenge to Western Theory.* Chicago, IL: University of Chicago Press.

Lutz, Catherine A., and Geoffrey M. White. 1986. "The Anthropology of Emotions." *Annual Review of Anthropology* 15: 405–436.

Magee, Wendy L., and Jane W. Davidson. 2002. "The Effect of Music Therapy on Mood States in Neurological Patients: A Pilot Study." *Journal of Music Therapy* 39, no. 1: 20–29.

Magrini, Tullia, ed. 2003. *Music and Gender: Perspectives from the Mediterranean.* Chicago, IL: University of Chicago Press.

Mahmood, Saba. 2005. *Politics of Piety: The Islamic Revival and the Feminist Subject.* Princeton, NJ: Princeton University Press.

─────. 2001. "Feminist Theory, Embodiment, and Docile Agent: Some Reflections on the Egyptian Islamic Revival." *Cultural Anthropology* 16, no. 2: 202–236.

Mandaville, Peter. 2011. "Transnational Muslim Solidarities and Everyday Life." *Nations and Nationalism* 17, no. 1: 7–24.

Marcus, George. 1995. "Ethnography in/of the World System: The Emergence of Multi-Sited Ethnography." *Annual Review of Anthropology* 24: 95–117.

─────. 2002. *The Sentimental Citizen: Emotion in Democratic Politics.* University Park, PA: Pennsylvania State University Press.

Marcus, Scott L. 1989. "Arab Music Theory in the Modern Period." Ph.D. dissertation, University of California, Los Angeles.

─────. 2002. "Music in Performance: 'Ud Lessons with George Michel." In *The Garland Encyclopedia of World Music* 6: The Middle East, edited by Virginia Danielson, Dwight Reynolds, and Scott Marcus, 45–46. New York: Garland.

─────. 2007. *Music in Egypt: Experiencing Music, Expressing Culture.* Oxford and New York: Oxford University Press.

Mardin, Şerif. 1989. *Religion and Social Change in Modern Turkey: The Case of Bediüzzaman Said Nursi.* Albany, NY: State University of New York Press.

─────. 2000. *The Genesis of Young Ottoman Thought: A Study in the Modernization of Turkish Political Ideas.* Syracuse, NY: Syracuse University Press.

─────. 2002. "Playing Games with Names." In *Fragments of Culture: The Everyday of Modern Turkey*, edited by Deniz Kandiyoti and Ayşe Saktanber, 115–127. New Brunswick, NJ: Rutgers University Press.

Markoff, Irene. 1986. "The Role of Expressive Culture in the Demystification of a Secret Sect of Islam: The Case of the Alevis of Turkey." *World of Music* 28, no. 3: 42–55.
———. 1990–1991. "The Ideology of Musical Practice and the Professional Turkish Musician: Tempering the Creative Impulse." *Asian Music* 22, no. 1: 129–145.
———. 1993. "Music, Saints, and Ritual: Sama and the Alevis of Turkey." *Manifestations of Sainthood in Islam*, edited by Grace Martin Smith, 95–110. New Jersey: Gorgias Press.
———. 1995. "Introduction to Sufi Music and Ritual in Turkey." *Middle East Studies Association Bulletin* 30, no. 2: 157–160.
Marx, Karl. 1976. *Capital: A Critique of Political Economy.* Vol. 1. Translated by B. Fowkes. Harmondsworth, UK: Penguin Books.
Massad, Joseph A. 2015. *Islam in Liberalism.* Chicago, IL: University of Chicago Press.
Massignon, Louis. 1982. *The Passion of al-Hallaj, Mystic and Martyr.* Princeton, NJ: Princeton University Press.
Massumi, Brian. 1996. "Becoming-Deleuzian." *Environment and Planning D: Society and Space* 14: 395–406.
———. 2002. *Parables for the Virtual: Movement, Affect, Sensation.* Durham, NC, and London: Duke University Press.
Mehmed, Haşim. 1864 [1853]. *Musiki Mecmuası.* İstanbul: Hariri Matb.
Mehmed, Nazmî, Efendi. 1864 [1853]. *Osmanlılarda Tasavvufî Hayat.* İstanbul: Insan Yayınları.
Meintjes, Louise. 2004. "Shoot the Sergeant, Shatter the Mountain: The Production of Masculinity in Zulu Ngoma Song and Dance in Post-Apartheid South Africa." *Ethnomusicology Forum* 13, no. 2: 173–201.
Menemencioğlu, Nermin. 1983. "The Ottoman Theatre, 1839–1923." *British Society for Middle Eastern Studies* 10, no. 1: 48–58.
Messick, Brink. 1993. *The Calligraphic State: Textual Domination and History in a Muslim Society.* Berkeley, CA: University of California Press.
Meyer, Rosalee K., Caroline Palmer, and Margarita Mazo. 1998. "Affective and Coherence Responses to Russian Laments." *Music Perception* 16, no. 1: 135–150.
Mills, Amy. 2010. *Streets of Memory: Landscape, Tolerance, and National Identity in Istanbul.* Athens, GA: University of Georgia Press.
Mitchell, Tim. 1991. *Colonizing Egypt.* Berkeley, CA: University of California Press.
Mizumura, Minae. 2015 [2008]. *The Fall of Language in the Age of English.* Translated by Mari Yoshihara and Juliet Winters Carpenter. New York: Columbia University Press.
Moglen, Seth. 2005. "On Mourning Social Injury." *Psychoanalysis, Culture & Society* 10, no. 2: 151–167.
Mohanty, Chandra Talpade. 2003. *Feminism without Borders: Decolonizing Theory, Practicing Solidarity.* Durham, NC, and London: Duke University Press.
Mourad, Suleiman. 2006. *Early Islam between Myth and History.* New York: Brill.
Muñoz, José Esteban. 2000. "Feeling Brown: Ethnicity and Affect in Ricardo Bracho's 'The Sweetest Hangover' (and Other STDs)." *Theatre Journal* 52, no. 1: 67–79.
———. 2006a. "Feeling Brown, Feeling Down: Latina Affect, the Performativity of Race, and the Depressive Position." *Signs: Journal of Women in Culture and Society.* 31, no. 3: 675–688.
———. 2006b. "The Vulnerability Artist: Nao Bustamante and the Sad Beauty of Reparation." *Women & Performance: A Journal of Feminist Theory* 16, no. 2: 191–200.

Mussell, Mary-Louise. 2004. "A Quest for the Divine and … the Tourist Dollar: The Dilemma Faced by Contemporary Dervish Orders." In *Inspired Speech: Prophecy in the Ancient Near East: Essays in Honor of Herbert B. Huffmon*, edited by John Kaltner and Louis Stulman, 347–353. London, UK: T&T Clark International.

Najmabadi, Afsaneh. 2005. *Women with Mustaches and Men without Beards: Gender and Sexual Anxieties of Iranian Modernity*. Berkeley, CA: University of California Press.

Nakano Glenn, Evelyn. 2002. *Unequal Freedom: How Race and Gender Shaped American Citizenship and Labor*. Cambridge, MA: Harvard University Press.

Nancy, Jean-Luc. 2007 [2002]. *Listening*. Translated by Charlotte Mandell. New York: Fordham University Press.

Naroditskaya, Inna. 2000. "Azerbaijanian Female Musicians: Women's Voices Defying and Defining the Culture." *Ethnomusicology* 44, no. 2: 234–256.

Nasuhioğlu, Orhan, ed. 1986. *Türk Musikisi: Raûf Yektâ Bey*. İstanbul: Pan Yayıncılık.

Navaro-Yashin, Yael. 1998. "Travesty and Truth: Politics of Culture and Fantasies of the State in Turkey." Ph.D. dissertation, Princeton University.

———. 2002a. *Faces of the State: Secularism and Public Life in Turkey*. Princeton, NJ: Princeton University Press.

———. 2002b. "The Market for Identities: Secularism, Islamism, Commodities." In *Fragments of Culture: The Everyday of Modern Turkey*, edited by Deniz Kandiyoti and Ayşe Saktanber, 221–253. New Brunswick, NJ: Rutgers University Press.

———. 2012. *The Make-Believe Space: Affective Geography in a Postwar Polity*. Durham, NC, and London: Duke University Press.

Negus, Keith. 1996. *Popular Music in Theory: An Introduction*. Middletown, CT: Wesleyan University Press.

Nelson, Kristina. 1985. *The Art of Reciting the Qur'an*. Austin, TX: University of Texas Press.

Nettl, Bruno. 1987. *The Radif of Persian Music: Studies of Structure and Cultural Context*. Champaign, IL: Elephant and Cat.

———. 2005 [1983]. *The Study of Ethnomusicology: Thirty-One Issues and Concepts*. 2nd ed. Champaign, IL: University of Illinois Press.

———. 2010. *Nettl's Elephant: On the History of Ethnomusicology*. Champaign, IL: University of Illinois Press.

Neuman, Daniel M. 1990. *The Life of Music in North India: The Organization of an Artistic Tradition*. Chicago, IL: University of Chicago Press.

Neuman, Dard. 2012. "Pedagogy, Practice, and Embodied Creativity in Hindustani Music." *Ethnomusicology* 56, no. 3: 426–449.

Nikolaisen, Bente. 2004. "Embedded Motion: Sacred Travel among Mevlevi Dervishes." In *Reframing Pilgrimage: Cultures in Motion*, edited by Simon Coleman and John Eade, 91–104. London, UK: Routledge.

Nooshin, Laudan. 1996. *The Processes of Creation and Recreation in Persian Classical Music*. Ph.D. dissertation, University of London (Goldsmiths).

———. 1998. "The Song of the Nightingale: Processes of Improvisation in *Dastgāh Segāh* (Iranian Classical Music)." *British Journal of Ethnomusicology* 7, no. 1: 69–116.

———. 2003. "Improvisation as 'Other': Creativity, Knowledge and Power—The Case of Iranian Classical Music." *Journal of the Royal Musical Association* 128, no. 2: 242–296.

Nora, Pierre. 1989. "Between Memory and History: *Les Lieux de Mémoire*." *Representations* 26: 7–25.

Nurbakhsh, Javad. 1976. *Samā in Sufism*. Tehran, London, and New York: Khaniqahi Nimatullahi.

Nussbaum, Martha. 2001. *Upheavals of Thought: The Intelligence of Emotion*. Cambridge, UK: Cambridge University Press.

———. 2013. *Political Emotions: Why Love Matters for Justice*. Cambridge, MA: Harvard University Press.

O'Connell, John Morgan. 1996. "*Alaturka* Revisited: Style as History in Turkish Vocal Performance." Ph.D. dissertation, University of California, Los Angeles.

———. 1998. "The Arab in *Arabesk*: Style and Stereotype in Turkish Vocal Performance." In *The Limerick Anthology of Arab Affairs*, edited by Nabil Adawi and Barry Wharton, 87–103. International Studies Series. Limerick, Ireland: University of Limerick Press, .

———. 2000. "Fine Art, Fine Music: Controlling Turkish Taste at the Fine Arts Academy in 1926." *Yearbook for Traditional Music* 32: 117–142.

———. 2002. "From Empire to Republic: Vocal Style in Twentieth Century Turkey." In *The Garland Encyclopedia of World Music, Vol. 6: The Middle East*, edited by Virginia Danielson, Scott Marcus, and Dwight Reynolds, 781–787. New York: Garland Publishers.

———. 2003. "Song Cycle: The Life and Death of the Turkish *Gazel*." *Ethnomusicology* 47, no. 3: 399–414.

———. 2005a. "In the Time of *Alaturka*: Identifying Difference in Musical Discourse." *Ethnomusicology* 49, no. 2: 177–205.

———. 2005b. "Sound Sense: Mediterranean Music from a Turkish Perspective." In *The Mediterranean in Music*, edited by David Cooper and Kevin Dawe, 3–25. Lanham, MD: Scarecrow Press.

———. 2006. "The Mermaid of the Meyhane: The Legend of a Greek Singer in a Turkish Tavern." In *Music and the Sirens*, edited by Linda Austern and Inna Naroditskaya, 273–293. Bloomington: Indiana University Press.

———. 2010. "*Alabanda*: Brass Bands and Musical Methods in Turkey." In *Giuseppe Donizetti Pascià: Traiettorie musicali e storiche tra Italia e Turchia*, edited by Federico Spinetti, 19–37. Bergamo, Italy: Fondazione Donizetti.

———. 2013. *Alaturka: Style in Turkish Music (1923–1938)*. Farnham: Ashgate.

———. 2015. "Sounds Humane: Music and Humanism in the Aga Khan Humanities Project." In *The Oxford Handbook of Applied Ethnomusicology*, edited by Svanibor Pettan and Jeff Todd Titan, 602–638. Oxford and New York: Oxford University Press.

Olick, Jeffrey K. 1998. "Introduction: Memory and the Nation: Continuities, Conflicts, and Transformations." *Social Science History* 22, no. 4: 377–387.

Önder, Sylvia Wing. 2007. *We Have No Microbes Here: Healing Practices in a Turkish Black Sea Village*. Durham, NC, and London: Carolina Academic Press.

Öngören, Mahmut Tali. 1986. "Radio and Television in Turkey." In *The Transformation of Turkish Culture: The Atatürk Legacy*, edited by Günsel Renda and C. Max Kortepeter, 179–196. Princeton, NJ: Kingston Press.

Oransay, Gültekin. 1983. "Cumhuriyetin İlk Elli Yılında Geleneksel Sanat Musikimiz." In *Cumhuriyet Dönemi Türkiye Ansiklopedesi*, 1496–1509. İstanbul: İletişim.

———. 1985. *Atatürk ile küğ: Belgeler ve virile*. İzmir, Turkey: Küğ Yayını.

Ortner, Sherry B. 1997a. "Introduction." In "The Fate of 'Culture': Geertz and Beyond," edited by Sherry B. Ortner, special issue, *Representations* 59: 1–13.

———. 1997b. "Thick Resistance: Death and the Cultural Construction of Agency in Himalayan Mountaineering." In "The Fate of 'Culture': Geertz and Beyond," edited by Sherry B. Ortner, special issue, *Representations* 59: 135–162.

Ouzgane, Lahoucine, ed. 2006. *Islamic Masculinities*. London, UK: Zed.

Ozak, Muzaffer. 1988. *Irshad: Wisdom of a Sufi Master*. Translated by Muhtar Holland. New York: Pir Press.

———. 1991. *Adornment of Hearts [Zintau-l Qulub]*. Translated by Muhtar Holland and Sixtina Friedrich. New York: Pir Press.

———. 2001. *The Unveiling of Love: Sufism and the Remembrance of God*. Translated by Muhtar Holland. New York: Pir Press.

Ozyegin, Gul. 2015a. *Gender and Sexuality in Muslim Cultures*. London, UK: Routledge.

———. 2015b. *New Desires, New Selves: Sex, Love, and Piety among Turkish Youth*. New York: New York University Press.

Özalp, Nazmi. 1986. *Türk Musikisi Tarihi*. 2 vols. Ankara, Turkey: Müziki Dairesi Başkanlığı.

Özbek, Meral. 2006. *Popüler Kültür ve Orhan Gencebay Arabeski*. İstanbul: İletişim.

Özgiray, Ahmet. 1995. "Atatürk ve Musiki": *Ankara Üniversitesi Türk İnkılap Tarihi Enstitüsü Atatürk Yolu Dergisi* 4, no. 15. 279–289

Özgür, İren. 2006. "Arabesk Music in Turkey in the 1990s and Changes in National Demography, Politics, and Identity." *Turkish Studies* 7, no. 2: 175–190.

Özkan, İsmail H. 1984. *Türk Mûsıkîsi Nazariyatı ve Usûlleri: Küdüm Velveleri*. İstanbul: Ötüken Neşriyat.

Özkırımlı, Umut, ed. 2014. *The Making of a Protest Movement in Turkey: #occupygezi*. London, UK: Palgrave MacMillan.

Öztuna, Yılmaz. 1969 [1955]. *Türk Musikisi Ansiklopedisi*. İstanbul: Millî Eğitim Basımevi.

———. 1990. *Büyûk Türk Musikisi Ansiklopedisi*. 2 vols. İstanbul: Millî Eğitim Basımevi.

Öztürk, Yaşar Nuri. 1997. *Mevlana ve İnsan*. İstanbul: Yeni Boyut.

Öztürkmen, Arzu. 1998. *Türkiye'de Folklor ve Milliyetçilik*. İstanbul: İletişim Yayınları.

———. 2005a. "Folklore on Trial: Pertev Naili Boratav and the Denationalization of Turkish Folklore." *Journal of Folklore Research* 42, no. 2: 185–216.

———. 2005b. "Staging a Ritual Dance out of its Context: The Role of an Individual Artist in Transforming the Alevi Semah." *Asian Folklore Studies* 64: 247–260.

Özyürek, Esra. 2006. *Nostalgia for the Modern: State Secularism and Everyday Politics in Turkey*. Durham and London: Duke University Press.

Pamuk, Orhan. 2004. *Istanbul: Memories and the City*. New York: Random House.

Panksepp, Jaak. 1995. "The Emotional Sources of 'Chills' Induced by Music." *Music Perception* 13, no. 2: 171–207.

Panksepp, Jaak, and Günther Bernatzky. 2002. "Emotional Sounds and the Brain: The Neuro-Affective Foundations of Musical Appreciation." *Behavioural Processes* 60, no. 2: 133–155.

Peirce, Leslie P. 1993. *The Imperial Harem: Women and Sovereignty in the Ottoman Empire*. Oxford and New York: Oxford University Press.

Pennanen, Risto Pekka. 2004. "The Nationalization of Ottoman Popular Music in Greece." *Ethnomusicology* 48, no. 1: 1–25.

Pennanen, Risto Pekka, Panagiotis C. Poulos, and Aspasia Theodosiou, eds. 2013. *Ottoman Intimacies, Balkan Musical Realities*. Helsinki: Foundation of the Finnish Institute at Athens.

Peristiany, John G., ed. 1966. *Honour and Shame: The Values of Mediterranean Societies*. Chicago, IL: Chicago University Press.

Perman, Tony. 2010. "Dancing in Opposition: *Muchongoyo*, Emotion, and the Politics of Performance in Southeastern Zimbabwe." *Ethnomusicology* 54, no. 3: 425–451.

Petrović, Ankica. 1988. "Paradoxes of Muslim Music in Boznia and Herzegovina." *Asian Music* 20, no. 1: 128–147.

Phelan, Peggy. 1993. *Unmarked: The Politics of Performance*. London, UK: Routledge.

Popescu-Judetz, Eugenia. 1996. *Meanings in Turkish Musical Culture*. İstanbul: Pan Yayıncılık.

Quataert, Donald. 2005. *The Ottoman Empire, 1700–1922*. 2nd ed. Cambridge, UK: Cambridge University Press.

Qureshi, Regula. 2006. "Islam and Music." In *Sacred Sound: Experiencing Music in World Religions*, edited by Guy L. Beck, 89–96. Waterloo, Canada: Wilfrid Laurier University Press.

Racy, Ali Jihad. 1976. "The Record Industry and Egyptian Traditional Music: 1904–1932." *Ethnomusicology* 20, no. 1: 23–48.

———. 1991. "Creativity and Ambience: An Ecstatic Feedback Model from Arab Music." *World of Music* 33, no. 3: 7–28.

———. 1998. "Improvisation, Ecstasy, and Performance Dynamics in Arabic Music." In *The Course of Performance: Studies in the World of Musical Improvisation*, edited by Bruno Nettl and Melinda Russell, 95–112. Chicago, IL: University of Chicago Press.

———. 2003. *Making Music in the Arab World: The Culture and Artistry of* Tarab. Cambridge, UK: Cambridge University Press.

Radden, Jennifer, ed. 2000. *The Nature of Melancholy: From Aristotle to Kristeva*. Oxford and New York: Oxford University Press.

Rahaim, Matthew. 2012. *Musicking Bodies: Gesture and Voice in Hindustani Music*. Middletown, CT: Wesleyan University Press.

Rasmussen, Anne. 2010. *Women, the Recited Qur'an, and Islamic Music in Indonesia*. Berkeley, CA: University of California Press.

Raudvere, Catharina. 2002. *The Book and the Roses: Sufi Women, Visibility, and* Zikir *in Contemporary Istanbul*. Stockholm: Swedish Research Institute in İstanbul.

Reddy, William M. 2001. *The Navigation of Feeling: A Framework for the History of Emotions*. Cambridge, UK: Cambridge University Press.

Redhouse, James. 1997. *Redhouse Türkçe-İngilizce Sözlüğü*. İstanbul, Turkey: SEV Matbaacılık ve Yayıncılık A.Ş.

Reicher, Stephen. 2001. "The Psychology of Crowd Dynamics." In *Blackwell Handbook of Social Psychology: Group Processes*, edited by Michael A. Hogg and R. Scott Tindale, 182–208. Oxford, UK: Blackwell Publishers.

Reinhard, Kurt, and Ursula Reinhard. 1969. *Turqie*. Vol. 4, *Les Traditions Musicales*. Paris: Buchet-Chastel.

———. 1984. *Musik der Türkei*. Wilhelmshaven, Germany: Heinrichshofens Verlag.

Reinhard, Ursula and Tiago Oliveira Pinto. 1990. *Sänger und Poeten mit der Laute Türkische Aşık und Ozan*. Berlin: Dietrich Reimar.

Renard, John. 2008. *Friends of God: Islamic Images of Piety, Commitment, and Servanthood*. Berkeley, CA: University of California Press.

Rice, Timothy. 1994. *May it Fill your Soul: Experiencing Bulgarian Music*. Chicago, IL: University of Chicago Press.

———. 1996. "Toward a Mediation of Field Methods and Field Experience in Ethnomusicology." In *Shadows in the Field: New Perspectives for Fieldwork in Ethnomusicology*, edited by Gregory F. Barz and Timothy J. Cooley, 101–120. Oxford and New York: Oxford University Press.

———. 2003. "Time, Place, and Metaphor in Musical Experience and Ethnography." *Ethnomusicology* 47, vol. 2: 151–179.

Ricoeur, Paul. 1978. "The Metaphorical Process as Cognition, Imagination, and Feeling." *Critical Inquiry* 5, no. 1: 143–159.

———. 1981. "The Narrative Function." In *Hermeneutics and the Human Sciences*, edited and translated by John B. Thompson, 274–296. Cambridge, UK: Cambridge University Press.

Rivers, William Halse Rivers. 1900. "A Genealogical Method of Collecting Social and Vital Statistics." *Journal of the Anthropological Institute of Great Britain and Ireland* 30, 74–82.

Ritter, Helmut. 1933. "Die Reigen der 'Tanzenden Derwische.'" *Zeitschrift für vergleichende Musikwissenschaft* 1: 28–48.

Rona, Mustafa. 1970. *20. Yüzyıl Türk Musıkisi*. İstanbul: Türkiye Yayınevi.

Rosaldo, Michelle. 1984. "Toward an Anthropology of Self and Feeling." In *Culture Theory: Essays on Mind, Self, and Emotion*, edited by Richard A. Shweder and R. LeVine, 137–157. Cambridge, UK: Cambridge University Press.

Rose, Nikolas. 2004. *Becoming Neurochemical Selves*. Piscataway, NJ: Transaction Publishers.

Roseman, Marina. 1991. *Healing Sounds from the Malaysian Rainforest: Temiar Music and Medicine*. Vol. 28. Berkeley, CA: University of California Press.

———. 2008. "A Fourfold Framework for Cross-Cultural, Integrative Research on Music and Medicine." In *The Oxford Handbook of Medical Ethnomusicology*, edited by Benjamin Koen, with Jacqueline Lloyd, Gregory Barz, and Karen Brummel-Smith, 18–45. Oxford and New York: Oxford University Press.

Rosenwein, Barbara H. 2006. *Emotional Communities in the Early Middle Ages*. Ithaca, NY: Cornell University Press.

Ruby, Jay, eds. 1982. *A Crack in the Mirror: Reflexive Perspectives in Anthropology*. Philadelphia: University of Pennsylvania Press.

Ruddick, Susan. 2010. "The Politics of Affect: Spinoza in the Work of Negri and Deleuze." *Theory, Culture & Society* 27, no. 4: 21–24.

Rumi, Mevlana Celaleddin. 1998a. "The Angel Is Free." In *The Rumi Collection*, edited by Kabir Helminski, 16. Translated by Kabir Helminski and Camille Helminski. Boston, MA: Shambhala Publications.

———. 1998b. "Expansion and Contraction." In *The Rumi Collection*, edited by Kabir Helminski, 189–191. Translated by Kabir Helminski. Boston, MA: Shambhala Publications.

———. 1998c. "The Human Shape Is a Ghost." In *The Rumi Collection*, edited by Kabir Helminski, 2. Translated by John Moyne and Coleman Barks. Boston, MA: Shambhala Publications.

———. 1998d. "There's Nothing Ahead." In *The Rumi Collection*, edited by Kabir Helminski, 7. Translated by John Moyne and Coleman Barks. Boston: Shambhala Publications, Inc.

———. 1999. *Signs of the Unseen: The Discourses of Jalaluddin Rumi*. Translated by Wheeler Thackston. Boston, MA: Shambhala Publications.

———. 2004. *The Essential Rumi*. Translated by Coleman Barks. New York: HarperOne.

———. 2004. *The Mathanawi of Jalālud'din Rūmī*. Translated by Reynold A. Nicholson. Lahore, Pakistan: Sang-e-Meel.

Sağman, Ali R. 1951. *Mevlid: Nasıl Okunur ve Mevlidhanlar*. İstanbul: Fakülteler Matbaası.

Şahin, Haluk and Aşu Aksoy. 1993. "Global Media and Cultural Identity in Turkey." *Journal of Communication* 43, no. 2: 31–41.

Said, Edward W. 1978. *Orientalism*. New York: Vintage Books.

———. 1993. *Culture and Imperialism*. New York: Knopf.

———. 2003. *Freud and the Non-European*. London, UK: Verso.

Saji, Alia, al-. 2004. "The Memory of Another Past: Bergson, Deleuze and a New Theory of Time." *Continental Philosophy Review* 37, no. 2: 203–239.

Sandoval, Chela. 1995. "Feminist Forms of Agency and Oppositional Consciousness: U.S. Third World Feminist Criticism." In *Provoking Agents: Gender and Agency in Theory and Practice*, edited by Judith Kegan Gardiner, 208–226. Urbana, IL: University of Illinois Press.

Sartre, Jean-Paul. 1962. *Sketch for a Theory of the Emotions*. Translated by P. Mairet. London, UK: Methuen.

Savage, Roger W. H. 2004. "Tradition and Imagination in a Transnational World." Paper presented at the Center for the Interdisciplinary Study of Music, University of California, Santa Barbara, May 12, 2004.

———. 2010. *Hermeneutics and Music Criticism*. London, UK: Routledge.

Saygun, Adnan. 1965. *Atatürk ve Musiki*. Ankara, Turkey: Ajans-Türk Matbaacılık Sanayii.

———. 1987. *Atatürk ve musiki: O'nunla birlikte, O'ndan sonra*. İstanbul: Sevda-Cenap And Müzik Vakfı Yayınları.

Schade-Poulsen, Marc. 1999. *Men and Popular Music in Algeria: The Social Significance of Raï*. Austin, TX: University of Texas Press.

Scheper-Hughes, Nancy. 1992. *Death without Weeping: The Violence of Everyday Life in Brazil*. Berkeley, CA: University of California Press.

Schimmel, Annemarie. 2001. "The Role of Music in Islamic Mysticism." In *Sufism Music and Society, in Turkey and the Middle East*, edited by Anders Hammarlund, Tord Olsson, and Elisabeth Özdalga, 5–27. Istanbul: Swedish Research Institute.

Schleiner, Winfried. 1991. *Melancholy, Genius, and Utopia in the Renaissance*. Wiesbaden, Germany: Harrassowitz.

Schoenewolf, G. 1990. "Emotional Contagion: Behavioral Induction in Individuals and Groups." *Modern Psychoanalysis* 15: 49–61.

Sedgwick, Eve Kosofsky. 2003. *Touching Feeling: Affect, Pedagogy, Performativity*. Durham, NC, and London: Duke University Press.

———. 2007. "Melanie Klein and the Difference Affect Makes." *South Atlantic Quarterly* 106, no. 3: 625–642.

Seeman, Sonia Tamar. 2002. "'You're Roman!': Music and Identity in Turkish Roman Communities." Ph.D. dissertation, University of California, Los Angeles.

———. 2006. "Presenting 'Gypsy,' Re-presenting Roman: Towards an Archeology of Aesthetic Production and Social Identity." In *Music and Anthropology: Journal of Musical Anthropology of the Mediterranean* 11. http://umbc.edu/MA/index/number11/seeman/see_0.htm

———. Forthcoming. *Sounding Roman: Music and Performing Identity in Western Turkey*. Oxford and New York: Oxford University Press.

Seremetakis, C. Nadia. 1991. *The Last Word: Women, Death, and Divination in Inner Mani*. Chicago, IL: University of Chicago Press.

———, ed. 1994. *The Senses Still: Perception and Memory as Material Culture in Modernity*. Boulder, CO: Westview Press.

Seroussi, Edwin. 1989. *Mizimrat Qedem: The Life and Music of R. Isaac Algazi from Turkey*. Jerusalem: Renanot.

———. 1990. "The Turkish *Makam* in the Musical Culture of the Ottoman Jews: Sources and Examples." *Israel Studies in Ethnomusicology* 5: 43–68.

Sezer, Fahri. 2013. "Professionals Working in the Field of Psychological Counseling Views on the Music Therapy [Psikolojik danışma alanındaki uzmanların müzik terapisine ilişkin görüşleri]." *Journal of Human Sciences* 10, no. 2: 219–232.

Shah, Idries. 1964. *The Sufis*. New York: Anchor Books.

Shankland, David. 2006. *The Alevis in Turkey: The Emergence of a Secular Islamic Tradition*. London, UK: Routledge.

Shannon, Jonathon Holt. 2006. *Among the Jasmine Trees: Music and Modernity in Contemporary Syria*. Middletown, CT: Wesleyan University Press.

———. 2011. "Suficized Musics of Syria at the Intersection of Heritage and the War on Terror; Or 'A Rumi with a View.'" In *Muslim Rap, Halal Soaps, and Revolutionary Theater: Artistic Developments in the Muslim World*, edited by Karin van Nieuwkerk, 257–274. Austin, TX: University of Texas Press.

Shelemay, Kay Kaufman. 1997. "The Ethnomusicologist, Ethnographic Method, and the Transmission of Tradition." In *Shadows in the Field: New Perspectives for Fieldwork in Ethnomusicology*, edited by Gregory F. Barz and Timothy J. Cooley, 189–204. Oxford and New York: Oxford University Press.

Shiloah, Amnon. 1995. *Music in the World of Islam: A Socio-Cultural Study*. Detroit, MI: Wayne State University Press.

———. 2000. "Jewish and Muslim Traditions of Music Therapy." In *Music as Medicine: The History of Music Therapy since Antiquity*, edited by Peregrine Horden, 68–83. Aldershot, UK: Ashgate.

Shissler, Holly. 2003. *Between Two Empires: Ahmet Ağaoğlu and the New Turkey*. London, UK: I. B. Tauris.

———. 2004. "Beauty Is Nothing to Be Ashamed Of: Beauty Contests as Tools of Women's Liberation in Early Republican Turkey." *Comparative Studies of South Asia, Africa and the Middle East* 24, no. 1: 107–122.

Shryock, Andrew. 1997. *Nationalism and the Genealogical Imagination: Oral History and Textual Authority in Tribal Jordan*. 23. Berkeley, CA: University of California Press.

Signell, Karl. 1967. "Mozart and the *Mehter*." *Consort* 24: 310–322.

———. 1976. "The Modernization Process in Two Oriental Music Cultures: Turkish and Japanese." *Asian Music* 7, no. 2: 72–102.

———. 1977. *Makam: Modal Practice in Turkish Art Music*. Washington, DC: Asian Music Publications.

———. 1980. "Turkey's Classical Music, A Class Symbol." *Asian Music* 12, no. 1: 164–169.

Silverstein, Brian. 2007. "Sufism and Modernity in Turkey: From the Authenticity of Experience to the Practice of Discipline in Sufism and the Modern." In *Sufism and the 'Modern' in Islam*, edited by Julia Day Howell and Martin van Bruinessen, 39–61. London, UK: I. B. Tauris.

Sinclair-Webb, Emma. 2000. "'Our Bülent Is Now a Commando': Military Service and Manhood in Turkey." In *Imagined Masculinities: Male Identity and Culture in the Modern Middle East*, edited by Mai Ghoussoub and Emma Sinclair-Webb, 65–91. London, UK: Saqi.

Sirman, Nükhet. 2000. "Writing the Usual Love Story: The Fashioning of Conjugal and National Subjects in Turkey." In *Gender, Agency, and Change: Anthropological Perspectives*, edited by Victoria Ana Godard, 250–272. London, UK: Routledge.

Slawek, Stephen. 1998. "Keeping It Going: Terms, Practices, and Processes of Improvisation in Hindustani Instrumental Music." In *In the Course of Performance: Studies in the World of Musical Improvisation*, edited by Bruno Nettl and Melinda Russell, 335–366. Chicago, IL: University of Chicago Press.

Small, Christopher. 1998. *Musicking: The Meanings of Performing and Listening.* Middletown, CT: Wesleyan University Press.

Solmaz, Metin. 1996. *Türkiye'de Pop Müzik: Dünü ve Bugünün İle bir İnfilak Masalı.* İstanbul: Pan Yayıncılık.

Soloman, Thomas. 2005a. "'Listening to Istanbul': Imagining Place in Turkish Rap Music." *Studia Musicologica Norvegica* 31: 46–67.

———. 2005b. "Living Underground Is Tough: Authenticity and Locality in the Hip-Hop Community in Istanbul, Turkey." *Popular Music* 24, no. 1: 1–20.

———. 2006. "Hardcore Muslims: Islamic Themes in Turkish Rap in Diaspora and in the Homeland." *Yearbook for Traditional Music* 38: 59–78.

Somakçı, Pınar. 2003. "Türklerde müzikle tedavi." *Erciyes Üniversitesi Sosyal Bilimler Enstitüsü Dergisi* 15, no. 2: 131–140.

Soyini Madison, D. 2012 [2005]. *Critical Ethnography: Method, Ethics, and Performance.* 2nd ed. Thousand Oaks, CA: SAGE.

Sözer, Vural. 1964. *Müzik ve Müzisyenler Ansiklopedisi.* İstanbul: Tan.

———. 1986. *Müzik ve Müzisyenler Ansiklopedisi.* 2 vols. İstanbul: Rezmi Kitabevi.

Spelman, Elizabeth V. 1998. *Fruits of Sorrow: Framing Our Attention to Suffering.* Boston, MA: Beacon Press.

Spillers, Hortense J. 1983. "A Hateful Passion, A Lost Love." *Feminist Studies* 9, no. 2: 293–323.

———. 1996. "'All the Things You Could Be by Now, If Sigmund Freud's Wife Was Your Mother': Psychoanalysis and Race." *Critical Inquiry* 22, no. 4 (Summer): 710–734.

Spinetti, Federico, ed. 2010. *Giuseppe Donizetti Pascià: Traiettorie musicali e storiche tra Italia e Turchia.* Bergamo, Italy: Fondazione Donizetti.

Spivak, Gayatri Chakravorty. 1988. "Can the Subaltern Speak?" In *Marxim and the Interpretation of Culture,* edited by Cary Nelson and Lawrence Grossberg. Urbana, IL: University of Illinois Press.

Starr, June. 1989. "The Role of Turkish Secular Law in Changing the Lives of Rural Muslim Women, 1950–1970." *Law and Society Review* 23, no. 3: 497–523.

Starrett, Gregory. 1998. *Putting Egypt to Work: Education, Politics, and Religious Transformation in Egypt.* Berkeley, CA: University of California Press.

Stearns, Peter N., and Carol Z. Stearns. 1985. "Emotionology: Clarifying the History of Emotions and Emotional Standards."*American Historical Review* 90, no. 4: 813–836.

Stewart, Kathleen. 2007. *Ordinary Affects.* Durham, NC, and London: Duke University Press.

Stokes, Martin. 1992. *The Arabesk Debate: Music and Musicians in Modern Turkey.* Oxford, UK: Clarendon Press.

———. 1995. "History, Memory and Nostalgia in Contemporary Turkish Musicology." *Past and Present Perspectives for the Anthropology of Mediterranean Music.* Meeting of the ICTM Study Group on the "Anthropology of Music in Mediterranean Cultures." Venice, Italy. June 1–3, 1995. http://www.muspe.unibo.it/peroid/ma/index/number1/stokes1/st1.htm/

———. 1997. "Voices and Places: History, Repetition and the Musical Imagination." *Journal of the Royal Anthropological Institute* 3, no. 4: 673–691.

———. 2003. "The Tearful Public Sphere: Turkey's 'Sun of Art,' Zeki Müren." In *Music and Gender: Perspectives from the Mediterranean,* edited by Tullia Magrini, 307–328. Chicago, IL: University of Chicago Press.

———. 2010. *The Republic of Love: Cultural Intimacy in Turkish Popular Music.* Chicago, IL: University of Chicago Press.

Stubbs, Frederick W. 1994. "The Art and Science of *Taksim*: An Empirical Analysis of Traditional Improvisation from 20th Century Istanbul." Ph.D. dissertation, Wesleyan University.

Sugarman, Jane C. 1997. *Engendering Song: Singing and Subjectivity at Prespa Albanian Weddings*. Chicago, IL: University of Chicago Press.

Summit, Jeffrey. 2016. *Singing God's Words: The Performance of Biblical Chant in Contemporary Judaism*. Oxford and New York: Oxford University Press.

Suurî. *Tadilü'l Emzice*. İstanbul Cerrapaşa Medical School, Medical History Department Library, No. 279.

Tambar, Kabir. 2011. "Iterations of Lament: Anachronism and Affect in a Shi'i Islamic Revival in Turkey." *American Ethnologist* 38, no. 3: 484–500.

———. 2012. "Islamic Reflexivity and the Uncritical Subject." *Journal of the Royal Anthropological Institute* 18, no. 3: 652–672.

———. 2014. *The Reckoning of Pluralism: Political Belonging and the Demands of History in Turkey*. Stanford, CA: Stanford University Press.

Tanrıkorur, Cinuçen. 1990. "Concordance of Prosodic and Musical Meters in Turkish Classical Music." *Turkish Musical Quarterly* 3, no. 1: 1–7.

———. 1991. "Introduction to Terennüm in Turkish Music." *Turkish Musical Quarterly* 4, no. 2: 1–8.

———. 1998. *Müzik Kimliğimiz Üzerine Düşünceler*. İstanbul: Ötüken.

———. 2003a. *Osmanlı Dönemi Türk Musikisi*. İstanbul: Dergâh Yayınları.

———. 2003b. *Sâz ü Söz Arasında: Cinuçen Tanrıkorur'un Hatıraları*. İstanbul: Dergâh Yayınları.

———. 2004. *Türk Müzik Kimliği*. İstanbul: Dergâh Yayınları.

Taşan, Turhan. 2000. *Kadın Besteciler*. İstanbul: Pan Yayıncılık.

Taussig, Michael. 1993. *Mimesis and Alterity: A Particular History of the Senses*. London, UK: Routledge.

———. 2009. *What Color Is the Sacred?* Chicago, IL: University of Chicago Press.

Taylor, Diana. 2003. *The Archive and the Repertoire: Performing Cultural Memory in the Americas*. Durham, NC, and London: Duke University Press.

Tekelioğlu, Orhan. 1996. "The Rise of Spontaneous Synthesis: The Historical Background of Turkish Popular Music." *Middle Eastern Studies* 32, no. 2: 194–216.

———. 2001. "Modernizing Reforms and Turkish Music in the 1930s." *Turkish Studies* 2, no.1: 93–108.

Tel, Mesut Cemil. 1947. *Tanburi Cemil'in Hayatı*. Ankara, Turkey: Sakarya Basımevi.

Temelkuran, Ece. 2016. *Turkey: The Insane and the Melancholy*. London, UK: Zed Books.

Terzioğlu, Derin. 2001. "Modernizing Reforms and Turkish Music in the 1930s." *Turkish Studies* 2, no. 1: 93–108.

———. 2002. "Man in the Image of God in the Image of the Times: Sufi Self-Narratives and the Diary of Niyāzī-i Misrī (1618–94)." *Studia Islamica* 94: 139–165.

Thrift, Nigel. 2000. "Still Life in Nearly Present Time: The Object of Nature." *Body & Society* 6, nos. 3–4: 34–57.

———. 2004. "Intensities of Feeling: Towards a Spatial Politics of Affect." *Geografiska Annaler: Series B, Human Geography* 86: 57–78.

———. 2008. *Non-Representational Theory: Space, Politics, Affect*. London, UK: Routledge.

Tolbert, Elizabeth. 1987. "On beyond Zebra: Some Theoretical Considerations of Emotion and Meaning in Music." *Pacific Review of Ethnomusicology* 4: 75–97.

———. 1990. "Women Cry with Words: Symbolization of Affect in the Karelian Lament." *Yearbook for Traditional Music* 22: 80–105.

Tomkins, Silvan S. 1962. *Affect Imagery Consciousness: The Positive Affects.* New York: Springer Publishing.

Tomlinson, Barbara. 2010. *Feminism and Affect at the Scene of Argument: Beyond the Trope of the Angry Feminist.* Philadelphia, PA: Temple University Press.

Topbaş, Osman Nuri. 2005. *Tears of the Heart: Rumi Selections.* Istanbul: Erkam Publications.

Tozlu, Musa. 2014. "Âsım Dîvânı'nda Mûsikî Unsurları [Musical Elements in Asım's Divan]." *Divan Edebiyatı Araştırmaları Dergisi* 13: 141–166.

Trix, Frances. 1993. *Spiritual Discourse: Learning with an Islamic Master.* Philadephia, PA: University of Pennsylvania Press.

Tsimouris, Georgios. 2004. "Musical Memories of the Greek Catastrophe and Local Bards as Emblems of Belonging: The Case of Maria Kouskoussaina." *Oral History Journal* 32, no. 1: 59–70.

Tsekouras, Ioannis. 2016. *Nostalgia, Emotionality, and Ethno-Regionalism in Pontic Parakathi Singing.* Ph.D. dissertation, University of Illinois at Urbana-Champaign.

Tucek, Gerhard. 1997. "Das Menschenbild in der Altorientalischen Musiktherapie." *Verlag für Angewandte Psychologie*, 8, no. 1: 21–34.

Tuğlacı, Pars. 1986. *Mehterhane'den Bando'ya: Turkish Bands of the Past and Present.* İstanbul: Cem Yayınevi.

Tura, Yalçin. 1988. *Türk Musikisi'nin Meseleleri.* İstanbul: Pan Yayıncılık.

Turam, Berna. 2006. *Between Islam and the State: The Politics of Engagement.* Stanford, CA: Stanford University Press.

Turino, Thomas. 1999. "Signs of Imagination, Identity, and Experience: A Peircian Semiotic Theory for Music." *Ethnomusicology* 43, no. 2: 221–255.

———. 2000. *Nationalists, Cosmopolitans, and Popular Music in Zimbabwe.* Chicago, IL: University of Chicago Press.

———. 2008. *Music as Social Life: The Politics of Participation.* Chicago, IL: University of Chicago Press.

Uludağ, Süleyman. 2001. *Tasavvuf Terimleri Sözlüğü.* İstanbul: Kabalcı.

———. 2004 [1976]. *Islam Açısından Musiki ve Sema.* İstanbul: Irfan Yayınevi.

Üngör, Etem R. 1980. *Türk Musikisi Güfteler Antolojisi.* İstanbul: Eren Yayınları.

Ünlü, Cemal. 2004. *Git Zaman, Gel Zaman: Fonograf —Gramofon —Taş Plak.* İstanbul: Pan Yayıncılık.

Van der Gaad, C., R. B. Minderaa, and C. Keysers. 2007. "Facial Expressions: What the Mirror Neuron System Can and Cannot Tell Us." *Social Neuroscience* 2, nos. 3-4: 179–222.

Walkerdine, Valerie. 2009. "Steel, Identity, Community: Regenerating Identities in a South Wales Town." In *Identity in the 21st Century: New Trends in Changing Times*, edited by Margaret Wetherell, 59–75. Basingstoke, UK: Palgrave Macmillan.

———. 2010. "Communal Beingness and Affect: An Exploration of Trauma in an Ex-Industrial Community." *Body & Society* 16, no. 1: 91–116.

Walter, Chip. 2006. "Why Do We Cry?" *Scientific American Mind* 17, no. 6: 44.

Warner, Michael. 2002. *Publics and Counterpublics.* London, UK: Zone Books.

Watson, Sean. 2003. "Bodily Entanglement: Bergson and Thresholds in the Sociology of Affect." *Culture and Organization* 9, no. 1: 27–41.

Wehr, Hans. 1994 [1979]. *The Hans Wehr Dictionary of Modern Written Arabic*, edited by J. M. Cowan. 4th ed. Wiesbaden, Germany, and Ithaca, New York: Otto Harrassowitz and Spoken Language Services.

Weidman, Amanda J. 2006. *Singing the Classical, Voicing the Modern: The Postcolonial Politics of Music in South India.* Durham, NC, and London: Duke University Press.

Werbner, Pnina, and Helene Basu, eds. 1998. *Embodying Charisma: Modernity, Locality, and the Performance of Emotion in Sufi Cults*. London, UK: Routledge.

West, Martin. 2000. "Music Therapy in Antiquity." In *Music as Medicine: The History of Music Therapy since Antiquity*, edited by Peregrine Horden, 51–68. Aldershot, UK: Ashgate.

Wetherell, Margaret. 2012. *Affect and Emotion: A New Social Science Understanding*. Los Angeles, CA: SAGE.

Wierzbicka, Anna. 2004. "Emotion and Culture: Arguing with Martha Nussbaum." *Ethos* 31, no. 4: 577–600.

Winegar, Jessica. 2006. *Creative Reckonings: The Politics of Art and Culture in Contemporary Egypt*. Stanford, CA: Stanford University Press.

———. 2008. "The Humanity Game: Art, Islam, and the War on Terror." *Anthropological Quarterly* 81, no. 3: 651–681.

White, Hayden. 1981. "The Value of Narrativity in the Representation of Reality." In *On Narrative*, edited by W. J. T. Mitchell, 1–24. Chicago, IL: University of Chicago Press.

White, Jenny B. 1991. "Women and Work in Istanbul: Linking the Urban Poor to the World Market." *Middle East Report* 173: 18–22.

———. 1997. "Turks in the New Germany." *American Anthropologist* 99, no. 4: 754–769.

———. 2002. *Islamist Mobilization in Turkey: A Study in Vernacular Politics*. Seattle, WA: University of Washington Press.

———. 2014. *Muslim Nationalism and the New Turks*. Princeton, NJ: Princeton University Press.

Williams, Raymond. 1977. *Marxism and Literature*. Vol. 1. Oxford, UK: Oxford University Press.

Wolf, Richard K. 2000. "Embodiment and Ambivalence: Emotion in South Asian *Muharram* Drumming." *Yearbook for Traditional Music* 32: 81–116.

———. 2001. "Emotional Dimensions of Ritual Music among the Kotas, a South Indian Tribe." *Ethnomusicology* 45, no. 3: 379–422.

Woodard, Kathryn. 2011. *Music in the Ottoman Imperial Harem and the Life of Composer Leyla Saz (1850–1936)*. Philadelphia, PA: Sonic Crossroads.

Wright, Owen. 1990. "*Çargâh* in Turkish Classical Music: History versus Theory." *Bulletin of the School of Oriental and African Studies* 53, no. 2: 244–444.

———. 1992. *Demetrius Cantemir: The Collection of Notations*. Vol. 1. Musicology Series No. 1. London, UK: School of Oriental and African Studies.

———. 2000. *Demetrius Cantemir: The Collection of Notations*. Vol. 2. Aldershot, UK: Ashgate.

———. 2013 [1992]. *Words without Songs: A Musicological Study of an Early Ottoman Anthology and Its Precursors*. New York: Routledge.

Yalçınkaya, Can T. 2008. "Turkish Arabesk Music and the Changing Perceptions of Melancholy in Turkish Society." *NEO 2008*. Accessed 24 September 2015. http://www.arts.mq.edu.au/current_students/new_and_current_hdr_candidates/hdr_journals/neo_journal/issue/2008/pdf/CAN-Turkish_Arabesk_Musicnd_the_Changing_Perceptions_of_Melancholy_.pdf

Yavaşça, Alâeddin. 2002. *Türk Musikisi'nde Kompozisyon ve Beste Biçimleri*. İstanbul: Türk Kültürüne Hizmet Vakfı.

Yavuz, Hakan. 2009. *Secularism and Muslim Democracy in Turkey*. Cambridge, UK: Cambridge University Press.

Yavuz, Hakan, and John Esposito, eds. 2003. *Turkish Islam and the Secular State: The Gülen Movement*. Syracuse, NY: Syracuse University Press.

Yektâ, Raûf. 1896. "Musiki Nazariyatı, Lisan-ı Elhan." *Resimli Gazete*, 10–28.

———. 1899. "Osmanlı Musıkisinde Çeyrek, Salis, ve Nısıf Sedalar." *İkdam*, 3.

———. 1902a. *Esâtîz-i Elhân I: Hoca Zekâi Dede Efendi*. İstanbul: Mahmut Bey Matbaası.

———. 1902b. *Esâtîz-i Elhân II: Hoca Abdülkadir Meragî*. İstanbul: Feridiye Matbaası.

———. 1910a. "Tarih-i Musiki." *Hale*, 1.

———. 1910b. "Tenkidât-ı Musikiye." *Hale*, 1.

———. 1912a. "Bestekâr ve Hanende Hacı Arif Bey." *Şehbal*, 39.

———. 1912b. "Risale-i Musiki." İstanbul: Mürettibhâne-i Husûsî-i.

———. 1919. *Millî Notamız ile Kıraat-ı Musikiye Dersleri*. İstanbul: Evkaf-ı İslâmiye Matbaası.

———. 1922. "La Musique Turque." In *Encyclopédie de la musique*. Part 1, vol. 5, edited by Albert Lavinac, 2945–3064. Paris: Delagrave.

———. 1925. *Esâtîz-i Elhân III: Dede Efendi*. İstanbul: Evkaf-ı İslâmiye Matbaası.

———. 1927. "Türk Musikisi Nasıl Islah Olunabilir?" *Telsiz* 18 August, 1–2.

———, ed. 1933. *Bektaşi Nefesleri*. İstanbul: İstanbul Konservatuvarı Yayını.

———, ed. 1934. *Mevlevî Âyinleri*. İstanbul: İstanbul Konservatuvarı Yayını.

Yığıtbaş, M. Sadık. 1972. *Musiki ile Tedavi*. İstanbul: Yelken Matbaası.

Youssefzadeh, Ameneh. 2000. "The Situation of Music in Iran since the Revolution: The Role of Official Organizations." *British Journal of Ethnomusicology* 9, no. 2: 35–61.

Zandi-Sayek, Sibel. 2011. *Ottoman Izmir: The Rise of a Cosmopolitan Port, 1840–1880*. Minneapolis, MN: University of Minnesota Press.

Zimmermann-Kalyoncu, Cornelia. 1980. *Deutsche Musiker in der Türkei im 20. Jahrhundert*. Frankfurt, Germany: Peter Lang Verlag.

Žižek, Slavoj. 2000. "Melancholy and the Act." *Critical Inquiry* 26: 657–681.

DISCOGRAPHY

Aydemir, Murat, and Derya Turkan. *Ahenk, Turkish Classical Music*. Golden Horn 1998.

Ayla, Safiye. *Safiye Ayla, No. 1*. Kalan, 2014.

Bezmârâ Topluluğu. *Mecmua'dan Saz ve Söz*. Kalan, 2003.

Çelik, Necati. *Sûzidil*. Fontimusicali, 2014.

———. *Yasemin: Classical Turkish Oud Music*. 7/8 Music Productions, 1998.

Cemil Bey, Tanburi. *Tanburi Cemil Bey*. Traditional Crossroads, CD 4264, 1994.

———. *Tanburi Cemil Bey Külliyatı*. Kalan, 2016.

Değişmez, Güzin. *Ah O Demler*. Kalan, 2015.

Deran, Erol. *Erol Deran*. Kalan, 2012.

Ergin, Dogan, dir., with Kani Karaca. *Returning: The Music of the Whirling Dervishes*. Interworld CD-916, 1995.

Erguner, Kudsi. *Turquie: Cérémonie des derviches Kadiri*. AIMP XII, CD-587, 1980, 1988.

Filiz, Aziz Şenol. *Beş Ayin IV (Şevk-u Tarab Mevlevi Ayini)*. Kalan, 2012.

Golden Horn Ensemble. *Music from the Harem: Harem'de Neşe*. Kalan, 1995.

Gülses, Melihat. *Hüznün Hikâyesi*. Akustik Yapım, 2004.

———. *Narçiçeğim 1*. Akustik Yapım, 2005.

———. *Narçiçeğim 2*. Akustik Yapım, 2005.

Hagopian, Harold G., ed. *Istanbul 1925*. Traditional Crossroads, CD 4266, 1994.

Hampartzum, Baba. *Besteler ve Şaranganlar*. Kalan, 2010.

Karaca, Kani. *Mevlana —Dede Efendi (Saba Ayini)*. Kalan, 1996.

———, with Salih Bilgin, Derya Turkan, Murat Aydemir, and Bahadır Şenel. *With Love . . . : Compositional Genres of Turkish Liturgical Music [Aşk ile . . . : Türk dinî musiki formları]*. Pan, 2002.

Karaduman, Halil, and Necati Çelik. *Classical Music of Turkey*. Near Eastern Music West (NEMW) 1001, 2003.

Kutbay, Aka Gündüz. *Aşk, No. 1*. Kalan, 2009.

———. *Aşk, No. 2*. Kalan, 2009.

Kutbay, Aka Gündüz, and Kani Karaca. *Meşk*. Kalan, 2009.

Mauguin, Bernard. *Turkish Music, Music of the Mevlevi*. BM 30 L 2019, 1962.

Özgen, İhsan. *Tanburi Cemil Bey: Peşrev ve Saz Semaileri*. Kalan, 1994.

Poché, Christian, and Bernard Moussali, eds. *Turquie: Archives de la musique turque*. Ocora, CDs C560081 and C560082, 1995.

Rifat Bey, Sermüezzin. *Ferahnak Mevlevi Ayini*. Kalan, 2003.

Signell, Karl, and Ercüment Aksoy, Münir Nurettin Beken, Talat Halman, Richard Spottswood, and Necdet Yaşar, eds. *Masters of Turkish Music, Volume 1*. Rounder, CD 1051, 1990.

———. *Masters of Turkish Music, Volume 2*. Rounder, CD 1111, 1996.

Tevfik, Neyzen. *Hiç'in Azâb-ı Mukaddes'i*. Kalan, 2000.

Yaşar, Necdet, and Niyazi Sayın. *Masters of Turkish Music: Niyazi Sayın & Necdet Yaşar*. Kalan, 2005.

———. *Masters of Turkish Music: Niyazi Sayın and Necdet Yaşar, No. 2*. Kalan, 2005.

INDEX

Note: Tables, figures, and musical examples are indicated by *t*, *f*, and *ex* following the page number.

spiritual perspectives on, 65–66, 150–152
of Turkish classical music, 33–35, 52, 57–60, 125–126, 176
Dede Efendi, Hammamizade İsmail, 38, 125–126
Dede Efendi, Zekai, 38, 79, 80ex
Deleuze, Gilles, 2, 98, 126
depression, clinical, 166, 196n3. See also melancholy, as illness
"Derdimi ummana döktüm," 134, 134ex, 135ex, 136
dialectic understanding, 196n6
"Dinle Sözümü," 180–181, 180ex
discourse analysis, 197n11
"dis-ease," 181, 209n2
diversity, in study of affect and emotion, 186
Donizetti, Giuseppe, 37, 58, 110–111, 125
duygu (emotion), 14
duymak (to feel), 6, 14

"east"–"west" bifurcation. See also orientalism
avoided in affective practice approach, 189
in framing and language of music, 31, 47, 155
in theory, 22
in visual and material arts, 205n8
edep (manners), 6, 192–193
Edirne Health Museum, 159
el-Hirî, Ebû Osman, 21
El Kanun fi't-tıbbi ("The Canon of Medicine"), 161
embodiment, boundaries of
Ahmed's model vs. ethnography, 185
dualistic categories insufficient for, 70, 84
gender difference and, 140–145, 186
hearing vs. listening in, 149
individual vs. social, 131, 139, 145, 152
language of, 129, 185–186
mundane vs. divine, 151, 153
naming practices and, 130
sacredness and, 70, 84–87
scope of term, 131, 152–153
separation and, 133

sonic and bodily melancholy, 132–140, 155–156, 193
in study of affect, 186
tears as, 148, 185
emotional contagion, 139
emotions
vs. affect, 14–16, 17
categories of, 15, 16
crossword puzzle metaphor for, 107
ontological assumptions of term, 14
pleasure and sadness from music, 146–147
scholarly approaches to, 186, 197nn8–9
social constructivist views of, 15, 184, 197n8
sociality of, 16–17, 185, 197n8
targeted by modes in music therapy, 160, 163, 166
term usage, 16
Turkish term for, 14
Emre, Yunus, 79
Enderun (school), 37, 103, 122
English language practices, 14
Ensari, Ünal, xvi, 133–138
Erdoğan, Recep Tayyip, 54, 202n15
Ersoy, Bülent, 143
eser (work), 129–130, 141, 208n1
ethnomusicology, in study of affect, 183–189
and introduction of bi-aurality, xiv, 114, 121-122, 126–127
in studies of genealogy, 97–100, 118–121
Eyüp Sultan district, 56
Ezgi, Suphi, 110, 207n7
Ezgi-Arel-Yektâ notation system, 110

Fado Resounding (Gray), 188
Fatih Book Fair, 52–53, 55
feeling(s), xiv, 14, 16, 184. See also affect; affective practice(s); emotions
Feld, Steven, 188
Feldman, Walter, 38, 59, 83, 111, 207n13
fez (head garment), 41
Fine Arts Academy, 49
Flatley, Jonathan, 11, 184
Foucault, Michel, 118, 197n11
Freud, Sigmund, 6, 166, 196n3

Gadamer, Hans-Georg, 196n6
gender
  God's genderlessness, 205n9
  harem and women musicians, 38, 124,
    202n9, 208n3
  melancholy and gender difference,
    140–145
  musical performance of femininity,
    141, 209n8
  musical structure and, 145–146
  music composition shaped by, 140
  music transmission and ideologies of,
    142, 208n3
  norms shaped by music, xvii, 140, 141
  public performance and circulation
    shaped by, 142–143
  queer phenomenology, 120–121
  reflexivity of author's own gender
    performance, xv–xvii
genealogical imagination, 118
genealogies, musical. *See* lineage
geographies, melancholic, 24, 97,
    114–118, 195n2
Gevrekzâde, Hasan Efendi, 161
Gezi protests, 69
God
  as *Allah*, 76
  genderlessness of, 205n9
  Hû as essence of, 76–77, 84
  Sufi understanding of, 72
  as ultimate cause of melancholy,
    1–3, 189
Gökalp, Ziya, 44–45, 202n16,
    203nn18–19
goygoy (ornamentation), 175
Gray, Lila Ellen, 188
Guattari, Félix, 98, 126
Gülses, Melihat, 138–140
Gülses, Necip, 140

habitus, 145, 147, 198n13
hadith, 21, 182, 189
halk (folk music). *See* Turkish folk music
Halman, Talat Sait, 59
Hamparsum notation, 36, 109
Hanım, Kevser, 141, 142, 144, 145
happiness, 135, 135ex, 136, 190
harem musicians, 38, 124, 202n9, 208n3
Hayâlî, 92
"Hay'dan gelen Hû'ya gider," 86

healing. *See also* music therapy
  in community, 157, 159, 163
  vs. medicine, 174
  sound as focus of, 154–155
  view of suffering and, 156
Heidegger, Martin, 196n6
Hicaz makamı (mode), 78, 79ex,
    161, 162
hicran (loneliness/vulnerability), 15
Hildegard of Bingen, 164
hissetmek (to feel), 14
Hood, Mantle, xiv, 114
Hû
  in Arab and Persian communities,
    76, 206n16
  calligraphic representations of, 71f,
    81, 82f, 93f, 206n21
  classifications transcended by, 94
  contemporary use of, 86–88
  as divine remembrance, 77,
    80–81, 84
  as essence/quality of God, 76–77, 84
  in every breath, 206n18
  as greeting and request, 71,
    81, 84, 87
  as instrument technique, 82–84
  as Istanbul, 87–89
  from life to death, 89–91
  meaning of, 71, 76
  as sacred embodiment, 84–87
  separation bridged by, 72
  social identity and, 84, 85–86
  as sound, 76–82, 84
  from sound to silence, 89–93
"*Hû Demek İster*," 78–79, 79ex, 206n17
Hume, David, 197n8
humors, bodily
  as fall from grace, 164
  melancholy as imbalance in, 10, 11,
    24, 157–158
  in music therapy, 160, 163
Hüseyni makamı (mode), 161, 162, 163
hüzün ("melancholy"), 12–13, 13f, 20–21
Hüzzam makamı (mode), 79

İçli, Selahattin, 138
İçli, Şerif, 134, 134ex, 135ex, 137
identity. *See also* selfhood
  dualistic categories insufficient for,
    70, 84, 85

Öztuna, Yilmaz, 112
Öztürk, Yaşar Nuri, 100

pain. *See* suffering and pain
Pamuk, Orhan, 12–13, 20
People's Houses, 47
Perman, Tony, 186
piety, 3, 18–22, 69, 133, 142–143,
    148–149, 154, 191
Post, Hafız, 77
power
    contexts for melancholic modalities, 13
    in discourse analysis, 198n11
    in practice theory, 198n13
    in scholarly approaches to affect and
        emotion, 186
practice (term), 17–18
practice theory, 198n13
privatization reforms, 53, 54, 55–56
psychology, western epistemologies
    and, 166

queer phenomenology, 120–121,
    126–127

radio
    music patronage and commodification
        through, 8, 44, 47–48, 55
    state control of, 203n20
    Turkish classical music banned from,
        47
    as vehicle for nationalism, 46–47
Rast makamı (mode), 160, 161,
    171, 172ex
reed bed (related to *ney*), 2, 64, 65, 89,
    126, 192
reforms, national
    categories created by, xx, 41, 46, 69
    death of genre and, 57
    effect on Arif Bey, 176
    language affected by, 43
    Law 677, 122–123
    master–apprentice relationships and,
        xix, 110, 112, 208n3
    Mevlevi Sufism influenced by, 74
    musical style shaped by, 7–8, 36,
        44–46, 122–123
    of music institutions, 50
    music patronage affected by, 47,
        122–123

music practice affected by, 46, 47–48
public performance by women and,
    142–143
secularization as goal of, 41, 112
structuration of cultural heritage
    affected by, 41, 44
reforms, Ottoman. See *Tanizmat*
    reforms
Rehavi makamı (mode), 161, 162, 163
reparation, 22, 181, 183, 190, 191,
    195n2. *See also* healing; music
    therapy
Republic of Turkey. *See also* reforms,
    national
    musical style negotiated in, xx, 7–8,
        36, 44–46
    neoliberalism and, 53, 55
    secularization of, 41–42, 44, 74–75
    Turkish classical music as
        a contemporary genre
        supported by, 8
    Turkish identity codified in, 40–42
rhizomatic analysis
    of affective practice, xiv, 6, 16,
        98–100, 191
    bi-aurality in, 97, 121–127
    concept of, xv, 2, 4, 23, 191
    horizontal listening in, 5, 8–9, 98,
        121, 187, 192
    of "may God increase your pain/
        suffering," 2–3
    in study of "Turkish classical music,"
        2, 4–5
rhizome
    as "anti-genealogy," 98–99, 126
    as figurative and literal metaphor, xv,
        2, 2f, 5, 6, 98–99, 191–193
rhythmic modes, xxi, 6, 8, 102–103, 136.
    See also usûl
Rufaî, Aziz, 206n21
Rumi, Mevlana Celaluddin, 61, 204n1.
    See also Mevlana

Saba makamı (mode), 160, 172, 172ex
Said, Edward, 7, 119
Salât-ı Ümmiye, 34ex
sama' (Ar. "listening")
    bodily boundaries and, 149, 152
    moral and spiritual implications of,
        149, 179

as necessary for happiness, 190
no medicine for, 174, 176, 177
piety and, 19
as remedy, 156, 157, 173–174, 177,
    181–182
as spiritually redeeming, 100
as theme in master–apprentice
    relationship, 100
Sufi (as a term), 204n5
"Sufi music" as a category, 55–56
Sufism, 3, 66, 67, 72–76. *See also* Mevlevi
Sultanahmet, 52–53, 55
Sunni Islam, 36, 41, 68, 72, 81
Suzidilârâ makamı (mode), 36, 36*ex*
Suzidil makamı (mode), 79, 80*ex*

taksim (improvisation)
    definitions of, xiv, xx
    example in *Segâh makamı,*34*ex*
    learning from recordings, 113
    melancholies heard through, 171, 172
    melodic movement in, 168–169, 172
    Mevlevi roots of, 83
    modal introduction to,29*ex*
    Tevfik's influence on, 171–173
talibeh (student), 100
tanbur (instrument), 8
Tanizmat reforms
    categories created by, 69
    mental health approaches shaped
        by, 169
    Mevlevi-s benefited by, 74
    military music house closed by,
        36–37, 125
    musical practices modernized by,
        36–39, 125
    palace orchestra established by,
        36, 125
Tanrıkorur, Cinuçen, 108, 168
tears. 146–148, 150 *See also* weeping
    biomedical understanding of,
        148, 209n9
    bodily boundaries manifested by, 148
    in emotional response to musics and
        sounds, 146–148, 150
    in musicians' rendering of
        melancholies, 139
"*Tekbir,*" 34*ex*
tekke-s (Sufi lodges)
    contemporary state of, 75, 75*f*, 123

history of, 44, 48, 49, 73–74, 122
music transmission at, 103, 115–116
terms, conventions for, xix
Tevfik, Neyzen
    improvisations, 156, 171–173,
        171*ex*, 172*ex*
    as melancholic musician, 156, 169,
        171, 172–173
    poetry by, 169
    statues of, 169–171, 170*f*
transcriptions, xix, xxi, 200n18
transitory melancholy, 165
translation, xix, 1–3, 13–14, 17, 100–
    101, 114–115, 151
transmission of affect, 139, 186
tree metaphors, 116–118, 119, 121, 126
Trix, Francis, 77
TRT (Turkish Radio and Television), 8,
    47–48, 55
Türk (term), 42
*Türkçülüğün Esasları (The Principles of
    Turkism),* 44–45
Turkey. xvii *See also* Ottoman Empire;
    Republic of Turkey
Turkish art music *(Türk sanat müziği),*
    47, 51
Turkish classical music. *See also* music
    therapy; music transmission;
    reforms, national; *Tanizmat*
    reforms
    affective character of, 3–5, 30,
        32–33, 127
    categories constructed for, 3, 7–10,
        41, 46, 68–69
    cultural framing of, 8–9,
        44–45, 48–51
    debates about musical style of, 7–8
    defined, 7–10, 31
    and embodiment, 129
    emotional maturity required by, 96
    as feminized, 143
    history of genre construction and
        invention, 7–8, 30–33
    listeners' connections to, 8–9
    loss narratives in, 30–31, 33, 37, 38,
        58–60, 111
    melancholies in composition of,
        95–96
    musical canon, 31
    musical style debates, 7–8, 36, 44–46

CPSIA information can be obtained
at www.ICGtesting.com
Printed in the USA
BVHW031756160419
545664BV00002B/32/P

9 780190 495015